EMPIRE'S
CROSSROADS

EMPIRE'S CROSSROADS

A History of the Caribbean From Columbus to the Present Day

CARRIE GIBSON

Atlantic Monthly Press
New York

First published in Great Britain in 2014 by Macmillan
an imprint of Pan Macmillan, a division of Macmillan Publishers Limited

Printed in the United States of America

ISBN 978-0-8021-2614-6
eBook ISBN 978-0-8021-9235-6

Atlantic Monthly Press
an imprint of Grove/Atlantic, Inc.
154 West 14th Street
New York, NY 10011

Distributed by Publishers Group West

www.groveatlantic.com

14 15 16 17   10 9 8 7 6 5 4 3 2 1

For Chris

Contents

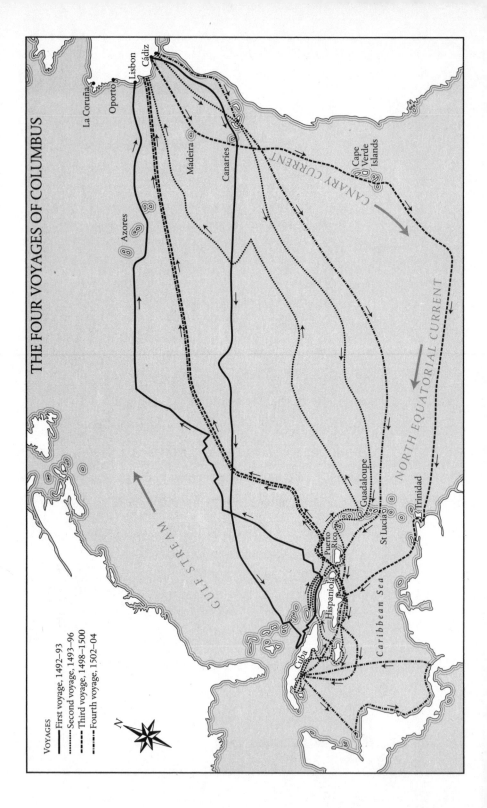

THE FOUR VOYAGES OF COLUMBUS

VOYAGES
—— First voyage, 1492–93
········ Second voyage, 1493–96
– – – Third voyage, 1498–1500
–·–·– Fourth voyage, 1502–04

La Coruña
Oporto
Lisbon
Cádiz
Azores
Madeira
Canaries
Cape Verde Islands
CANARY CURRENT
NORTH EQUATORIAL CURRENT
GULF STREAM
Cuba
Hispaniola
Puerto Rico
Guadaloupe
St Lucia
Trinidad
Caribbean Sea

N

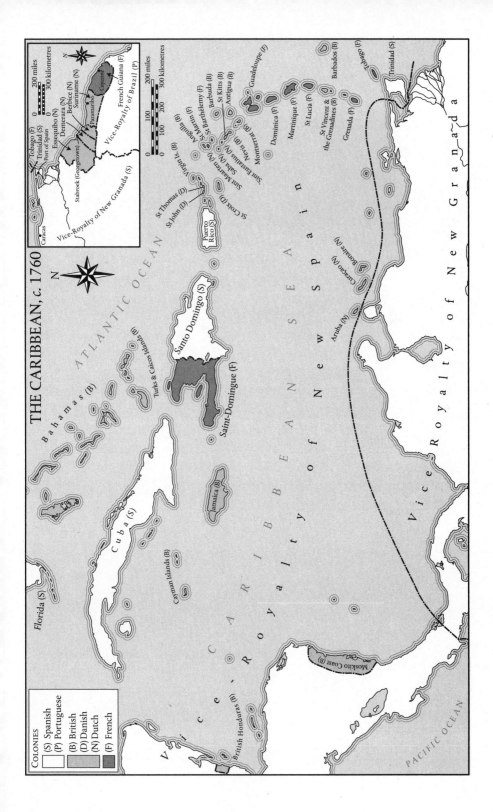

THE CARIBBEAN, c. 1760

COLONIES
(S) Spanish
(P) Portuguese
(B) British
(D) Danish
(N) Dutch
(F) French

ATLANTIC OCEAN

CARIBBEAN SEA

PACIFIC OCEAN

Florida (S)

Bahamas (B)

Cuba (S)

Cayman Islands (B)

Jamaica (B)

Turks & Caicos Islands (B)

Santo Domingo (S)

Saint-Domingue (F)

Puerto Rico (S)

Virgin Is. (B)

St Thomas (D)
St John (D)
St Croix (D)

Anguilla (F)
St Martin (F)
Sint Maarten (N)
St Barthélemy (F)
Barbuda (B)
Saba (N)
Sint Eustatius (N)
St Kitts (B)
Nevis (B)
Antigua (B)
Montserrat (B)
Guadeloupe (F)
Dominica (F)
Martinique (F)
St Lucia (F)
St Vincent &
the Grenadines (B)
Grenada (F)
Barbados (B)
Tobago (F)
Trinidad (S)

Curaçao (N)
Aruba (N)
Bonaire (N)

Moskito Coast (B)

British Honduras (B)

Viceroyalty of New Spain

Viceroyalty of New Granada

Vice-Royalty of New Granada (S)

Vice-Royalty of Brazil (S)

Caracas

Tobago (F)
Trinidad (S)
Port of Spain

Essequibo (N)
Demerara (N)
Berbice (N)
Suriname (N)
French Guiana (F)

Stabroek (Georgetown)
Paramaribo
Cayenne

200 miles
300 kilometres

100   200 miles
100 200 300 kilometres

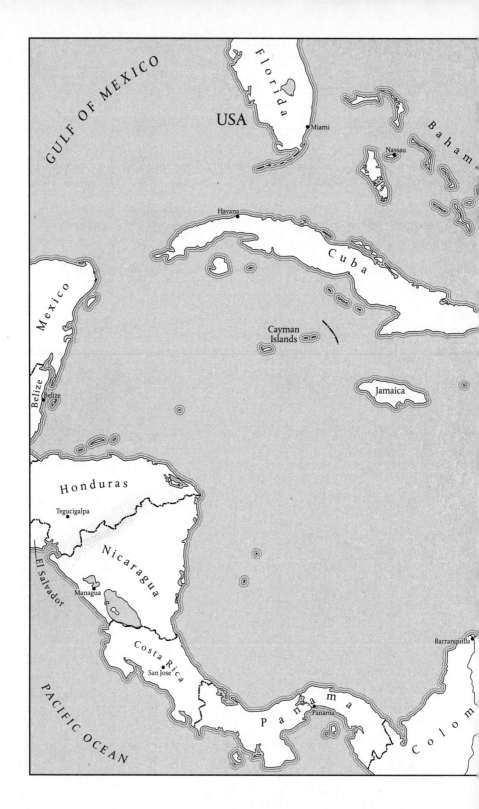

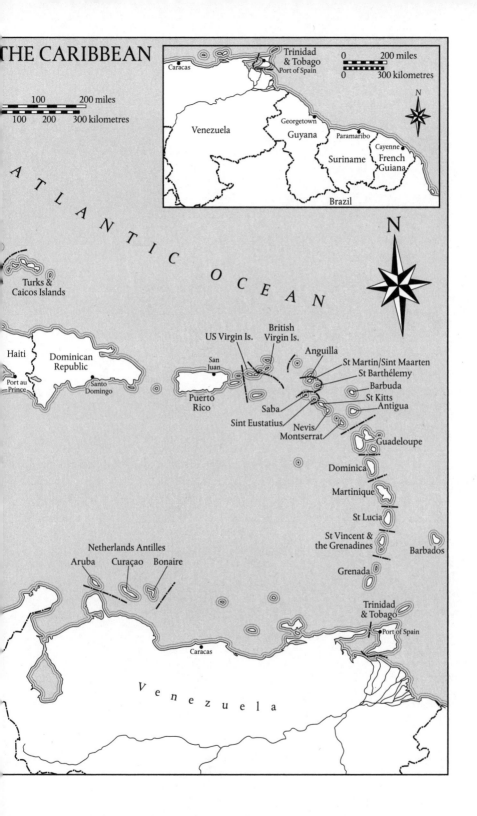

List of Illustrations

Introduction

On the mountainous island of Martinique, at the edge of La Savane park, in the capital, Fort-de-France, there is a statue of a headless woman. Under the shade of leafy trees, and mounted on a sturdy plinth, she is dressed in the type of empire-waist gown that was fashionable in the late eighteenth century. In her right hand she holds a rose to her chest, her left is resting on top of a large cameo, on it carved the profile of Napoleon Bonaparte. The statue is of his first wife, Marie-Josèphe-Rose Tascher de la Pagerie, perhaps the most famous (or, indeed, infamous) daughter of Martinique. She was born to sugar-planter parents in Trois-Îlets, across the bay from Fort-de-France.

No one is certain when she was decapitated, but the head is long gone and there has never been any effort to fashion a new one for the Rose of Martinique, as she was known. Lashings of red paint now adorn her body. The antipathy from Martinicans comes not just from the fact that she was a planter's daughter, or that she was Napoleon's wife, but from the convergence of the two: many islanders believe she convinced him to reinstate slavery in the French colonies eight years after its abolition in 1794 in order to protect her family's fortunes. There is no evidence that she said anything to Napoleon about slavery, but the myth lives on.

Something about this story captures almost every element of Caribbean history: the connection between the tiny island and powerful people in Europe; the legacy of slavery; the persistence of myths and legends; and the idiosyncratic way that it has been memorialized. The statue remains in the island's capital, headless and daubed with paint, facing the sea.

*

'Empire' might seem an anachronistic term to use in the title of this book. The trend in scholarly arenas is for the more encompassing 'global', which conjures fewer images of pith-helmeted imperialism, and allows for the inclusion of a wider range of nations and people. But the reality is that the modern Caribbean, from 1492 onwards, was the product of an encounter between Europeans and other peoples. That is not to say Europeans *made* the islands what they are, but that they started a process both destructive and constructive that has led them to become what they are today. Europeans eradicated most of the islands' indigenous past. Indeed, it is increasingly accepted that Columbus did not 'discover' the Americas, but rather that he led a march on their people while thinking he was in the Far East. The early period of West Indian, and by extension American, discovery and settlement was a time of upheaval made all the more unusual and deadly because of the toxic combination of guns and germs. To be sure, disease did its part in wiping out large swathes of the Amerindian population, but Europeans did not stand idly by as smallpox swept through. They took advantage of the situation. The clash between the new and old worlds brought about death and destruction, of course, but it also allowed for the development of new processes, including transatlantic slavery. It was the creation, quite literally, of new worlds on top of old lands that gives the islands their unique place in history. This was also aided by the fact that so little was known, understood, or recorded about indigenous life on the islands, whereas, in contrast, a great deal more of the nearby Aztec and Inca states survived and was discussed – not always without problems.

However, the credit for making the diverse islands of the West Indies what they are today lies with the people: the surviving Amerindians, the large number of Africans, the smattering of Europeans, and, later, the people born and raised in the Caribbean, the 'creoles'. This is reflected by a diversity throughout the islands' music, food, art, dance and other cultural forms – but also, paradoxically, between the shared history of that diversity. Yet even the recognition of this has been a long time coming. Europeans were hardly kind in writing about the islands, or the people in them. The English novelist Anthony Trollope, in an 1859 account of his tour around the islands, wrote about the island-born people of African descent he met in Jamaica: 'They have no country of their own, yet have they not hitherto any country of their adoption for, whether as slaves in Cuba, or as free labourers in the British isles, they are in each case a servile people in a foreign land. They have no language of their own . . . they have no idea of country, and no pride of race.'[1] St Lucian poet Derek Walcott, in his Nobel Lecture of 1992, made reference to 'Trollope's "non-people"' in a passage about Port of Spain, a city in which it was possible to embrace what Trollope had rejected. The city, Walcott wrote, had 'a downtown babel of shop signs and streets, mongrelized, polyglot, a ferment without a history, like heaven. Because that is what such a city is, in the New World, a writer's heaven.'[2] But the white European and later North American views and all the racist ideas embedded in them dominated the written accounts of the Caribbean in the eighteenth and nineteenth centuries, and often these and documents written and organized by white colonial officials may be all the interested historian has reference to. It was not until the later decades of the twentieth that many of these ideas were refuted and rejected, though some ongoing stereotypes seem to have been carved in stone.

Empire is crucial, because the more than five hundred years of European rule in Caribbean waters cannot be washed away, even if many people would like it to be. Many of the islands are now independent, and the era of imperial rule is a fading memory. But there is no ignoring the legacy. At the same time, the history of the Caribbean is not simply a tale of European powers and African slaves; a much wider global story has developed that stretches from the United States to China. Empire is not a static word either – its meanings range from asserting direct political control to more indirect economic dominance.

However, 'empire' in this book does not offer a reassuring narrative about how the Spanish or British or French or Dutch brought order or civilization to these islands. To be clear: Europeans brought destruction, chaos, and disorder. They may have built roads and set up bureaucracies, or maintained a semblance of control through the repression of dissent or uprising, but as becomes clear early on, resistance and rebellion was all around.

Making sense of these multiple and conflicting strands is far from straightforward. For every tranquil planter there was a rebellious slave. For every bored colonial administrator there was a subordinate

subverting the system. But there was also a great degree of cooperation, and assimilation, too. Life was often not as dichotomized as it
has frequently been presented. If there is an overarching narrative here,
it is not of progress, or development, but persistence: this is what
happened, good and bad, after Europeans arrived. If all the islands of
the Caribbean could be amalgamated and anthropomorphized, the
resulting person would have been taken from the African coast, worked
as a pirate, been forced into slavery, toiled in a cane field, fought in a
war, been freed, squatted on land, become a unionized labourer, and
run a tourist resort. This is an exaggeration, of course, but the character
of the West Indies has everything to do with surviving the many brutal-
ities, restrictions, and challenges served up by people from Europe,
and later the United States. And that is not to mention the ongoing
struggles against nature in a region regularly battered by hurricanes,
as well as periodic earthquakes and volcanic eruptions. If there is one
thing at the heart of this story, it is the genius of adaptation. This is
what the clash of worlds – as violent as any force of nature – demanded.
Adaptation – to diaspora, to disease, to slavery, to racism, to earth-
quakes, to poverty, to tourism – was the response to an exhausting
series of events. Yet, as the cultural theorist Stuart Hall has pointed
out, the Caribbean, to Western eyes, is 'very much "the same". We
belong to the marginal, the underdeveloped, the periphery, the "Other".
We are at the outer edge, the "rim", of the metropolitan world – always
"South" to someone else's *El Norte*.'[3]

*

History is no mere collection of inert facts and dates. It can be manipulated, shaped, stretched, and moulded. Sweeping historical narratives
have a complex social psychology. They often speak to a collective
need to feel that transgressions of the past were not so bad, or perhaps
that they were worse than we could have possibly imagined, or that
things were awful and we helped to change them. Histories help a
nation define what it is, or indeed what people would *like* it to be. Yet
the past cannot so neatly be packed into boxes, and the story that
unfolds in this book is often one of extremes: brutality and liberation,
oppression and freedom. History has long been used for political ends.
Consider the more recent examples: the appropriation of the Boston
Tea Party by right-wing Republicans in the US; or, in Britain, the

ongoing debate between the government and professional historians about the narrow, Anglocentric school history curriculum. In relation to the Caribbean, by extension, the idea that somehow Columbus and other Europeans brought civilization rather than destroyed it has been a tenacious myth, though it is one that is finally being chipped away.

Thinking about the wider West Indies and how to place them means piecing together a story that has long since fragmented. Histories tend to be linguistically and imperially grouped, not least because so much archival or source material is in English, Spanish, French, or Dutch, and so language often guides research. But there is also the issue of nationalism. As islands like Jamaica or Cuba make sense of their own history, they necessarily push aside a wider story in favour of a more focused one.

The second half of the book's title – *Crossroads* – references the history of the West Indies as one of connections and crossings, such as the planter's daughter from Martinique who married a self-proclaimed emperor of France. Today, to many people, the idea of the islands is best represented by a generic image of blue water and palm trees, yet each of the islands has its own rich, dense history that extends across the globe, far beyond the Caribbean. There is a spiritual dimension too, as religious scholars Ennis Edmonds and Michelle Gonzalez point out: 'In Afro-Caribbean religions, the spiritual entity Papa Legba, or Elegguá, rules over the crossroads – the symbolic juncture between the human and the realm of the spirits, the pathway between present realities and the African past, the point that separates the present and the future, the place of ritual transformation and empowerment, and the site of decision and opportunity.'[4]

The shipping lanes in and out of these islands brought the world together. Silks moved from China to Panama to Spain and onwards. People moved, too; the seas could be a means to liberation and living outside the law, or a conduit to the living hell of enslavement. The sea also was the bringer of goods. Eager islanders awaited shipments of European wares, while Europeans demanded ever more shiploads of commodities to give them their sugar fix, or tobacco hit. The sort of global commodity chains we take for granted today – the ones that bring us iPads and cheap shoes – were forged in this period.

But some caution should be exercised. Claiming to be the first 'modern' place or the earliest 'globalized' nation is a bit of an ivory-tower arms race. Historians in many areas – medieval Europe, seventeenth-century India, fifteenth-century China – have claimed the roots of the modern world are to be found firmly planted in Westphalia, Bengal, or Shanghai. This is a contest with no clear winner. However, the links between the West Indies and the rest of the world certainly made them a contender for claims to early global connections. Within a relatively short space of time, the rise of European colonialism in the West Indies linked Santo Domingo to Manila, and Trinidad to India. There were other trade circuits, to be sure, but none that spanned east and west to such a degree – the route becoming faster still after the awkward trek across the Panamanian isthmus ended with the opening of the Panama Canal in the twentieth century.

The Caribbean was both factory and marketplace. Fortunes were made and lost growing sugar and other crops; smaller islands could trade in global goods, at times flouting both commercial laws and tax regimes. It was an important hub in the development of the modern world economy. But, like the sweatshops of the present, the cost of such economic development was borne by the exploited workers; these islands were also the site of demographic upheaval and displacement in the name of profit, as African labourers were brought to their shores. Then, as the era of slavery drew to a close, Indians and Chinese followed these imperial paths to the doors of Trinidad, Guyana,* and Jamaica, with some even diverting to Cuba. In these small places, people from around the world lived together. The story was not always a happy one, but the outcome made the islands like nowhere else.

Another critical aspect of the Caribbean is the emotions it fostered. It was at once a place of dreams, of fantasy, of riches, of sexual excess. And it was feared as a graveyard, in both a physical and a spiritual sense. Millions of people – Europeans, Africans, Asians – died from tropical diseases until scientific advances and public health reined in the killing power of the mosquito and other carriers. But there were also concerns that life on these islands could ruin a European's moral health, making them lascivious and corrupt degenerates, revelling in

---

* Guyana is the modern, post-independence spelling of British Guiana, the former colony. I use the nomenclature appropriate to the time and status of the country.

their ill-gotten gains. Columbus set about his mission looking for gold; the sugar planters arrived seeking their fortunes; and today's tourist steps off the plane to be whisked away to a villa where all cares are to be swept aside. The islands have continued to foster fantasy, often completely at odds with their reality. At first glance it does look like paradise: the blue sky, and impossibly clear turquoise water, the sand, the palm trees, the gentle caress of the sea breezes. Yet most islanders face an everyday struggle for survival amid such natural splendour. The dreams work both ways as well – many islanders cannot find what they are looking for in the Caribbean, and instead set off to the United States or Europe in pursuit of whatever that may be.

It is perhaps unfashionable to say so, but there is a great deal of the present in the Caribbean's past. Although the adage that history repeats itself is tiresome, there are patterns here that cannot be ignored. Certain themes arise again and again in today's world: slavery (waged, or otherwise); environmental crises; wild and destructive stock-market bubbles; unfair trade; political repression. It is perhaps best left to the philosophers to question the seemingly repetitive quality of human malfeasance, but the parallels and precursors are clear for all to see. Before there was a campaign against sweatshop labour, there was one against buying Caribbean sugar; before there was the toppling of Saddam Hussein, there was the overthrow of the government in Guatemala. The answers are not necessarily to be found in the past, but the clues are. The history of the Caribbean is a history that belongs to everyone.

*

My own relationship to the Caribbean is born of two things. The first is a nagging disquiet over the fact that so much of Caribbean history was transformed – deformed – by the worthless commodity of sugar. Of course, it wasn't financially worthless, then or now, but the human body does not need it to survive. A system of suppression and enslavement underpinned a human desire for the superfluous. The initial hunt for gold and silver is easier to understand – these metals had a value, which is why the Spanish were searching for them. But sugar, a useless by-product of a breed of grass, shaped not only West Indian history, but the rise of consumer society. There had to be a hunger there, greed. It also needed a large labour supply, empty land with the right climatic conditions, a philosophical moment when agriculture was seen as the route to riches, and a trade network that put a high value on it. There also had to be a gap between the production and consumption of a good, which was soon in place as well, and European sugar use expanded and a blind eye was turned to the source. There are clear parallels to be made about more modern commodities, for instance sweatshop-produced clothing, or the illegal drug trade. The dream of easy wealth at the expense of someone else's misery is one that refuses to die.

The second entry point is more personal. I am not of Caribbean origin, nor, as far as I know, did any of my family have interests in the islands. But I spent my childhood in the Deep South of the United States in the 1980s, moving there less than twenty years after segregation had ended. The scars from that period were real and visceral. It seemed at the time that the Caribbean, or at least what little I knew or understood of it, offered a different story, one that provided a more positive ending to an ugly period in the history of the Americas. It is a shared history, after all. The elements are similar – encounter, exploitation, slavery, emancipation, displacement, migration – but they seem to be jumbled up, like a box of puzzle pieces. This, certainly, was a child's perspective, and what I came to discover was not better or worse but, of course, different. There were nasty episodes and triumphant ones. But it instilled in me a lasting curiosity about the region that has developed into a passion over the past decade of writing and research. There is a long shared history between the US and the West Indies, and especially between the Southern states and the islands, but one that is too rarely thought about or acknowledged. In many ways the historical glow that continues to radiate from the American War of Independence overshadows other narratives: the story of the *Americas*. The thirteen colonies and later the US were far more than a backdrop or trading partner, but a steadily rising behemoth that the whole hemisphere, for better or worse, had to learn to coexist with. The obsession with the 'exceptionalism' of the US can push aside any wider or often more nuanced view of this relationship.

Then again, comparing one place that was fairly homogeneous – the Southern US – to a collection of more than twenty islands and numerous coastal countries with different languages and people is like comparing one orange to a barrel of fruit. To write about the

'Caribbean' at all seems a bit outdated. With all the islands' internal diversity, is there any point? Some of these islands are independent nations, others are colonies; some speak English, others Papiamento. Some are prosperous, some are bankrupt. Some are stable democracies, others are failed states. Is it too much of a stretch, then, to try to bring them together? There is a shared heritage that goes all the way back to their very formation. Although the islands stretch across a territory of around 3,000 miles, under the water there are ancient links. Some 50 million years ago, the Greater Antilles islands of Cuba, Jamaica, Hispaniola, Puerto Rico, and the scattered islets of the Bahamas, the Turks and Caicos, and the British Virgin Islands were forged out of tectonic plates, giving the larger of these islands dramatic interior mountain ranges, and carving out deep oceanic troughs, such as the Puerto Rico trench. The backbone of the Caribbean, the small islands of the Lesser Antilles, were formed when the small Caribbean tectonic plate collided with its neighbours, resulting in a string of volcanoes, as the Barbadian writer George Lamming has poetically described it, scattered in a 'curve of dots and distances'.[5] For all that shared past, physical and historical, the twentieth-century fragmentation has persisted. Over the course of my research I realized there was a bumpy road in trying to follow their path, and an even rockier one in putting it in the context of the Americas more broadly. The history of the US is one expressed more confidently, often with narrative arcs involving good guys and bad guys. The story of the Caribbean is more diffused, dappled, a ramble with shadows and light rather than a march to triumph under a blazing sun. The water between the islands has seemingly widened, and they have become consumed, not unreasonably, in understanding their own individual histories.

*

It is a regrettable inevitability that a work such as this must, by its very nature, be the product of a net cast deep and wide. Trawling produces a range of sources – not least of which are the numerous excellent studies in which many dedicated historians mine archives and reveal new insights as to how the West Indies functioned in the past and how it continues to function today. This is the foundation for any general history, and my debt to these historians is great. There are also the limitations of the writer: my primary research interest was the

Spanish Caribbean, while the many years I have lived in Britain took me to the shores of the Anglophone islands. It is not my intention to give short shrift to the French and Dutch (and Danish) islands, but I will be the first to say that my French does not measure up to my Spanish, and my Dutch and Danish require outsourcing. But whatever the language, English included, any mistakes or oversights are most certainly my own. The Caribbean lends itself to the mosaic approach to history – there are so many fragments to use and arrange.

Archives presented more of a challenge – it is far more straightforward to find recent or crucial scholarly books and journals. Looking for undiscovered archival gems can be a needle-in-a-haystack activity, often made more difficult by the elements. For instance, a hurricane can wipe out almost all the holdings, as happened in Bluefields, Nicaragua. Many other repositories have been neglected, though this can be turned around by political will, as the impressive results in the Dominican Republic illustrate. In recent years, too, there have been enormous efforts to preserve what remains by organizations such as Florida International University's Digital Library of the Caribbean. National institutions such as the Archivo General de Indias in Seville have also done a great deal of digitizing, and the wealth of material that can be accessed from home seems to multiply exponentially with every log-on. Though it may seem like a colonial legacy, many important documents about Caribbean history remain either to the north in the United States, or across the Atlantic in Europe. Given that this is the case, and given the rather woeful state of many archives throughout the area, why go there at all? There were hot, flustered, frustrating moments when I asked myself that very question. Yet experiencing the places themselves was an essential part of the writing of this book. Sadly, I could not spend months in each archive, any more than I could hope to visit every place that can be considered part of the region. But for the record, I spent time (in order of appearance) in: Belize, Guatemala, Honduras, Nicaragua, Panama, Dominican Republic, Haiti, Cuba, Jamaica, St Martin, St Eustatius, St Maarten, St Bart's, St Kitts & Nevis, Antigua, Dominica, Martinique, Barbados, Grenada, Trinidad, Guyana, Suriname, Curaçao, Bonaire, and Aruba.

My focus is more on the islands than the surrounding shores, but the area is huge, and the interconnected stories converge and diverge, which means that I cannot claim to have treated each and every island and all the surrounding countries equally. Bermuda, the Bahamas, Venezuela, Colombia, Central America, and some of the smaller islands get relatively little attention against Cuba or Haiti. This is also the case with Mexico. Although Veracruz was an important trade centre within the Caribbean, I limit its role here, as the history of pre- and post-Columbian Mexico have rightly been the subject of numerous books. The same goes for Brazil – a country with a large and complex history of which there are many accounts, and likewise with Colombia and Venezuela.

It may seem contradictory to include Guyana, Suriname, and French Guiana; but I would contend that these three places, two of which are now independent nations, were established in the same spirit as the islands, and in the case of Guyana (Britain) and Suriname (Netherlands), were also in the sugar-and-slavery circuit. French Guiana followed a somewhat different path when sugar failed to take root. Modern Guyana especially is part of the British West Indies; its cricketers and writers part of a Caribbean tradition, rather than a South American one. And, in a way, these three territories are like islands, hemmed in as they are not only by rivers and jungle, but also linguistically, on a continent where Spanish and Portuguese dominate. For this reason, I have given their story more weight than other parts of South America.

In the same vein, tiny Dutch St Eustatius was a key intersection in Atlantic trade networks in the 1700s, though its twentieth-century story is somewhat more muted, whereas Cuba had a quiet beginning while the conquistadors were elsewhere searching for El Dorado, yet by the mid-1800s it dominated the other islands in terms of population and wealth. It is impossible to treat each island equally across time and space; rather, I am trying to put together a large, disparate puzzle. The great French historian Fernand Braudel elegantly summed up this quandary in the introduction to his seminal work on the Mediterranean:

> The basic problem, however, remains the same. It is the problem confronting every historical undertaking. Is it possible somehow to convey simultaneously both that conspicuous history which holds our attention by its continual and dramatic changes – and that other, submerged, history, almost silent and always discreet, virtually unsuspected either by its observers or its participants, which is little touched by the obstinate erosion of time?[6]

This book does not contain every fact about every island. There are no extensive indexes or appendixes on every battle, every sugar shipment, and every planter. Rather, the aim is twofold. The first is to present a picture of this complex region, and how this new world grew out of the violent combination of many others: European, African, Amerindian, Asian, North American, while becoming a crucial link in the global chain of goods, peoples, and ideas. Second, a history of the Caribbean is a chance to meditate on a few modern issues, not least so-called 'globalization' and consumerism. Alongside this, a history of the Caribbean is a chance to think about the contradictions and complexities of the past, and of the present.

Chapter One

A PASSAGE TO THE INDIES

The story of the modern Caribbean does not begin with Christopher Columbus's famous voyage. It starts, instead, in a small port town in northern North Africa, almost within sight of the Iberian peninsula. On 25 July 1415, the feast day of St James, Prince Henry* of Portugal – later known as the 'Navigator' – led a fleet of around 200 ships down the Tagus, which would carry them out of Lisbon and into the Atlantic Ocean. Of an estimated 45,000 soldiers on board, only a handful were aware of their final destination. Rumours had been circulating about the expedition but very few people had actual facts.

Preparing that number of ships and men had been no small operation, and it had attracted some attention. The Portuguese fleet was not sufficient for the plans, whatever they were, so another hundred ships had to be chartered from Castile, Flanders, Brittany, and England.[1] A Castilian agent in Lisbon could not help but notice the ships being readied, and he reported to King Ferdinand I that by his count there were around 5,400 men at arms, 4,900 bowmen, and 9,000 foot-soldiers.[2] This was a worrying development for Castile, as both agent and king expected the Portuguese to head for neighbouring Granada, which was the last Islamic foothold in Catholic Iberia. Once a mighty empire that spread almost over the entire peninsula, Islam was now contracting. As the Islamic caliphate was riven by its own internal crises, the Catholics were able to retake their kingdoms, bit by bit. Granada, at the foothills of the Sierra Nevada mountains, home of the mighty Alhambra palace, was the final – and most highly sought – prize.

---

* For the sake of consistency I will use the anglicized versions of the names of royals throughout the book.

Ferdinand I was surprised by the rumours, not so much because of the scale of the operation but because he thought Henry would have known Castile had laid claim to the right to invade and reconquer Granada.[3] Portugal had reconquered its southern Algarve territories in 1249, but the continued Islamic governance of Granada was a Muslim thorn in the side of the Catholic rulers of Castile. Ferdinand I also considered the idea that the vessels could have been heading for Gibraltar, which was still under Muslim control. He was wrong on both counts.

As the ships set sail, details of the plan emerged. The target was the North African port of Ceuta, 150 miles from the Portuguese coast. Most, if not all, of the soldiers on board would have been surprised when they found out where they were going. Ceuta was a small, peninsular outpost in North Africa with a fortress; it was not a dazzling jewel of a city, like Granada. But what it lacked in splendour it made up for in bustling trade. In Henry's time this port was known for its commerce in wheat and in gold. Ceuta sat at a crucial location; mirrored by the rock of Gibraltar in the north, it was the southern part of the 'Pillars of Hercules' – the gateway to the commercial world of the Mediterranean. It was also the exit to the terrifying and mostly unknown waters of the Atlantic. Whatever the reason, Ceuta was a puzzling choice for an attack. The call to arms against the infidel was not a new motivating factor but the target was. Although battling Islam contributed to Prince Henry's idea for an invasion, it was not his only reason. Gold and wheat loomed large in his mind.

Wheat was a problem for Portugal. The small kingdom had a mountainous interior, and could grow very little, making it dependent on imports. These were too often manipulated by the state of political relations with the Genoese, Dutch, or other exporters of wheat, or more volatile still, the vicissitudes of the climate, which could lead to surpluses in some years and shortages in others. Access to a steady, dependable source of grain could have manifold benefits, and Ceuta was the place to access it. And then there was the matter of gold. Many people believed that Ceuta was the last link in the long supply chain that connected the Mediterranean with the rumoured riches that lay deep in the unknown African interior. When it came to gold, no European ruler could stockpile enough of it. Certainly not Henry, the third of five surviving sons of John I of Portugal and Philippa of Lancaster and raised to expect the courtly splendour of his counterparts in England. But unlike England,

Portugal's population was tiny – only about a million people, most of whom were eking out an existence; taxing them would not raise sufficient revenues. Indeed, Portugal did not even issue its own gold currency. What money there was had to be spent on the ongoing struggle against the growing power of Castile, which had been brought to a temporary halt under a treaty signed in 1411.

Born in Porto on Ash Wednesday, 4 March 1394, Henry was a devout Catholic. He was schooled in the chivalric ways of England, as imparted by his Plantagenet mother, while also being infused with a hatred of the 'infidel' Moors by his family.[4] This attack on Ceuta was to be his moment, his stance against Islam, but it was also his chance to improve his own fortunes. This was not unusual. In Castile, the armies that had fought against the Moors were led by noblemen who were allowed to keep some of the spoils of war. Henry was acting within this tradition, but hoping, by extending his geographical reach, to find something more.

Into the mix of grain, gold, and God would also be added the figure of Prester John, a mythical Christian who had travelled to a faraway land (often Ethiopia), where he had become king and had access to enough gold and soldiers to defeat all enemies of Christendom. He had an army strong enough to fend off any rising menace from Islam and the growing power of the Ottoman world. If only Prester John knew what dangers were in store for his Christian brothers, so the thinking went, he would send his armies to defeat the infidels. And, of course, he had a lot of gold. Although Prester John haunted the medieval world, no evidence proves that he actually existed, though he was alive in the minds of Henry and his contemporaries. The account of who Prester John was varies through the centuries, changing with the wishes and anxieties of whoever wrote and talked about him. Henry certainly appeared to believe the story. He thought that by securing Ceuta, the Portuguese would not only have a stronghold in the Muslim Mediterranean and access to wheat supplies, but that they could then penetrate into the hinterland, find Prester John, and share in his riches. Henry was not alone in this desire – the legend of Prester John had existed since the Crusades began more than 300 years earlier, and the story compelled people to search for him and his treasure. Henry's unwavering belief in Prester John and his desire for gold would have ramifications that would reach well beyond the confines of Ceuta's fortress.

As Henry's ships set sail that July across the Straits of Gibraltar, there was an ominous eclipse of the sun. The storm that followed drove the fleet back to Algeciras, on the southern coast of Andalusia, where they had to lie at anchor. Meanwhile, the governor of Ceuta, Salah ben Salah, had received word of the fleet's arrival and was on the brink of calling in reinforcements when he heard that the would-be attackers had turned away and presumed they had changed their minds. Ben Salah's assumption would prove to be disastrous. He called off the extra troops, and so was in for a very unpleasant surprise on 21 August when, after a thirteen-hour fight, the Marinid people of Ceuta were defeated.[5] In the style of the victorious, the Portuguese troops looted the city, searching everywhere for the fabled gold. They found little precious metal, but in their lust for it, they managed to destroy stocks of valuable spices, ignorant of the fact that these exotic flavourings were often worth their weight in gold.

As the Portuguese settled into occupation and the local inhabitants fled, it soon became clear that the enterprise was an economic failure. Henry's troops had taken over Ceuta, and the prince established his reputation, but it was a hollow victory. The Muslim traders – the vital conduits of wheat and gold – had left, and no Muslim merchants from the wheat-growing interior would do business with the Portuguese. With such slim economic prospects, no one from the mainland wanted to settle there, and so soldiers were forced to stay in the colony.* The longed-for gold was nowhere to be found. But Henry was not deterred. The search had begun.

Despite his sobriquet, there is little evidence Henry the Navigator ever sailed beyond Ceuta.† Instead, it was in his role as a leading ship owner that Henry contributed to the rise of Portugal's maritime domi-

---

* This, however, did not prevent another attack, this time a disastrous failure, in 1437, on Tangiers, led by Henry's brother, Ferdinand. After complicated negotiations, Henry reneged on his deal to exchange his captured brother for Ceuta, leaving him to die. Ceuta stayed under Portuguese control until 1668, when it passed into Spanish hands under the Treaty of Lisbon, and is today an autonomous city governed by Spain. Tangiers was eventually won by Portugal in 1471, though today it is part of Morocco.

† With Henry's partial English heritage, the English liked to claim him as their own. Seventeenth-century geographers Samuel Purchas and Richard Hakluyt hailed Henry's exploits as exemplifying the natural English gift for navigation, and it is around this time the nickname emerged. Henry's image was later appropriated by Portugal's dictatorships from 1926 to 1974.

nation in the fifteenth century, which resulted in part from his triumph in Ceuta. Although something of a false victory, Henry and others had tasted overseas conquest – not peninsular reconquest. The prince and fellow elites understood that access to gold was crucial not only to their own personal fortunes, but for overall prosperity, to fund the ongoing struggle against Islam, and to find Prester John. Henry was buoyed by his success, and he pushed Castile to invade Granada in 1419 and 1434, but that battle would be not be fought for decades yet.

Around the time of Henry's foray into North Africa, there were profound changes in maritime techniques in the Mediterranean. Sailing in the fifteenth century was a cumbersome process, as it had been for hundreds of years. Galleys needed oarsmen, which meant they could neither go far nor carry much. Space was needed for the gangs of men on the oars and sufficient water and food for everyone on board. Explorers were limited as well, though the Vikings are believed to have reached parts of North America centuries earlier. But as shipbuilding design changed, some intrepid Portuguese were able to engage in a more systematic exploration of the Atlantic, then known as the 'Ocean Sea', well beyond the limits of the known waters of the Mediterranean. The crucial element in this change was the design of the caravel. Many of the earlier ships were cogs, which were Baltic in origin, and had rounded hulls. They were designed to sail using currents, not wind – although they had a square-rigged sail – and could only go relatively short distances. The design of the caravel – which, and it is no coincidence, bears a relation to the Arab *dhow* – used lateen, or fore-and-aft, sails which allowed the ships to manoeuvre with more ease and sail closer to the wind. The Chinese, too, had used new technologies to travel further, arriving on the African coast in the 1400s. They also had gunpowder and compasses – but that was because they had invented them.[6] And while these discoveries may have seemed very exciting and new to the Portuguese, it was only because Western Europe was so very far behind much of the rest of the world. In the fifteenth century China, the Indian kingdoms and the Islamic world had produced scientific discoveries well ahead of those coming out of a Europe emerging from the Dark Ages. But shifts were happening again, and the combination of Islamic weakness and a European resurgence meant the balance of power in the Mediterranean was changing.

For Portuguese and other European sailors, the switch from

manpower to wind power would prove a dramatic one. These ships needed fewer men, and could go further than their predecessors. Around the time of the attack on Ceuta in 1415, the known southern limit of the world was around 27°N, near Cape Bojador (on the coast of today's Western Sahara). It was infamous for having a violent current, frequent dense fog, and difficult prevailing winds that could frustrate any attempt to sail back north to Lisbon. Arab geographers were more familiar with this region than the Portuguese and called it the 'Green Sea of Darkness'. To many sailors and map-makers it marked a true point of no return. But the Portuguese caravels could weather the journey and soon began to round the cape and find they could, with the help of the wind, make their way back. The sailors' newfound confidence helped override their fear of the blank spots on their maps.

Bit by bit, wave by wave, Portuguese sailors began to make sense of the currents and winds, realizing there were patterns that would allow them to go beyond the Pillars of Hercules into the unknown, and return in one piece. Using their intuition, logic, and experience, they soon discovered they could bump southwards along Africa's western coast by harnessing the winds to sail further into the Atlantic and catch the westerlies back home. Ocean currents in the northern hemisphere move in a clockwise direction. Understanding this was the trick – if they sailed too close to the coast on the way back, the northerlies could wreak havoc, as had happened in the past, sending ships into oblivion. By expanding their loop, sailors could catch the winds they needed. Soon mariners saw there was a mostly reliable pattern to these winds. The stars helped, too; after crossing the equator, sailors familiar with navigating using the position of Polaris in relation to the horizon were able to make calculations using different celestial bodies.[7]

New realizations dawned on map-makers as well. Some of the earliest known European maps from around the eighth century are called T-O maps, which were symbolic rather than cartographic. They were framed in a circle, with Asia taking up the top half, and the bottom half split between Africa and Europe. The T shape represented the Mediterranean, the Nile, and the River Don in Russia, which separated Europe and Asia.[8] Maps were the physical embodiment of a Christianized world, and they became almost devotional objects. They charted spiritual realities, not geographic ones. Jerusalem was usually at the centre, as it was supposed to represent the spiritual heart of the Christian universe. But over time, and fed by reports from sailors, maps began to change shape. Newer maps reflected geographic realities. Portolan charts had emerged by the 1300s as a navigational aid, the maps often looking like spiders' webs of criss-crossing lines and compass points of sailing routes. The Crusaders had brought back to Europe a physical knowledge of parts of the East, and now sailors were adding to the understanding of the seas outside the Mediterranean.[9] Some places became hubs of cartographic activity, such as the Balearic island of Majorca, which lies close to the port of Barcelona. It had a community of influential Jewish mapmakers, including Abraham Cresques, whose famed and elaborate Catalan Atlas of 1375 marked the location of the elusive River of Gold in Africa.

There were new political realities too, as kingdoms such as Castile and Aragon consolidated into stronger political entities. Port cities throughout Europe were no longer outposts, but increasingly vital commercial and strategic arms of an expanding continent. Combined with the ongoing battle with Islam, a Europe began to emerge that was pushing at the limits of knowledge and of the known world. As commerce now took an ever-increasing role not only in Portugal but also in emerging economies elsewhere, the need for gold and silver, in short supply in Europe, grew.[10]

As the Portuguese sailors, funded by the optimistic Henry and others, made their way along the coast of Africa, they soon encountered the people who lived there. By 1482, when Diogo Cão pushed inland and made contact with the kingdom of Kongo, there was already a good deal of commerce with the people along the coast. These Africans, like the Portuguese, were quite happy to trade, and soon Portuguese sailors had established settlements to trade and continue their hunt for gold. A new age was beginning, reflected even in the language. In Portugal, by 1472, the verb *descobrir* – to discover – had emerged, and the use of *descobrimento* – discovery – dates to 1486.[11] Sailors based in Lisbon could expect to go to these African outposts as a matter of course, as well as to points further north, such as Bristol, Ireland, and even Iceland, as a young Genoese mariner named Christopher Columbus* was said to have done in the 1470s.

---

* Columbus is a man of many names. The Genoese version is Cristoforo Colombo, Portuguese Cristóvão Colombo, and Spanish is Cristóbol Colón. This text will use the anglicized spelling.

Understanding Columbus requires more than just knowing about his maritime record. It means going back to his world; not the ports of Lisbon, nor the courts of Castile, but Genoa, circa 1451–2, the given time of his birth. He was not born with a map in hand and an idea of the New World. Rather, he was the product of a time and a place; a small but significant Ligurian port which sits in the shadow of the Apennine mountains. At first, Genoa appears a simple city. But a closer look reveals a self-contained world, cut off from the rest of the Italian peninsula, with only the sea as an exit. Its cramped streets accelerate into an ever-increasing jumble as they near the docks, with only the coming and going of ships providing an outlet into the wider world.

Like its rivals Venice and Pisa, Genoa had prospered during the Crusades, when the Christian soldiers in the Middle East established trade agreements with those ports, using them to their advantage, not only to launch ships and move troops, but also to trade goods with the markets in the Levant. This line of commerce proved lucrative, and soon these city-states grew very wealthy. However, the waters were awash with Muslim ships and pirates ready to plunder, and despite their growing disputes – Genoa, Pisa, and Venice often fought among themselves – these cities were united in the effort to repel them. In these and earlier times, Islam had dominated Mediterranean trade. Muslim sailors had more advanced navigation techniques than Christians, and from the eighth century their piracy was also striking terror into Europeans on sea and land. Their technical prowess and ruthlessness made them a constant worry.

Trade was not only to the Levant, though, and despite the religious animosity, Genoa often made commercial transactions with ports along the coast of North Africa. Venice, in contrast, looked more to the East and became more enmeshed with Byzantium. The East was known as the land of riches, and luxury goods such as silks and spices came up to Europe along the Silk Road, though often in very limited supply, thus commanding the high prices which made them available only to the wealthy.

Although Genoa did not have the same access as Venice to the riches of the East, it prospered and soon became not only a centre for the distribution of goods and the circulation of currency, but also – its tangled streets full of sailors and tall tales – an important place for map-makers, shipbuilders, and adventurers. Perhaps one of the most significant sailors to wash up in Genoa was Marco Polo. The thirteenth-century Venetian explorer had been thrown in a Genoese prison after being captured in a naval battle between the two city-states.

While in prison, he told the story of his amazing (and no doubt exaggerated) travels to the East to his cellmate, a man called Rustichello of Pisa. Rustichello later published this traveller's tales of meeting and his subsequent service to Kublai Khan and his voyage to Persia and other exotic locales. The work captured the imagination of the public, who were ignorant of but curious about these parts of the world. But the book also mentioned some familiar figures, and even Prester John made an appearance. Soon the work was translated, copied and distributed throughout Western Europe. Although the Silk Road from East to West, along which gold and spices were traded, had long been in operation, Polo's tales made the splendours of the Far East come alive for the growing number of European readers with descriptions of the Orient. Polo recalled of the palace of Kublai Khan: 'The walls of the chambers and stairs are covered with gold and silver, and adorned with pictures of dragons, horses, and other races of animals. The hall is so spacious that 6,000 can sit down to banquet; and the number of apartments incredible.'[12] But more importantly, these tales whetted the appetites of sailors and merchants keen to find an easier route to these treasures. Columbus would have read Polo at some point as his tales were still circulating many decades later. But even putting Polo's stories aside, Genoa would have provided a cosmopolitan hothouse for the young and ambitious Columbus.

He was the son of a weaver, which put him at a social and economic disadvantage in a town where the wealthy made their fortunes in trading. His family were from the mountains, not the sea. Like most people in Genoa, they were very politicized, and Columbus's family were linked with anti-Aragonese factions in the city, as the kingdom of Aragon was also a competitor in the world of Mediterranean trade. His education in complex Mediterranean and Iberian politics would later serve him well. Despite Columbus's humble beginnings, Genoa was still a city in which an eager and willing young man could seek his fortune, and he planned to do so through the sea. Indeed, in his time the city was particularly dynamic, and Genoa had spread its control to Corsica, and indeed as far as the Aegean island of Chios, a place that Columbus may have sailed to around 1474 or 1475, not long before he arrived in Portugal.

This was a period of intense commercial activity in the Mediterranean, one which stretched from Egypt to England. Columbus's contemporaries would have sailed to Southampton and Alexandria and many points in between. Trading posts were set up as oils, sugar, spices, and cloth circulated. Olive oil and nuts went from Sicily to Egypt.[13] Other goods were sent to Flanders and traded for cloth, which would be taken around the Mediterranean. Ships would dock in Spain and trade wool and gold, with the wool going either to Tuscany or to weavers in Genoa such as Columbus's father. Cities began to fill with traders, and ships were dispatched all over the region. Venetian ships went East; Aragonese ships arrived in Genoa; Pisan ships went to Sicily.

There was another, darker trade as well – one in humans. Slavery had long been a part of Mediterranean life. At first, it was the Moorish sailors who brought non-believing captives from other regions of Africa to the Iberian peninsula, where they were traded throughout European kingdoms. But Moors were also captured and sold as slaves, and Columbus no doubt would have seen Moorish slaves in the streets of his native city. The slave trade, however, was not limited to people from the Islamic world. Slaves in this period varied in background – there were Germanic and Slavic people,[*] Tartars from the Black Sea, Saracens, and even Jews. Nor were they all men, to be worked to an early death, but often women. The whiter they were, the higher the price they fetched. The more olive or darker-skinned, the lower their value.[14] A few Africans began to arrive at the ports, too. But unlike what was to come later, they were not sent out to work in fields. Instead, many lived as servants in ports such as Lisbon or Seville.[15]

Most slaves lived in households, and in Genoa they were owned in small numbers, yet there were numerous social restrictions in place. For instance, shopkeepers were not permitted to sell keys to slaves, or to buy gold or silver from them, and slaves in apothecaries were not allowed to sell arsenic. Slaves also needed passes from their owners to leave the city, and masters could chain their property to prevent them from running away.[16] By this point, the Catalan port of Barcelona had also joined the slave trade. The city had grown throughout the

---

[*] The word 'slave' has linguistic roots in the enslaved 'Slav'.

1200s, and it was in a prime location to buy human cargo from the Muslim slave traders of North Africa. At the same time, Sicily was beginning to experiment in the production of sugar, as knowledge of its cultivation spread from east to west, south to north. As this precious food additive moved through Genoa, Antwerp, and Barcelona, a new class of wealthy consumers began to acquire a taste for it. All these developments were disrupted, however, when the Black Death killed tens of thousands of people across the Mediterranean and the rest of Europe in 1348–9.

By the time of Columbus's birth, Genoa's fortunes were waning somewhat. After the fall of Constantinople in 1453 to the Ottomans, it began to decline, soon relinquishing its colonies and settlements. The Turks took outposts in Phocaea and Lesbos, while the Venetians grabbed Cyprus. Chios, however, persisted under Genoese control until 1566. Genoa adapted, and many merchants began to realize that, rather than trading in goods, it was much safer to be in control of the capital that financed expeditions. Many Genoese would later become important financiers of European royal houses and Atlantic expeditions.

The rhythms of trade were also changing. While Genoa and Venice had been active in commerce with the Crusader states, there was a shifting to the north as Catalan ships sailed to Flemish or even English waters, searching for goods such as wool. Genoa could no longer look to the East for trade, and its merchants saw Catalan and Portuguese traders in strong positions. At the same time, the labour dynamics were transformed as the price of slaves more than doubled owing to the fall in supply, and by the 1470s there were fewer than 1,000 slaves in the port. Genoese traders tried to find new slaves from the Balkans, but many of these were Christian women, and there was some concern about enslaving fellow believers, a question that would also later reson-ate in distant lands. By the time Columbus decided to go to Lisbon, Genoa was not quite the beacon of commerce it had been, but there is no doubt its history left a deep impression – the bustle of the port, the lure of wealth, the normality of slavery, the taste of sugar – on its most famous son's earliest years.

*

Columbus's move to Portugal around 1476, whether by design or accident, was an astute one. He had left a port on the decline for one that was not only on the rise, but also on the cutting edge of navigational knowledge. Sailors returned from voyages with tales of coastal Africa and of the Atlantic islands. In addition, the public imagination had been gripped by the growing accounts of these new worlds. Sailors and scholars alike reinvigorated the art of discovery. Ptolemy's second-century *Geographia*, and *Almagest*, which described how the sun rotated around the earth – considered the foundation of the universe until Copernicus shattered the idea in the mid-sixteenth century – were translated into Latin in the twelfth century. Now there was a thirst to revisit this classical knowledge. The boom in navigational work meant many sailors and map-makers were once again keen to read Ptolemy's ideas, which included dividing the world into latitude and longitude segments. Sailors were also paying attention to the sun and stars, and while on board Columbus learned lessons that would serve him well on later voyages.

In a similar vein, Polo's tales were once again read with renewed enthusiasm – a 1485 translation into vernacular languages published in Antwerp was popular – but this time they were also infused with possibility. In addition, the development of printing technology allowed for a larger and wider readership. Like many sailors, Columbus would have read these books, or at least discussed their ideas while making tavern small talk about big dreams of what was to be found in the Ocean Sea. The Far East, perhaps, was not so far after all. There is a copy of Polo's book in Seville that, it is claimed, has Columbus's annotations in it. If this is the case, he marked a passage about Polo's arrival in Ciampagu (or Cipango), which is thought to be Japan:

> There is gold there in very great abundance, but the monarch does not easily permit it to be taken away from the island, and consequently few traders go there, and rarely do ships from other regions land at its ports. The king of the island has a large palace with a very fine gold roof, in the manner in which we line churches with lead. The windows of this palace are all trimmed with gold, and the paving in the halls and many rooms is covered with slabs of gold, which are two fingers thick ... There are also many precious stones, and for this reason the island of Ciampagu is marvellously rich.[17]

Later on in the work, Columbus also noted a section that mentions India as having many islands, as Polo claims: 'The number of islands in India is so numerous that no living being could recount all their qualities. So the sailors and pilots of those regions affirm, and from what is known from the sea charts and from observing the compasses of the Indian sea, there are 1,378 islands at least in the sea, and all, they say, are inhabited.'[18]

Though it is difficult to know if those truly are Columbus's annotations, it is easy to see how he could be misled. Reading Polo, it was possible to believe that a route to the East was not so hard to find after all, and that when he got there he would find many islands and lots of gold. Yet everyone – including Columbus – knew of the dangers of such dreams. However rapid the changes and developments in navigation, the likelihood of sailing into oblivion was still high. Tales circulated about the daring souls who ventured beyond the known boundaries and did not live to come back, such as Flemish mariner Ferdinand von Olmen, who set out with a commission from the Portuguese crown to find new lands in 1487 and was never heard of again.[19]

Sailing, even in the new caravels, was a tough life. The distances were significant – it still took about five days to go from Lisbon to the Gibraltar Straits. And there were persistent fears of attack or capture by Islamic pirates in the Mediterranean. Proper provisioning was also a worry – even if sailors were in a caravel, they needed their daily ration of half a kilogram of sea-biscuit each. Likewise, there needed to be plenty of fresh water and, of course, wine.

Throughout this period, Columbus was becoming not only an experienced mariner, but a very ambitious one. By his calculations, he believed he could navigate a passage to the East – he just had to convince someone to pay for it. After failed attempts elsewhere, he arrived in Seville in 1485 with no money, but with plans to turn to the united crowns of Ferdinand II of Aragon and Isabella I of Castile and hope they would believe in his vision.

Such an enterprise, however, was far from the minds of the Catholic monarchs. They had married in 1469, and in 1474, after the death of Isabella's half-brother King Henry IV, began to rule as one the two kingdoms that would give them control of most of the Iberian peninsula, which by this time was made up of the three Christian realms of Castile, Aragon, and Portugal. 'Spain', such as it was, took its name from the Roman Hispania, and in the Middle Ages the word described the Iberian peninsula, not a country in any modern sense. The monarchs' concerns were focused on Granada, which remained under Muslim control. The issue that had so bothered Prince Henry more than fifty years before still had not been resolved. The fall of Constantinople to the Ottoman Turks in 1453 had not been so long ago, and Christian ascendancy was far from assured in this long-running battle. There had been a distraction, however, as the marriage of Ferdinand and Isabella had been followed from 1474–9 by a war of succession over control of the crown of Castile. Had Isabella's half-sister Joanna la Beltraneja been victorious, Castile would have been united with Portugal, not Aragon. At this point, Castile comprised about 65 per cent of the peninsula's area, and Aragon about 17 per cent, including Catalonia and Valencia and their crucial ports, as well as Sardinia and Sicily, of which the Aragonese had wrested control by 1409, and Naples.

By late 1481, the Catholic monarchs had started to attack parts of Granada, and by the 1490s they began what would be the final push. They were firm believers in the need to Christianize the world, though at this point the world to them meant the land bordering the Mediterranean Sea. The year 1492 was a landmark one for Ferdinand and Isabella. On 2 January, almost 800 years of Muslim rule on the Iberian peninsula was brought to an end. They made a triumphant entrance into Granada on 6 January. Not only was there a celebration of the immediate victory, but, like Henry's victory in Ceuta seventy-seven years earlier, this defeat of Islam marked the arrival of a renewed confidence. The Reconquista, as it was known, was followed by a bloody attempt to rid the peninsula of non-Christians. Ferdinand and Isabella soon demanded that any remaining Muslims convert or leave, and the same applied to Jews, many of whom were forced into exile around Europe. This was not the first time this had happened to the Jews – the pogroms of 1391 had forced many of them to convert or leave, and it was in this period that the seeds of the obsession with limpieza de sangre – purity of blood – were planted.

Although the Portuguese shared the fierce Catholicism of Castile and Aragon, their king realized it was better to tolerate the unconverted – with their capital and mercantile links – than to drive them off the peninsula altogether. Jewish people therefore found a home in Portugal, albeit a short-term one (they were expelled once more in 1497). Many Muslims and Jews, however, opted for conversion, though others felt compelled to leave under the relentless persecution of the Inquisition. These Muslim *moriscos* and Jewish *conversos* would play an important part in events on the other side of the Atlantic, though in many cases the Inquisition would give them no respite there either.

Columbus, in his initial forays to find financing for his expedition before coming to Seville, had turned to Portuguese, English, and French investors, all of whom declined to take part in what they thought was a rather unlikely adventure. Many were not persuaded by his calculations. But Columbus did manage to convince two friars in Andalusía, Juan Pérez and Antonio de Marchena, who had the ear of Isabella and could give him credibility in court. With the Reconquista finished, and the expulsion or conversion of non-Christians in progress, the monarchs could once again turn their attention away from domestic affairs.

They were both enticed by the riches of the East, which could also help to recoup the cost of fighting in Granada. They, too, would have known the stories of Marco Polo and of the work of the Jesuit missionaries who had travelled the long route to the East, and later sent reports back to Europe. They would have been delighted at the prospect of their newly united and powerful kingdom of Castile and Aragon making its presence known among other non-believers. It was almost too tempting to resist: the gold and spices of the Orient, as well as new peoples ripe for conversion. Columbus, by this point, had been following the court around the peninsula, using every opportunity to drum up support for his venture. Many of the crown's advisers, however, were reluctant to believe this unknown Genoese sailor. Although he had made some important connections in Portugal and married well, his relative obscurity did not inspire confidence. Columbus was not unique in wanting to find a sea route to Asia, though he was original in believing that it could be reached from the west, via the Ocean Sea. Some palace advisers checked his calculations and found them lacking. As it turned out, Columbus thought there were 2,400 nautical miles separating Castile from Cipango, when it was closer to 10,600.[20] Still, the queen was intrigued. Perhaps it was the promise of wealth, or the crown's own spirit of adventure, or simple post-Reconquista confidence. Perhaps, as some historians have argued,

Columbus won over the queen for more sentimental reasons – Isabella's great-grandfather was King John I of Portugal, her grandfather was Prince John, and her great-uncle was Prince Henry. Although Columbus was Genoese, his Portuguese connections did him no harm.[21]

Negotiations began, and Columbus stood firm in many of his demands, not least in the matter of what he would receive for his efforts. He demanded the title of admiral in addition to that of viceroy over any lands he claimed on behalf of the crown, and one-tenth of the profits, including a share of the rights to those lands; perhaps it was greedy, or simply the worldview of a Genoese merchant who, tradition dictated, should receive a share of the spoils.[22] He was also a weaver's son with ambitions to outdo his father and bequeath his sons not only money but also a title. While the rewards were full of promise, the failure of such a mission would have a high price: humiliation, monetary loss, and perhaps even death. The Ocean Sea was still the great beyond. But the race to the East had been on for some time, inching ever closer to the coveted route: the Portuguese navigator Bartolomeu Días rounded the Cape of Good Hope in 1488.

By 17 April 1492 Columbus had received the backing and the terms he wanted for his voyage. The preparations started in earnest. There were two caravels and a larger ship called a não. The caravels were the *Santa Clara*, which became known as the *Niña* after the owner, Juan Niño, and the *Pinta*, owned by Cristóbal Quintero. Columbus also chartered the *Santa María*, owned by Juan de la Cosa, which was called *La Gallega* because it was built in Galicia. Columbus then engaged shipowner Martín Alonso Pinzón, and his brother, Vicente, to raise the crew and take command of the *Pinta* and *Niña*. It was a bold mission, and an uncertain one, but the Pinzón brothers still managed to find around ninety men, only three of whom were prisoners. The rest wanted to sail into these unknown waters and were willing to join in the adventure.

Four months later, on 3 August 1492, Columbus set off from Palos, near Huelva, on the Costa de la Luz. It was not quite a launch into the unknown: Columbus stopped at the Canary island of La Gomera along the way. The winds from there gave the ships a solid start. Setting off from La Gomera on 6 September 1492, they caught the north-east trade winds, which blew them west. But after that, the only certainty was Columbus's obsession with finding the East.

It would be more than a month from La Gomera until the next landfall. They had calm seas and good weather, and were soon sailing through the grasses of the Sargasso Sea, which might have scared them into turning back had Columbus not already been warned about them – in a fortuitous turn – by an old mariner.[23] Columbus and his men then spotted birds, a sign that land must be near. They still had enough water to last for some time, and there was plenty of sea-biscuit and salted meat. On 25 September the *Pinta* issued a signal that land had been spotted, but it turned out to be a mirage. Despite the smooth sailing and a good stock of provisions, there was a near-mutiny by 6 October as worried sailors on the *Santa María* wanted to turn back. However, these fears were assuaged, for the time being. Then, six days later, the *Pinta* signalled yet again that land had been found. As it was almost midnight, crew members did not row ashore until the following morning. When they did, they took a royal banner, with a green cross and the letters F and Y on it, planted it in the sand, and declared the land for the Catholic monarchs.* Columbus called the island San Salvador.† They had done it. They had made it to Cipango.

When Columbus later recounted the journey he wrote that 'I found a great many islands inhabited by countless people.' If this is what he indeed found, it should have raised some alarm in his mind. The overland route to the East was well travelled by Columbus's time, and although there was every possibility that there indeed were islands in the Indian Ocean, as Polo claimed, the story Columbus began to tell does not add up to anything approximating Japan, India, or the East at all.

This landing must have been the most confusing moment of Columbus's life. No one can know the expanse of his fecund imagination, fed by stories of Oriental splendour. Whatever he dreamt the East looked like, to be certain it did not match what he saw. There was no gold, there were no palaces. He spoke with some of the Amerindians on this island but soon decided to keep looking. So on he sailed, certain that there must be something, anything. Columbus had encountered the islands of the Caribbean, and it was not what he had bargained

---

* The letters I and Y were often used interchangeably in this period, e.g. Ysabel.

† There is some dispute as to where this original landing took place, but the consensus is that it was on an island in the Bahamas today known, again, as San Salvador, but which used the name Watling Island for many years.

for. So he was going to make his dream come true in quite a literal way. Desire would triumph over reason.

After meeting a few people, and realizing there was little to trade, and little sign of gold, Columbus continued to push the ships to explore the area, landing in Cuba, which he gave the short-lived name of Johanna, later incorrectly remarking that 'I can say that the island is bigger than England and Scotland taken together.'[24] Before long they found a much larger island, which they christened Hispaniola, although its aboriginal name is thought to have been Quisqueya (meaning 'mother of all lands') and also Ayti (meaning 'mountainous lands').[25] Once they arrived in Hispaniola, Columbus later noted, he saw that 'its inhabitants (and those of all the other islands that I saw or learned of) always go naked as the day they were born, except that some women cover their private parts with a leaf or a spray of foliage, or a piece of common cloth which they make for the purpose'. This might have been another clue that he had not landed in the Orient: given that silks came from there, that he had landed among people who wore no cloth at all might be considered a significant fact. But despite all evidence to the contrary, Columbus insisted he was in the East.

He faced a considerable problem when the *Santa María* ran aground and was no longer seaworthy. With the support of one of the local rulers, known as Guacanagarí, Columbus decided to leave thirty-nine of his men to erect a settlement he called – it was close to Christmas – La Navidad. He charged the men with setting up a gold mine and left Hispaniola.

He then decided to return to Europe on 16 January 1493 with the few nuggets of gold he had managed to find, tropical produce, colourful parrots, and some Lucayo people they had baptized and whom Columbus wanted to show to Ferdinand and Isabella as proof of his success. The native people, he wrote, were convinced 'that I have come down from heaven'. Whether or not they were frightened by this, Columbus managed to persuade, no doubt with force, some of them into his ship. He said of these captives, 'whenever we made landfall, some of them [called] to the rest, "Come, come and see the men from heaven".'[26] Historian Matthew Restall has pointed out that the word for heaven in Spanish is the same as sky: *cielo*. There is, of course, no way of knowing what native word Columbus heard, or whether *cielo* is correct in the first place. But the ambiguity means that Columbus and his men could have been described as coming from the sky, or as gods from heaven, the latter having much more serious implications.[27]

The Europeans were quick to attempt to communicate, and try to find native peoples to act as interpreters. It is impossible to know what was understood or lost in translation, but Columbus claimed that 'in a short time we got to understand them, and they us, by combination of sign-language and words', though no one could really answer the question 'Where is the gold?' quite to the admiral's satisfaction. They would need a return voyage to work that out, by which time the islanders would not be so quick to welcome these strange-looking men in their large boats.

The ease of the journey out was not matched on the return. Although the Caribbean current snakes up from the south through to the west, Columbus and his men only had a limited notion of the trade winds, and had yet to understand how to harness the west-to-east flow of the Gulf Stream. It was a slow trip. There were terrible storms and problems with the ships. They had to land in the Azores on 18 February to make repairs. They set off again, and were separated through bad weather. The Niña, with Columbus on board, finally limped into Palos after being forced to stop near Lisbon, while the Pinta had washed up to the north, in Bayona, Galicia, before returning to the southern port. Despite the difficult journey back, to say nothing of the fact that the East he had discovered bore no resemblance to any East ever written about, Columbus was triumphant. He showcased the products and people he found in this New World, and all of Europe was enthralled. He brought with him 'Indians', as well as gold, plants and animals. The public was mesmerized.

Word spread across Europe, to Rome, Paris, Antwerp, and Basel, aided by the rapid circulation of a copy of Columbus's letter to the Spanish monarchs. This correspondence was said to have been translated from the original Castilian to Latin by Leandro de Cosco in 1493. It was so popular it went through nine printings in that year alone. Even a German version was published. There is no way of knowing or measuring exactly how far the story of the voyage spread, but the tales of Columbus's crossing into the unknown and his discovery of another world must have captured the imagination of thousands. Soon, Columbus's exploits were enshrined in verse, when a Florentine priest named Giuliano Dati turned the letter into a poem, *Lettera delle isole nuovamente* *trovate.* Columbus also kept his own journal of the trip, which was lost but is alleged to have resurfaced in the sixteenth century.*

In many ways, Europe's initial encounter with the Caribbean was more accident than destiny, and Columbus was a stubborn egotist rather than navigational genius. He never admitted he had found something other than the East. But his journey, its consequences for better or worse, emerged out of a Europe in flux, a Christianized world gaining ground against its more advanced rivals. Europe's trade and commerce were growing, and its people were developing new ideas about the world, and the things (and people) that could be bought and sold within it. Meanwhile, sailors were going further and understanding winds and tides with more scientific precision. Within decades, Europe, Africa, the Americas, and the Far East would be connected by the sixteenth century's superhighway: the sea. And for decades to come, satisfying the desire to see these new places would entail a long, arduous, and dangerous journey, but the number of people who took to the seas never diminished. The New World was the missing link. It is here that the development of the Caribbean and its slavery and sugar fields begins. However, there were a few more places between the Old World and the New that were crucial in linking their fortunes: the islands of the Atlantic.

---

* Columbus's journal was transcribed and annotated by a Dominican friar, Bartolomé de las Casas (see Chapter 2). That Columbus's journal ended up in this particular friar's hands is, if not a simple historical irony, perhaps cause for a degree of wariness. Indeed, Casas inserts his own ideas into the text by summarizing Columbus's notes so that the text flits between first person and 'the Admiral said'. But it is all that remains.

Chapter Two

STEPPING STONES TO THE
NEW WORLD

Columbus's stop in La Gomera, in the Canary Islands, on his first voyage was no accident. By the time his fleet had set off, this archipelago off the coast of North Africa was already a well-known colony of Castile. Indeed, as early as the first century AD, Pliny the Elder had mentioned the Atlantic islands in his writings, calling them 'Canaria'. How much was known about the islands then is difficult to ascertain, but in the new age of exploration it was only a matter of time before these seven islands, sixty miles off the coast of North Africa and hundreds of miles from the Iberian peninsula, were rediscovered. Some accounts put the re-entry of Europeans into the Canaries sometime around 1312 when a Genoese sailor, Lanzarotto Malocello, was said to have arrived on one of them, though little is known about what transpired.[1] Other expeditions followed, including one claimed to be commissioned by Portugal's Afonso IV in 1341. Details are scarce, but the islands began to appear on maps.

After an initial flurry of exploratory activity from the Genoese, Castilians, and Portuguese, the islands lay quiet for a while. By the time two Normans, Jean de Béthencourt and Gadifer de la Salle, met in La Rochelle in 1402, interest in the islands had waned. Béthencourt was a noble who was possibly in search of a fortune to pay off debts. He had tried to convince the French crown to back his plans, to no avail, which is why he ended up turning to Castile.[2] He may have been on the hunt for gold, but he might also have been looking to enslave some of the native Guanche people to sell. There were also trees on the islands whose resin had been sold to be transformed into a valuable dye known as 'dragon's blood'. Of course, Béthencourt also had to claim they wanted to introduce Christianity to the unbelievers. Salle, a knight, told Béthencourt he was looking to find his fortune. So on 1 May 1402 they, along with a crew, embarked for the 'lands of Canary, to see and explore all the country, with the view of conquering the islands, and bringing the people to the Christian faith', according to an account written by a friar and a priest who participated in the voyage.[3]

Soon they met a 'foul wind' and were forced to stop in Galicia for a few days, and then headed south, stopping in the Andalus port of Cádiz. Béthencourt got into trouble there, as he had made no friends in Galicia and 'Genoese, Placentian, and English merchants . . . brought accusations against him . . . that he and his crew were robbers'. While Béthencourt was trying to straighten out this misunderstanding, a rumour spread that his ships did not have enough supplies for the journey, and twenty-seven men left the expedition. Finally, the situation was resolved and eight days later they arrived on a tiny island they named Graciosa, which is near the larger island of Lanzarote, the easternmost of the chain. These volcanic islands were formed thousands of years ago, and their climate is mostly arid; the desert-like desolation is augmented by sand blown in by Saharan winds for part of the year, though there are pockets of tropical lustre, such as on the northern part of Tenerife.[4]

The men crossed over to Lanzarote, but did not get off to the most auspicious of starts, as the friar and the priest reported. Realizing they were not alone, their early attempts to greet the natives were summarized as 'great efforts to capture some of the people of Canary, but without success'. Eventually, some of the native Guanche people came down from the mountains. With a fragile friendliness established, Béthencourt ordered a fort built once he had received their leader's permission. He left Bertin de Berneval in charge and he and Salle went to the next island, Fuerteventura, which lies to the south. Again, they made 'great efforts to find their enemies, and were much vexed that they could not fall in with them'.[5] Béthencourt and Salle stayed eight days, after which Béthencourt returned to Lanzarote and then to Spain to resupply and meet with the king. While Béthencourt was awaiting his audience with Henry III of Castile, Berneval captured Lanzarote's ruler, and also stranded Salle on the small island of Los Lobos, off the coast of Fuerteventura, after which Berneval wrested control of a ship to take him back to Spain.

Once Béthencourt returned, he was ready to conquer – Henry III had named him lord of the islands, and granted him the right to collect one-fifth of the colony's profits in exchange for claiming them for Castile. Béthencourt and Salle soon began a more aggressive attempt to colonize. They got off to a straightforward start when the ruler of Lanzarote, 'who had so often been taken and escaped again', decided to give in and 'yield obeisance to M de Bethencourt', meaning that he would accept Christian baptism. When the occasion at last arose, the king 'shewed every appearance of sincerity . . . and received . . . the name of Louis'.

But the Norman pair met resistance elsewhere, and soon the financial and material support Béthencourt had collected in Spain dwindled. A frustrated Salle left for Seville, as did Béthencourt, and there their paths diverged. Béthencourt returned to the islands, this time with more settlers, and Salle did not. Upon Béthencourt's return, he persisted in his attempts to subdue the people of Gran Canaria, but the island's people stood firm. After this, Béthencourt decided to leave, and put his nephew, Maciot de Béthencourt, in charge of Lanzarote and Fuerteventura. Béthencourt went to Spain, Rome, and then France in 1406. He sent more men to settle the islands, but he never returned, and died in Normandy in 1425.[6]

Well before Béthencourt's death, Henry the Navigator had heard what had been taking place in the Canaries. Like Afonso IV, Henry, too, wanted Portugal to control these islands. In 1424, he organized an expedition of 2,500 men – although he did not join it – ordering them to capture Gran Canaria. But unlike the Ceuta campaign a decade earlier, it was a disaster. The Guanche were prepared, and they fought off the soldiers. Undeterred by Castilian claims to the island and native resistance alike, Henry continued attacking intermittently for decades to try to take the islands, failing every time.

Lanzarote and Fuerteventura had not been as heavily populated as the islands to the west, and Europeans were able to to live there. By 1455 there were reports of 'Christians' living on both as well as on the smaller La Gomera and El Hierro, while Gran Canaria, Tenerife, and La Palma were still inhabited only by 'pagans'.[7] Castile, too, would later struggle to subdue the Guanches, and Gran Canaria, La Palma, and

Tenerife would not become part of Castile until the last decade of the fifteenth century.

Like the indigenous people of the New World nearly a century later, the existence of the islands' native inhabitants opened up questions in the minds of Europeans, people whose worldview was still narrowly constrained by the precepts of Christianity. The priest and the friar who wrote about Béthencourt's exploits pointed out on the first page of their account that the islands 'are inhabited by unbelievers of various habits and languages'. Such men were accustomed to the 'unbelievers' in Islamic lands, but the people on the islands were puzzling because they were not part of the Muslim world.

Little is known about the Guanches, except what was recorded by Europeans, who no doubt had little understanding of their languages or customs. The Guanches – itself a broad term used to describe people across all the islands – were probably connected to North African Berber tribes. The estimates of the population across the islands vary, ranging from 6,000 to more than 60,000. They did not survive into the seventeenth century, and because the only written records were European, the recorded descriptions have a familiar ring. For instance, the priests describe the people of Gran Canaria as going 'quite naked, save for a girdle of palm leaves . . . [and] print devices on their bodies . . . their hair tied behind . . . They are a handsome and well-formed people.' But whatever Europeans thought about them, they had been able to keep those Europeans at bay until Béthencourt's time, and even then he had not managed to take all the islands – there was an active and sustained resistance.[8]

However, this came to an end over time as all the islands were put under Spanish control, and larger-scale settlement began. The merchants and artisans arrived, as did large estate-holders with their peasants. Portuguese, Genoese, Catalans, Jews, Moors, and moriscos displaced the Guanches.[9] By the mid-1500s, even the English had arrived, and traders on the islands were exchanging cloth for sugar and dyes extracted from wood.[10]

None of these settlers, however, found any sign of the mystical river of gold, despite the proximity of the African coast. But instead of exploring further, they looked to the ground and planted something that was almost as valuable – sugar. The climate on some of the islands was suitable for raising the crop and there was a growing market for it. Before long the remaining natives were enslaved and working in the fields, and Africans brought from the Portuguese posts in Guinea were not long in joining them. The Genoese, with their interest in capital investments, were heavy backers in this enterprise, and they made handsome profits. From the beginning, the exploration of the Atlantic and the development of the sugar trade could scarcely be called 'Spanish' at all – Castilian, Portuguese, Genoese, even Norman. Much of western Europe was involved in the enterprise, even though the islands were under the Castilian crown.

But despite Henry's failure to take any one, much less all, of the Canary Islands, Portugal still managed to find some Atlantic islands of its own – and with no fighting at all.

*

In 1420, navigators João Gonçalves Zarco and Tristão Vaz Teixeira were blown off course in a storm, and they took refuge on the small island of Porto Santo.[11] They would have disembarked into silence, with only the waves lapping against the flat shore and the sound of birds. No signs of life were present. There were no Moors to vanquish, no Africans to enslave, no Canarians to suppress. There was no one. The only thing nearby was the looming volcanic island of Madeira, and they soon sailed over and began to explore it. It must have come as a surprise, for Madeira is green and mild, and it would have felt like a spring day to the men. The fertile landscape was imposing, with near-vertical volcanic slopes.

The mariners were quick to spot the island's potential. They could see it was rich in wood and had a climate that supported flora and fauna, a stark contrast to the arid Canary Islands. While many other sailors might have been dissuaded from going inland or would have been unable to see the value of the craggy hillsides, these experienced navigators could. Of equal importance was that Gonçalves and Vaz were not so off course as to be unable to return home, that great occupational hazard of this period.

Madeira lies about 965km (600 miles) from Lisbon and some 482km (300 miles) north of La Palma, in the Canaries. It is volcanic, and its peak had been spotted by other sailors before Gonçalves and Vaz's expedition. Yet the Portuguese crown had little inclination to find out more until reports arrived in 1417 that Castilian ships had been seen sailing nearby, though nothing came of it. Although an empty island would seem to have more obvious attractions because there were no native people to contend with, the opposite was the case: no money could be made there capturing slaves. However, Portugal's King John I decided not long after Gonçalves and Vaz's expedition to send around a hundred people to settle the colony and ward off future incursion from Castilians or anyone else. The group was led by Gonçalves and Vaz, and they were joined by Bartolomeo Perestrello, whose family came from the Italian peninsula. Perestrello was given control of Porto Santo, the smaller, flatter island to the north-east of Madeira. By 1425 a stream of settlers began making their way to the fertile islands. Madeira and Porto Santo prospered, and at one point, around 1478 or 1479, Columbus arrived and lived there for a while. He married Perestrello's daughter, giving him ties to a prominent Portuguese family, even if they, like Columbus, had their roots in Italy. The seas might have been infinite, but the world of the sailor was much smaller. And so Columbus's colonial education continued.[12]

On the main island logging began because, as in the Canaries, there were trees whose resin could be used for dye. The few trees of Porto Santo suffered a different fate as they were cleared to make way for livestock and other grazing animals. Some of Madeira was also cleared for growing crops, especially much-needed wheat, but also sugar. Sugar thrived there because there was enough rain. When it was grown in Sicily or the Algarve, farmers had to construct irrigation systems to give the plant sufficient water. The climate on Madeira enriched the canes with a higher natural sugar content, making it easier to grow and refine. But the island's steep slopes made it difficult to grow the crop in large plantations. As in the Canaries, it was the Genoese who brought the capital to spend on sugar mills, and the Portuguese who brought the labour. However, the settlers were soon using Africans brought up from the Gulf of Guinea and Guanches captured on the Canaries to produce the crop as well. Despite the success of sugar, little of the profit went to the settlers; most went to the Genoese investors.

Madeira was also producing around 12,000 bushels of grain a year by the middle of the fifteenth century.[13] In addition, the island was well suited to growing grapes, and islanders began to produce the fortified wine that bears its name to this day. It was not long before the Genoese became even more involved in the control of trade and development of the island, though other merchants, such as the Flemish, began to arrive as well. With a steady supply of sugar now guaranteed for Portugal, the market opened up.

By 1455, Madeira was in profit. By around 1500 it had 211 sugar producers, with many of the estates being owned by the Genoese and Florentines. More Africans were sent to the island, along with enslaved Canarians, to help increase output, which reached around 1,360 tons, by the early 1500s, though by the 1520s – when New World sugar was beginning – this would drop significantly and the island would never again reach its previous peaks.[14]

For a while, however, Portugal's sugar island was the envy of other nations. With Madeira and Porto Santo established, sailors began to press further into the Atlantic, where they soon came across another uninhabited group of islands, known as the Azores, which lie to the north-west of Madeira. Ilhas dos Açores means Islands of the Goshawks, a reminder of how an understanding of the natural world was part of early navigation.[15] Portugal began to settle these islands in 1439. Although the Azores were too far north for sugar production, they prospered with wine and grain. Both they and Madeira were soon incorporated into the expanding Portuguese world.

Further south, sailors were refining the *volta da Mina*, which was the name used to describe the return trips between Africa and Portugal that were facilitated by the growing understanding of winds and currents. Mina was also the name of the first Portuguese settlement, today's Elmina, in Ghana. Once contact with Africans had been established, traders were quick to set up *feitorias*, around the 1440s. These 'factories' were basic trading posts. The first was at Mina, but they were soon dotted all along the coast. The Portuguese brought textiles, beads, horses, and brass goods, as well as guns and other weapons, and in exchange loaded their ships with gold, spices, ivory, and slaves to take back to Europe. From the middle of the fifteenth century until around 1530, estimates put the number of enslaved Africans at around 156,000.[16]

The Portuguese were able to add another link in their Atlantic chain near these African forts. About 650km (400 miles) from mainland West Africa is an archipelago of ten islands. The Portuguese called them the Cape Verde Islands, though ironically, as the *verde* (green) refers to the verdant land of coastal Africa around Guinea and Senegal, not the islands themselves. Like the Canaries to the north, these islands are mostly arid deserts, though some, such as Santiago, the largest, are more mountainous and tropical. While undertaking the *volta da Mina*, sailors had begun to stop off on these islands and by the 1460s there was an official settlement on Santiago. As on Madeira, the sailors found no other human beings. Unlike the mainland territories, where the Portuguese would have encountered the Jolof, for instance, the sailors to Santiago were met, as far as is known, with silence. If there were humans, all traces of them had been swept away by the island's ever-present winds. But the archipelago was soon repeopled. Like Madeira and the Azores, Cape Verde too saw a mix of people come to its shores – sailors and merchants – although before long it was overwhelmingly Africans, as the islands – especially Santiago – became ever more bound up in the slave trade.

Soon Santiago bore the hallmarks of a European colony, a process hammered out in the Atlantic and replicated in the Caribbean. First there needed to be a well-situated harbour, in this case Ribeira Grande, which has a sandy beach encircled by steep, vegetation-lined hills, and a river offering a supply of fresh water. Then a few streets of houses sprang up along with a church. Convents further up the hillside soon followed, and at the top, a fortress, with vistas stretching for miles.[17] Such settlements could be established quickly. And of course there were variations. Sometimes the fort came first, then the monastery, and then the settlers. The elements were often the same, even if the order differed. Settlements were not usually secured inland, but on the sea fronts. Ships could call in, and goods be loaded and exchanged.

The arid and windy climate – the islands receive uncertain and often scarce amounts of rainfall and winds off the Sahara – meant they were not suitable for sugar. Some of the archipelago could, however, produce salt, as the name of one of the islands, Sal, attests. But the main purpose of the development of these islands was as a stopping point for the burgeoning maritime traffic and slave trade.

The papacy had been taking note of these Atlantic developments with growing interest. On 8 January 1455 Pope Nicholas V promulgated his *Romanus Pontifex*, praising the Afonso V for his role in overseeing the colonization of Madeira and the Azores, as well as the crown's foray into Africa and the attempts to convert the natives. He also granted permission to enslave the non-believers. The Catholic Church still held and exercised an enormous amount of power in Europe during this time, and the direction of expansion was in no small part due to papal policies and the Church's support. The colonization of the Atlantic and later the Caribbean was a project not only of the evolving marketplace or Genoese merchants (though of course they were crucial to its development), but of Church and state. Claiming of territories and enslaving 'unbelievers' required the support of the crowns of Portugal, Castile, and Aragon, as well as the permission of the Vatican.

The Reconquista roots to this are traceable. For instance, the papal bull *Dum Diversas* of 18 June 1452 gave the king of Portugal permission to attack and conquer unbelievers and take their lands, which was considered especially important as parts of the Iberian peninsula were still under the control of the Islamic caliphate. Even though Portugal had driven Islamic rule out of the Algarve in the south in 1249, attacks on non-Christians were still permitted. Indeed, one of the longest-running preoccupations of Christian Europe was the threat of the infidel, a tradition that dates nearly to the beginning of Islam. That this spills over into the early years of discovery should come as little surprise. Although concepts about conquest and colonization would undergo numerous transformations (especially when the Protestants arrived), the starting point is here, in the rocky terrain of the Iberian peninsula. It was not the case that one thing led to another – that the fight against Islam *led* to overseas expansion. Rather, it was the case that there was an institutional framework in place, via the Catholic Church, that legitimized what was happening. The Portuguese, Castilians, Aragonese, and Genoese were pushing into new worlds, and encountering people who were so vastly different that they grappled to find a vocabulary to explain it, and so they turned to what they had.

However, the continued relay race of discovery and conquest was straining the already fragile relations between the Castilian crown and Portugal, both of whom wanted to claim these new territories – and the right to find more – as their own. It would take the power of the papacy to put it to rest, and a series of treaties were issued to stop the claims and counter-claims between these two kingdoms. The 1479 Treaty of Alcáçovas that brought the Castilian War of Succession to an end also stipulated that Portugal would recognize Castile and Aragon's right to the Canary Islands, and in exchange receive recognition for its claims on Madeira, the Azores, and Cape Verde. This would set a precedent for what followed in *Inter Caetera*, a papal bull issued in 1493 by Alexander VI – who was from the notorious Valencian Borja (or Borgia) family – after Columbus's voyage, and the Treaty of Tordesillas in 1494, which established the line of demarcation of Portuguese territory at 370 leagues (around 1,185 nautical miles) to the west of Cape Verde, with the area beyond that going to Castile. This invisible line would have very concrete ramifications.

After 1492, as the Iberian nations pushed out the non-Catholics who refused to convert, many soon spilled into this expanding Atlantic world. Jewish people played a large part, especially when, in 1497, Portugal decided to follow Spain in forcing the Jews to convert. Thousands were killed, and thousands more were deported to the colonies, especially São Tomé in the Gulf of Guinea. Some of them converted to save their lives but then left the country, and these 'new Christians', or *cristãos novos*, would make their way to Cape Verde and onward from there.

When Columbus set off, he not only had his Mediterranean experience, but had also played an active part in the early years of European colonization in the Atlantic. Before he arrived in Porto Santo, he had already been to Chios, as well as Tunis and Marseille before that, and even Iceland and Ireland. He may have also done the *volta da Mina* in the 1480s, and he knew about the Canaries and Cape Verde. He was aware of Africans and Guanches, and he realized that sugar was a money-maker. Columbus had been no dreamy-eyed map reader, but an active player in this new Atlantic colonization.

*

When the admiral sailed into the West Indies on his first voyage and saw unbelievers, he reverted to what he knew from the example of the Canary Islands and the Mediterranean. Here were slaves to capture, and people to convert. His initial encounter on these islands may not have matched his grandiose vision; it would have seemed familiar, rather than exotic. In his journal, Columbus noted that the 'Indians' he met were 'very handsome and not small; and none of them are black, but the colour of Canary Islanders'. Yet Columbus and hundreds of people after him could not – or did not want to – find a way to explain this new world and its people on their own terms. Instead, they created new words.

The diary of Dr Diego Álvarez Chanca, a physician on Columbus's second voyage (September 1493 to June 1496), could perhaps be considered the starting point for the vocabulary devised to describe the people they met in this new world: the so-called Taino and Caribs. Although the words Taino and Carib (and Arawak, at times) are used today to describe the indigenous people of the Caribbean, there is a great deal of uncertainty about their meaning. Almost from their inception they gave a sharp contrast: the Taino was a peaceful islander, happy to aid and work for the Spaniards, while the Carib was a warrior who killed Tainos and often ate them, and fought the newcomers. Chanca's account of what happened when the expedition stopped on the island later named Guadeloupe offers a vivid commentary on the differences between the two peoples. The doctor observed that 'the captain went to the shore in the boat and made his way to the houses . . . he brought away four or five bones of the arms and legs of men. As soon as we saw this, we suspected that those islands were the Carib islands which are inhabited by people who eat human flesh.'[18] Indeed, Columbus himself wrote, regarding his first voyage, that this New World was said to have people who 'feed on human flesh'.[19]

Later, Chanca observed 'many men and women [who] walked along the shore near the water wondering at the fleet . . . and when a boat came to land to speak with them, saying to them tayno, tayno, which means "good", they waited as long as our men did not leave the water, remaining near it, in such a way that then they wished they could escape'.[20] Columbus used this terminology, and Chanca recorded it, and so the dichotomy was established and enshrined. The people of the Greater Antilles – Hispaniola, Cuba, and Puerto Rico – were considered to be peaceful Tainos, while those of the smaller islands were deemed violent Caribs.

However, in the past thirty or so years scholars across a range of disciplines have challenged the notion that the Amerindian past divided so sharply. They have also questioned whether these people were made 'extinct', as generations of writers have repeated in their histories of the islands. Studies have found not only biological persistence (through DNA) but cultural practices and even archival evidence that have survived.[21] What is beyond dispute, however, is that life as all parties knew it was altered to the limits of recognition because of the encounter. People from different backgrounds who had never seen each other before – American, African, or European – converged and diverged. Diseases were unleashed on everyone, as was violence. Similar investigations have been conducted into the differences among the indigenous people of the Caribbean, whose identity was defined for centuries by historical sketches or first-hand accounts by Europeans such as Chanca, who understood neither their culture nor their language.

That there was inter-island warfare and hostility is no surprise. Like other nations and peoples, alliances changed and wars began and ended. One group describing another as good or bad did little to help these newly arrived foreigners make sense of what they were encountering. Instead, the Europeans often based their judgements on which groups offered help and which groups preferred to shoot arrows at them. Generally speaking, Taino came to mean helpful, and Carib hostile. There was plenty of resistance from the indigenous people in the Greater Antilles, but the myth of cooperation there persisted. Caribbean Indians became symbolic of the encounter of old and new worlds. Even as the Indians died by the thousands, these dichotomies lived on: they were cannibals, they were peaceful; they were barbaric; or sometimes, they were both. How they were viewed reflected the success or failure of attempts to settle in these new lands. This was not helped by the proliferation of writings, such as Peter Martyr's *De Orbe Novo*, published around 1516, from Europeans who had yet to set foot on the islands. They were basing their accounts on reports of men who were there primarily to find gold and convert heathens, not on a mission of cultural understanding. Martyr's work was a misleading compilation of reports and letters from explorers, and it was soon translated and disseminated throughout Europe to an eager readership.

Although it is fruitless to judge that world against our own – disciplines such as anthropology or archaeology did not exist until the nineteenth century at the earliest – it bears noting that the idea and use of Taino and Carib continue today. It is ironic that, at the same time, the people doing the naming were perhaps not very clear about their own identity. Hispania had been a Roman invention. Spain in its present guise was not quite fully formed, and the Genoese were independent of what would become Italy in 1861. It was religion in this period that served as a way of dividing and categorizing people.

If the people were not Carib or Taino, what were they? Recent archaeological scholarship reveals a far more specific history.[22] In a wide sense, these peoples were mostly from the Orinoco and other river basins in South America. There is a growing consensus that some of these first peoples had learned how to harness the currents of the rivers and sea to travel northward, thousands of years before the Genoese sailor set off on his mission. They too were looking for some-thing – not gold, but food, plants, perhaps new places to settle. They too were sailors, but of canoes (a word which derives from the Arawak). They are thought to have arrived around 6,000 years ago, which, in terms of human history, makes them quite recent immigrants, the Caribbean being – to the best of current knowledge – one of the later places of human settlement.[23] By around 4,000 BC many of the islands had sizeable communities, and different waves of migration from the Orinoco valley and other parts of South America continued. Included in this was the later and significant arrival of the Saladoid people, who travelled from South America and inhabited the islands between approximately 500 BC and AD 600, with settlements scattered from Trinidad to Puerto Rico. Others may have gone to Hispaniola and Cuba directly from coastal South America.[24]

As the archaeologist Samuel Wilson has pointed out, these early colonists, like the later Europeans, 'refashioned the island environ-ments, unintentionally and intentionally, to suit their purposes'.[25] They brought their own plants, insects, and germs as well, and settled these islands. They too needed to grow plants and chop down trees, and fish in the waters. By the time Columbus arrived there were areas of dense settlement, and 'villages' that contained thousands of people. Although Taino became the catch-all term for the peoples in the Greater Antilles, there were actually other groups, such as the Lucayans of the Bahamian islands who traded with the Tainos. There was vari-ation in the Arawak language spoken throughout the region, though the Arawaks lived in northern South America and have been often conflated with Tainos and Lucayans.[26] Indeed, there is evidence that most islanders thought themselves culturally distinct from those on neighbouring islands, or even a different part of the same island.[27]

The people Columbus called Tainos, then, had their roots in the archaic pottery-making Casimiroids and Ostionoids, while many on the smaller islands were the descendants of the Saladoids.[28] But after

Columbus, the incarnation of the Carib took a variety of turns: Kalinago described the people of Dominica and Grenada, and the people of St Lucia and St Vincent were later called 'black Caribs' because there was intermixing between runaway slaves and indigenous people – and they were known for their fierce resistance. Because a variety of the Arawak language was spoken, people in the smaller islands were called Arawaks at times. Despite the stories, there is no evidence that anyone on any island was a cannibal: that remains in the realm of folklore. Yet the idea of the Carib remains, extending even to the sea surrounding the islands.

From this Taino/Carib misunderstanding has sprung a long debate about the origins and ethnic demarcations of the native peoples of the Caribbean, but the idea of the cannibalistic 'Carib' is perhaps the most persistent. By the time Daniel Defoe published *Robinson Crusoe* in 1719, most of the native peoples in the New World would have been long dead, yet the Europeanized idea of them was clearly quite alive.

After the narrator, Crusoe, survives shipwreck and sets up on the desert island, he frets, 'I had heard that the people of the Caribbean coast were cannibals or man-eaters, and I knew by the latitude that I could not be far from that shore.' Later on, he spots five canoes on the island and proceeds to spy on the people who had come ashore. What he saw confirmed his suspicious, as 'two miserable wretches dragged from the boats . . . were now brought out for the slaughter'. He grew alarmed as one victim made an escape but was not followed very far. But he was soon cheered up, as he recalled that 'it came very warmly upon my thoughts . . . that now was the time to get me a servant . . . and that I was plainly called by Providence to save this poor creature's life'.

Crusoe helped this man kill some of his captors, and took him under his protection. This was, of course, Friday. A while later they revisited the scene of Friday's near-death and found it 'covered with human bones . . . and great pieces of flesh left here and there, half-eaten, mangled, and scorched . . .' While this revolted Crusoe, he noted that 'I found Friday had still a hankering stomach after some of the flesh, and was still a cannibal in his nature' but made it clear that 'I would kill him if he offered it'.[29]

In a few pages, the native person of the Caribbean was enshrined in literature not only as a perfect candidate for servitude, but also as a cannibal by his very nature. Other writers perpetuated the myth of the native cannibal, though some put it down to a vicious type of revenge, rather than something innate. Père Labat, a French missionary who travelled to the Caribbean in 1693 and wrote extensively on the islands, said of the people of Dominica, 'I also know, and it is quite true, that when the English and the French first settled in the Islands many men of both nations were killed, *boucanned*, and eaten by the Caribs. But this was due to the inability of the Indians to take revenge on the Europeans for their injustice and cruelty, and it was done with impotent rage, not custom.'[30]

On the eve of Columbus's arrival, the peoples of Hispaniola were living in organized settlements, some as large as 5,000 people. The men hunted and fished, and the women worked the land, raised children, and performed other duties, and the communities were in general quite hierarchical.[31] The depiction of Amerindians as sensual or lazy is, of course, a European fantasy, or at least a false impression. In Hispaniola there was intensive agriculture and fishing. Estimates of the pre-Columbian population of the West Indies range widely, from hundreds of thousands to millions across the islands. What is certain is that most of them died early as a result of the encounter with Europeans, be it through disease, labour, or murder.

Columbus and his men, and the sailors who soon followed, had technology and germs on their side. The native people had poor resistance to European diseases; and the Europeans had firepower for which spears were usually no match. By Columbus's time, there had been great changes in guns and other arms, especially in the development of the musket.[32] By the middle of the fifteenth century, sailing ships were carrying increasing amounts of armaments. The evolution of such weapons gave Europeans tactical advantages against Africans, Canarians, and native peoples in the Americas. Weapons were also later used as a means of barter, as guns were sold for slaves in West Africa.[33]

Despite the diseases, the horses, the ships, and the weapons, the native peoples did not necessarily give themselves up easily. There are numerous accounts of hostility. For instance, a Spaniard, Pedro Arias de Ávila, arrived in 1514 with nineteen ships to take the island of Dominica, but he and his 1,500 men were greeted with a hail of poisoned arrows. They anchored in a bay on the north-west shore, later called Prince Rupert Bay. Over time, the Spanish were able to convert a tiny bit of the island to a small resupply station for ships, but they remained under continual attack. Further to the south, on the island of St Vincent and the scattered Grenadines, Caribs (and later black Caribs) put up a fight against European settlement until 1796, when they were shipped out of the islands.[34] The Central American coastline, too, faced similar incursions, and in places such as Nicaragua and Honduras the Miskito people gave the Spanish constant problems. Europeans also encroached around the littoral of South America. Further south, along the Guyana territory (which later would be British Guiana, Suriname, and French Guiana) the indigenous peoples of the Amazon interior would remain largely untouched in the dense and virtually impenetrable jungle while settlements were established along the fertile coast. The problems began when the imported African slaves ran away into the forest, where they could regroup and plan attacks.[35]

But there was also more commonplace resistance, as the historian Matthew Restall has pointed out. This took place in numerous ways, from working slowly to sabotaging equipment to simply picking up and leaving for more isolated places to live, out of the reach of Europeans. Attacks and revolts were often local, and usually straightforward to put down, and so less likely to be enshrined in the pages of the histories of these islands being written in Europe.[36]

On the other hand, collaboration between the Spaniards and the people they enslaved and killed played a significant part in the settlement of the Caribbean. Indeed, according to Restall, such cooperation began on the ships. Those armour-plated 'conquistadors', so often depicted as white Spaniards, could actually be a more diverse crew. Africans were part of the early colonization process. They had been brought enslaved to Spain and Portugal and were many times put to use in high-status servant roles. They frequently accompanied their masters on voyages, and became involved in the settlement of the islands. Men like Juan Garrido, a West African taken to Lisbon who was later involved in expeditions to Puerto Rico and Cuba, were part of the development of this world. Garrido arrived in Hispaniola in 1502 or 1503, making him one of the first Africans to go to the New World. He was later freed and lived in Mexico City after joining the expedition to Mexico around 1519.[37]

In the same vein, many indigenous people in Hispaniola, and later elsewhere in the Americas, considered it in their interest to aid these new people. From the outset, Columbus and his men needed at the very least interpreters. Sometimes alliances were for strategic political reasons, other times for more personal ones. Sex was also part of the encounter, and shiploads of Spanish men came without women. Some women were willing concubines, others were the bargaining chip of powerful fathers, and still others victims of brutal rape. The result was known as *mestizaje*: the merging and blending of the indigenous and Spanish. Through this, the indigenous past of Hispaniola and other islands was kept alive, even if the number of Amerindians continued to decline. The lines between the two groups were not rigid, and in fact were quite easily crossed.

Modern historians and social scientists only know fragments of the pre-Columbian world of the Caribbean. There are very few written sources revealing what any of these native people felt or thought when they saw Columbus and his ships, or in the turbulent time thereafter. There are records of what Europeans *thought* the indigenous people said, and there are accounts of the Caribs not cooperating. Over time, cultural artefacts were ruined and practices interrupted and transformed though the encounter, so working with what remains means examining what indigenous people did, rather than what they were reported to have said. The myth of the compliant Indian is one that permeates the entire American continent, from Canada to Argentina. The idea of the first Thanksgiving, when the native peoples saved the English settlers from starvation, is one of the foundation myths of the United States. The docile Taino, and his Janus twin the Carib likewise have left an indelible imprint on the history of the Caribbean.

*

In 1493, Columbus was eager to return to Hispaniola and see how La Navidad was faring. This second expedition was a much larger one, with seventeen ships. He had plans to turn his outpost into a commercial centre, a *feitoria*, like that of Mina, but he would be trading in gold.[38] He had varied the route, and he and his entourage sailed further to the south, which brought the ships in between Guadeloupe and Dominica. On this voyage he gave names to the islands he passed: Santa María de Guadalupe (Guadeloupe), Santa María de Montserrat (Montserrat), Santa María de la Antigua (Antigua), San Cristóbal (St Kitts), Santa Cruz (St Croix), and San Juan Bautista (Puerto Rico). He did not arrive on Hispaniola until November, which gave his dreams time to develop, but they would have died a quick death when they reached the settlement. There was nothing. No signs of life, no people. Just silence and stillness. Dr Chanca described the scene: 'We went to the place where the town had been, and we saw that it was entirely burned and the clothes of the Christians were found in some grass.'[39]

Where many others might have been deterred from attempting another settlement, Columbus was not. He had brought farm animals, sugar cane, grapes, and wheat for planting. He had a vision, and it did not include eerie silences and failed settlements. His men were quick to find a new location, also along the north coast, and this time named it after the queen of Spain, La Isabela. In many senses, Columbus's determination at this juncture marked the true beginning of the colonial enterprise in the Americas. Undaunted by the possibility of death, not fearful of the native peoples, Columbus and his men pressed forward, like the conquistadors who would follow him, straight into a rugged physical terrain, and an even more terrifying spiritual one. La Isabela had a shaky start; there was not enough food or water. Soon the colonists were heading inland to find the riches they had been promised, either taking from the native people or trying to make them work. The native anger, already stoked during the collapse of La Navidad, only increased. Columbus made two brutal campaigns in 1494 and 1495 against the Amerindians on Hispaniola, killing and conquering, and he took some 1,600 people into slavery, sending around 550 of them to Spain.[40] In this sense, Columbus continued to reflect the moral codes of the Old World. He knew the Portuguese had been enslaving Africans, with papal approval – indeed, a 1436 bull by Pope Eugene IV called Africans 'enemies of God'.[41] Closer to home, the Guanches in the Canary Islands had been forced into slavery. In 1495, the Spanish crown authorized the sale of captured people from the Caribbean. Those Columbus did not sell or force to scrabble for gold, he left to raise cassava and other crops.

There were other problems. The *feitoria* idea did not sit well with some of the settlers. Many of the men were minor nobles and felt the hard work of settlement was beneath them, especially when there were native peoples who could do the labour. The blueprint of the Reconquista was set in their minds. They believed they had come under the *repartimiento* system, which had been used to resettle land taken from

Muslims, and later in the Canary Islands as well. It is, in essence, an agreement that the settler would be granted land if he promised to work it for a set number of years. But such a system was a square peg for the round hole of the island's problems.

In March 1494 Columbus left again, this time to explore further, still believing he was in the East. He left Bartolomé, his brother, in charge. During that voyage, Columbus sailed around more of Cuba, and the island of Jamaica (St Jago). His brother, meanwhile, was contending with a full-on rebellion. It did not start immediately. Indeed, by that August, a decent vein of gold had been discovered in the south of the island, and Bartolomé had moved the capital to a new settlement nearby, calling it Santo Domingo. It was a strategic location as well, as it had a good harbour. But that was about the only happy decision he had made. By this point he had so enraged the settlers that there had been a revolt, led by Francisco Roldán. This breakaway faction had moved to the west of the island, taken over native lands and forced people to work outside the auspices of the sanctioned leader. Columbus, in the meantime, had returned to Castile, having left in March 1496. Unfortunately for him, news of the colony's failure had reached the crown, too. But Bartolomé did not have time to worry about that, as tensions with the Amerindians had rekindled.

By this point, the Catholic monarchs had become concerned about the state of this colony. It was obvious to all that while Columbus had found something, it bore little resemblance to what he had claimed he would find. Although the crown continued to have serious misgivings, Columbus's campaign for a third voyage was a success, and he set off once again from Spain on 30 May 1498, albeit with a much smaller fleet of six ships. His journey took him via the Cape Verde islands, where he hit a becalmed section of water – the infamous doldrums. When he eventually spotted land on 31 July, he had arrived much further south, between Trinidad and the South American continent. He returned to Hispaniola a month later, where the situation was so grave that Columbus began to grant *encomiendas* to the angry settlers.

This system functioned by making use of some existing structures: the distribution of labour on the island was such that native peoples often already worked under their chief, or *cacique*. Indeed, this was not unlike the labour system on the Iberian peninsula, which, like much of Early Modern Europe, used vassalage. But under the Spanish in Hispaniola, these *caciques* then paid tribute to the Spanish land-holding *encomenderos*. In exchange, the *caciques* and labourers received some pay, conversion to Christianity, and, as vassals of the Spanish crown, protection – in theory – from further abuses or attack. It was a system that could benefit powerful local rulers and the Spanish, though many of the workers who laboured in the mines and fields fared less well.

Queen Isabella's displeasure increased when she heard that Columbus was issuing such grants, since in doing so he was acting well above his station. The exasperated monarchs sent Francisco de Bobadilla over to govern the colony in place of Columbus, who had disappointed them, and they also began to grant licences to other explorers. In addition, Isabella decided to issue a *cédula* (decree) in 1500 that freed the Amerindian slaves who had been brought to Spain by Columbus. For his part, Bobadilla's solution to the ongoing unrest between Spaniards resulted in Columbus, Bartolomé, and another brother, Diego, being sent to Spain in chains the same year. Nicolás de Ovando was appointed governor soon after, and he arrived on the island in 1502. Accompanying him were 2,500 settlers, one of whom was an eager young man named Bartolomé de las Casas.[42] Casas's father, Pedro, had been a member of Columbus's large second expedition, and he returned to Spain with a Taino slave in tow. Only a few years later, Bartolomé had joined his father on the Ovando expedition, ready to make his fortune. Bartolomé's journey, however, would not be merely physical, but also spiritual.

When Ovando arrived, he was determined to make Hispaniola productive. He sent the troublesome Roldán back to Spain, and put more native people into the mines to pick at rocks in order to fill ships to Spain, delivering the promises of gold. These settlers were doing themselves no favours, laying a foundation for the *leyenda negra*, the black legend that casts these peninsular interlopers as cruel and heartless conquistadors. In 1503, seeing no other option, Ovando told the crown that the Indians had to be forced to work in the mines. He had also gone on slaving expeditions to neighbouring islands to replace the high number of people who were dying. He was partly able to do this by capitalizing on the conceptual gap that Columbus had opened between the cannibalistic 'Caribs' and the other indigenous people. Queen Isabella was convinced enough to allow, in 1503, the enslavement of people from other islands, 'in order that if the said cannibals still resist and will not be taught of our holy Catholic faith and be in my service and under my obedience, you may capture them and shall capture them in order to bring them to whatever lands and islands you so deem'.[43] A royal *cédula* of 20 December 1503 approved the system, but reports of mistreatment were relayed to Spain on a regular basis.

Ovando managed to squeeze profits from the colony, at the expense of the native people whose numbers were fast diminishing through overwork and disease – and at his own hand. In 1504 he massacred many of the chiefs. In 1509, the native population was thought to be 60,000; by 1518 a census recorded only 11,000. The small supply of gold, too, had been exhausted. Dreams of exporting expensive Asian silks, exotic spices, and valuable porcelain were dimming, replaced by the harsh tropical realities of Hispaniola.

Columbus set off on one last voyage on 11 May 1502, with four ships and under strict orders not to go to Hispaniola. He attempted to take shelter there from a brewing hurricane in June, but was denied permission to land. He weathered the storm, and after it passed he sailed on to Honduras, exploring the Bay Islands and the Central American coast. He set off once again for Hispaniola in April the following year, but ended up beached in Jamaica by the end of June. He and his men were stranded, and at one point some of the crew used a canoe to reach Hispaniola and ask for help. Ovando refused at first, though nearly a year later relented, and allowed ships from Santo Domingo to go and fetch them. Columbus was able to return to Spain in 1504, where he died, in Valladolid, in 1506. Although he had been stripped of the titles admiral and viceroy of the Indies, he ended his life a wealthy man thanks to the gold he had saved, but his quest for riches had been an uneven journey, and one that left him at the end of his life gripped by a strong religious fervour. And he never admitted that he had not found the East. The lands he encountered would never bear his name, but rather that of a later Florentine navigator, Amerigo Vespucci. Vespucci, who had sailed to the New World around the late 1490s and whose writings about his travels were widely read, differed from Columbus in that he felt that what he had seen was not the East but another world altogether. In 1507 a map attributed to the German cartographer Martin Waldseemüller appeared to agree with this assessment, and a landmass across the Atlantic from Europe was labelled 'America'.[44] Although Columbus's name does not directly survive in the nomenclature of the Americas, its presence lives on in the names given to the islands he sailed around: the West Indies and Caribbean.

Meanwhile, Bartolomé de las Casas had been enjoying the fruits of his *encomienda*, which was making him a wealthy man. He was also teaching religion to the native people, and helping suppress any rebellions among the Amerindians in Hispaniola. During this time, Ovando stepped down and Diego, Columbus's son, was given command of the island in 1509. Other expeditions around this time were yielding the establishment of settlements on Puerto Rico (1508), Jamaica (1509), and Cuba (1511). Casas joined the settlers in Cuba in 1513. He went as a chaplain, having been ordained a few years earlier. And it was in Cuba that he would undergo his true conversion. There had been a growing awareness of the mistreatment of the native workers, and another cleric, Antonio de Montesinos, had given controversial sermons on the subject in Santo Domingo in 1511 which were quickly circulated, having upset the Spanish population on the island, and which deeply influenced Casas.

Casas began to realize that the Amerindians under Spanish control were being mistreated, and that the *encomienda* had to end. He gave it up and began his campaign. Orders issued in 1512, known as the Laws of Burgos, attempted to regulate the system and curb mistreatment with stipulations such as 'we order that no person or persons shall dare to whip or abuse any Indian, or call him dog or any other form of address except his proper name'.[45]

It is difficult to know if the many edicts of the Laws of Burgos were actually fulfilled – one of the defining characteristics of the Spanish empire is the concept of *obedezco pero no cumplo*, meaning 'I obey but I do not comply'. Although this might sound like a way of obfuscating official orders, the system that evolved gave men on the ground in these far-flung colonies a pragmatic way to apply royal policies as best they could, while also giving the Spanish imperial bureaucracy some flexibility to respond to problems as they arose. Like most systems of governance, however, it was also subject to abuse.

Cuba, Jamaica, and Puerto Rico followed a similar trajectory – gold (quickly depleted), some rearing of livestock, depopulation, and neglect.

However, the Amerindians who continued to work the mines provided the settlers with some sixty tons (US) of gold to export to Spain in the first half of the sixteenth century.[46] It was not all the pursuit of metal, though. As in the Atlantic islands, land was cleared and planting began. The beginnings of a profound agricultural transformation were under way. The first sugar mill in Hispaniola was opened around 1513, and soon there were mills in Puerto Rico as well.

Casas began to make a case to the king, and indeed was given the title 'Protector of the Indians'. But there was still a labour shortage, especially in running the new sugar operations. As early as 1502 Ovando had tried to bring some Africans over, but they had run off and taken refuge with the native people, so he banned the importation of any other slaves.[47] But with the decline of the indigenous population, the island was losing its workforce. In 1517, Casas thought he had hit upon the solution – try again to use Africans. He would later rue the decision to promote this idea, as the scale of African slavery would well outstrip the use of Amerindians. In 1510 King Ferdinand had authorized a shipment of around 250 Africans to be taken to Hispaniola. But by the end of the 1500s around 100,000 people from Africa had been distributed throughout Spain's New World colonies.[48] Since the Africans came from the papal-designated Portuguese zone, it also meant that Spain could not buy the slaves at source, so the crown allowed traders to bring a fixed number of slaves to Spanish territories, while also forcing them to pay it for the privilege – an added bonus.[49] Over time this arrangement for the importation of slaves formalized and became known as the *asiento*.

In the decades that followed, Casas continued his campaign throughout the conquered territories, trying to protect the indigenous people of Peru and Mexico. He also managed to bring the conquest of Nicaragua to a halt for a couple of years, after petitioning Charles V, of Spain, who issued a *cédula* calling for its cessation. All the while, he worked on his *History of the Indies*, which would not be published until after his death, although in 1540 he did give Charles V a shortened version of the book, later printed as 'An Account, Much Abbreviated, of the Destruction of the Indies', pointing out to the king that 'in these forty years [i.e. since 1502] there have been above twelve million souls – men, women, and children – killed, tyrannically and unjustly, on account of tyrannical actions and infernal works of Christians'.[50] He reminded his reader of the brutality: 'They would enter into the villages and spare not children, or old people, or pregnant women, or women with suckling babies, but would open the woman's belly and hack the babe to pieces, as though they were butchering lambs shut up in their pen. They would lay wagers who might slice open the belly of a man with one stroke of their blade.'[51]

Over time, Africans supplanted the remaining Amerindians and an entirely new system of production began.[52] Further to the south, the colonization project continued as well. The conquistadors managed to get a foothold in the deep and deadly jungles of Central America around 1510, near Darien, Panama, in the area known as Tierra Firme, land that stretched from Central America along the coast to Venezuela. Three years later, Vasco Núñez de Balboa crossed the isthmus to the Pacific, and the years that followed under his governorship were violent and bloody, wiping out more of the native population there. The town of Panama was established in 1519, moving the settlement from Darien. Around the same time, Cuba became a launching point for other expeditions to the mainland, not least of Hérnan Cortés to Mexico.

As the settlers moved around, pearls from the Venezuelan coast were added to the exports of gold and sugar. Spaniards set up *rancherías* off the coast of Margarita island, and smaller nearby islets called Cubagua and Coche, and by 1520 there were around a hundred. The pearls were gathered by native peoples (and later Africans), who were forced to dive into oyster beds.[53]

Reports of Spanish activity, delayed as they would have been, still reached eager ears in Europe. This was the height of the Renaissance, and, with the development of printing in the 1450s, the dissemination of ideas – and stories of adventure and exploration – was rapid. Ideas could and did move. Intrepid English, Dutch, and Frenchmen began to seek backing for such adventures of their own, and before long the passage between Europe and the Caribbean was becoming increasingly well travelled. As the sailors of Europe brought their ships to the shores of this new world, one thing was clear: the Caribbean was a place for fantasy, a place beyond rules, and social norms. It was also a land of riches, lust and power. Identities were challenged, and the social stratifications of Europe easily peeled off under the heat of a tropical sun. At the same time, it was brutal and violent, a certain death for many, and a rude awakening for people who believed the tales they heard back home. But by the end of the sixteenth century, the old and the new were soldered together. The pulse of medieval and Renaissance Europe still gave a faint beat, but by crossing the Atlantic, Columbus and those who followed him were – for better or worse – not just attempting to control the 'New World' but forging one of their own. Not everyone was eager to go to the West Indies, however. In 1497 the Venetian explorer Giovanni Caboto – John Cabot – with a commission from the English, worked out an Atlantic crossing further to the north, from Bristol to Newfoundland. And in 1498 the Portuguese Vasco da Gama stepped ashore having found at last a sea route to the true India. The age of exploration was under way.

As for the West Indies, another chapter was about to begin, as western Europeans arrived in earnest on its shores, intent on claiming their share of the riches they had heard so much about. But they would not come away with gold, and had to find their wealth in other ways.

Chapter Three

PIRATES AND PROTESTANTS

With such dramatic events in the Americas, it was impossible for Spain to keep its news secret. Throughout Europe people were talking about the 'New World', and relating the stories they had heard or read, inspiring many mariners to consider making the Atlantic crossing. However, in theory, these new lands were off limits to anyone besides the Spanish. The Pope had divided the New World into spheres of influence for Portugal and Spain, and there was little the English or French could do – except ignore such rules and sail where they liked. They had an added impetus by the early decades of the 1500s, after Spanish explorers and conquistadors had arrived on the mainland territories, encountering the great civilizations of the Inca, Maya, and Aztec, and extracting their great gold and silver wealth. If simple curiosity was not enough of a lure, the prospect of riches certainly was, and reports of English and French ships in West Indian waters began to appear from around the 1520s onwards.

However, during this time of exploration around the Caribbean, a transformation was taking place in Europe that would have profound consequences for the next stage of European settlement in the West Indies. When the disgruntled German friar Martin Luther nailed his ninety-five theses to the door of the church in Wittenberg in 1517, he made public his many complaints about corruption in the Catholic Church. And while his intention was to reform the Church, what followed was far more dramatic, and far-reaching. It was not long before Christianity in Europe was riven: the Protestant Reformation had begun. In subsequent years, there was an intense period of debate, hostility, and the establishment of new Protestant sects, while the Catholic Church attempted to respond to this crisis with the Council of Trent (1545–63). There were dissenters throughout Europe – in the Low Countries and the German states, and by 1534 England's Henry VIII had broken with the Catholic Church as well. But this was not limited to a war of words over theology: within a decade of Luther's ninety-five theses, armed conflicts spurred by this religious division began to spread across the continent, and across the sea.

The most obvious manifestation of this religious divide in the Caribbean was the anti-Catholic sentiment expressed by non-Spanish sailors: Protestant sailors considered ships under the Spanish (i.e., Catholic) flag fair targets. Northern Europeans became more emboldened to enter these waters, exploring and plundering. Soon English, French and Dutch ships became a regular presence in West Indian waters, and on some of the islands. Inevitably on such long journeys, ships would have to stop for water and other supplies. It was during this period that these sailors began to have contact with the chain of Lesser Antillean islands, many of which had few Spanish settlers. The native peoples across these islands were often happy to help and trade with the other Europeans, realizing that they, too, were enemies of the Spanish. The Spanish, however, began to resent the people they often called *corsarios luteranos* – Lutheran corsairs.[1] Another name for these interlopers was, of course, pirates. Such high-seas raiders were not unknown: around the same time, sailors from Morocco, Algiers, Tripoli, and Tunisia were raiding Christian ships, taking infidels captive and raising money for the Ottoman treasury – and causing havoc in the Mediterranean. They were known as Barbary corsairs, and they inspired terror among seagoing European Christians. Between 1600 and 1644 they captured some 800 English, Scottish, Welsh, and Irish ships – not to mention thousands from elsewhere in Christendom – totalling around 12,000 people.[2] But while the Barbary corsairs captured those they considered non-believers, the northern European sailors in the Caribbean took advantage of the religious schism in Europe to justify attacks on valuable Spanish ships.

Despite the hostility towards the Church in Europe and towards the Catholic Spaniards in the Caribbean, Spain's Philip II, who came to the throne in 1556, had one very significant consolation: the metals from the New World, of which there seemed to be an endless supply. Indeed, in 1545 a rich vein of silver had been discovered in Potosí and the town, which sits up at around 4,050m (13,300ft) in the Andes, soon boomed, its population hitting 150,000 well before the end of the century, dwarfing that of anywhere else in the New World. Above the clouds, the silver miners dug into the earth, providing the capital to pay for wars thousands of miles away. Yet no matter how much silver Philip had, he always needed more. Around this time, a more systematic way of getting the gold and silver to Spain had been developed, a convoy known generally as the *flota*. Every spring an armada would set off downriver from Seville (and later direct from Cádiz because the Guadalquivir river had become too full of silt for ships to travel to Seville) laden with all manner of Spanish goods, such as olives and wine, as well as cloth produced in other parts of Europe. Upon reaching the Caribbean, it split into two groups, the *galeones* destined for New Spain (Mexico), and the *flota* destined for Tierra Firme (Panama). In the Tierra Firme port Nombre de Dios, and later Portobello, the merchants would sell wares, the sailors would go to the taverns, while mules would carry bags of precious metal across the isthmus from ships that had sailed up the Pacific coast from Peru. They would also wait for the galleons to come in from Spain's Pacific colony in Manila, bringing luxury goods that would have to be carried across to the Caribbean ports. By the 1560s, the Spanish had almost reached China, and set up a Pacific outpost on the nearby island of Cebu, in the Philippines. From there, they were able to make contact with the isolationist Chinese, whose merchant ships, or junks, were soon trading their wares for the one thing Spain could give them that they could not supply themselves: silver.[3] The Spaniards with their galleons were the 'missing link' connecting an early global market.[4] Months later, when the gold, silver, and other goods had been loaded in Panama and New Spain, the ships set sail for Havana, where the fleet reunited and then sailed up the Florida Straits, along the North American coast, and across the Atlantic.

When other European sailors learned about this system, many were willing and eager to try to capture one of these silver- or gold-laden ships. It was also an incentive to continue to sail west, rather than east, as many other European sailors had been doing. And, with the moral context provided by the anti-Catholic sentiment, increasingly hostile and aggressive ships began to arrive in the Caribbean, bringing Dutch, English, and French crews. The Dutch had a particular issue with Spain, in that their United Provinces, as part of the Holy Roman Empire, had been put under Spanish Habsburg rule. There was much resentment when the Holy Roman Emperor Charles V gave the Habsburg Netherlands territories to his son, Philip II, which meant that the region would be governed from Spain. Sporadic revolts culminated in a rebellion in 1568 by the Holland and Zeeland provinces, and this soon segued into a wider battle for independence, known as the Dutch Revolt, which would last for eighty years. The sea became an extension of this battleground in the West Indies too, as Dutch ships attacked the Spanish fleet. But the Dutch were not the only ones causing problems for Spain. The English had started their own battle against Spain. England's Elizabeth I sent ships to aid the Protestant Dutch in their efforts at independence, and they attacked Spanish vessels. Such raids were known as privateering, which meant that what would otherwise be called piracy was in fact granted a semblance of legitimacy. For instance, a sailor might carry a letter of marque from the English monarch allowing him to attack Spanish ships, and claim a portion of whatever booty he found – the rest, of course, going to the crown. Pirates, however, worked outside this structure, as did sailors known in English as freebooters, as *flibustier* in French, and in Dutch as *vrijbuiters*. They did raid and plunder, though at times they would also go on privateering missions. These seafarers were usually a motley crew, comprising adventurers of both sexes together with people of colour both enslaved and free. They ranged widely in years; boys often lied about their age in order to secure a berth. Most freebooters were from the lowest social classes, and by the seventeenth and eighteenth centuries runaway slaves were thought to have made up about a quarter of pirates – ships often provided an alternative to bondage and servitude, though some aboard remained enslaved or were sold illegally.[5]

Sailors who undertook these privateering missions during a time of war, however, were often acting in place of an official navy, a component of the military that had not been completely developed in this period. England and the Dutch relied on these freelance operators to score political hits, if not also financial ones. In England, one of the most famous privateers (to the English – the Spanish prefer to think of him as a pirate) of this period was Francis Drake. Under his leadership, English ships made impressive raids on Spain, and in the West Indies. Although he failed to capture their treasure fleet he shocked the Spanish with his daring in 1586, including a raid on Santo Domingo in which he burnt down much of the city, followed by one on

Cartagena, and rounded off by an attack on St Augustine, Florida, which he also set on fire. Philip II decided to strengthen the defence at Spain's key West Indian outposts, and during this period he instituted a large fort-building programme in the Caribbean that was the basis for the massive Castillo de los Tres Reyes Magos del Morro in Havana and the imposing Castillo San Felipe del Morro in San Juan, as well as fortifications in San Juan de Ulúa, in Mexico, Portobello on the isthmus of Panama, and Cartagena on the South American coast. Many of these undertakings were so vast they took another century to complete, forcing Spain to often rely on increased *guarda costa* ship patrols to intercept any suspicious vessels.

Drake's exploits reached a dramatic climax in 1588, when Spain sent its Armada, with about 130 ships, up the English Channel to seek revenge. But it was met with a humiliating defeat; and one that did not result in the loss of a single English ship. Drake and fellow privateer John Hawkins helped Lord Howard of Effingham secure an English victory, after which the privateering continued. Drake died of dysentery near Portobello in 1596, but piratical attacks at sea continued until the English and Spanish signed a treaty in 1604. But this did not guarantee a lasting peace. In 1618 the devastating Thirty Years War began. Underpinned by religion, the conflict would draw in most of the continent.

*

Although this was a period rife with political instability, religious intolerance, war, and piracy, other aspects of the ongoing settlement of the Caribbean were also changing the way Europeans understood the world. The islands and the surrounding coast were full of plants and animals unlike anything Europeans had ever seen – there was an immediate and intense curiosity about the natural world in these new lands. With the increase in maritime traffic, so too was there a rise in the specimens being brought across the Atlantic.

Nicolás Monardes, a physician from Seville, was an enthusiast who often waited with anticipation for the arrival of new plant species, especially those thought to have medicinal properties. One plant in particular excited him very much, and he included a detailed description of it – and its many virtues – in a multi-volume work first published in Seville in 1574 and translated into English three years later as *Joyfull Newes out of the Newe Founde Worlde*.[6] The plant's leaves, Monardes claimed, have a 'particular virtue to heal griefs of the head, and in especially coming of cold causes . . . the leaves must be put hot to it upon the grief, and multiplying them the time that is needful, until the grief be taken away'.[7] It seemed to be a wonder plant, efficacious in treating ailments of the chest and the stomach too. Monardes also thought it could 'cast out matter and rottenness at the mouth', as well as killing internal worms and providing relief for aching joints. The plant could be used in many forms, whether applying the leaves directly, grinding them in a mortar, or indeed smoking them. Ground-up leaves could be mixed 'and with Sugar made a Syrup' in order to 'expel the Matters, and rottenness of the breast marvelously'.[8] What was this wonder plant? Tobacco.

No one outside the Americas had ever seen tobacco. It was indigenous to the New World, and its cultivation may have started as long ago as 5000 BC.[9] It was used throughout the Americas, and it also spread to the Caribbean. As Monardes realized, it had many uses, not just medicinal ones. Drawing from the accounts of travellers he had read, Monardes explained that native priests used tobacco leaves in ceremonies, claiming that 'Indians for their pastime, do take the smoke of the Tobacco, for to make themselves drunk withal, and to see the visions, and things that do represent to them, wherein they do delight'.[10] However, smoking was only one of many ways it could be ingested: native practices included sniffing, chewing, drinking, or using the leaves in creams.[11]

Indians also used tobacco, Monardes claimed, 'to take away the weariness, and for to take lightsomnesse of their labour'.[12] Its stimulating properties appear to have already spread to African users, too, as Monardes reported that 'the black people that have gone from these parts to the Indies, has [sic] taken the same manner and use of the Tobacco, that the Indians have, for when they see themselves weary, they take it at the nose, and mouth'.[13] The nicotine in tobacco stimulates the brain and numbs pain. As a result European apothecaries and herbalists were eager to study the plant and use it as a medicine. However, for quite some time they were the only people putting it to any use. Two of Columbus's men, Rodrigo de Jerez and Luis de Torres, were Europe's first smokers when, in 28 October 1492, they sampled the tobacco offered to them by Amerindians.[14] However, Columbus did not bring tobacco back to Spain on that voyage, as he was suspicious of its association with the Amerindians' heathen practices. The

Inquisition took a similar view and made its stance on the plant clear: Jerez was jailed for three years for smoking in public.[15] But curiosity was too great and soon tobacco seeds were being smuggled into Spain and France, where the plants were grown and examined by expert eyes.

It is the English, though, who are thought to have popularized the herb in the 1560s, after John Hawkins brought it back from one of his voyages, and turned this medicinal plant into, in the view of some people, a social menace.[16] England's King James I saw the tobacco craze as a source of national weakness, the product of 'barbarous *Indians*'.[17] He wanted smoking and tobacco use banned, complaining:

> Have you not reason then to bee ashamed, and to forebeare this filthie noveltie, so basely grounded, so foolishly received, and so grossely mistaken in the right use therof? In your abuse thereof sinning against God, harming your selves both in persons and goods, and raking also thereby the markes and notes of vanitie upon you . . . A custome lothsome to the eye, hatefull to the Nose, harmefull to the braine, daungerous to the Lungs . . .[18]

But it was too late. By the time the king published his *Counterblaste to Tobacco* in 1604, pipes and spittoons had proliferated among his subjects, and they had long been trying to find a cheaper way to source their habit. James's predecessor on the English throne, Elizabeth I, had approved attempts to establish a tobacco colony in Roanoke on the North American coast in what is now North Carolina, although this was unsuccessful. And although taxes on tobacco and restrictions on its cultivation in England both rose under his rule, they did little to stem its use, or the proliferation of tobacco houses.

It was not only England that had become consumed by the weed. By the 1600s, Europeans had taken tobacco to the Far East, where it was also a success.[19] Once it became clear that there was a great deal of money to be made, and despite the Inquisition's wariness, the Spanish continued to sell it. Most tobacco leaf grown in the New World was shipped to Seville for processing, and the city set up its first tobacco factory in 1620, producing snuff, and tobacco shops followed.[20] But this monopoly was a source of ire to others. Reluctant to pay the high prices set by the Spanish tobacco trade, the English were soon ready to try to find their own source of supply once again – and this time they succeeded. A North American colony in Virginia, established in

1607, managed to survive a shaky start and began growing the crop. By 1618 it had exported 20,000lb; by 1627, the total shipped was 500,000lb.[21] It was followed by another colony in Bermuda. Indeed, William Alexander mentions it in his 1624 tract *An Encouragement to Colonies*, which was meant to entice Scots to the colder climes of New Scotland (Nova Scotia), noting, 'This Plantation of the Bermudas, a place not knowne when the King came to England, hath prospered so in a short time, that at this present, besides their ordinary (and too extraordinary valued) commodities of Tobacco, they have growing Oranges, Figs, and all kinds of fruits that they please to plant, and doe now intend to have a Sugar worke.'[22]

Tobacco had taken England – and the world – by storm. It had also given English investors the impetus to risk setting up colonies across the Atlantic. Tobacco was quickly losing its indigenous spiritual and medicinal basis and becoming a global fashion for people wealthy enough to afford it. Across the world, a range of tobacco-related paraphernalia followed in its wake, such as shiny silver snuff-boxes or ornate carved pipes, making the addiction more than purely chemical. But the popularity of the plant also proved the perfect opportunity for other European kingdoms to challenge Spain at its own game. There was a growing awareness that much of the land in the New World and many islands in the Caribbean were poorly guarded by the Spanish, and might thus be ripe for settlement.

Throughout the early decades of the 1600s, many of the islands of the Lesser Antilles were claimed by either the French (part of St Kitts, Guadeloupe, Martinique, St Lucia, St Barthélemy, Grenada, part of St Martin), the English (Barbados, Nevis, Antigua, Montserrat), or the Dutch (part of St Martin, Tortola and Anguilla, which was temporarily taken from England, Saba, St Eustatius, and Curaçao, Aruba, and Bonaire), with many of the settlers aiming to get into the lucrative tobacco trade. Even the Order of the Knights of Malta became involved, buying up St Kitts, St Martin, St Barts, Tortuga, and St Croix for 120,000 livres, though France bought the islands back for 500,000 livres in 1665.[23] They established basic settlements, whose inhabitants were at the mercy of the elements and which were occasionally wiped out by a hurricane. There were also attacks by native people – it was one thing for Europeans to trade with them, but claiming land was another issue altogether. Settlement was far from straightforward. But slowly, they evolved; land was cleared for growing, merchants began to provision passing ships, houses began to withstand tropical winds. Land grants were issued from monarchs, bestowing legitimacy on the enterprise. Settlers arrived, left, arrived again, perhaps died. Many of the settlers who lived there were northern Europeans, ranging in dogma from French Huguenots to Dutch Calvinists to English Puritans.[24] But these Protestant islands lacked the gridded streets and imposing cathedral plazas that were quick to be built under Spanish rule in Hispaniola, Cuba, and Puerto Rico, growing instead in fits and starts.

*

Although tobacco – as opposed to piracy – was a legitimate enterprise, it was still a source of consternation for the Spanish. In addition to competing with their own crop, many Spanish officials worried that tobacco growing was simply a cover for illegal trade. Smuggling, as much as piracy, could offer lucrative profits. The Spanish colonies operated a trading system by which settlers in the colonies could only buy Spanish goods from Spanish ships. The mechanics of smuggling were straightforward. For instance, Spanish settlers in Cuba needed cloth. That cloth might very well be sitting in a warehouse in Seville, or indeed merchants in that city might have been waiting for Catalan merchants to send cloth they had imported from the English or the Flemish. Because very little of the extracted gold and silver was invested in the Spanish economy, it failed to develop industry, and as demand grew from colonists, Spain was forced to import goods from elsewhere in Europe to put on the ships. Delay drove up demand, and hence the price. Very early on, merchants realized that because they had a monopoly on exports, they could control the price. In the meantime, anxious Spaniards in the islands who needed new dresses, or wanted wine, would be forced to wait. When the ships came in, they had to pay high prices and sometimes import duties as well.

It did not take long for British and Dutch contrabandists to realize they could undercut Spanish prices and still make a handsome profit, while at the same time giving the eager customers the cloth or whatever other scarce goods they wanted, and without paying any tax. They could cut Spain out completely. The islands were perfect for such illicit activity – caves and coves offered places to stash goods, and no one was able to patrol the waters effectively enough to stop it. Of course this did not mean that Spaniards in the Caribbean were opposed to or above such activity – many were all too eager to profit from this illicit commerce as well, or at least willing to take the bribes offered by the illegal traders. Life on the Spanish islands in the early seventeenth century was often difficult, and dependent on the ebb and flow of the *flota*. In fact, these islands subsisted in a large part on silver payments, known as the *situado*, from the larger metal haul to pay for defence and administration.[25] But it was never enough, and the people who lived there, even if they were officials, had to find ways to supplement their income.

Smuggling would soon bring to Hispaniola's northern coast a painful episode, known in Dominican history as the 'devastations' of 1605, when there was a forced depopulation. By the 1600s the *flota* routes had stopped calling at Santo Domingo, opting instead for the better harbour of Havana; as a result, the island's economy had slumped. Its small population was struggling, and many settlers lost interest once its gold mines petered out, moving throughout the 1500s to Mexico or South American territories. Even the slave ships that were meant to bring labour to the island's sugar plantations were in short supply, meaning that most people only had a few slaves living in proximity to the family, rather than large plantations. Cattle, rather than sugar or tobacco, became the mainstay of the economy, as their hides had a high trading value. The economic isolation of Hispaniola's residents from the main currents of Spanish trade forced them to turn to the illicit goods being sold by other Europeans. Buying from anywhere other than a Spanish ship was deemed illegal, but often it was a case of buy illegally or don't buy at all. In Hispaniola, the easiest trading point was along the north coast, in places such as Monte Cristi and Puerto Plata, rather than on the other side of the island around Santo Domingo.

Smuggling, by its nature, cannot necessarily follow a routine, but common practices emerged which notified eager buyers that there were goods for sale. For instance, a ship would drop anchor, a signal would be given, such as a cannon shot, and a launch would go out to the ship full of eager locals. Most merchants did not go ashore for fear of kidnapping. If a ship was anchored somewhere more secluded, both parties could exchange wares on the beach. Often slaves or free blacks who worked on the ships were sent as go-betweens.[26] Island officials knew what was going on, but turned a blind eye (or indeed, took advantage of their position to trade, or profit in some way themselves). But because of this illicit trade, the hides produced by the islanders seldom reached Spain in any significant quantity. By 1598, some 80,000 hides were smuggled a year.[27]

This problem took up much of Baltasar López de Castro's attention. He had held an important administrative post in the colonial Audiencia, but he lost the job in 1597 as a result of a political squabble. His punishment mandated that he stay twenty leagues away from Santo Domingo for four years, so he went one better and sailed to Madrid to plead his case. In trying to return to the crown's good graces, he crafted a plan, outlined in a couple of *memorias* in 1598 about the natural abundance of Hispaniola and how its potential was being undermined by illegal trade with non-Spaniards. What was more, he argued, these foreigners were not Catholic, and they were putting souls at risk. He suggested numerous measures to end the contraband, one of which was simply to depopulate the north of the island, where most of the trading took place, and force people to live closer to Santo Domingo. Similar measures had been proposed earlier – the crown was well aware of the contraband problem – but the idea had not only found its time but was heard by an enthusiastic audience. By early 1602 the Council of the Indies approved the measures, and López had his old job back.

However, the plan, as might be expected, was not well received by the residents of the north coast or indeed those in other parts of the island. The governor, Antonio Osorio, who assisted the implementation of these orders (and was later considered the cruel mastermind behind them), had spent much of his career in the service of the Spanish military, which was fortunate for him because he needed battle experience to combat the resistance and anger of the people of Hispaniola. Orders went out that Puerto Plata, Bayaha, Monte Cristi, and La Yaguana should be depopulated, and the settlers moved to new towns. There were clashes with resistant residents who did not want to move their homes, or their cattle ranches, to the south. Osorio struggled for compliance, and by 1605 had to bring in 150 soldiers from Puerto Rico to help. In a rather unfortunate irony, one of Osorio's letters to Spain that year, in which he complained about the difficulties he was having, was confiscated by smuggler-privateers who had attacked a Spanish ship. It turned up in Santiago, Cuba, a year later. Once the policy had been carried out, the overall ramifications for the island were significant, as it severely damaged the island's trade in cattle hides, as well as the small amounts of sugar and ginger it was producing.[28]

*

For the Dutch jurist and philosopher Hugo Grotius the new global seascape presented a problem: to whom did the waters belong? This may not be such a surprising question – when he practised as a lawyer one of Grotius's clients was the Dutch East India Company (EIC).[29] In his 1609 *Mare Liberum*, he argued that the seas did not belong to any one nation or kingdom, and should be free for all to navigate, and many Dutch and English mariners enthusiastically agreed. However, conflicts on the high seas now represented a legal problem. One of the issues sailors and settlers alike faced in the West Indies was the absence of law, or, at least, an absence of clarity about how the laws of their own homeland applied to this new world. To add to the confusion, in these early years there was also an absence of accurate maps of these waters.[30]

In addition to the freedom to navigate, Grotius thought that during a state of war, the ships – and the loot within them – of any enemy were fair game.[31] But others had disagreed, arguing that plunder needed to be authorised by a nation's sovereign, such as in letters of marque. In practice, external events usually decided who was a privateer and who was a pirate. Captains and crews often wanted to be sure their booty was considered legal.[32] In fact, some sailors would claim they were forced into raids against their will as a defence, just in case something went wrong.[33] And when some seventeenth-century sailors are today thought of as operating as 'pirates', it is because they are being judged against modern ideas. During this period, at least, the question of who owned the seas – and how one was to behave upon them – was a long way from having a clear answer.

Grotius published his pamphlet around the time that the Dutch had negotiated a truce with Spain, halting the war for independence for twelve years. For Grotius, anything that was public – the sea, the air – could not be private property. No nation could claim the sea, as Portugal had tried to do in deflecting growing Dutch interest in the southern Atlantic. In 1609, however, Spain granted the Dutch rights of navigation in the East Indies, and their ships had lost no time heading east. But resentment lingered in the United Provinces and by 1621 many people were ready to resume the fight for independence, realizing Spain's earlier entry in the Thirty Years War had created the ideal opportunity. The same year saw the establishment of the Dutch West India Company, for which privateering was one of its main orders of business, as were expanding its settlements in Brazil and increasing its shipments of Africans.[34] And despite the difficulty of attacking the Spanish fleet, the Dutch scored a stunning success in 1628, when a West India Company ship managed to take a ship from the *flota* around Veracruz and made so much money on that one haul that shareholders were paid a 50 per cent dividend that year.[35]

As the relations between Spain and England again soured, the idea of setting up a similar English West India company emerged, modelled on the Dutch. But the plans never materialized. The English had set up an East India Company in 1600, but not a monopoly company for West Indian trade.[36] The East India Company acted as imperialists by proxy in the East, taking what started out as a trade monopoly to move goods from India to England and transforming it through centuries of violence into colonial rule in India and south-east Asia. The English and Dutch companies constantly fought in Indian Ocean waters during this period, as the Dutch was also trying to expand its reach, but as far as the West Indies were concerned, any such ventures were on a much smaller scale.

There was enough interest, especially after the success of the Virginia colony, for private financiers to make similar efforts to establish tobacco colonies on Caribbean islands that had not been settled by the Spanish, although such experiments were fraught with difficulty and often ended in disaster. The fate of two English colonies, Providence and Barbados, illustrates the pitfalls and rewards that might await the risk-takers. Providence Island was, in many respects, a daring choice for the investors of the Providence Island Company. It is a small volcanic island of only 17 square kilometres (6.65 square miles), stumbled upon by the English during earlier privateering raids on the Spanish mainland. At the time the company was created, around 1629, the island was surrounded by Spanish territories; it lay off the coast of Nicaragua, to its west and south was the Spanish Main, while to the north was Jamaica, then still claimed by Spain.

The backers included earls and baronets, and many of the men had been involved in the financing of the Virginia and Bermuda (Somers Isles) colonies. They knew the risks, and that the rewards

could be a long time coming. The Plymouth colony (1620) in Massachusetts had taken a decade to pay off its debt, and Jamestown, Virginia
(1607), took fifteen years to find its financial footing.[37] Still, they were
confident of the enterprise, and on Christmas Eve 1629, the first settlers
stepped ashore on Providence Island, led by their newly appointed
governor, Philip Bell. The colonists were Puritan, and they named the
island in accordance with their beliefs that they were aligned with
divine will. In February 1631, about a hundred more settlers left London
aboard the *Seaflower*. The Catholic Spaniards, for their part, were immediately suspicious of these heretic settlers, and thought they were only
planting tobacco as a cover for smuggling and piracy. The Dutch had
been known to use Providence and neighbouring islands in their raids
before the settlers arrived.

The intention of the English was to use indentured servants as
labour to grow tobacco, and later cotton, but it did not go to plan. The
crops did not thrive, and abuse of servants was rife – by 1634 the
company could not find enough willing settlers to fill a ship; many
people in England had heard reports of mistreatment.[38] There were
indigenous people from the mainland – the Miskito – who came to
the island to hunt turtles, but they were supposed to be left alone and
not forced into labour. And as people free of indenture left when their
contracts expired, the settlers could not find replacements. The fact
that the people working the land did not own it either added to the
growing discontent. It was not long before the islanders started to
consider African labour. Bell was said to have brought his own slaves
from Bermuda, and in 1633 he wanted to buy more to undertake public
works because there was not sufficient manpower. Some of the stricter
Puritans were concerned that enslavement would be the end of the
godliness of their colony. To add to the problem, the Spanish raided
Providence Island in 1635, and appeals to New England for more
settlers to join them were met with no result. By 1638 a later
governor, Nathaniel Butler, was given permission to buy a hundred
slaves. For some of the landless settlers, owning slaves was a way to
compensate for the lack of land, and soon the island had several
hundred Africans. None of England's other fledgling colonies had
acquired Africans at such a rate, and in such numbers. In that same
year, the slaves rose up in the first rebellion in the British colonies, on
1 May 1638. The island's fortunes continued to deteriorate, and another

raid by the Spanish, in 1641, finished off the colony. A Spanish fleet arrived on 19 May 1641, bringing 1,400 troops. They found 350 English men and women, and 381 slaves, though it is believed that many slaves had been sent to St Kitts and Bermuda in anticipation of such an attack. By 25 May, Spain had retaken the island.[39]

Geography, among other factors, helped make the fate of Barbados very different. Not only was it much larger than Providence Island at 431 square kilometres (167 square miles), its position was outside the Spanish territories. Barbados sits on the edge of the Caribbean, like an accidental drop of ink just outside the graceful dots of the Lesser Antilles islands. There is nothing but water to its east, and to the west are only the small islands of St Vincent and St Lucia, neither of which then had European inhabitants. Unlike Providence – and many of the other islands – Barbados was flat. It was also uninhabited. Amerindians had lived there but were gone by the time Europeans arrived.

It sounded very promising indeed to Anglo-Dutch London merchant Sir William Courteen, who was willing to take a risk investing in tobacco and what sounded like just the place to grow it. One of his associates, Captain John Powell, had come across Barbados in 1625, calling in during a voyage back from the South American mainland (some accounts say from Guiana, others Brazil). Powell saw at first hand how ideal the island was. The captain's brother, Henry Powell, arrived in 1627 on the *William and John* with around eighty settlers and ten slaves captured from a Portuguese ship. They named their settlement James-town (today's Holetown). The early settlers worked for Courteen's company and were not given land. Instead, the company paid the settlers wages. They soon got to work clearing forests to make fields and planting edible crops. Indigenous people from mainland South America were brought in to assist in planting (there are varying accounts of whether or not these people were enslaved). In 1628 they exported 100,000lb of tobacco, and this success lured more settlers from England, often indentured for terms of three to ten years. As a result of a dispute over the island's ownership, Courteen's settlement was eventually taken over by the Earl of Carlisle in 1629. Carlisle gave the planters land in exchange for 40lb of tobacco, but from that point they had to organize and pay for their own labour and find their own capital.[40]

This worked for a while – but when the price of the crop dropped, many could no longer make a living. In fact, the quality of Barbados tobacco was considered poor compared with that of other colonies, with one writer calling it 'earthy and worthless' – even the settlers themselves imported better smoking tobacco from Virginia or the Spanish colonies.[41] Also, the market was oversupplied, and prices plummeted despite tobacco's global popularity. Worried planters turned to cotton and indigo, a valuable dye, but a drought in 1631 made conditions desperate, and the 1630s were known as the 'starving time'. Each switch to a new commodity brought about cycles of boom and bust, which continued into the 1640s. But the island's agricultural uncertainty was about to come to an end.

In 1640 a young planter named James Drax left the island for Recife in Brazil, where he had heard the Dutch were growing sugar cane. He went to observe and learn their techniques, and when he returned to Barbados he started experimenting, at first with mixed results. Unlike in Providence, planters like Drax were still relying on indentured labour; they had not yet fully turned to African slavery. Indentured servants arrived through many means – some came after agents in England scoured rural villages for people poor and desperate enough to risk the passage to the New World. People who had the means to pay for their own passage did so, and then they indentured themselves upon arrival in Barbados, usually on shorter contracts.[42] Others, like Irish Catholics, who faced persecution from the English during this period, were forcibly sent over. Indenture was often little better than slavery. The life was hard and dirty, and the masters often unkind, if not downright brutal. By 1649, a group of indentured servants planned to revolt and murder their masters, but the plot was uncovered. Freedom for those servants who served out their term offered few prospects. By 1652, near the peak, there were 13,000 indentured servants in Barbados. This dropped to 2,301 in 1683, and to 1,500 by 1715.[43] Labour would have to be found elsewhere.

*

Like Providence and Barbados, St Kitts had been initially settled with the intention of growing tobacco. Englishman Thomas Warner had sailed to Guiana in 1622 to establish a settlement but was run off by the Spanish, so he turned to the Caribbean. He left England in 1623 for St Christopher's, as St Kitts was then called, where he 'met with a friendly reception from the Caribees'.[44] Later that summer a hurricane destroyed ot only the tobacco crop, but other foodstuffs and homes, though they managed to survive and eventually turned a good crop. Reinforcements and more settlers arrived in 1625, and it was after this that Warner was able to send a proper first harvest back to England. But his troubles continued. There was an uprising by the indigenous people in 1626 that led to a bloody massacre by the English.[45] Passing Spanish ships that had taken a different course en route to Panama saw the settlements and attacked, taking the island back briefly in 1629. In the meantime, the French had taken part of the island as well. Like the English, the French had combined settlement and piracy. And although early settlers needed a hiding place, later ones wanted to start growing tobacco. Many French began to arrive in St Kitts, Guadeloupe, and Martinique, also trying to grow tobacco and also using indentured servants – engagés – who were contracted to work for periods ranging from just over a year to more than three years. It was not the smoothest start, though over the intervening decades the colonies began to take root.

However, skirmishes between the Europeans and the native peoples, and between the French and English, continued. In theory, the French and English could hold off attacks by the native people and Spaniards. In practice, the politics of Europe spilled into St Kitts, and the period was marked by ongoing violence. The French and English managed to wrest control of the island from its indigenous inhabitants, and Warner continued to expand into other islands, first into Nevis (1628), which sits just across a bay at the thin end of the drumstick-shaped St Kitts, then Antigua and Montserrat (both in 1632). He amassed a fortune and died in 1648. However, Warner was rumoured to have had a bastard son with an indigenous slave taken from Dominica. The boy, known as Indian Warner, went to live on that island and soon was made a chief among his mother's people. In 1664 he brought Kalinago men from Dominica to assist the English with a raid on the French in St Lucia. But this was not enough to establish his status among the English, and he would meet a tragic end. According to a French account, Philip Warner – Indian's half-brother – plied him with brandy and killed him when he was drunk. Other versions of events say Indian was killed during a drunken feast. The details are unclear, the truths and embellishments of Indian Warner's life and death having blurred in the intervening centuries, but the story captures the brutal and bloodthirsty nature of settlement.[46]

Warner's old friend and lieutenant John Jeaffreson had also joined the colonization effort, and when he died, his son, Christopher Jeaffreson, inherited some of this West Indian land, as well as property in East Anglia. So in 1676, at the age of twenty-two, he embarked for St Kitts to inspect his inheritance. His letters to England survive, and they show how St Kitts was, like Barbados, making the transition to sugar and slavery. In a letter to his father-in-law, Christopher lamented that 'I intend, God willing, to try my fortune in planting canes, notwithstanding the great discouragement I meete with, upon the attempt of the French, who are twice as strong as wee.'[47]

Sugar by now was the priority, but it was still an inexact science, as Jeaffreson remarked: 'I goe on expending money upon my plantation, in hopes it will repaye mee with interest; but I must have patience, for it will require tyme, as well as a large expense, before the sugar-worke can bee perfected. It is now esteemed here a great folly for a man to expose his tyme or goods to the hazard of indigo or tobacco, sugar being now the only thriveing and valuable commodity.'[48] He mentions that the island was not yet an important part of the trade routes, as 'forty or fifty saile of ships . . . come to this island and Nevis every year; but few of them to this island as yet, it being not so well settled'.[49]

And in a letter to his cousin, William Poyntz, he bemoaned the lack of white labour on the island, saying,

I am necessitated to reiterate my sayd request to you, not only for a clerke or tradesman, but for any sorte of men, and one or two women if they can be found. They are generally wanted in this island; and all my bond-servants are gone free. [This was in his fifth year on the island] . . . It is seldome seene that the ingenious or industrious men fail of raising their fortunes in any part of the Indies, especially here, or where the land is not thoroughly settled. There are now several examples of it to my knowledge – men raised from little or nothing to vast estates. And I can assure you our slaves live as well now as the servants did formerly.[50]

But his nascent sugar operation was swept away by a hurricane on 27 August 1681. He wrote in a letter to his sister that October that 'I had not a house standing on my plantation, in which I could shelter myself from the weather'. His new 'sugar-work' was 'flatt with the ground, – the stone wall overturned, and the timber scattered in divers places' and there were thirty-two slaves and some white servants to give food and shelter.[51] He eventually decided to return to England, departing in July 1682 having entrusted Edward Thorn with the post of manager. There was no guarantee his plantation would thrive; life on these islands was full of uncertainty, not only for planters like Jeaffreson, but for everyone involved.

The Dutch, in the meantime, had been shoring up their salt supplies. They had been banned from the lucrative Iberian salt trade in 1585. The Portuguese had a large supply of salt, but in 1580 Portugal became part of the Iberian Union, under which it and Spain were united and which lasted until 1640. This coincided with the end of the twelve-year truce between Spain and the Dutch, after which the Dutch found themselves with insufficient salt supplies to preserve their herring, which was a key export. Sailors were quick to look around Panama and the Venezuelan coast to find new supplies, and they took Curaçao from Spain in 1634, as well as neighbouring Bonaire and Aruba soon after, all of which lie very near to the South American mainland, and all of which are arid and thus held the possibility of some salt pans. The Spanish were so concerned about the Dutch encroachment in South America on their quest for salt that they went as far as building a large fort in the Araya peninsula on the Venezuelan coast to stop any attempts at extraction.

The human body doesn't need tobacco or sugar, but it does need salt. An average person contains about 250g (0.6lb) of salt, which is depleted through bodily functions and must be regularly replaced.[52] Considering that the heat and humidity of the tropics drew out salt through never-ending perspiration, there would have been reason enough to find a source for local consumption alone. But there was a greater need – salted fish was big business. Cod from Newfoundland and herring could be preserved by salting and there was a large Catholic market ready to eat it on holy days. And as slavery began to expand, imported salted fish also became a staple of the slave diet.

The Dutch wasted little time setting up salt pans; by 1640 Dutch West India Company employees were being given instructions 'concerning the saltpans, both here and upon Buenairo [Bonaire]'. They were 'to pay close attention that the seasons are observed and during the dry period that as much salt as possible is made [i.e. collected], dried and preserved, so that all incoming ships, whether belonging to the Company or private, shall be so served thereby'.[53]

The English, too, had been searching for a source of salt but they managed to make a deal with the Portuguese to use their salt flats in the Cape Verde islands of Maio and Boa Vista. (A third island the Portuguese used for salt was called Sal.) The Turks and Caicos, which are scattered across the water to the north of Cuba and Haiti, also became part of the salt circuit, as settlers from Bermuda landed on the uninhabited islands looking for better sources of the mineral in the late 1600s.

Records from around the 1640s show that the Dutch islands, while a decent source of salt, were difficult places to live, and food was often scarce. Aruba, Bonaire, and Curaçao have arid climates, and their rocky soil makes them ill-suited for growing crops. The colonists therefore had to rely on cattle and what little foodstuff could be produced. Indeed, a 13 March 1643 resolution from Curaçao asking for shipments of supplies raised the 'fear of being involved once again in a similar or worse famine, which could happen if food is not supplied from the fatherland'.[54] Despite the difficulties, by 1635 the Dutch had built a fort on Curaçao, and it had become an important link in their Atlantic routes, which spread north to New Netherland (today's New York), and as far south as West Africa, where the Dutch were active in the slave trade.

It was a difficult life on those dry, rocky islands. Daily existence was tough enough, but the Spaniards also raided them, sometimes in retaliation for Dutch attacks on their territory; one attack on Bonaire in 1642 destroyed the nascent fort and salt works. Everything had to be imported. One receipt listed the arrival in Curaçao of: '2 sturdy four-wheeled farm wagons, horse harness and equipment for the afore-said wagons for eight draft horses, 1 plow with the appropriate equip-ment thereto, some sturdy wheelbarrows for moving salt . . .'[55]

Slaves were brought in to work in the salt pans, but there were also a few Amerindian people left as well, which reports claimed had 'given us great service' and shown 'loyalty' towards the Dutch. By 14 April 1643 another report noted that the salt works were back up in Bonaire, and orders were given 'to send all the Company's Negroes over there' even though there was still a food problem: '[A]fter making a calculation concerning the food supply and realizing that it would not be sufficient until relief came from the fatherland or New Nether-land, even if we maintain the employed Blacks with flour, beans and fish, as has been done in the past, and whereas it is still necessary that those working the saltpans have proper nourishment; therefore it has been decided to send a sloop . . . to catch some turtles, if possible, for the Negroes.'[56]

The island was then under the command of Petrus (Peter) Stuyvesant, the last Dutch governor of New Netherland. He arrived in Curaçao in 1635, and from 1642 to 1646 he served as director of that island and neighbouring Bonaire and Aruba, for the Dutch West India Company, which at that point was in charge of the colonization. In 1651 João de Illan (also Jeudah), a Jewish man who had lived in Brazil, petitioned the WIC to establish a colony and bring some settlers with him, but his efforts were thwarted by Stuyvesant, who was hostile towards the Jews.[57] The following year, the directors of the WIC allowed Joseph Nunes da Fonseca (also known as David Nassi) and his partners to 'establish a colony on the island of Curaçao', and they were given a number of freedoms, including 'permits to sell wood and salt, as well as a commission . . . in order to be permitted to seize and capture Portuguese ships, provided the prizes be brought to this country . . .'[58] In 1659 Isaac da Costa, who had been working as a sugar planter in Brazil, obtained a charter to establish a colony, and he brought some seventy people with him, adding to the small but significant Jewish community on the island.[59] This would be the foundation for the reinvention of the island, soon turning this outpost into a major trading centre.

There was one more substance left to add to the mix of tobacco, salt, and sugar – coffee. Coffee, unlike tobacco, was a crop already known around the world. From its roots in Ethiopia, it spread through the Arab world via Muslim traders, arriving in Europe around the 1500s. The first of London's famed coffeehouses opened around 1650 and fifty years later there were more than 2,000 in that city alone, but the coffee bean would lose its lustre once the delicate tea leaves of China arrived.

Other Europeans, however, continued to need their coffee fix. Coffeehouses spread through the major cities, such as Venice and Paris.[60] The Dutch took coffee beans to their settlements in Java and Ceylon, while French planters brought them to Martinique. Some of the islands – those with mountainous interiors – had the right mix of heat and coolness, light and shade, for growing the plant. Once they are ready to harvest, beans have to be picked, and then dried in the sun (or in drums), and their skins removed, so it is a fairly labour-intensive crop. Coffee took root across the Caribbean, including Cuba and Jamaica, but nowhere more so than in the French colony of Saint-Domingue, which, by the 1780s, would supply half the world's coffee – in addition to the mountains of sugar it also produced.[61] By 1788, its coffee exports had increased sixfold from what they had been as recently as 1765.[62] Although coffee was not the impetus to colonize, like tobacco, nor the source of vast wealth like sugar, it would soon be an important component of West Indian trade. It also spread to a number of the smaller islands, and was cultivated there, too.

Drinking chocolate had also become popular; cacao was grown in Central America and, like tobacco, spread throughout Europe, spawning crazes and becoming a staple in European – and North American – homes. Another important beverage was being produced in the Caribbean during this time as well: rum. By 1664–5, the island had exported 102,744 US gallons, and the numbers would keep rising. Other sugar colonies would soon follow.[63]

Tobacco would retain an important place in the Caribbean imagination and indeed as a crop – witness the longevity of the Cuban cigar's popularity – but as a cash crop it was soon eclipsed by sugar. Taken together, these new substances captured the imagination – and bloodstream – of a European public in transition. They were complemented by other West Indian crops, such as ginger, cacao, cotton, and indigo. Tobacco and coffee stimulated and excited the public, and they were now well within the reach of the growing middle classes. At the same time, global sea routes were connecting the world, and by the start of the eighteenth century the results were clear. Commodities were being transplanted and transported halfway across the globe to reach a new class of people. Much as tobacco spawned an industry that produced decorative storage and smoking devices, so too did tea bring the desire for fine porcelain pots and cups from which to serve and drink it. And such goods found their way to Europe and the Americas via the Far East. Demand and fashion became as potent a mix as caffeine and tobacco, and more ships sailed and more debts were incurred as more goods were taken to more houses.

Consumption was not limited to Europe. The settlers of the Caribbean, too, had to keep up with the latest fashions, despite obvious differences in climate and lifestyle. For instance, the St Kitts heir

Christopher Jeaffreson, while on the island, sent over a shopping list to a relation in England asking to be sent 'per the first shippe':

> A demi-castor hatt . . . a good perrewig . . . a laced cravat and cuffs . . . as much broad cloth as will make me a fashionable suit . . . A suitable lining and trimming of any colour, except blew or yellow, which I now weare . . . A douzaine yards at least of ribbons for cravatt and cuffs . . . a fashionable and handsome belt . . . a payer of silke, and 4 payer of thread stockings . . . Enough silver and gold lace to lace my hat round . . . 8 payer of shoes, which is more, I hope, than I shall weare out here, after the arrival of these things.[64]

It did not take long for the arms of European commerce to reach into these new colonies. By 1686, the value of English goods exported from London to Barbados was nearly £70,000 and to Jamaica around £30,000, or £9.7 million and £4 million, respectively, in today's money.[65] Foods and fashions converged and diverged across a commodity trail that was now linked around the world. Merchants like Manuel Bautista Pérez, whose life took him from Portugal to Seville to Peru, traded not just in the West Indies, but across the globe. He had contacts in Veracruz, Panama, and Cartagena, but also in Guatemala, Angola, and Santiago de Chile, through which he moved African slaves and Chinese textiles, as well as Caribbean products such as indigo. His trade network extended to India and the Far East.[66] The Caribbean was in the centre of this action, connecting the East and West, as well as North and South. There was also a lot of inter-colonial trade. By this time, North America had seen the arrival of Europeans, from the English and French fur-trappers in the north of Canada down along the Atlantic coastline, to the Spanish in Florida.* These settlements had more natural resources at their disposal than the islands, especially timber. Yet they wanted tropical products that were scarce or difficult to produce, such as sugar or molasses for making rum. Soon these routes between north and south were thriving, from Rhode Island to Barbados, or Martinique to Louisiana, though there was of course plenty of illegal cross-over, with British goods from Delaware somehow washing up in Cuba, for instance.

---

* Prior to the settlement of Jamestown and Plymouth, the area around the St Lawrence River in Canada saw the arrival of the French in the 1530s, while Newfoundland was settled by the English in 1583.

The growth of settlements did little to stifle the spread of illicit maritime activity. At the very least, the emerging material needs of the settlers gave some sailors all the more reason to continue with contraband trade – there was a growing market for their wares. But, alongside the Peace of Westphalia in 1648, which ended both the Thirty Years War and the Dutch Revolt between the Netherlands and Spain, there had also been an agreement to ban privateering by prohibiting letters of marque. The peace agreements gave independence to the northern United Provinces (today's Netherlands), while the Low Countries (modern Luxembourg and Belgium) remained under Habsburg control. Some aspects of the settlement would last. The prohibition of privateering would not. But this time, some of the clashes would be between the Dutch and the English. During England's civil war from 1642 to 1651, the Dutch had seen their shipping and commercial prowess expand, so much so that it became a concern to the English. But by 1653, with the war over and Oliver Cromwell established as Lord Protector of the Commonwealth of England, Scotland, and Ireland, some attention could be given to the state of oceanic trade. Cromwell's government passed the Navigation Act of 1651, which targeted the Dutch. It stipulated that goods from English colonies or foreign countries had to be transported in English ships, meaning neither the Dutch nor any other foreigners could bring their products to England's ports, including those in the Americas. The act aggravated relations between England and the Netherlands and triggered the first Anglo-Dutch War, which ended in 1654. This was followed by a war between England and Spain over trade, one that would have important consequences for the West Indies.

By this time, Cromwell and 'empire' were spoken of in the same breath, and talk turned to his 'Western design'. Catholic Spain, unwilling to meet trade demands, seemed the more obvious target for the Protestant Commonwealth.[67] Into this political setting stepped Thomas Gage, a Dominican friar turned Puritan. He was one of the few Englishmen to have spent significant time in Spanish America during the early years of conquest. After a voyage that entailed hiding in an emptied biscuit barrel on board one of the convoys to the Americas – non-Spaniards were prohibited from the New World – he stayed on as a friar in Mexico and Guatemala from 1625 to 1637. Upon his return, he wrote an account of his adventure, which was published in 1648 and widely read. By this point, Gage had converted to Puritanism, and his writings reflect a politically astute antipathy towards the Spanish and Catholicism. There is little doubt that they influenced Cromwell's West Indian policy.[68] There was a growing feeling that a successful attack against the Spanish would – in accordance with biblical metaphor – prove the fall of 'Romish Babylon', as Gage put it.[69] Reprints – or, rather, selectively edited and translated versions – of Bartolomé de las Casas's *History of the Indies* were circulating around this time as well, and anti-Spanish feeling ran high.

The idea was that a defeat of Spain would result in God making the Commonwealth – and by extension Cromwell – ruler of the Indies, and grant them what seemed like all the gold in the world. Indeed, in 'Some Briefe and True Observations Concerning the West-Indies', which Gage presented to Cromwell, he pointed out that there are 'no people more sinfull then the Spaniards in America, both greate and smalle, viceroys, judges, and poore pesants, who in general sinne, and hide not their sinne . . . therefore their sinnes will betray them and fight against them, if ever any nation shall oppose them'.[70] Gage then took it a step further and virtually incited Cromwell to attack by claiming, 'It hath been for these many years their owne common talke, from some predictions, or (as they call them) prophecies, vented out amongst them, that a strange people shall conquer them, and take all their riches from them.' He reminded Cromwell that the Spanish had regularly attacked England's fledgling colonies, where settlers were 'unhumanly and most barbarously treated'.

But Gage, with his first-hand knowledge of the Spanish Main, could also tell Cromwell with confidence that large parts of it were 'very thinnely peopled by Spaniards', and that he was aware of native and slave hostility, too. To Gage, Hispaniola was an attractive target, not only because it was Spain's oldest colony and 'therefore would bee to them a bad omen to beginne to loose that', but also because it had few settlers. Gage confessed that the riches there were not 'comparable with those of the maine', but that ginger, hides, and sugar could be found, and there were rumours of silver mines. Gage went on to comment on Cuba and New Spain, but in the end Cromwell decided to attack Hispaniola. The austere Cromwell cannot be said to be in the same category as gold-hungry conquistadors; for him money was, as it remains, a form of power. By conquering Hispaniola, England would have the means to take forward its Puritan revolution.

The expedition force, led by Admiral William Penn and General Robert Venables, left England in 1654. After stopping in Barbados to gather more troops, they landed on Hispaniola in April 1655. The soldiers were unprepared: not for the Spaniards they faced, but for the heat and disease. Venables later explained that, on Hispaniola, 'The Ennemy suffered without lett our Men to march on, who went just into the midst of danger (being ready to faint with thirst, having march'd eight miles without water), and then Charg'd them.'[71] Even he admitted to being ill at that point with 'a grievous Flux'.[72] After two attempts they gave in. The fabled riches of the Spanish world – which by this point had been well depleted on the island anyway – would elude the English. Yet, they did not want to leave the expedition empty-handed and tried to take Jamaica, whose name comes from the indigenous word *xaymaca*, which was thought to mean 'land of wood and water'. On 10 May 1655 they landed on the island, 'gaining with little Opposition the Enemy's Fort with some Guns'. They made a treaty and, as Venables recalled, 'I told them we came not to pillage, but to plant.'[73]

For Cromwell, the humiliation severely dented his confidence, and he never stopped questioning the failure of something about which he had felt so certain. When the reports of the debacle in Hispaniola reached him on 24 July 1655, he shut himself away for a day.[74] He later wrote to Admiral Goodson, in Jamaica, in October 1655, 'It is not to be denied but the Lord hath greatly humbled us in that sad loss sustained at Hispaniola; no doubt we have provoked the Lord, and it is good for us to know so.'[75] In fact, the defeat was so profound that on their return to England Penn and Venables were incarcerated in the Tower of London.

Cromwell died in 1658, and the Commonwealth collapsed. Charles II returned to the throne in 1660. In the same year, another Navigation Act was passed that stipulated all goods were to be carried to and from the colonies in English ships, with a mostly English crew, again trying to force out the Dutch. As before these measures proved difficult to enforce and, once again, in 1665 they sparked a war.[76] The Peace of Breda in 1667 stopped the fighting for a while, and gave the Dutch the colony of Suriname in exchange for ceding to England its struggling New Netherland outpost in North America.

*

By this point, France had become the fourth major power in the Caribbean. It too set up a West India company, the Compagnie des Indes occidentales, in 1664. France in this period was, like Spain and to a degree the English, operating a protectionist market. The policies of Louis XIV's finance minister Jean-Baptiste Colbert, who was in office from 1665 until his death in 1683, and who advocated a mercantilist system, imposed many restrictions on what the island colonies were allowed to do. In theory colonists should buy French wares, and in exchange France would receive goods from the colonies, such as sugar. This policy was extended to all the colonies in France's growing global empire, which could trade with each other. But many French people in the Caribbean were also operating outside of this system. A few years after the death of Colbert, in 1685, Louis XIV's revocation of the Edict of Nantes stripped French Protestants of their religious freedoms and ended France's policy of religious tolerance. Many Huguenots fled the country, making their way to North America and the Caribbean. Some became involved in privateering and piracy.

One such person was Alexandre Olivier Exquemelin. He claimed that he did not seek this profession but, rather, found himself in it, working as a barber-surgeon on the ships after starting out as an employee of the French West India Company. Born around 1645 in the port of Harfleur, at the age of twenty-one he joined the French WIC and on 2 May 1666 he set sail on the *St John*, bound for Tortuga, an islet just north of Hispaniola. He kept an account of his life at sea, later publishing it in 1678, first in Dutch, and then upon its success in other European languages. Exquemelin brought to Europe's attention the world of the Americaensche Zee-Roovers (as it was in the original title), or the buccaneers. These buccaneers became associated with Tortuga, no doubt thanks to Exquemelin. A small settlement had already been established in 1659 to grow tobacco, do a bit of logging, and to attempt to trade illegal goods to the nearby Spanish territories, though by the time he arrived there it was not faring well. Even with the addition of WIC investment, the colony eventually went bust, and Exquemelin found another living on the high seas. But even before the colony was set up, sailors – many of whom were French – had long been using the island as a base for raids, or for hunting wild boar and cattle, from which they could eat the meat and sell the hides.[77] These early squatters, who may have included runaway slaves as well, survived by learning what they could from the remaining native peoples in Hispaniola about how to live in the yet untamed wilderness. They were taught how to smoke-dry their meat, hanging strips of it over a frame, or *boucan* – which is the name the French gave it, and led to the men being called *boucaniers*, and later in English buccaneers – made of sticks and allowing it to cook above a fire and let it smoke, making it a forerunner to the modern barbecue.[78]

But it was not for hunting wild boar that buccaneers became infamous. They also took to the seas, raiding and ransacking coastal communities, like pirates. The distinction lay in the fact that some of them hunted and traded illegally on land – but they would also sack a Spanish ship when the occasion presented itself. Although these men were often depicted as lawless, their ships were no floating vessels of anarchy. The sailors agreed by a vote as to where they would cruise, and they made an arrangement with the captain with regard to their share of loot and any payment to the injured, for instance 'for the loss of a right arm, 600 pieces of eight or six slaves'.[79] Buccaneers and pirates alike needed hideouts, ideally beyond national jurisdictions; for a time Tortuga proved ideal. Others headed for the Central American coast, where European settlement was scarce and sailors were often able to establish relationships with the native peoples. Towns such as Bluefields, Nicaragua, began as pirate hideouts before becoming port towns, with British and Dutch sailors arriving and settling, some engaging in trade (illegal or otherwise).[80]

Exquemelin's own journey took him into the crew of one of the most infamous pirates of the time: Henry Morgan. Welsh-born Morgan had arrived in the Caribbean around 1658, though other accounts claim he went earlier, as an indentured servant. Using Jamaica as a base, as many English sea-dogs were doing, he could privateer and raid. He made a number of successful attacks on the Spanish: with French privateers – including Exquemelin – he attacked Puerto del Príncipe, Cuba, in 1668, and later that year Portobello, Panama. Portobello, despite its reputation for being well guarded because of the arrival of the treasure fleet, was not the most difficult target. The fortress of Santiago de la Gloría was finished around 1629, and sat on a hill overlooking the bay, but it was possible to sneak up and attack it from behind, which Morgan did. Construction of another fort along the water, San Jerónimo, close to the *aduana*, or customs house, had begun, but was yet to be completed when Morgan landed. Portobello, with its seasonal flow of silver and other goods, had become a linchpin of East–West trade, and was of significant interest to European pirates. The fact that the *aduana* was built so close to the water illustrated either a certain confidence, or lack of awareness on the part of the Spanish; it was as if they believed that no one would dare to threaten territory that had been claimed by the Spanish crown. Morgan, and others before and after him, showed them the folly of their thinking. Morgan celebrated immediately and he and his men 'began making merry, lording it with wine and women', as Exquemelin recalled.[81] They stayed there about a month, gathering ransoms and plundering – often torturing residents on a rack until they told them where they were hiding money, even if they were not. They brought back a haul worth somewhere between £9 million and £14 million in today's money. But Portobello was only the beginning of Morgan's incursions and the following year he successfully raided Maracaibo, on the coast of Venezuela, netting the equivalent of around £4 million.[82] However, he had a more audacious target in mind: Panama City.

Unlike Portobello, which sits on the northern edge of the Caribbean side of the isthmus, attacking Panama City, which lies on the Pacific, was a major challenge. Morgan led some four hundred men over river and land, in an expedition that left them so hungry that, upon coming to a deserted village where leather bags that had contained bread and meat were lying around, the starving men 'ate the leather bags, with as much gusto as if the leather were meat'.[83] After marching for another eight days they reached Panama City, having survived ambushes by the Amerindians and battles with Spanish cavalry. Morgan and his men sacked the city and took 200 prisoners, treating many of them with great cruelty. Exquemelin described one as a 'poor cripple' with a silver key, who swore he did not have the coffer it was supposed to open:

> When it became plain this was all he was going to tell them, they strappado'd him until both his arms were entirely dislocated, then knotted a cord so tight round the forehead that his eyes bulged out, big as eggs. Since he still would not admit where the coffer was, they hung him up by his male parts, while one struck him, another scorched him with fire – tortures as barbarous as a man can devise. At last, when the wretch could no longer speak and they could think of no new torments, they let a Negro stab him to death with a lance.[84]

Morgan and his men spent three weeks pillaging the city, and on 24 February 1671 they left with 175 mules laden with treasure and 500 captives held for ransom. They marched them back over land and river, and in the end, according to Exquemelin, 'each man found his share came to no more than 200 pieces of eight'. Not only that, but 'many jewels were missing – for which Morgan was publicly accused by the buccaneers'.[85] Exquemelin decided to leave Morgan, and travelled with a few others to Cape Gracias a Dios, on the Honduran coast. Morgan and his cronies, meanwhile, went to Jamaica and celebrated their haul in Port Royal, the main town on the island and their base. Morgan received a half-hearted official reprimand for his actions in England – albeit including a stint in the Tower of London in 1672 – but he was made lieutenant-governor of Jamaica in 1674, much to the consternation of the Spanish. Only a few years earlier Spain and England had signed the Treaty of Madrid, in which the Spanish recognized England's settlements, including Jamaica and Virginia. It was also meant to end hostilities at sea between the two, especially the privateering raids.

Morgan returned to Jamaica in 1675, overseeing the island's profitable privateering, which had continued to thrive in his absence. Indeed, Morgan was adamant about the legality of his actions, and when Exquemelin's book came out in English in 1684, Morgan sued for libel over his depiction in the work, taking offence at being called a buccaneer.

Under his watch, Jamaica continued to be a haven for contrabandists and privateers. Although it was an English colony, agriculture had yet to take hold on the same scale as on the other islands. Morgan later lost his post owing to local political infighting, but he still amassed a personal fortune. He died there in 1688. A few years later, in 1692, the pirate town of Port Royal – considered to be the wickedest place on earth – was destroyed by an earthquake. Many law-abiding English people – not to mention the Spanish – thought the town got what it deserved.

*

The waters of the Caribbean were not only the site of plunder and violence – they had excited scientific minds too. Some men were drawn to a life at sea not for the possibility of riches, but out of curiosity. One such mariner was William Dampier. Although he was involved in raids and dubious pirate-related activity, he was more interested in the wonders of the world around him. Dampier was born in Somerset in 1651, and at the age of twenty-two he took a post at a sugar plantation in Jamaica. It did not take long for him to want to leave, remarking, 'I was clearly out of my Element there.'[86] After sailing around Jamaica for a while, he spent some time logging wood near Campeche, Mexico, before returning to England. But he did not stay away from the sea for long, and he made many epic voyages, observing and recording everything he could. Over the course of his seafaring life, he became highly regarded for his skills as a hydrographer, navigator, and naturalist. He was famed for his accounts of sailing around the world, which he did three times. His writings, such as A New Voyage Round the World (1697) and A Voyage to New Holland (1703), influenced later scientists, including Charles Darwin.[87] The project of colonization needed science as well – and knowledge was not benign; there was a need to categorize, record, and observe.

*

By the end of the tumultuous seventeenth century, there were stirrings in Scotland about foreign settlement. The Scots were eager to avoid Westminster and the English as much as they could, and increasingly believed that they could do this by having their own empire, or at the very least a prosperous colony. Around 1691, William Paterson, from Dumfriesshire, hit upon the idea of establishing a port on the isthmus of Panama and found an eager audience. He had travelled a bit around the West Indies and thought the location ideal for trade, even though he had not been to Panama himself, an oversight that would prove catastrophic.

By 1695, an Act of the Parliament of Scotland had established the 'Company of Scotland trading to Africa and the Indies', giving it a monopoly over trade between Scotland and Asia, Africa, and the Americas for the next thirty-one years. Feeling that this venture could give the country much-needed financial security, more than 1,400 Scots staked a staggering £400,000 on the scheme, representing between one-quarter and one-half of Scotland's liquid capital.[88]

In July 1698, the colonists loaded five vessels with 1,500 Bibles, woollen goods, tartan blankets, 25,000 pairs of shoes, 14,000 needles, and wigs.[89] Some 1,200 passengers joined the cargo, and the whole of

Edinburgh turned out to see them off.[90] They landed on the isthmus on 2 November 1698, after a crossing in which forty-four people died. They set to work building a fort, which they called St Andrew, and a settlement, New Edinburgh. The Spanish gave them the usual welcome of raids and gunshots in February 1699, but the settlers managed to drive them off. They attempted to trade with the Amerindians in the region, known as the Cuna (or Kuna) people, who were quite bemused by the strange goods these people had brought.

The site was marshy, and disease soon spread – Paterson's wife died in the first few weeks there, along with thirty-one others.[91] The Bibles, while perhaps offering spiritual sustenance, could not feed the needs of the body. The settlers had not brought enough food, and much of what they had perished in the dense humidity. They could not grow crops either, and were driven to eating birds, monkeys, and turtles. Their letters home shielded readers from these realities, and remained positive, and by 1699, another 1,300 settlers were on their way over. These hopefuls were not aware, however, that all but six of the 700 or so surviving original members had by this point boarded three ships and left for Europe. The six who stayed behind were dying of fever.

When the second ship arrived, their passengers must have been dismayed by the scene – the failure of the colony, and the obviously lethal conditions. The jungle was probably reclaiming what little the rain had not washed away. The Spanish attacked again, and more people died of malaria and yellow fever. In the end, fewer than a hundred from the second ship made it back to Scotland. Overall, out of the 2,500 settlers who went to Darien, only around 500 survived, and the company posted losses of £219,000 – or the equivalent of around £27 million today.[92] The English crown offered to pay the debt and reimburse the shareholders, but by accepting the offer the Scots could no longer secure their independence, and their dream of an empire vanished. In 1707, when the Acts of Union took effect, Scotland joined England (which included Wales) to become one nation: Great Britain.

*

It is uncertain when the English settled – if it could be called that – around the shore of Honduras. Although the terrain could be as hostile as that of Panama, which contributed to the Scottish disaster, there was no grand scheme along the Honduran coast. Rather, it was a gradual arrival. Some accounts date a settlement around 1630, as privateers drifted into logging, but it may have been after Jamaica was ceded to England in 1655, giving the English a contact point, and more showed up during the temporary privateering lull that followed the 1670 Treaty of Madrid. Men at a loose end went inland, and the logwood trade boomed all along the coast, up to the Yucatán peninsula in New Spain (Mexico). By 1671, one estimate calculated that 2,000 tons (US) of logwood, worth £40,000, had been shipped.[93] Logwood, a tree that produces a dye used by the wool industry, was much in demand.

The loggers there had skirmishes with the Spanish for some time, as the pirate-naturalist William Dampier recounted after his own lucrative spell there in 1675. 'Our Cargo to purchase Logwood was Rum and Sugar; a very good Commodity for the Logwood-Cutters, who were then about 250 Men, most *English*, that had settled themselves in several Places hereabouts.'[94] But he did not romanticize the life of the Baymen: 'During the wet Season, the Land where the Logwood grows is so over-flow'd, that they step from their Beds into the Water perhaps two Foot deep, and continue standing in the Wet all Day, till they go to Bed again.'[95] It was hard, wet, unpleasant work. But it paid well.

What became known as the Mosquito Coast is a strip of shore that runs from Cape Gracias a Dios, discovered on Columbus's final voyage in 1502, south to the San Juan river in Nicaragua. 'Mosquito' here does not refer to the flying pest, but rather the indigenous Miskito people, who managed to avoid the demographic destruction suffered by the native peoples on the West Indian islands. This was in part due to the fact that the inland areas were almost uninhabitable for Europeans, with disease in the jungle and swamps being the most significant threat. Also, the Miskito people put up a tough fight against the Spanish, and, in the spirit of 'my enemy's enemy is my friend', were willing to tolerate and trade with the anti-Spanish English and Dutch. Though the area only had about 2,000 English, Scottish, and Irish settlers by the 1700s, it was considered important for its proximity to Jamaica. Some settlement had started in the age of piracy, around the mid-1600s. The English captured the Bay Island of Roatán (also Rattan) in 1642 but its subsequent occupation was not recognized by the Spaniards and it became a long-running point of contention between the two nations.

Inland, however, the British could take advantage of the Miskitos' hostility to the Spanish to set up trading posts, such as Bluefields in Nicaragua and Black River. As the English and Dutch ships arrived, they also were eager to capitalize on the relative isolation of the shoreline for contraband. This was the Wild West of the Caribbean, a place that had a very different trajectory from the islands. As these European ships called in, Africans who either ran away or were free mixed with the Miskitos and they and their offspring were known in the terminology of the time as zambos. Some remained slaves in the lumber trade, but others found their freedom in the swamps of the Miskito territory.

While William Pitt the Elder was forging his political career in the British parliament, another William Pitt, a distant cousin, was expanding the empire into the mangrove swamps of Central America.[96] It was not a case of bringing shiploads of Puritans, as had happened earlier. Rather, the British subjects were already there, not planting tobacco but felling trees. Many of them were perhaps less desirable members of that kingdom – pirates, contrabandists, general ne'er-do-wells – but some of them had stumbled into the lucrative wood trade.[97]

Well before Pitt arrived in Honduras, the Miskito had made their alliances with the English. In 1637 the Earl of Warwick, one of the members of the Providence Island Company, took a young Miskito man to England after one of his voyages. Three years later, when that Miskito returned, he was made a chief and he asked for the territory to be placed under English sovereignty. A Miskito named Oldman visited London in 1655 and was given a 'crown' that was little more than a laced hat, and in 1687 Oldman's son went to Jamaica and renewed his loyalty to the crown to the governor of Jamaica, whence he was named King Jeremy and given some royal trinkets.[98] This marked the start of a dynasty and future Miskito kings would go to Jamaica or Belize for their coronation, where they took names such as Jeremy I and George II. Royal princes were often educated in England or Jamaica.[99]

In 1702, Philip V of Spain issued a royal order to destroy the English camps in Campeche, which were in New Spain and operated in a similar way to those in Miskito territory. There were ongoing disputes until the English were finally expelled around 1716. By the time Pitt arrived from Bermuda around 1725, the Spanish were again attacking the logwood cutters from Yucatán and around Belize, so many moved further down the shore, to Honduras.[100] These loggers were in the hinterlands of the Spanish empire, yet by basing themselves in wealthy, powerful New Spain, they were also in the heart of it. Protestant sailors felling trees amid the animosity of the Spanish illustrates how unclear the demarcations at the edge of empire could be.

In many ways, the modern idea of empire – certainly when it comes to the British version – is formed by late nineteenth-century notions: patriotism, commercial packaging, flags, songs, propaganda, parades, monuments. This would be true to a degree in the British Caribbean, but in this period, in these places, such a narrative did not exist. The English had fledgling colonies, and the Englishmen drifting around the Central American coast in the late 1600s and early 1700s were living on the margins of the law. Indeed, in the case of the kings of the Miskito, it was as if they were the ones to dictate their relationship with the English, rather than the other way round. Pitt established a settlement along the Black River in the early 1730s, which had space around it for raising cattle and growing some sugar, and there the fish and turtles were plentiful as well. He saw that the site had smuggling potential, too, trading British cloth and metalware for Spanish gold and silver. The town also sat on a lagoon, helping protect it from invasion.[101]

In 1740 Captain Robert Hodgson paid Pitt a visit during the War of Jenkins' Ear (see Chapter 7) to make sure the Miskito were still England's allies, and he organized raids on the Spanish in the region. Around this period, there had been a declaration that 'Edward King of the Mosquito Indians' would, along with his people, 'hereby become Subjects of Great Britain' and that they acknowledged that they 'desire the Assistance of Great Britain to recover the Countries of their Fathers from their Enemies the Spaniards'.[102]

Although there was settlement along the area, it continued to be informal and it was not until 1749, when Hodgson became the first governor of the colony, that the situation became more orderly. Hodgson had to report to the governor of Jamaica and he was to be paid £500 a year, with orders to use the appointment to 'regulate and superintend the Settlement upon the Mosquito Shore, which has been subsisting several years, under the Protection of Our Friends and Allies the Mosquito Indians'.[103] A census made around 1757 put the population of the region – from Cape Gracias a Dios to Bluefields – as 1,124 souls, the majority of whom were black and native slaves. There were 154 whites, 170 free people of colour, and 800 slaves.[104] The whites, few though they were, were reported to 'live much after the European manner in every thing. The Houses, in general, (no Brick having yet been made) are of wooden Frames, thatched . . . white washed; but there are some which make a good Appearance, built entirely of Wood Two Stories high.'[105]

Demand for logwood dropped, but the wood trade rebounded, albeit through a new luxury product: mahogany.[106] The hardwood was first used in ship-building, but soon furniture-makers saw its value. By the 1720s there was a growing demand for mahogany pieces, and tables, chairs, dressers, and other decorative furniture for the home were crafted from it. While the English were eager to march into the forests and jungles around the Bay of Honduras to take the wood, the cutting was often done by native or African slave labour. Mahogany logging required better organization than previous timber exploits, which had been somewhat haphazard. Slave labour, organized in gangs of ten to fifty, found the trees, cut them down, rolled them to the river, and floated them to the bay where ships waited to take them away.[107] At first some of the wood also came from the islands, such as Santo Domingo, but eventually Honduran wood dominated and by the 1770s, it was a key export. The pursuit of luxury had come to the jungle.

*

The seventeenth century was a time of transition in the Caribbean. New practices in this new world were taking shape. International law regarding piracy and settlement was established up to a point, and the life of privateering and raiding was giving way to settlement and trade. Indeed, the golden age of piracy was more or less over by the beginning of the eighteenth century. Britain had organized a campaign to eliminate piracy – and the government was no longer supporting privateering raids – and other imperial powers were happy to join in, the result being a large number of hangings in those years, around the Atlantic.[108] That is not to say that it completely ended, but it tapered off, as would-be or former pirates instead joined the expanding – and legitimate – Royal Navy, set up as planters, or continued working among the logwood cutters, and by 1725 there were thought to be fewer than 200 still at sea, though piracy has never completely disappeared.[109]

Although the globe had been criss-crossed numerous times over the course of the century, and the fear of unknown waters had subsided to a great degree, life at sea continued to be dangerous. Journeys on the ocean were fraught with dangers. Even if the destination could now be seen on a map, without a method of finding longitude, the ship's position could not be fixed accurately. The sea could be cruel, dashing ships on rocks or becoming so becalmed a crew might die of starvation and thirst. Disease could pass through a ship with fearsome speed, wiping out most of its passengers and crew. Or just over the horizon there could be an enemy vessel, ready to take and plunder whatever was on board, including lives. Yet the sea brought with it freedom and opportunity, and there were people who were open to its possibilities. As the century wore on, the space between Europe and the West Indies grew smaller in the public mind. This no-longer 'new' world had also created new markets, and new forms of commerce. Piracy gave way to purchasing. But it was not solely economic. The establishment of colonies throughout the seventeenth century by their very nature demanded the creation of new forms of governance and bureaucracy, new means of implementing order and control, and new ways of organising labour. These developments would converge, and the resulting system would underpin an enterprise that made many far richer than the most successful pirates had been: the sugar plantation.

Chapter Four

SUGAR

Historical time, seemingly driven by dates and events, is far more fluid and amorphous than it first appears. This is nowhere more true than in the story of sugar in the Caribbean, which cannot be neatly packaged. It was a series of stops and starts, failures and successes, requiring both capital and labour, and of course, sugar cane itself.

By the time sugar arrived in the Caribbean, it had already been everywhere else in the world. Although the plant has an intimate association with the West Indies, sugar, like the people who were forced to cultivate it, was not native to the islands. The true origins of sugar lie on the other side of the world, in the grasslands of Papua New Guinea, where islanders domesticated the plant and chewed its husks for energy. As trading networks in south-east Asia grew, cuttings of the grass were carried in ships further afield, to China and India. Indians extracted the juice, which was widely drunk, and the plant, known as *iksu*, caught the attention of visiting Greeks. From there, cane was carried to Mesopotamia around the fourth century AD, and thence to Persia. When the Arabs invaded around the seventh century, they took the plant with them, spreading it throughout the Mediterranean, the Middle East, and the Nile Delta. The spread of sugar coincided with the Islamic golden age, and some of the technological innovations in processing the plant led to the development of better sugar-refining techniques. Mills soon appeared in Palestine, Morocco, and even Sicily, which was about as far north as it was possible to cultivate what was, essentially, a tropical plant.[1]

It was not until the Crusades that most northern Europeans would come into contact with sugar. Crusaders saw the cane fields in the Levant, and tasted their fruits. With the sweetness lingering on their tongues, they brought refined sugar back with them. Before this, food was sweetened with honey or fruit juice. Soon, however, sugar's popularity – and value – soared throughout Europe. During this period it was one of the most valuable spices, preserved for special occasions or used to show off wealth. In England, the records of Edward I show that the royal household had quite a sweet tooth – some 6,000lb were used in 1288. Sugar was indeed the food of kings. Its scarcity and high cost in Europe made it a luxury. Some was set aside for medicinal uses, especially for tricking the taste buds into swallowing bitter concoctions, though this sweetened medicine was also largely the preserve of the wealthy. But simply as a sweetener, sugar continued to grow in popularity, and distributors in Venice and Genoa grew rich by catering to the palates of wealthy Europeans. However, the sources in the Levant were beginning to dry up, and Islamic production was falling. Sugar cultivation was tried further north even than Sicily, in the Algarve and other parts of the southern Mediterranean. There were also experiments with planting the crop in Tuscany and Provence. Sugar, however, needs abundant water, and the hot, dry Mediterranean summers proved disastrous. So when the opportunity arose to plant cane on the wetter Atlantic islands of the Canaries and Madeira, Europeans seized it.

The refining process that had by then developed would remain largely unchanged for generations. Although there were regional variations, the basic procedure was to chop the cane, crush it, then mill it between two grindstones which could be powered by oxen (or men), and run what was left under a beam or screw press to force out the final drops of juice. Eventually a three-cylinder mill was developed, which made the process far more efficient as the cane did not have to be so finely chopped before milling. Such an intensive process was not done by peasants alone, and the patchwork of records that exist about Mediterranean sugar production indicate that it, too, relied on slaves, for example those brought to the Maghreb through Saharan slaving expeditions. Although northern Europeans could not grow cane, they could participate in the processing of sugar, and refineries capable of turning the coarse product from the West Indies into more highly refined varieties began to spring up in places such as Bologna and Antwerp, allowing them to speed up the delivery of sugar to hungry consumers. By the 1400s this, coupled with the success of the crop in Madeira and the Canary Islands, began to fill the gap in the market.

Columbus was said to have taken some sugar cane cuttings to Hispaniola on his second voyage, though little came of those plantings. Settlers tried to grow it again around 1503, but there were scarcely enough willing or enslaved workers to harvest and process it, and the experiment came to a halt. The fields lay fallow once more. Finally, men who knew the sugar business from the Canaries arrived on the island a few years later and managed to make cane grow there. By 1571 Puerto Rico was exporting around 212,000lb and Santo Domingo 1,290,000lb.[2]

The Portuguese, while being active slave traders, stuck to their papal bargain and stayed within their demarcated limit, which meant they did not colonize any of the Caribbean islands. However, a portion of South America fell under their jurisdiction, and it was also well located near the Cape Verde islands and the west coast of Africa: Brazil. With the right mix of climate, and the access to slave labour, Portuguese planters could take northern Atlantic knowledge of sugar production and use it south of the equator. By 1570 there were sixty *engenhos* (sugar mills) in the region. Fifteen years later there were 120, including sixty-six in Pernambuco and thirty-six in Bahia, and this figure rose to 192 by 1612.[3] As with the earlier sugar colonies in the Atlantic, labour was brought in from Africa or forced out of the indigenous people. This colony was soon outstripping the Spanish islands in sugar production by a large margin – it was producing 25,000 US tons a year by 1610, compared to less than 1,000 from the Spanish islands.[4] Hispaniola and Puerto Rico were further hindered by ongoing pirate attacks, which added to the cost of transporting sugar. In addition, many settlers turned to the production of ginger, which at the time was far more cost-effective, sending large shipments to Seville, though these too had dropped off by the end of the 1500s. By the mid-1600s, however, the dynamics had shifted once again, as the British and French entered the sugar market, turning away from tobacco. However, like the Canarians who went to Hispaniola, and the Madeirans who influenced Brazil, the French and British would need help in getting their sugar plantations started, as they had no experience growing the crop in either the Mediterranean or the islands of the Atlantic. But help would come from an unexpected quarter: the Netherlands.

*

The Dutch played an important role in the development of sugar in the New World, despite the islands they controlled being too dry or too mountainous to grow it in any serious quantity (although this was not the case with Suriname). What they did have was the money to back plantations and to pay for expensive machinery and labour. Dutch investors were eager to put up capital and technical knowledge. By 1630 the Dutch West India Company was in control of Pernambuco and other northern territories in Brazil, setting up more sugar mills with direct trade links to Antwerp.

Some of the people involved in this trade were Jewish. Holland had long had a sizeable Jewish community – many Jews arrived in Amsterdam in the 1590s, and prior to that, when Portugal followed Spain's discriminatory example in the late 1400s and forced them to convert or leave, they had gone to the tolerant city of Antwerp. Antwerp, like Amsterdam, was fast becoming a city of commerce, and as its connections with the New World expanded, some Jews from there decided to go out and see what opportunities there were in the islands. These Jewish investors and merchants were critical in the development of the Caribbean, yet at times their story is omitted or obscured under the labels of 'Portuguese' or 'Dutch'.

During the period in which the Dutch – and with them the Jewish people and other Europeans who were involved in their project – had taken control of northern Brazil, the Iberian Union had ended, and from 1640 Portugal was once again a separate kingdom from Spain. Portuguese independence combined with growing local hostility in Brazil to banish the interlopers from the country, and by 1654 the Dutch and all those associated with them had been driven out.

Some of these exiles had learned of French and English efforts to grow sugar. Some planters on these islands, like James Drax from Barbados, had gone to Brazil to learn the techniques being used there. The Dutch knew that the French too were beginning to plant in the west of Hispaniola, land to which France was given legal entitlement under the 1697 Treaty of Ryswick. This area became known as Saint-Domingue, and many of the former buccaneers who had used nearby Tortuga as a base were now switching to agriculture.

Meanwhile, in Barbados, the settler population had fluctuated during the English Civil War. Royalist exiles came to the island – which itself succumbed to Cavalier and Roundhead politics – as did political prisoners.[5] One such royalist was Richard Ligon, who made the journey to Barbados in 1647. He stayed a few years, spending time on a sugar plantation. His plan was to go to Antigua to set up as a planter, but soon he had two partners and 500 acres, where 'there was imployed for sugar somewhat more than 200 acres; above 80 acres for pasture, 120 for wood, 20 for Tobacco, 5 for Ginger, as many for Cotton wool, and 70 acres for provisions: viz Corne, Potatoes, Plantines, Cassavie, and Bonavist; some few acres of which for fruit; viz Pines, Plantines, Milions, Bonanoes, Gnavers, Water Milions, Organes, Limons, Limes, &c'.[6] He returned to England in 1650 and, in 1657, published an account of his time on the island. His observations show a society in transition. Even on the journey over the signs were there; they stopped on the islands of Cape Verde 'where wee were too trade for *Negros*, Horses, and Cattell; which we were to sell at the *Barbados*'. When they finally arrived, the passengers, however, were greeted with death and illness, and 'the living were hardly able to bury the dead'.

Ligon's experiences coincided not only with the transition from tobacco to sugar, but also with the move away from white indentured labour to African slavery. His book illustrates early on the cruelties of the slave trade that would persist for more than 200 years: 'When they are brought to us, the Planters buy them out of the Ship, where they find them stark naked, and therefore cannot be deceived in any outward infirmity. They choose them as they do Horses in a market . . . Thirty pound stirling is a price for the best man Negre; and twenty five, twenty six, or twenty seven pound for a Woman; the Children are easier rates.'[7]

Ligon observed the impact of Brazil and the Dutch while he was in Barbados: 'Some of the more industrious men, having gotten Plants from *Fernambock* [Pernambuco], a place in *Brasill*, and made tryall of them at the *Barbadoes*; and finding them to grow, they planted more and more.' However, the initial experiments did not take so well, and the Dutch soon were 'content to make a voyage thither [to Brazil], to improve their knowledge in a thing they so much desired . . . And so returning with more Plants, and better Knowledge, they went on upon fresh hopes.'[8] A later writer, Sir Dalby Thomas, claimed the 'Hollanders' who arrived on the island saw the good sugar cane, and realized that the English 'knew no other Use of them, than to make refreshing

Drinks for that hot Climate'.[9] The Dutch were knowledgeable, but more importantly they also had capital, and were soon lending to and teaching the French and English settlers.

Yet there was still some overlap with the old ways. Indeed, when Heinrich von Uchteritz was forced off a ship that called in to Barbados in 1652, he realized he was going to be put to work in the fields. By this point, some 80 per cent of arable land was being used for sugar. Von Uchteritz was a German soldier who had been captured at the Battle of Worcester in 1651 while fighting as a royalist mercenary. After languishing in prison in London for three months, von Uchteritz, like many other captives, was put on board a ship bound for the West Indies – or in the terminology of the time 'Barbadosed'. He later wrote of his experiences, describing how '1300 of us were sent on ships to the West Indian island of Barbados, which the English possessed. As far as I know no one returned except myself.'[10]

Sugar was the key to his experience there; it was behind his initial sale, his labour, and his later freedom. He was traded, like each of his fellow passengers, in exchange for sugar. Currency was in limited supply on the island, and planters often had little choice but to use their produce instead of money. His new master was a Count Weitecker, who 'had one hundred Christians [whites], one hundred Negroes, and one hundred Indians as slaves'. Von Uchteritz's four months of work on the island consisted of sweeping the plantation yard and feeding pigs, though later he 'had to do the kind of work usually performed by slaves', which implies he may have been sent into the fields. A short time later, Weitecker discovered von Uchteritz was a nobleman and wanted to hold him for ransom. Eventually a plan was concocted with the help of some German merchants on the island who realized von Uchteritz's identity and were willing to pay to have him released – and the price of his freedom was set at 800lb of sugar.

As the Portuguese took over Dutch territory, other people cast out of Brazil began to settle land on the north littoral of South America, from Suriname to Essequibo in Guiana, though the population was sparse. However, the climate was right for sugar, and plantations would do well there.[11] Some of the Jewish settlers who left Brazil had good links across the region, and a few went to Curaçao, fast becoming a thriving centre for trade, with sugar shipments and other goods bound for New Netherland – one receipt from 16 May 1659 records 3,789lb of sugar.[12] But not all the goods shipped from the island were agricultural – Curaçao was also turning into a slave depot.

*

Establishing a sugar plantation entailed a number of prerequisites. Vital conditions included soil that was not prone to flooding, and a hot climate with plenty of strong sunlight but not too dry an atmosphere – all of which existed in the Caribbean. Trees, however, were a problem. They had to be cut down and land cleared to make way for sugar. Swathes of timber fell across the islands, never to be replanted, and were replaced instead with fields of tall green cane. Not only did this change the long-term ecology of each island, it had quite severe immediate effects as well. Hans Sloane, a physician from London, arrived in Jamaica in 1687, eager to see the plants and animals of the New World that he had read about; better yet, he, like other budding naturalists, was hoping to observe even more new species. He was struck by the forests in Jamaica, noting that they had very good trees, but he also realized that the landscape was changing very rapidly:

> 'Tis a very strange thing to see in how short a time a Plantation formerly clear'd of Trees and Shrubs, will grow foul, which comes from two causes; the one the not stubbing up of the Roots, whence arise Young Sprouts, and other the Fertility of the Soil. The Settlements and Plantations of, not only the *Indians*, but even the *Spaniards*, being quite overgrown with tall Trees, so that there were no Footsteps of such a thing left, were it not for old Palisadoes, Buildings, Orange Walks, &c which shew plainly the formerly clear'd places where Plantations have been.[13]

What he saw was part of a process that had begun with Columbus. The landscape, the animals, even the people, entered the growing global commodity chain, with very mixed results. For instance, Columbus and his men had brought horses, cattle, sheep, and crops like sugar cane, grapes, and wheat from Europe, as well as plants from further afield, including coffee. But with them came all manner of insects, from cockroaches to worms.[14] New flora, fauna, microbes, and bacteria entered these islands. At the same time, Europeans there were tasting new fruits, such as papaya, guava, and pineapple. And there was also an exchange of disease. Indian susceptibility to smallpox and various influenzas was more beneficial to the Europeans than any weapon. Malaria, too, took root in the Caribbean; current scientific consensus maintains that human malaria did not exist in the pre-Columbian Americas, but it did in the fenlands of East Anglia and throughout the southern Mediterranean.[15] So when ships began to arrive in the Caribbean they often carried a strain of the disease on board, while another variant arrived with the Africans who were forced over to the New World.

And, at the time, no one understood the connection between cleared land and the proliferation of mosquitoes in pools of stagnant water in the newly exposed fields, let alone the onset of illness. As a result the West Indies were often seen as a graveyard – it was too often a ticket to the afterlife for Europeans. But African slaves had a higher survival rate because many were immune to malaria, having already been exposed to a strain of it, as well as to yellow fever, another unwelcome arrival in the West Indies. Yellow fever had no past in the Mediterranean world; its roots were in Africa and it was no doubt brought on slave ships. It is only spread by the *Aedes aegypti* mosquito, and in the late seventeenth and early eighteenth centuries it killed half its victims. It is a particularly vicious disease, causing the sufferer to vomit black blood and making the skin yellow with jaundice, hence the name. Survivors, however, develop immunity.[16]

This immunity – normally a welcome biological adaptation – would have profound consequences for Africans.[17] It did not take long for white settlers to realize that something was different. Lacking an understanding of biology, they ascribed the slaves' high survival rate simply to their being 'African'. Thus, it was soon accepted that slaves were more 'suited' to the climate, and the work; it was easier to 'season' them. White indentured servants were as likely as white indentured masters to die of disease. Planters began to realize their money was better spent investing in Africans than in Europeans.

*

Barbados planters began to bring in black slaves rather than find more white indentured servants in this period; the black population more than doubled between 1645 and 1665 while the number of whites dropped. According to research on plantations in Barbados by Hilary Beckles, there were no slaves and only 114 servants in 1639–40 across

six estates, but by 1668–70 there were 421 slaves and twenty-one servants on four estates. He also points out that in 1640 there had been
about thirty servants for every one slave but by 1680 there were seventeen slaves per servant, a dramatic demographic reversal. However,
there was still a white population of more than 20,000 people.[18]

The growth in the number of African slaves was bolstered by the
growth of the sugar trade itself. It became more cost-effective to buy
slaves rather than contract with indentured servants, who increasingly
saw little reason to go to Barbados.[19] Servants had contracts that would
end on average after six years, but slaves could be used for much longer.
Unlike in Jamaica, indentured servants would not receive land at the
end of their term of service. In addition, people from England, Scotland,
and Wales were increasingly reluctant to leave, as economic prospects
at home improved after the restoration of the monarchy in 1660.[20]

The figures speak volumes: between 1600 and 1650, 27,751 Africans were brought to the islands in the Caribbean; between 1650 and
1700, the number rose to 464,743, mostly in ships registered to English
and Dutch merchants.[21] The English islands were by far the largest
recipients in this period. Over the second half of the seventeenth
century, 156,099 Africans were brought to Barbados. Indeed, before
long the pursuit of sugar took up 80 per cent of the arable land and
90 per cent of its labour force.[22] By 1654, Drax for his part had 200
slaves, making him the wealthiest man in Barbados.[23] The slave populations on other islands were not quite as large, but still significant.
The years 1650–1700 saw the arrival of 38,140 Africans to the French
islands; 124,158 to the Dutch islands and Suriname; and even 18,146
to the Danish West Indies.[24] And this was only the beginning.

*

So much labour was needed because sugar demanded it. It was not a
case of plant, till, and harvest. The process as practised in the Caribbean began with a slave taking a two-foot cutting of old cane and
planting it in the ground – it would take a year for a full stalk to grow.
Sugar cane stalks have a hard exterior, like a large bamboo shoot. They
contain only about 10 per cent sugar by weight, so the key to producing
sugar, and making any profit from it, is scale – one hectare of land
properly planted and harvested can produce up to ten tons of sugar.

But harvesting the crop is difficult and requires great technical knowledge to do it well. It can only take place in the dry season, from around
November to April. Once the cane is cut, it must be processed within
twenty-four hours, otherwise it begins to ferment and becomes un-
usable. Production was therefore complex, yet had to be done quickly.
Plantations needed a variety of outbuildings and an extensive labour
force that could work long hours in difficult conditions. Although it
may not have been rainy, it was hot, and the work of cutting cane by
hand was exhausting.

The refining process also placed great demands on the labourer.
Edward Littleton, one of the largest plantation owners in Barbados in
the 1670s, described the risks: 'If a Mill-feeder be catch't by the finger,
his whole body is drawn in, and he is squees'd to pieces. If a Boyler
get any part into the scalding Sugar, it sticks like Glew, or Birdlime,
and 'tis hard to save either Limb or Life.'[25] The 'Mill-feeder' and 'Boyler'
were two of the vital jobs in the process. When the cane arrived at the
mill, the stalks had to be passed through rollers in order to extract the
juice from the fibres. The Dutch had funded the development of a
three-roller mill, which had proved crucial in making Caribbean sugar
extraction more efficient. Then it was the turn of the 'Boyler'. Once
the brown juice was collected it was taken to the boiling house, where
it was refined through a series of vats. These houses would have been
unbearably hot anywhere in the world, with temperatures of 60°C
(140°F) during the day, but in the tropics they would have felt like an
inferno. Even at night, there was scant relief for the slaves, as the internal
temperatures were still around 50°C (approximately 120°F).

Most boiling houses contained a series of kettles, which began
large and relatively cool and became progressively smaller and hotter.
As the brown cane juice was moved from the larger kettles to the
smaller ones it began to crystallize, then it was put in a cooling cistern
before being decanted into pots that were left in a hot curing house
to dry. While they were drying, the liquid that was produced was
collected; this molasses was used to make rum.[26] Once the pot dried,
the 'loaf' of crystals that remained was reboiled and placed under the
sun to dry further. Finally, the loaves of the resulting unrefined *musco-
vado* were packed into hogsheads – casks that held 16 cwt – and placed
on board a ship bound for Europe, where they were further processed

in refineries in Amsterdam or Liverpool and transformed into the white crystals that were becoming a fixture in European kitchens.

The extraction of cane also meant that everything necessary for establishing a sugar plantation needed to be imported. As one tract explained:

> But the field experiences are trifling, in comparison of the utensils necessary in the sugar works, such as coppers, mill cases, ladles, skimmers, mills, stills, and almost numberless other articles, to which may be added nails, locks, hinges, bolts, and lead, employed by the planter in his other buildings, and the almost innumerable kinds of iron work that are used in waggons, carts, mill works, and other things not only exceedingly expensive at the first setting out, but which from their being in continual use, constantly wear out and require fresh supplies. All these, at whatever price, must be had from *Britain*, and even the lumber, that is timber, cattle, &c though it coms from the northern plantations, is paid for by sugar planters, and goes in discharge of the *balances* respectively due from those colonies to *Britain* . . .[27]

The author pointed out that all furniture and clothing too had to come from Britain, and as a result the British planters were of 'immense importance to the grandeur and prosperity of this their mother country'.[28]

Unsurprising then, that Littleton, like other planters, thought that the English government should be more grateful to the planters for their efforts in bringing this valuable – and complicated – commodity to its shores, as well as their overall contribution to the national economy. He wrote, 'We by our Labour, Hazards, and Industry, have enlarged the English Trade and Empire – the English Empire in America, whatever we think of it ourselves, is by others esteemed greatly considerable.'[29] Littleton wrote those lines in the concluding paragraph to a pamphlet he had distributed around England, with the eye-catching title *The Groans of the Plantations*. The Shropshire-born, Oxford-educated lawyer had become a tireless advocate for abolition – not freedom for the slaves who laboured on his plantation, but the end of what he considered to be unfair duties on sugar. Having spent seventeen years in Barbados, this was a subject close to his heart. At the peak of his career on the island, he owned 600 acres and 120 slaves; he later sold some of his holdings and eventually returned to England to retire in 1683. By this point, Caribbean planters were at the mercy of what Littleton saw as unfair taxes. In the case of sugar, there were rising duties on the crop between 1605 and 1705, and planters were forced to pay 4.5 per cent duty on exports as well. For Littleton, it amounted to a policy that would bankrupt Barbados, which in its short time as a colony had already come back from the brink of ruin after the failure of its tobacco plantations. Littleton was unrelenting, if not a touch melodramatic, claiming that he wrote his 1689 pamphlet 'so the World may know, by what cruel Methods, and by what fatal Degrees, the once flourishing English Colonies have been brought to ruine'.[30] Of course, the ruin of the people actually doing the labour seems not to weigh on his mind. And the sugar came. From 1669 to 1700, the amount that West Indies planters sent to England increased from 11,700 tons to 27,400 tons, with Barbados at the centre of the trade.[31] They would not hold that position for long, but the planters made of it what they could.

*

Caribbean sugar changed the way the world ate, and created untold wealth for plantation owners. The trade was larger and more exploitative than anything that had come before. Sugar money would pay for the Dutch masters' paintings and build mighty mansions in Bristol. But sugar has no value to the human body. What was really being produced in the Caribbean was luxury. The foodstuff of kings now appeared on more humble tables. But while the European middle classes delighted in its sweetness, sugar produced nothing but bitterness for those who were forced to plant, harvest, and process it. By now the natives were mostly gone, and the white indentured servants freed or departed. That left only one group, the imported Africans, to provide the free labour upon which so many across these islands would grow rich.

Chapter Five

THE RISE OF SLAVERY

Amid the wonder at the scientific and material developments in the New World there was a growing sense of unease. By the beginning of the 1700s, anyone who had been to these new lands could not fail to be aware of both the riches being generated and the cruel regime under which the plantations operated. African slavery was now too widespread to be ignored. While in Jamaica, Hans Sloane observed:

> The *Negros* from some Countries think they return to their own Country when they die in *Jamaica*, and therefore regard death but little, imagining they shall change their condition, by that means from servile to free, and so for this reason often cut their own Throats. Whether they die thus, or naturally, their Country people make great lamentations, mournings, and howlings about them expiring, and at their Funeral throw in Rum and Victuals into their Graves, to serve them in the other world.[1]

Slavery was already a living death for millions, and in the course of the eighteenth century this brutal trade only got worse. By this point, Africans had been enslaved in the Caribbean for more than 200 years. The Portuguese had been the first to start trading with Africans on the West Coast, and although other private traders muscled in – especially when Portugal and Spain were at war in the 1640s – they dominated the early years of the trade, taking Africans to the Spanish Main ports of Cartagena and Veracruz, with at least 487 ships calling into the former between 1573 and 1640, and 78,453 slaves disembarking, many from Angola and Upper Guinea, and some from Lower Guinea.[2] Throughout the sixteenth century many slaves were moved in ships flying Portuguese flags. Once they disembarked in the mainland ports, slaves might stay in the city, be sent to work in rural areas, or be sent to the Peruvian mines. But over the course of the following century the English, French, and Danish began to infiltrate the trade. By the 1600s they all had forts or some sort of presence in West Africa: the English along the Gold Coast and Sierra Leone; the French around Senegambia (today's Senegal and Gambia); and the Dutch also in the Gold Coast. When the Portuguese ran Dutch settlers out of Brazil in 1654, they took their slaves and resold them around the Caribbean.[3]

In the West Indies, Curaçao, with its proximity to the Spanish Main, was swiftly established as a slave transhipment point. Matthias Beck, a WIC vice-director who took over the running of the island from Pieter Stuyvesant, wrote to the company directors on 28 July 1657 concerning some early illicit trade with the Spanish Main: 'This is important regarding the Negro trade because [a] Biscayer [Basque privateer], who is now here in person, has informed me specifically . . . one should trade not only in shiploads of Negroes but successively more in good current merchandise'. Beck then outlined a complicated plan for the privateer to sell slaves, saying, 'at any time when there is a ship ready here with Negroes, from now on, he shall be informed thereof'. He added that he was enclosing some of the Biscayer's proposals in writing, pointing out, 'as he told me, a trail would thereby be blazed by which they would come here in the future to trade for Negroes and other merchandise.'[4]

By the 1660s other European kingdoms had also entered the slave trade. In 1666, the Danish African Company agreed terms to take over the Dutch forts at Christiansborg, Frederiksborg, and near Cape Coast in the Gulf of Guinea. In addition, they colonized the West Indian islands of St Thomas in 1672, St John in 1718, and St Croix, which they bought from the French in 1733. During this period Danish vessels were recorded as having made an average of 450 departures a year from the African coast.

The Danes, however, were not the only Nordic people to come to the tropics. A Swedish African Company, with many Dutch backers, was established in 1649, but – probably because at the time the Swedes had no sugar colonies nor any territory in the West Indies – it was conspicuously unsuccessful. Indeed, the Dutch paid the Swedish crown to get out of the slaving business – and for access to the few forts they had set up, which were later taken over by the Danes. Would-be colonizers also came from the Baltic duchy of Kurland, who set up Fort St James in the estuary of the Gambia river around 1651, and later added seven more forts. A few years later, eighty Kurland families went to Tobago to establish a colony, with the intention of growing tobacco to sell to Russia. But the Dutch soon invaded, and by 1691 Kurland's West Indian enterprise was over.[5]

Others kept coming, however. In 1682 the elector of Brandenburg, Frederick III, set up the Brandenburgisch Afrikanische Compagnie (BAC), again backed by the Dutch. The BAC established a fort on the Gold Coast and obtained permission from Denmark to bring its slaves to St Thomas to sell them. This did not please the Dutch West India Company, and it soon drove the BAC out of business. However, a successor company, the Brandenburgisch Afrikanisch-Amerikanische Compagnie (BAAC) – again with Dutch backers – was formed, and, since Holland and Brandenburg were by then allies, it was allowed to flourish, transporting some 19,000 slaves to the West Indies between 1680 and 1706.[6] Nonetheless, by 1717 the WIC had paid the BAAC to leave the slaving business and was keen to take control of the Brandenburg fort. But in one of the odder episodes of this period, an African named John Conny took over the fortress, claiming it for himself. For seven years, he sold slaves, while apparently always wearing a Prussian uniform. Or so the story goes.[7]

By 1700, English ships had taken around 400,000 slaves from Africa, although such statistics inevitably obscure the number of slaves who died at sea, were stolen by pirates, or were smuggled.[8] In addition, the eighteenth century – whose broad historical movements spill over into the centuries before and after, extending to a period often referred to as the long eighteenth century – started with another conflict, the War of the Spanish Succession, which began in 1701. It was triggered by the death of the last Habsburg king of Spain, Charles II; there were fears that the French claimants would create a Franco-Spanish bloc, upsetting the balance of power in Europe. Its conclusion, under the Treaty of Utrecht in 1713, put the Bourbons on the Spanish throne and ceded much of the rest of Spain's territory in Europe to the Austrian Habsburgs. It allowed the British to keep Gibraltar and the Balearic island of Minorca, which they had captured in the course of the war. France was forced to part with its share of St Kitts, while also handing over to Britain Canadian territories including Hudson Bay,

Newfoundland, and Nova Scotia. And Britain was also granted a thirty-year contract to provide slaves from Africa to Spanish America, the valuable *asiento*.

This trade agreement would come to underpin the South Sea Company, which had been set up by Robert Harley, the First Lord of the Treasury, in 1711. Harley was concerned about England's high levels of debt, run up through costly decades at war. At around the same time, London's fledgling financial sector was beginning to grow – the Bank of England was established in 1694 – and so was overseas trade, as evidenced by the success of the East India Company. Harley thought the South Sea Company could reap similar income, especially when factoring in the slave-trade monopoly, income that could be used to offset government debt. The company was presented as an investment offering an almost assured profit, and people began to flock to it, buying shares. (They did not appear to give the slave-trading aspect of it much thought.) Eager investors from a broad range of backgrounds, not just the elite, were able to buy because the company could offer credit, which was to be paid back in instalments. At first the company seemed to prosper – in 1715 it shipped 2,090 slaves, or around 20 per cent of England's total that year. By 1717, the figure had reached 3,953, about 23 per cent of the total trade.[9] But its overall profitability was far from clear, although this did little to dim public trust, and the share price continued to rise. In 1720 the company converted the government debt into shares, convincing creditors to swap their bonds for shares in the company. The share price went up tenfold – and by the autumn of 1720 the bubble burst when the share price collapsed. There were a number of factors in this decline, including the fact that company could no longer afford to extend credit to investors; foreign backers – including many Dutch – had earlier pulled their money out of the shares and out of London; and the uncertainty that surrounded the question of profits. However, that was not the end of the South Sea Company. It continued to engage in the slave trade, and later moved into North Sea whaling, staying in business until the nineteenth century.

*

Europeans were quick to profit from the slave trade, but they did not introduce it to Africa. It had been a long-running practice throughout the continent, as it had been both in the Mediterranean and in the Islamic world. And unlike Europe, where land was a generator and signifier of income, in some African kingdoms having slaves was a sign and form of wealth, as it would later be for planters in the West Indies. The Europeans who ventured there had trouble making sense of this; they did not understand that land was not held privately, but in common, nor that a powerful ruler might have no land, but would own many slaves.[10] Enslaved people within African societies were often prisoners of war, and many were put into slave armies. Others were more like extensions of family, while those less fortunate were made to undertake tasks no one else would do. And, of course, they were also traded for guns and other goods.[11] It was a profitable business for Africans, too, and European demand stimulated supply, altering previous practices. However, many Europeans could not see past their own slaving forts and made little or no attempt to understand Africans' distinctions and traditions. With so few Europeans directly involved in the trade – sea captains, crew, and administrators at the fortresses – it was not difficult to obscure the horror that lay within and beyond it. Slaves were no longer brought to Europe, as they had been by the Spanish and Portuguese in the 1500s. Instead, they were taken to the Americas and West Indies. Their suffering was hidden away, buried under contracts and behind ledger books thousands of miles away in London and other European cities that were enjoying the fruits of the trade's profits.

After the enslaved Africans were on a ship, their voyage into terror began; a journey known as the Middle Passage. Although each trip provided new horrors for the Africans, there were some constants for the crew, who showed little sympathy for their cargo: they would pack in as many people as they could; they would chain them together; they would not feed them much; they would force them on to the deck to move about; some of the Africans would die; some would try to jump overboard; many of the women would be raped. The crew might make the passage safely, or they might be attacked by pirates, or wrecked. In rare instances, an inattentive crew might find the slaves try to launch a rebellion.

Indeed, such were the circumstances in which Danish surgeon Paul Erdmann Isert found himself aboard the *Christiansborg* in 1786.[12] Isert was on his way back to Denmark after nearly three years of living in Guinea, working at the Danish forts. In his letters, published in 1788, he claimed that his desire to live there was nothing to do with slavery but rather 'was solely an interest in natural science'. However, in order to return to Copenhagen, he had to board a slave ship first bound for Danish islands in the West Indies:

> Picture the tumult in front of a ship of black slaves, a ship which, when used in the king's service would hold no more than 200 people, now holding more than 452 slaves, who have to be kept in check by 36 Europeans. Imagine the sight of such a multitude of miserable people – some who were by chance born to slave parents; some who were captured in war; some who were stolen and innocent of any crime; some who, for other casual reasons, were sold to the Europeans . . . Furthermore, they give no credence to all the assurances from the Europeans that they are going to be taken to a beautiful country, and other similar cajolery. On the contrary, whenever the opportunity presents itself they take flight or kill themselves, since they fear death far less than slavery in West India. Indeed, all precautions must be taken to prevent their having the opportunity of committing suicide. For this reason on the French ships they are not even allowed a narrow strip of loincloth for fear they will hang themselves by it, which has in fact happened.

On the second day of the voyage, rebellion broke out. As Isert recalled,

> at that moment I found myself alone among the Blacks, and since I understand the language of the Akras I was exchanging pleasantries with some of them and with some Dunkos . . . Because there is always a great tumult with such a number of people, I noticed that it had suddenly become extremely quiet. Since most of the crew were below, eating, I decided to go to the bow of the ship to see if everyone was at his post, in case the Blacks had some kind of rebellion in mind.

As he was doing this there was a loud cry, and Isert felt the full weight of iron shackles hit his head – the slaves were rebelling with their chains still on.

Isert crawled away and managed to reach the bulwark door when 'such a number of Blacks seized the door that the crew had great difficulty in closing it'. He knew the situation was perilous because 'it is established policy that it is better to let a European be killed than to allow the Blacks to gain control of that door, since they could then make their way to the stern of the ship, which is full of weapons hanging there'.

As Isert struggled, one slave who had procured a shaving razor began to slash the Dane's forehead and was stopped only when he was shot by one of the crew. Soon there was more gunfire as the sailors tried to suppress the slaves, some of whom 'had, in the meanwhile, hammered off their irons', while some of the others 'when they saw that they could not succeed, all sprang overboard into the sea'. The sailors tried to catch those who dived off the ship, and Isert remarked on the brutal struggle that took place, 'It was astounding how some pairs, although they each had only one hand and one foot free (because they were chained together by the other hand and foot), were very adept at staying above water. Some were stubborn even in the face of death, defiantly casting away the rope which had been thrown around their bodies from the ship in order to draw them up, and diving under with force'. In the end, after two hours of struggle, thirty-four slaves died, all by drowning. Isert found out later why he had been singled out for harm – some of the slaves thought because he boarded the ship very late, he must have been its owner, and 'that it would be best to send me into the other world first, after which the Europeans, like mercenaries, would surrender all the sooner'.

Despite his experience, Isert decided to return to Africa. But this time he had bigger plans – to set up a plantation there. Rather than use slave labour, he would pay workers a small wage to grow tropical products for export. If it was successful, he reasoned, there would be no need for slavery. He wrote in one of his letters: 'Should we break our habit of using sugar, coffee, chocolate and other luxuries brought from this place to Europe – articles now become so necessary? No! That would make as great a number of Europeans unhappy as it would probably make the Blacks happy. Why were our forefathers not sensible enough to establish plantations of these products in Africa? There one could get enough workers for only a small wage!' He set about this scheme in 1788, but it was a failure. However, his book brought the horror of a slave-ship voyage to the attention of thousands of European readers.

Up to this point, accounts of the slave trade and the horrors of slavery had been written by European observers. However, the following year, in 1789, another account was published – this time by an African who had suffered the humiliation of the Middle Passage and the indignities of slavery first-hand.[13] In telling the story of his bondage and freedom, Olaudah Equiano gave a chilling account of his voyage across the Atlantic.[14] A slave in North America who had bought his freedom, according to his narrative Equiano was born to the Igbo people, in what is today modern Nigeria, and grew up with a father who, in the tradition of the time, kept slaves. He was one of seven children and was the youngest son. When he was eleven, his childhood came to an abrupt end when raiders came to his house: 'One day, when all our people were gone out to their works as usual, and only I and my dear sister were left to mind the house, two men and a woman got over our walls, and in a moment seized us both'.[15] The siblings were soon separated, and he 'cried and grieved continually; and for several days did not eat anything but what they forced into my mouth'. At first he was sold internally, but soon enough he ended up at the coast, where he saw the slave ship he would be forced onto, which, he would later recall, 'filled me with astonishment, which was soon converted into terror'. Once on board he saw 'a multitude of black people of every description chained together, every one of their countenances expressing dejection and sorrow, [and] I no longer doubted of my fate, and, quite overpowered with horror and anguish, I fell motionless on the deck and fainted.'

He gives a vivid description of life below deck, where he 'received such a salutation in my nostrils as I had never experienced in my life'. He endured illness, and lost his appetite, and when he refused to eat he was flogged, a punishment he had never previously experienced. Eventually he found slaves from his own nation, asked what was happening, and was told he was being taken to 'these white people's country to work'. This did not ease his mind; he was concerned he might yet die because he had 'never seen among any people such instance of brutal cruelty; and this not only shewn towards us blacks, but also to some of the whites themselves'.

Once at sea, Equiano found 'the shrieks of the women, and the groans of the dying rendered the whole scene of horror almost inconceivable'. As if Equiano's account were not vivid enough, drawings of slave ships were also circulating, showing in stark detail how the slave traders crammed human beings into every spare inch of space. It was a torture inflicted on millions of Africans throughout the eighteenth century. From 1700 to 1807, it was recorded that British ships took an estimated 2,530,969 slaves from West Africa, the French 1,139,381, the Dutch 333,504, and the Danes 83,444.[16] Millions of them were destined for the West Indies. And the journey was only the start of their suffering.

*

What awaited slaves on the other side of the Middle Passage was little better. Some Africans would be taken straight to their owners, but many more were shipped again, or faced the humiliation of the auction block. Mary Prince, who was born into slavery in Bermuda, although she later obtained her freedom and published a memoir of her experiences, recalled:

> At length the vendue master, who was to offer us for sale like sheep or cattle, arrived, and asked my mother which was the eldest. She said nothing, but pointed to me. He took me by the hand, and led me out into the middle of the street, and, turning me slowly round . . . I was soon surrounded by strange men, who examined and handled me in the same manner that a butcher would a calf or a lamb he was about to purchase, and who talked about my shape and size in like words – as if I could no more understand their meaning than the dumb beasts. I was then put up to sale. The bidding commenced at a few pounds, and gradually rose to fifty-seven, when I was knocked down to the highest bidder; and the people who stood by said that I had fetched a great sum for so young a slave . . . When the sale was over, my mother hugged and kissed us . . . It was a sad parting; one went one way, one another, and our poor mammy went home with nothing.[17]

Other slaves were moved through transhipment points such as Jamaica or Curaçao to other islands. When they arrived at their plantation, they found Africans from a wide geographical range. In addition, there would have been enslaved blacks, like Mary Prince, born on the islands, and known as creole slaves. These slaves often had certain advantages as a result of being born in the Caribbean and speaking the same language as their masters, such as roles as overseers,

which set them apart from the new arrivals. Slaves were not a homogeneous group of people – creoles had their own diverse histories, and
Africans who were brought to the West Indies came from many parts
of western Africa: around Guinea, the Bight of Benin, the Gold Coast,
and Sierra Leone, while others were sent from Angola and the kingdom
of Kongo. Still others would have come from further afield, from places
like Mozambique. There was linguistic diversity as well. Which Africans ended up where was also significant – there is evidence that the
Twi-speaking people of the Gold Coast and Ghana were the dominant
group in Jamaica, while in Haiti, it was the Ewe-Fon speakers of Benin
and western Nigeria.[18] Hans Sloane, while in Jamaica in the 1680s,
observed that those from 'several places of *Guinea*' were 'reckoned
the best Slaves', while 'those from the *East Indies* or *Madagascins*, are
reckoned good enough, but [as Muslims] too choice in their Diet . . . and
do not well here, but very often die. Those who are *Creolian*, born in
the Island, or taken from the *Spaniards*, are reckoned more worth
than the others in that they are season'd to the Island.'[19] Europeans like
Sloane, as well as creole planters, liked to imagine that they understood
the world that the slaves came from, a practice that did not abate
over the years the trade persisted. In his 1808 account of his twenty-one
years in Jamaica, John Stewart noted:

> The Eboe is crafty, saving, and industrious . . . The Coromantee
> is fierce, savage, violent, and revengeful. This tribe has generally
> been at the head of all insurrections, and was the original parent-
> stock of the Maroons. The Congo, Chamba, Mandingo, &c. are
> of a more mild and peaceable disposition. The Mandingos are a
> sort of Mahometans . . . The Creole negroes are, of course, the
> descendants of the Africans, and may be said to possess in
> common the mingled dispositions of their parents or ancestors.
> But they affect a greater degree of *taste and refinement* than the
> Africans, boast of their good fortune in being born a Creole, and
> the farther they are removed from the African blood, the more
> they pride themselves thereon.[20]

As might be imagined, such a diverse group of people did not often
share either language or tradition, only the fact of their enslavement,
although sometimes certain islands or plantations might have many
slaves from one particular place, or who shared a language. But the

reality of slavery demanded an abrogation of the past, which whites attempted to replace by their inadequate understanding of African cultures; and so slaves were often given labels such as Coromantees (many of whom went to Jamaica, and were from the Gold Coast or Bight of Benin), based on the nearest fort of their enslavement, Kormantin.[21] Yet this enforced mixing was the precondition for new identities and traditions to emerge from the ones brought across the Middle Passage, and to grow under the shadow of slavery.

*

There was also diversity in the way slavery was implemented across the West Indies. The experience of slaves in the Caribbean varied according to the codes that had been developed to govern how they *should* be treated; whether they were followed or not is a matter of speculation. In the seventeenth-century Spanish Caribbean, slaves were under the jurisdiction of the wide-ranging legal framework known as the Siete Partidas (Seven-Part Code), which had its roots in Roman law. Although it was later adjusted to account for the changes that the opening up of African slavery in the Atlantic world had wrought, at its core, the code still conceived of slavery as an acquired and not a natural state, and in doing so allowed for a system of *coartación*, in which slaves could negotiate the price of their freedom and pay their masters in instalments. Slaves in the Spanish Caribbean also had recourse to the courts, and had knowledge of their rights, such as they were. However, this is not to say the system was in reality any more benign.[22]

The French king Louis XIV issued a slave code in 1685, which reflected the rise of the slave colonies and the plantation economy. Known as the Code Noir, among other things it prohibited any sort of sexual relation (concubinage) between a free French person and a slave. However, if such a relationship occurred and the man was single, the code prescribed that he must both marry the slave and free her and any children of the union. One of the unintended consequences was that some slave women sought out single white men. The Code Noir also, among other things, expelled the Jews from France's colonies; demanded slaves be Catholic, not Protestant; permitted slaves to rest on Sunday; fined owners 2,000lb of sugar for each child of concubinage;

enslaved the children of a slave woman; prohibited the slaves of different masters from gathering under any pretext, even a wedding; required slaves to have a master's permission to sell their own fruit and vegetables; ordered masters to look after the health of their slaves; and punished by death a slave who struck a master while permitting masters to chain and beat slaves (but not torture or mutilate them).[23]

A century later, José de Gálvez, the Spanish Minister of the Indies, thought new ordinances based on the Code Noir would stimulate the economy of Santo Domingo, which continued to lag behind the some of the other sugar colonies, including neighbouring Saint-Domingue. Slavery had never taken root on a large scale in Santo Domingo, and most cattle ranchers and small farmers only had a few slaves, who usually lived in close contact with the family. The resulting legislation, first the Código Negro Carolino and, a few years later, the Código Negro Español, called for more holidays for and better care of the slaves, and made provision for educating the slave population. However, some historians have argued that, far from an attempt to be more benevolent – not that the French lived up to the prescriptions of their code – the intention was to lay the foundation for large slave plantations similar to those that prospered on the French side of the island.[24] These codes would do little to foster the development in Santo Domingo, which by this point was doing a brisk trade in animal hides to its neighbour.

Even the Swedes implemented a slave code for their island, St Barthélemy, which they bargained for in 1784, in exchange for a trade deal with France involving the North Sea port of Gothenburg. It was similar to the others, prohibiting, for instance, people of colour from carrying arms, or assembling without permission. Nor were they allowed to buy gold or silver. They, too, would be punished for striking a white person. Their masters, however, were allowed to chain and whip them, up to twenty-nine lashes. A runaway slave found with a weapon could be put to death, and innkeepers were prohibited from giving them liquor, under a penalty of 200 livres.[25]

Barbados was the first British colony to develop a slave code, and this, too, was influenced by its Spanish and French predecessors.[26] But all these codes were in essence a set of rules that a minority tried to impose on a majority. There was not an island in the West Indies where white European colonizers made up the majority of the population. In the Spanish islands, however, there was a large number of creole inhabitants and a low number of slaves at this point, though this would begin to change towards the end of the eighteenth century, as slave importation increased there. There might have been more free people than slaves in some places, but a proportion of those free people would have had African blood and been enslaved or had a forebear who had been.

As with the differences between the slave codes, so, too, was there a difference in management. The British plantation owners more often than not lived in Britain, not the West Indies. Many were serving Members of Parliament and thus could vote for legislation that favoured their interests. The day-to-day running of their estates was undertaken by white overseers. Back in England, wealthy planter families built stately homes, while merchants in port cities such as Bristol and Liverpool thrived on the slave trade and sugar riches. The French planters, likewise, tended to set up profitable concerns in Saint-Domingue or Martinique and then return to France as quickly as possible. Both English and French families based in the Caribbean usually sent their children to Europe to be educated. On the Spanish islands, however, most of the planters were island-born, so there was little of the absenteeism that marked the British model. They often had a good deal of local political power; this was especially the case in Cuba.

Not all Europeans in the West Indies were plantation owners, of course, but it would have been very difficult to be white and not also to be implicated in the buying, selling, or controlling of other human beings. Merchants, chaplains, ship captains, soldiers – their daily lives were all intertwined with the continuation of the slavery regime. In addition, these slave societies subsisted on fear – rumours, conspiracies, and misinformation that fed the imaginations of slave and master alike. Violence, whether stipulated by law, such as a permissible number of lashes that could be inflicted on a slave, or outside it, which could be any manner of torture, was used to suppress slaves; keeping social order intact was a never-ending worry for the outnumbered whites, haunted by the nightmare of a rebellion, or, closer to home, the prospect of poison in that evening's soup.

In French Saint-Domingue in the 1750s, a period of heightened panic about poisoning and even the casting of spells against whites, a runaway slave named Macandal (also Makandal) was burnt at the stake, accused of leading attacks on plantations, poisoning white people, and teaching others how to do so.[27] Crimes such as his soon became known as macandalism, though whether or not Macandal actually poisoned anyone is unclear; what is significant is that he represented the prospect of poisoning.

Alleged poisonings would also play a part in one very public display of planter cruelty in Saint-Domingue. Although France's slave code stipulated that slaves were not to be tortured, little interest was paid to the definition of torture – until the Lejeune case.[28] Nicolas Lejeune inherited a plantation in the 1780, in Plaisance, Saint-Domingue, near the northern port city of Cap Française. As on most plantations, slaves there were beaten, often on charges of attempting to poison their master. By 1788, however, slaves in the colony had a legal right to complain about treatment that was not in line with the code, including torture. Planters' abuse of slaves was becoming widely known – and opposed – in France. In the spring of 1788, fourteen slaves arrived in Plaisance asking for protection from Lejeune, claiming he had twice burnt his slaves with a torch. The first time had been a year earlier, but a few days before two slaves called Zabeth and Marie-Rose had had their legs scorched, and were then locked in a cell.[29]

The town's judicial administrators took up the case. One of the investigators found the two women incarcerated at the plantation, with burns on their feet and legs. Lejeune claimed they had poisoned another slave named Julie, and that he had survived an attempt to poison him as well. Although Zabeth and Marie-Rose had wounds so severe that they soon died, they were able to tell the investigators that their pain caused them to confess to whatever crimes Lejeune had invented. It also became clear that this sort of torture was not a new occurrence on that plantation. Lejeune's defence was that if he were brought to justice, the colony would go up in flames because the slaves would become insubordinate. Soon the worried planters were calling for the case to be dropped.

However, a warrant for Lejeune's arrest was issued, and he went on the run, with the charges against him elevated from torture to murder after the women's deaths. In a letter to the court, the colony's planters pleaded, 'Our fortunes, your life, ours, the existence of ten thousand families in France all depend on the subordination of the slaves . . . Humanity may be revolted by the rules that ancient and modern

policies have adopted; [but these] conventions have been made . . .'
Lejeune's father also tried to have the charges dropped, and Lejeune
was eventually acquitted. However, the white planters' fears would soon
become a reality and France would no longer be able to ignore the
brutality on its most valuable island. The slaves would eventually have
their revenge on all the Lejeunes of Saint-Domingue, but there would
still be plenty of brutality ahead for the slaves on the island as France
continued to grow wealthy on the profits of sugar.

*

The British islands were experiencing similar sugar riches; by the
middle of the eighteenth century, about 60 per cent of slaves in the
British Caribbean worked in sugar. Smaller-scale planters had been
pushed aside, and other goods were also forced to the margins. Like
the French islands, cruelty to slaves ran rife there too. Mary Prince
gives a horrific account of the punishment meted out to one of her
fellow slaves:

> Poor Hetty, my fellow slave . . . led a most miserable life . . . One
> of the cows had dragged the rope away from the stake to which
> Hetty had fastened it, and got loose. My master flew into a terrible
> passion, and ordered the poor creature to be stripped quite naked,
> notwithstanding her pregnancy, and to be tied up to a tree in the
> yard. He then flogged her as hard as he could lick, both with the
> whip and cow-skin, till she was all over streaming with blood. He
> rested, and then beat her again and again. Her shrieks were terrible.
> The consequence was that poor Hetty was brought to bed before
> her time, and was delivered after severe labour of a dead child.
> She appeared to recover after her confinement, so far that she was
> repeatedly flogged by both master and mistress afterwards; but
> her former strength never returned to her. Ere long her body and
> limbs swelled to a great size; and she lay on a mat in the kitchen,
> till the water burst out of her body and she died.[30]

But many planters presented the world with a more benign account
of enslavement. Bryan Edwards had first-hand experience of plantation
life in the British colonies. In 1759 he was sent to live with an uncle
in Jamaica, from whom he inherited substantial estates ten years later,
including more than 1,000 slaves. After around thirty years on the

island, he returned to England and stood for Parliament, where he was, unsurprisingly, a vigorous defender of planters in the face of growing opposition to slavery. In 1793 he published, in two volumes, *The History, Civil and Commercial, of the British Colonies in the West Indies*. Writing in England, far removed from the island, he painted a picture of eighteenth-century Jamaica that persisted into modern times. On the matter of slavery, he argued that most people who owned slaves 'came into possession of their plantations by inheritance or accident', and that many had never even seen their estates.[31] He went on to explain how the plantations worked – that the slaves were divided into three gangs, the first being the most robust men who planted the crop and then cut the cane and worked in the sugar mills after the harvest; the second were children, pregnant women, and convalescents who weeded the cane and did other 'light' work; and the third were young children who worked the garden or 'some such gentle exercise, merely to preserve them from habits of idleness'.

The first group was woken before sunrise and immediately put to work in the fields. They had a break around 8 or 9 a.m. for a breakfast of 'boiled yams, eddoes, okra, calalue and plantains' and 'by this time most of the absentees make their appearance, and are sometimes punished for their sluggishness by a few stripes of the driver's whip'. They worked until noon, then had food and a siesta before returning to the fields from 2 p.m. until sunset. He pointed out that 'in the crop season, however, the system is different; for at that time, such of the negroes as are employed in the mill and boiling houses, often work very late, frequently, all night', taking turns in watches. Slaves also had some land where they had to grow their own food, with masters seeing this as some sort of indulgence because the slaves were allowed to sell the surplus. Edwards was keen to deny any notion that the 'excessive whipping, and barbarous mutilations, which have lately awakened the sympathy of the public' might be true: 'I . . . aver that, although such enormities have certainly *sometimes* happened, and may happen again, that the *general* treatment of the negroes in the British West Indies is mild, temperate, and indulgent.' His account was of course designed to obscure many of the large horrors and small indignities of daily life in a slave society, such as those Mary Prince witnessed. But, as Edwards himself acknowledged, there was growing disquiet – and gradually the public learned the truth.

Edwards also wrote about the other people on the island, dividing Jamaica's 30,000 whites and estimated 250,000 blacks into four groups: European whites, creole or 'native' whites, mixed-race creoles and free blacks, and slaves.[32] In a world increasingly riven by colour, Edwards wrote that there is 'an independent spirit' among the whites: 'The poorest white person seems to consider himself nearly on a level with the richest.' He noted that there were some 'peculiarities' that would surprise the visitor from Europe, 'one of which is the contrast between the general plenty and magnificence of their tables (at least in Jamaica) and the meanness of their houses and apartments; it being no uncommon thing to find . . . a splendid sideboard loaded with plate and the choicest wines, a table covered with the finest damask . . . and all of this in a hovel not superior to an English barn'. More shocking was the 'strange incongruity' whereby the slave butler wears shoes and stockings but 'all the others, and there is commonly one to each guest, wait at the table in *bare footed majesty*; some of them perhaps half naked'.

Creole women, based on his description, appeared to live a stultifying existence, 'except the exercise of dancing, in which they delight and excel'; otherwise,

> they have no amusement or avocation to impel them to much exertion of either body or mind. Those midnight assemblies and gambling conventions, wherein health, fortune, and beauty are so frequently sacrificed in the cities of Europe, are here happily unknown. In their diet, the creole women are, I think, abstemious even to a fault. Simple water, or lemonade, is the strongest beverage in which they indulge; and a vegetable mess at noon, seasoned with Cayenne pepper, constitutes their principal repast.[33]

Visual culture appeared to follow suit. The paintings of Agostino Brunias, for example, depict a seemingly ordered and peaceful West Indian world. He was an artist from Rome who, through his connection to Sir William Young, the commissioner of Dominica, Grenada, St Vincent, and Tobago, travelled to the Caribbean and spent some thirty years during the latter half of the eighteenth century painting the people of the West Indies, dying in Dominica in 1796. Part of the reason Young encouraged Brunias was that he thought a positive depiction of life on these islands – which had previously been under French control – might encourage more settlers to come there.[34] Brunias did not focus on slaves in the field, but instead the world of the free people of colour. By the eighteenth century, across the Caribbean there were growing communities of free people, often because of the allowance for manumission in the slave codes, and so over time many islands built up large populations of free people of colour. They still faced violence and discrimination, but they had their liberty. Brunias's work depicts a lively, elegant society among these people – with whom he may have also socialized, being a craftsman rather than a landowner – in the 'ceded' islands.[35] One of his most arresting works is *A Linen Market*. In the centre are two elegant free women of colour, dressed in white with elaborate hats, buying cloth from darker-skinned women on St Vincent. Off to the left are Caribs, with one pipe-smoking man watching them. In the distant background, two slaves appear to be having a cudgelling match with sticks, while other men watch. The sky is blue, the trees green. The market seems a lively place, but also a peaceful one, and all the shades of people are depicted as knowing their place. Brunias's work, interestingly, showed the many social and perceived racial gradations on the island, and they were far more complex than simply black, white, mulatto. Free people of colour were not homogeneous – some had white parentage, others were completely African – and the numbers varied across the islands. By the early 1800s there were some 70,000 free people of colour across all British territories.[36] In Cuba, there had been a significant free population for at least a century, and the French islands – especially Saint-Domingue – all had large free communities.

Many of the illegitimate and free children born to African mothers and European fathers in the Spanish and French colonies, and to a lesser degree to the English, were recognized by their fathers, and they were often sent to Europe to be educated. Their presence is sometimes hard to trace, though literature can offer a glimpse, and also illustrates European attitudes to such people. For example, in Thackeray's novel *Vanity Fair*, Miss Swartz, a minor character who appears early in the book, is described as 'the rich woolly-haired mulatto from St. Kitt's'. Later she returns as a society marriage prospect, thanks to her numerous plantations and the 'three stars to her name in the East India stockholders' list'. She is also in possession of 'a mansion in Surrey and a house in Portland Place'. An orphan, her father was said to be 'a German Jew – a slave-owner they say – connected with the Cannibal Islands in some way or other', with a fortune of £200,000. For George Osborne, the money was not the issue. "'Marry that mulatto woman?" George said, pulling up his shirt-collars. "I don't like the colour, sir. Ask the black that sweeps opposite Fleet Market, sir. I'm not going to marry a Hottentot Venus."'

Most women of colour, however, were not so financially fortunate, nor did they live in European cities. Many free people of colour worked hard to survive as tradesmen or market-sellers, and relied on fellow freedmen and women in their communities. Attitudes to colour in the colonies were arbitrary and changed over time; they were also influenced by European practice. For example, in France the notion that nobility could be passed along in the blood became a problem when there was a *mésalliance* with a commoner or when a newly ennobled person joined an old family.[37] The offspring of an alliance between a noble man and a non-noble woman was known as a *métis*. This became the basis for a 'quasi-biological' type of social hierarchy that would spill over into the colonies. In French Canada, for instance, there were efforts to bring the French and converted Indians together, with France issuing instructions in 1667 to the colony requiring the natives to embrace Christianity so that 'having one law and one master, they may form one people and one blood'. But the policy failed, and Indian women who lived as concubines with French men were blamed for any number of social ills. In the Caribbean, mixed marriages were recorded before 1700, a time when French colonists were supposed to marry women they had impregnated. But this soon changed; men in Martinique were fined 1,000 livres, payable to the Church, if they were found to have fathered a mulatto child. And in Guadeloupe, as early as 1680 an edict was passed forcing mulatto children to follow their mothers into slavery. Equally, though, such diktats were often simply ignored.

For other free people of colour, owning land was a way of asserting autonomy, as well as a means to make money. In Saint-Domingue, free people of colour – also known as *affranchis* – were involved in the lucrative coffee trade, and others in the cultivation of the indigo crop. The sugar plantations were in the north of the island, but the south, which juts out like an arm reaching for Cuba, was far less developed. Many free people of colour lived in the south, away from the plantations, allowing them also to participate in the contraband economy nearby.[38] Planters realized coffee would grow well in the hills in these southern regions, as would indigo. Indigo, like other Caribbean crops, was labour intensive, requiring planting, weeding, and harvesting, before a series of soakings and drainings.[39] Yet it did not require many slaves to grow it in order to turn a profit – some plantations had as few as thirty-five slaves – and it brought prosperity for some free people of colour, including the family of Julien Raimond. Raimond's father, Pierre, was a Frenchman who arrived in Saint-Domingue and married a free-born mulatto woman named Marie Begasse in 1726. She brought a dowry of 6,000 livres with her and by the time of Pierre's death in 1772, the family had 115 slaves on their indigo plantation. Some of their surviving ten children went to school in France. Two of their sons, François and Jean-Baptiste, managed to quadruple the value of the estate, and Julien joined them, later buying his own estate. By 1782, Julien's wealth was estimated to be 202,000 livres, and he married a free mulatto who had an 80,000-livre dowry.[40] His family and business dealings stretched across the Atlantic, and his name would come to prominence in an attempt to bring equality to the island.

In Cuba, many freed people, and sometimes slaves, of African or creole birth were members of a *cabildo de nación*, or council. Such organizations were grouped by a shared African origin and often language as well, reflected in the name, such as Konga Masinga or Mina Guagni. These societies provided services such as housing or loans, and even at times purchased freedom for a member who was still in bondage, and there were more than thirty across the island by the late eighteenth century.[41] They were outside the plantations and the racism of daily life, yet tolerated by officials and planters, some of whom saw them as a safety valve that could allow slaves and free blacks to channel their frustration without it leading to a rebellion. They have their roots in the European tradition of confraternities (*cofradías*), or mutual-aid societies with links to the Catholic Church. In Cuba, people of African heritage were recorded as taking part in their processions and ceremonies during religious festivals as early as the mid-1500s. But there was an African antecedent to this as well, because some peoples, such as the Yoruba – who had a significant presence in Cuba – had similar social organizations in place in Africa.[42] Over time, these developed into the *cabildos*, blending old world and new, bringing

African traditions to Catholic holy days, such as the feast of the Epiphany (also known as Día de los Reyes), when people of colour paraded through Havana's streets in costume, drumming and dancing. But by the nineteenth century there would be growing concern that such celebrations might lead to unrest, and eventually they faced severe restrictions or were completely abolished.[43]

But blending old and new was not unique to Cuba; the spiritual realm was a place where the convergence of these worlds – African, Muslim, Amerindian, European – was perhaps best expressed. The most famous of these is Haitian voodoo (also voudou or vaudon). The word itself is from Dahomey (today's Benin) – *vodu*, which means spirit or deity. When slaves from West Africa were taken to Saint-Domingue and ripped out of their polytheistic belief system, they were simultaneously exposed to Catholicism. The many saints of the Catholic faith provided a cover under which people could continue to worship their spirits, or loas (*lwas*). An example of this would be the Dahomean goddess of love who is related to Oshun in Nigeria and became Erzulie in Saint-Domingue, and in Catholic iconography is represented by the Virgin Mary. Or the god Damballa, who is often associated with serpents, being depicted as St Patrick.[44] Voodoo is a community-based religion and the rituals often involve a group. Yet the spiritual dimension is intensely personal as the spirit 'mounts' the human 'horse' (*cheval*) and possesses them temporarily. The ceremonies often last for hours, and involve drumming and dancing. These foreign practices – the chanting, drumming, dancing – and the fraternizing among slaves, as well as free people of colour, would give French officials and planters cause for concern and there would follow the inevitable attempts to ban the ceremonies.

Similarly, in Cuba santería developed from Yoruba traditions, and has many similarities to voodoo, especially in the *orishas*, or spirits, which also overlapped with Catholic saints. Catholic religious orders had been on the Spanish islands since the earliest days of colonization, and so Christianity was most deeply entrenched there, though Catholic orders established themselves on the French islands too. Religious ceremonies in santería also involved spirit possession, drumming, offerings to the gods, and the coming together of participants. Both religions have local leaders – for instance, the male *houngan* and female *mambo* in voodoo – but no overarching centralized hierarchy, or official places of worship. In colonial times, their decentralized nature made it easier to organize and practise away from official eyes.

Religion on the Protestant islands had significant differences. Best known in the English-speaking islands was Jamaica's obeah. It is not so much a religion as a system of beliefs connected to the supernatural and the spirit world. Its roots lie in the Ashanti practices of the Gold Coast of Africa – obeah is a corruption of the word *obayifo* – and many slaves from this part of West Africa were taken to the British colonies.[45] Contact with the spirit world could be for good or bad purposes, and the obeah-man or -woman also made potions from natural substances such as plant leaves or feathers in order to 'put on' or 'take off' ghosts, also known as duppies, or jumbees, the spirits of the dead. Obeah – also sometimes called obi – is concerned with solving problems too, such as worries over health or money. Although it is most associated with Jamaica, the practices of *quimbois* on the French islands of Martinique and Guadeloupe are similar. With its mixture of spirits of the dead, potions, and communion with the supernatural, the planters were very nervous about obeah practitioners, who also were often leaders of their communities, and often associated by whites with slave revolts.

The Jamaican planter Bryan Edwards blamed a 1760 slave revolt – known as Tacky's rebellion – on an 'old Koromantyn negro' of that name who was the 'chief instigator and oracle'. The rebellion involved rebel slaves seizing guns and powder from a fort in Jamaica, and there were related uprisings in the south-west parishes which lasted for six months and unnerved the planters and officials. It comes as no surprise that the obeah practitioners, involved or not in such plots, would come under white scrutiny. According to Edwards, this obeah-man 'administered the fetish or solemn oath to the conspirators, and furnished them with a magical preparation which was to render them invulnerable'. But he was later caught and hanged 'with all his feathers and trumperies about him'.[46]

However, there were Christian variations, too, as many slaves and free people of colour added their own variants to what the missionaries were teaching them; variants that the same missionaries often tried to stop or suppress. The Moravians were some of the earliest Protestants to try to convert the slaves; they did so on the Danish islands in the early 1700s, and soon a wide variety of Protestant sects, such as

Lutherans, Methodists, Anglicans, and the Dutch Reformed Church were doing the same. Not all planters were eager for their slaves to convert; if they were Christian the validity of their captivity might be called into question and they might have to be set free. In the end, the planters prevailed, although the slaves were told the 'emancipatory' story of Christianity while held in bondage. However, over time the number of slave and free coloured followers began to grow, with many people being attracted to evangelical Christianity. This would fuse with much older traditions to form uniquely West Indian churches, often evangelical and charismatic, for instance the Shouter Baptists. This is a mostly Trinidad-based denomination, which acknowledges its African roots yet remains firmly Christian, and its modern incarnations include possession (or speaking in tongues), chanting, and hand-clapping. Its services and communities worried the British colonial authorities sufficiently that in 1917 they prohibited the religion, but the ban was repealed in 1951.

*

While religion offered a modicum of amelioration for those who remained enslaved, life continued to be a constant battle. Small acts of resistance were a daily occurrence, and there were also large-scale rebellions. But there was also the possibility of *marronage* – running away to join a maroon colony. Maroons, from the Spanish word *cima-rrón* (wild), were slaves who left plantations and lived in remote areas – mountains, forests, and jungles – out of the reach of planters. Often they lived with or were helped by surviving indigenous people. This was especially the case around Honduras, as well as the lesser populated islands like Dominica. Some of these smaller islands had rugged, mountainous interiors that Europeans had not mapped and into which they were wary of treading far.

Certain islands were better suited to maroons than others. The flat, cultivated fields of Barbados and Antigua offered few places to live outside the reach of planters. But in other islands, such as Jamaica, the wooded hills of the interior provided many hiding places. Indeed, relations with the maroon colonies in Jamaica were a long-running issue not only for the planters but also the colonial administration. In the 1730s there had been ongoing raids by the maroons on local plantations, and retaliation by British troops. This escalated into a full-scale conflict, known as the First Maroon War. There had been maroon colonies in the island's mountains since the Spanish administration, and thus under British rule there were already established communities for runaways to join. One such runaway was Cudjoe, who was one of the war's leaders. He was later ambushed and forced to sign a peace treaty stipulating that he and his fellow maroons could continue to live in their mostly autonomous communities if they stopped the raids and agreed to help capture other runaways and suppress any rebellions. Another chief, Quao, was forced into a similar bargain. Women also participated, among them Nanny, who has become one of Jamaica's national heroes, and who established a settlement in the mountains – Nanny Town. She stands out in a male-dominated world, where accounts of slave women tend to depict them as household servants or concubines. Nanny, however, was acknowledged to be a fearless warrior and known for her obeah powers, including feats such as being able to stop bullets and throw them back at the person who shot them.

Uprisings were another option for the slaves. Throughout the enslavement of Africans, there had always been acts of rebellion. Sometimes they were large-scale attempts, such as trying to overpower a crew on a slave ship; on other occasions there were localized protests over poor treatment. Often they were organized among Africans who still shared a similar language or were from the same places, rather than island-born slaves. No colony was immune, and the tales are numerous. For instance, in 1733 there was an insurrection on Danish St John's, partly in response to a new, stricter code brought in to further control the slaves, as the island was struggling to recover from a drought followed by a hurricane. It stipulated punishments such as cutting off the leg of captured runaway slaves, or flogging as a punishment for religious practices, or 'witchcraft'. That November a small group of slaves described as 'Amina' – in this instance believed to be Akwamu people from the Gold Coast – attacked a fort on the island, and fired a cannon to signal other slaves to attack the whites, triggering six months of fighting.[47] In 1763 there was an uprising in the Dutch South American colony of Berbice (Guyana) involving some 4,000 slaves from which the colony took more than a year to recover.

But such rebellions were not limited to slaves. In Dominica, in the late eighteenth century, Governor Sir John Orde continued to have problems with the surviving Amerindians, the Kalinagos. Many of the slaves who were brought to the islands ran into the mountains and survived thanks to the help of the indigenous people. By 1786, three years into his governorship, Orde had made little headway in suppressing the native people and recapturing the runaway slaves. He reported to London – and to the 'great satisfactions' of King George III: 'Our success against the Runaways has been as good as from the Nature of the Country and other Circumstances would well be expected – we have killed and taken between 30 & 40, some have also surrendered – the rest are in general dispersed and under the greatest distress for provisions &c.'[48]

To the south, on the island of St Vincent, which was half the size of Dominica, the governor, Valentine Morris, was facing similar problems. Runaway slaves there were also joining the indigenous people living in the island's volcanic interior. By early 1777, Morris claimed to have 'happily effected a breach of that alliance between the runaway negroes, and . . . [the] greater part if not all the Charibs [sic]' after 'eating a little dirt' – which he underlined in his letter – to seal the deal. He offered them protection and a pledge not to take their land if they were willing to assist: 'I convinced them that these must still greatly encrease [sic] by being an Asylum to all of our runaway Negroes, which must end soon in the falling on them, & taking from them their Lands.'[49] This arrangement did not last for long.

Runaways faced stiff punishments when they were caught – they were to be taught a lesson but not rendered incapable of labour, unless they continued to rebel. The Code Noir stipulated that 'the fugitive slave . . . shall have his ears cut off and shall be branded with a fleur de lys on one shoulder. If he commits the same infraction for another month, again counting from the day he is reported, he shall have his hamstring cut and be branded with a fleur de lys on the other shoulder. The third time, he shall be put to death.' In the Danish islands, runaways were to receive similar harsh punishments such as being 'pinched three times with red-hot iron, and then hung', while informants were to be paid a fee for each slave found to be involved in a plot.[50] But in a society where the rules stipulated that 'a slave meeting a white person, shall step aside, and wait until he passes; if not, he may be flogged', there were reasons to be punished every day, making the risks involved in fleeing eminently worth taking.[51] Hans Sloane wrote about the many penalties that were inflicted on runaway or rebellious slaves in late-seventeenth-century Jamaica:

> The Punishments for Crimes of Slaves, are usually for Rebellions burning them, by nailing them down on the ground with crooked Sticks on every Limb, and then applying the Fire by degrees from their Feet and Hands, burning them gradually up the Head, whereby their pains are extravagant. For Crimes of a lesser nature Gelding, or chopping off half of the Foot with an Ax. These Punishments are suffered by them with great Constancy. For running away they put Iron Rings of great weight on their Ankles, or Pottocks about their Necks, which are Iron Rings with two long Necks rivetted to them, or a Spur in the Mouth. For Negligence, they are usually whipt by the Overseers with Lance wood Switches, till they be bloody, and several of the Switches broken, being first tied up by their Hands in the Mill Houses . . . After they are whip'd til they are Raw, some put on their Skins Pepper and Salt to make them smart; at other times their Masters will drop melted Wax on their Skins, and use several very exquisite Torments.[52]

Slavery demanded violence, and colonial societies were shaped by it. No island could escape the rebellions, nor ignore the runaways. Yet Europeans kept feeding Africans into the great sugar machine; imports throughout this period rose, adding to the number of slaves already on the islands. White people became ever more outnumbered, forcing them to turn to increasingly inhumane means to maintain control of their plantations and slave societies.

*

In Europe, many people were trying to make sense not only of the transatlantic trade, but of the people of Africa, and the New World itself. Race, as it is understood today, was not yet part of the eighteenth-century worldview, although a language was evolving. For instance, there was already a clear distinction between the Amerindians and the Africans.

The indigenous people of the Americas were either gentle or fierce, civilized or cannibalistic, depending on who was writing about them. The New World seeped into the consciousness of Old World writers, and the result was often contradictory. For instance, the sixteenth-century

French writer Michel de Montaigne notes in his essay 'Of Cannibals' that Europeans were all too capable of being savage, observing, 'I find, that there is nothing Barbarous and Savage in this Nation, by any things that I can gather, excepting, That every one gives the Title of Barbarity to every thing that is not in use in his own Country.'[53] But he nonetheless goes on to describe the people of the New World as having

> no manner of Traffick, no knowledg of Letters, no Science of Numbers, no name of Magistrate, nor Politick Superiority; no use of Service, Riches or Poverty, no Contracts, no Successions, no Dividents, no Proprieties, no Employments, but those of Leisure, no respect of Kindred, but common, no Cloathing, no Agriculture, no Mettal, no use of Corn or Wine, and where so much as the very words that signifie, Lying, Treachery, Dissimulation, Avarice, Envy, Detraction and Pardon, were never heard of.[54]

Of course, writers of that era were necessarily limited to travellers' accounts, often translated from other languages, and many times infused with the author's particular agenda. Sifting fact from fiction could be nearly impossible, and because of this the idea of the Amerindian, and later slave, could be abstracted and refashioned to reflect anxieties related to European society. Being reduced to metaphor did little to preserve with any accuracy the changing – or, indeed, dying – traditions of these people. At the same time, high-profile intellectuals were also brought into the ever-widening orbit of the colonial sphere. Men like Grotius were not sitting in a tower thinking and writing – they had first-hand experience of these new places, or at the very least of the institutions that were underpinning imperial expansion, such as the Dutch East India Company.

The English writer John Locke was another thinker whose life straddled these worlds. In 1689, he set out a theory of slavery in his *Two Treatises of Government*, arguing that man should 'have only the law of nature for his rule' before going on to say that the 'perfect condition of slavery' is related to war, and that slavery is 'but the state of war continued, between a lawful conqueror and a captive'.[55] Oppression by a despot or a ruthless monarch was illegitimate slavery. Concern about the powers of a monarch would seem probable enough, given that he was writing in the context of the accession of Holland's William of Orange in 1689 to the thrones of England, Scotland and Ireland in the Glorious Revolution. Yet, through his work, Locke was pulled across the Atlantic as well. He was a shareholder in the slave-trading Royal Africa Company, and in 1667 he had begun working as a personal secretary for Anthony Ashley Cooper, later Earl of Shaftesbury, and also was secretary to the Board of Trade and Plantations, and later one of the Lord Proprietors of Carolina, in North America. Locke, therefore, was employed at the heart of the imperial project, and was also profiting from it. In his working life, he would have access to the ongoing arrival of accounts and reports from Europeans in the New World. He could not have been writing about slavery in the abstract, yet in his work, he does not speak with any explicitness about this aspect of the evolving colonial world. But he would have known that a New World slave was not the prisoner of a just war.[56] This is not to enter a debate on Locke's meaning, but to point out how the developing colonies and expanding imperial world infiltrated every level of society.

His thoughts on land, however, are clearer: he promoted the idea that land should belong to people who could put it to use or who were willing to 'improve' it, declaring that 'as much land as a man tills, plants, improves, cultivates, and can use the product of, so much is his property.'[57] This was a sentiment that would come to infiltrate political thinking for the next century in England and France.[58] It not only underpinned England's hierarchical land-use system, but provided justification for taking untilled fields in the New World from native peoples who, in the eyes of Europeans who had little understanding of their often sophisticated agricultural systems, were perceived as not 'using' them.

The Spanish were more concerned with codifying difference, for instance regarding 'purity' of blood, which was related to Old World prejudices against Muslims and Jews. Yet in the New World, Spain introduced the somewhat contradictory *gracias al sacar* – a royal order granted to non-whites to make them legally white.[59] Although it was used for people who were part native, or mestizo, it was later extended to blacks or mulattos, i.e., people who had one white and one black parent. At the same time there was a growing obsession with classifying the children of inter-racial relationships, best articulated in the *casta* paintings, physical representations of the many new combinations of human beings. They were an art form unique to New Spain, but they encapsulate what was taking place across the region. The paintings are often on one canvas, divided into twelve or sixteen squares, although there are series of individual paintings. Almost all of them show a man, woman, and child – usually in an idealized home, or in a bucolic landscape setting – and underneath is written what the combination is supposed to be. For instance, there might be a Spanish man in modern clothes with a porcelain complexion, alongside a woman in a full-skirted indigenous outfit, depicted with dark skin. The child, holding the mother's hand, would wear a smaller version of the father's clothes, while his complexion would be a shade between that of his parents. Underneath there would be a caption reading 'De Español y Yndia, Mestizo' – of a Spanish man and female Indian, a mixed child. These paintings are a vivid indication of the colonizers' need to control and define what was happening in the New World, across all possible combinations of people. For instance, the offspring of an Amerindian and an African would be called a zambo, or also a 'lobo' (which means wolf in Spanish). Despite these efforts at creating a nomenclature, there was a great deal of regional variation, though the terms mestizo and mulatto were widely used. Other colonies followed this pattern, coming up with terms like half-caste, or quadroon (someone who is one-quarter African), or octoroon (someone who is one-eighth African).

As Europe entered the nineteenth century there would be an ever more relentless drive to name and classify everything in the known world – plants, animals, and people. This urge would cause heated debates between scientists and slave traders. Who were the Africans? Should they be enslaved? And what about the offspring of African and European? The spectre of racial categories and stereotypes loomed. As James Sweet has pointed out, 'Europeans invented themselves as whites, Africans as blacks, and later, Indians as reds', and of course put white at the top of the hierarchy that they themselves had invented.[60] Or as historian and later prime minister of Trinidad and Tobago, Eric Williams, wrote in his seminal work *Capitalism and Slavery*, 'slavery was not born of racism: rather, racism was the consequence of slavery'.[61] Someone had to do the work, and occupy the bottom rung of the ladder – the economic hierarchy now demanded it.

By the 1700s the colonies and the colonial powers were locked into a financial pact. Hans Sloane had recognized the value of trade between the West Indies and England on his visit to Jamaica:

The Trade of *Jamaica* is either with *Europe* or *America*. That of *Europe* consists in bringing thither Flower, Bisket, Beef, Pork, all manner of Clothing for Masters and Servants, as Osnabrigs, blew Cloth, Liquors of all sorts, &c. *Madera* wine is also imported in great quantities . . . The Goods sent back again, or Exported from the Island, are Sugars, most part *Muscavados*, Indico, Cotton-wool, Ginger, Pimento All-Spice or *Jamaica*-Pepper, Fustick-wood, Prince-wood, *Lignum Vitae, Arnotto*, Log-wood, and the several Commodities they have from the *Spaniards* of the *West Indies* . . . such as *Sarsaparilla, Cacao*-Nuts, Cochineel, &c on which they get a considerable profit.[62]

By 1700 Caribbean sugar output was worth around £1.7 million, approximately £4 billion in today's money, and it quadrupled over the next seventy years.[63] So planters had a lot of money to spend, and they wanted to show what they were worth. Many in the British and French colonies were younger sons of titled families who went to the colonies to make their own wealth because they could not expect to inherit, while others were from less exalted circumstances. Most wealthy West Indian planters fell prey to the lure of an ever-expanding range of expensive goods: fine porcelain from the East, furniture made from the finest mahogany, the latest fashions from Paris and London. In a few generations, the hard life of a sugar planter had been transformed into one fabled for its idleness, luxury, and lasciviousness. This was partly due to the generous extension of credit, which was offered to planters throughout the British Atlantic world. Planters ordered goods from London, the cost of which was added to the debts they already owed. It also meant that the London factor had control over what was sent over, or was not, in the case of orders that went missing or arrived in the wrong port.[64] No matter how wealthy a person, someone across the Atlantic could be undercutting or mismanaging him. Even George Washington, after he married into a great deal of money, could not buy the service he wanted, complaining to his London factor in 1759 that instead of getting things 'good and fashionable in their several kind, we often have articles sent to us that could only have been us[e]d by our forefathers in the days of yore'.[65] No doubt the situation would have been similar, if not worse, in the West Indies, because not only were planters there beholden to London, they also required a lot of staples from the North American colonies.

The historian Christopher Berry has argued that luxury 'acts as a barometer of the movement from the classical and medieval world-view to that of modernity', dividing luxury into four categories: food and drink; shelter; clothing; leisure. The basics of human existence were now a vast world of choice, and West Indian planters were at the vanguard of such vanities. Indeed, in the wake of new objects and new ways of consuming (not least owning slaves), manners followed suit, with snobbish elites and clamouring middle classes eroding the idea that privilege was something that money could not buy. If human beings were for sale, then anything could be bought.[66]

In Britain, capital earned through slavery and sugar was invested in the building of factories; mass production had begun. Mill workers would have seemed familiar to the slave owner. The enforced poverty, ignorance, and brute treatment of the people (often children) in the factories had their counterparts in the West Indies. And while the workers were free, their lives were ones of misery. But the ever-increasing number of goods they made were sold to the colonists who bought them with the profits from the tropical produce they sold to England, profits which also funded more expeditions to sell more slaves to the islands to grow more things to exchange for more wares. The triangle was complete. But such a system could not bear these burdens for ever.

Chapter Six

A WORLD AT WAR

As dramatic flourishes go, displaying a severed ear that had been preserved in a jar for seven years to a room of parliamentarians was a pretty memorable one. But to add extra insult to the injury, Captain Robert Jenkins told the politicians that the man who lopped off his ear, Spanish Captain Juan de León Fandiño, had said to him at the time of the incident: 'Take this to your King and tell him if he were here I would do the same to him.'[1]

Tensions between Spain and Britain were again heightened in the early decades of the eighteenth century, this time over ongoing raids on British ships. León Fandiño had boarded Jenkins' brig, *Rebecca*, in April 1731 claiming the British were engaged in smuggling goods and raiding Spanish *flota* ships.[2] Yet while on board, León was unable to find any contraband, though he did spot some Spanish gold, which was proof enough for him.[3] It is entirely possible that Jenkins was trying to smuggle dyewood from Honduras or Campeche, and he was caught out by one of Spain's *guarda costa* patrols.[4] Words were exchanged, and insults flew. Enraged, León Fandiño took out his sword, and Jenkins lost his ear, not an uncommon infliction at the time. The *Rebecca* returned to London in June, and León Fandiño continued stopping and searching British ships in Caribbean waters. London merchants were increasingly irritated because it was disrupting trade and costing them money, and they wanted to see Spain punished.

However, Robert Walpole, the British prime minister, was against taking action, despite being told that fifty-two ships had been plundered by the Spanish since 1729.[5] Jenkins was summoned to the House of Commons in June 1738. Whether or not he really did take his ear is a matter of speculation – and what he said when he got there only caused the angry parliamentarians to rattle their sabres louder. Walpole tried the diplomatic route, but Spain refused to ratify the Convention of Pardo, which had been drawn up to resolve issues around contraband and smuggling. With few options left, and popular support for a war, Walpole finally gave in.[6]

Battle began in 1739, and the British attacked the Panamanian port town of Portobello. Vice-Admiral Edward Vernon led the fleet to victory, which was celebrated throughout Britain, with Vernon declared a national hero.[7] The rest of the war was not so successful. The British attack on Cartagena was rebuffed by a much smaller Spanish fleet, led by Blas de Lezo, whose career on the seas had left him with only one eye, one arm, and one leg. Lezo was further aided by tropical diseases, which wiped out many of the British troops.

Despite the other losses, the victory in Portobello was commemorated in Britain for a larger symbolic reason as well – the British had failed to capture that port only a decade earlier. Not so long before Jenkins was separated from his ear, Spain and Britain had already fought the Anglo-Spanish War (1727–29), during which the British attacked Portobello unsuccessfully in 1727. The Treaty of Seville in 1729 was meant to end the conflict and also put a stop to various complaints about trade and privateering, but as Jenkins could tell Parliament himself, it clearly had not been effective. The British were called home before there could be any decisive result, because by that point another European conflict had erupted – the War of the Austrian Succession (1740–48).[*] Until now, the eighteenth century's many wars had begun in Europe, albeit with battles fought in Caribbean waters; in the latter half of the century conflicts also began in the American and West Indian colonies.

As Enlightenment ideas spread throughout eighteenth-century Europe, the old order was called into question: the divine right of kings, the nature of commerce, how agriculture, finance and manufacturing could best benefit the nation. And on issues relating to the New World and the Caribbean – empire, slavery, trade – there were numerous conflicts and contradictions in the most important writings of the time.

---

* The Treaty of Aix-la-Chapelle in 1748, which ended the War of the Austrian Succession, contained provisions regarding some of the Caribbean territories. It declared Dominica, St Lucia, St Vincent, and Tobago as neutral and reserved for the 'Carib' people, though this was never really enforced.

For instance, Montesquieu's 1748 *The Spirit of the Laws* initially takes a decidedly anti-slavery tone, arguing that one man's ownership of another is 'not good by its nature; it is useful neither to the master nor to the slave'. Montesquieu admitted that slavery is more bearable in a land where the entire population is already in 'political slavery', but in a democracy or an aristocracy slaves 'are contrary to the spirit of the constitution; they serve only to give citizens a power and luxury they should not have'.[8] Yet he went on to argue that in tropical climates the condition of slavery is more 'natural' and thus justified.[9] And he showed little compassion to the slaves themselves, arguing that sugar would be too expensive were it not for slave labour, and that 'One cannot get into one's mind that God, who is a very wise being, should have put a soul, above all a good soul, in a body that was entirely black.'[10]

It was an ugly contradiction, though perhaps not a surprising one from the man who presided over the Bordeaux parliament; Bordeaux was one of the richest ports in France, its ornate buildings constructed with the profits of the slave trade.[11] Like Locke before him, Montesquieu was also tied to colonial trade and his writings contributed to a European racism that would later be almost enshrined in science, using the idea of 'race' as a means of deciding who should be enslaved and who should not. Indeed, in the same year, the Scottish philosopher David Hume, in a footnote to his essay 'Of National Characters', said, 'I am apt to suspect the negroes, and in general all the other species of men (for there are four or five different kinds) to be naturally inferior to the whites. There scarcely ever was a civilized nation of any other complexion than white, nor even any individual eminent either in action or speculation. No ingenious manufactures amongst them, no arts, no sciences.'[12]

Denis Diderot, in his vast *Encyclopédie*, however, refuted such ideas. The entry on slavery, written by Louis de Jaucourt, argued that the purchase of Africans was 'a negotiation that violates all religion, morals, natural law, and human rights' and went on to say that 'if a trade of this kind can be justified by a moral principle, then there is absolutely no crime, however atrocious, that cannot be legitimized'.[13] In addressing the widely held belief that the sugar colonies would collapse without slave labour, Jaucourt conceded their commerce would 'temporarily suffer' but was adamant that slave colonies should be 'destroyed rather than create so many unfortunates'.[14] Adam Smith, too, was opposed to slavery, and argued that the richer a society was, the worse it would be for slaves as the gulf in conditions between master and slave widened. And the more free the society, the worse for the slaves, saying 'in a democracy they are more miserable than in any other'.[15] Yet Smith, like many other fellow Britons, had a weakness for sugar.[16]

Some thinkers were prejudiced not only against African slaves but also against the Europeans born in the colonies. Creoles, many of whom had been on the islands for generations, were taunted as weak and degenerate in body and mind. Montesquieu, who believed that hot climates made people timid, while cold ones bolstered courage, wrote that 'Indians are by nature without courage; even the children of Europeans born in the Indies lose the courage of the European climate.'[17] But unlike Africans of this period, they could try to defend themselves. One such angry creole was the Santo Domingo cleric Antonio Sánchez Valverde. In a 1785 tract, he lambasted the Dutch philosopher Cornelius De Pauw, then reputed to be Europe's greatest authority on the Americas, for his views on creole 'degeneracy', saying that De Pauw's 'fecund imagination added much to his writings'.[18] He went on to ask De Pauw, who had never been to the Americas: 'In what part of Europe is one able to obtain, still with all the determination of the Monarchs, a *plátano*, a *piña* or *ananás*, a *guanávana*, a *mamey*, a *zapote*, a *cacao*, an *aguacate*, a *molondrón*, or any of the innumerable species of fruit of the island?' citing these fruits as symptomatic not of decline, but abundance.*

One of the most famous creoles in English literature is Mrs Rochester in Charlotte Brontë's novel *Jane Eyre*. Bertha Rochester was a Caribbean-born woman forced to live in the attic of her wealthy husband's manor, and considered to be insane, eventually starting a fire which leads to the destruction of the house and her death. The twentieth-century Dominican writer Jean Rhys sought to redress her literary silence by making Bertha the heroine of her novel *Wide Sargasso Sea*, which imagines the events – set in the Caribbean – that prefigure *Jane Eyre*. In Rhys's reworking, Mr Rochester observes of his new wife,

---

* A *plátano* is a plantain or banana, a *piña* is a pineapple and *ananás* are also pineapples (*piña* was in reference to the plant's similarity to a pine cone), *cacao* is cocoa, *aguacate* is avocado, *guanávana* is soursop, and *mamey* another version of *zapote* or sapote – a small tropical fruit not widely exported from the Americas – and *molondrón* is okra.

'She wore a tricorne hat which became her. At least it shadowed her eyes which are too large and can be disconcerting. She never blinks at all it seems to me. Long, sad, dark alien eyes. Creole of pure English descent she may be, but they are not English or European either.'[19]

This hostility to creoles fits in with a wider spirit among some writers against ongoing imperial expansion. There was a discernible anti-imperialism during the Enlightenment expressed in works by thinkers such as Diderot and Adam Smith.[20] They found the existence of the colonies a problem. Smith, for his part, claimed that 'the establishment of the European colonies in America and the West Indies arose from no necessity; and though the utility which has resulted from them has been very great, it is not altogether so clear and evident'.[21] The idea of luxury was very much part of this debate. Diderot had called for a discussion of luxury and what it meant, publishing an article on the subject in the *Encyclopédie* written by the Marquis de Saint-Lambert. The historian István Hont has explained that, for Saint-Lambert, luxury was 'the central moral and political issue of modernity'.[22] Saint-Lambert begins his lengthy *Encyclopédie* entry by saying that luxury 'is the use that one makes of wealth and industry to obtain a pleasant way of life' but soon attacks it, claiming its primary cause is 'our lack of satisfaction with our situation, our yearning to be better off'.[23] He conceded that all nations and peoples have their own idea of luxury, 'the savage has his hammock . . . the European has his sofa'.[24] However, in the end, he thought if luxury goods created demand, that could perhaps – if the ill effects were carefully managed – be of benefit to the nation. Smith, like many others, came to see that luxury was simply part of progress, and indeed one chapter in his *Wealth of Nations* is entitled 'Of the Natural Progress of Opulence'.[25] Other philosophers thought luxury was reprehensible – it corrupted monarchs and made people neglect agriculture, which they believed was the true source of national prosperity and happiness.

By the end of the eighteenth century, notions of luxury had changed. Enlightenment thinkers had begun to cast it, as John Shovlin has said, as 'a harmless byproduct of commercial prosperity and a stimulus to economic development'.[26] The middle classes in Europe were on the increase, wanting lumps of sugar for their tea and garments made from Chinese silk, as well as manufactured goods, and their values had filtered into the philosophical debate. Across the Atlantic, the consumption did not cease in the New World, as sugar was traded for expensive furniture, Paris fashions, and more slaves. But those philosophers who worried about the dangers of luxury perhaps could see something that the planters could not – by the end of the century it would contribute to the downfall of France's Saint-Domingue, the richest colony in the Caribbean.

*

In the meantime, the Enlightenment in Spain had a different set of preoccupations. The Inquisition continued to ban books – including Diderot's *Encyclopédie* in 1759 – and there were no real challenges to the monarchy or the Church; instead, change came from the crown. Charles III ushered in a period later known as the Bourbon reforms, which instituted many changes at home and in Spain's American colonies. Some of the more significant ones included a governmental reorganization that saw many creole officials supplanted by new appointees from the peninsula; the creation of stronger militias throughout the region; and the expulsion of the Jesuit order from the Americas, as well as Spain in 1767.

And just as England and France had watched with envy as Spain mined and spent its metal wealth, now Spain was all too aware that British and French sugar colonies were bearing financial fruit. For so much of the previous two and a half centuries, Spanish policy in the Caribbean had focused on mining, protecting the *flota*, and fighting contraband trade; it had failed to develop the potential of its island colonies. Some blamed this on the Habsburgs but the Bourbon regime had done little to change things. The contrast between Saint-Domingue and Santo Domingo was stark. Indeed, Montesquieu criticized Spain's reliance on gold and silver: 'Gold and silver are a wealth of fiction or of sign . . . The more they increase, the more they lose their worth, because they represent fewer things. When they conquered Mexico and Peru, the Spanish abandoned natural wealth in order to have a wealth of sign, which gradually became debased.'[27]

Increasingly, Spanish thinkers encouraged the crown to look to its fertile colonies for more than metal. José del Campillo y Cossío noted the 'islands Martinique and Barbados give more benefits to their masters than all . . . of America give to Spain'.[28] Most of Spain's riches had been poured into war, and the country's infrastructure was deficient, yet the commercial sea routes were well worn, and the turn to agriculture – more specifically sugar – was an enticing one. Voices from the islands echoed the sentiment, too. Fray Íñigo Abbad y Lasierra was a Benedictine who had arrived in Puerto Rico in 1771 and wrote what is considered its first history in 1782. In it, he complained that the island needed more people – it was still little more than a garrison – and that the few farmers there needed better trade links rather than being forced to scrape a living engaging in contraband. He lamented,

> In the early years of discovery of this island, during which the land was not fatigued with the crops of the Indians, and the activity of the new settlers was regular, they enjoyed good harvests of cacao, indigo, ginger, cotton, and tobacco, with the hides and other goods of industry, maintaining a lucid commerce; but after the attacks of the Caribs and the pirates interrupted them, and their bodies, dominated by the effects of the climate, lost their strength and activity . . .[29]

In addition, contraband trade was undercutting what was produced on the island. One Spanish official, Alejandro O'Reilly,* lamented in a 1765 report to the crown that, during a visit to Puerto Rico, it was obvious that 'Illicit trade very frequently takes place all over the island,' explaining how a vessel would drop anchor and then canoes or small launches would be used to conduct trade. 'The Dutch carry away most of the tobacco, the English the mulberry and Guayacan wood, the Danish provisions and coffee, and they all take the cattle, and as many mules as they can obtain.'[30]

Reforms were slow, but around the late 1770s, Spain phased out the creaking *flota* system, and smaller ships were given licences to make journeys. Even more radical was the decision in 1778 to experiment with 'free trade'. Up until this point, only one port had had permission to trade with the colonies: first Seville, then, from the late seventeenth century, Cádiz. Now, other cities could compete against the Cádiz monopoly; soon ships from Barcelona, Bilbao, and Coruña, among others, were sending their cloth or salted cod directly to the colonies,

---

* O'Reilly was from an Irish family, and like many Irish at the time, entered the army or the service of the Catholic king of Spain rather than Protestant Britain.

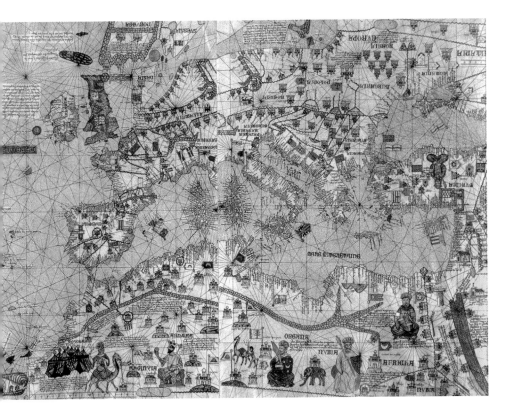

1. The Catalan Atlas of 1375 is attributed to mapmaker Abraham Cresques and was presented to France's Charles V. Its detail of Europe, the Mediterranean, and North Africa made it one of the most cartographically advanced maps of its time.

2. Christopher Columbus landing on the island of Hispaniola for the first time, as later imagined by Flemish printmaker Pieter Balthazar Bouttats (1666–1755).

3. 'Carib' Indians, from an engraving in a 1593 account by Johannes Lerii, complete with ceremonial tobacco pipes though no obvious cannibalism.

4. A portrait of Welsh-born pirate Henry Morgan, who attacked Spanish settlements in Cuba, Panama, and Venezuela, and was later named lieutenant-governor of Jamaica in 1674.

5. A Dutch engraving (1678) depicting Henry Morgan's devastating attack on Panama City in 1671, where he and his men spent three weeks pillaging the Spanish city, taking as much treasure as they could find.

6. A seventeenth-century map of Santo Domingo, on Hispaniola, which was by that point the capital of the island.

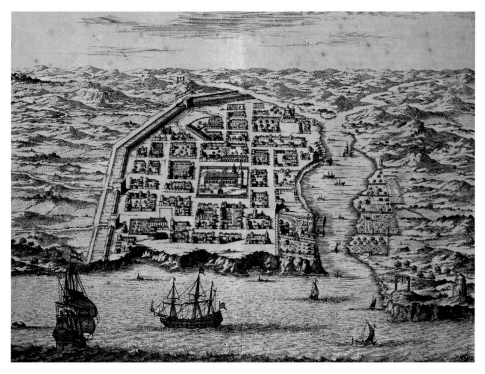

7. Detail of a Mexican 'casta' painting (c. 1715), this one showing the 'mestizo' offspring of a Spanish man and an indigenous woman.

8. The sixteenth-century Alcázar de Colón, in Santo Domingo, was built to house Diego Columbus, the son of Christopher, who became the island's governor in 1509.

9. An engraving (c. 1585) of Dutch traders arriving in West Africa (Guinea) to negotiate a shipment of slaves.

10. Gold mining in Hispaniola, as imagined in the nineteenth century. The mines were so dangerous that the brutal conditions often quickly killed the indigenous people and African slaves who worked in them.

11. A romanticized depiction of sugar cane harvesting in Antigua, c. 1820s, displaying none of the brutality that was part of daily life for slaves.

12. An engraving of the sugar refining process in the mid-seventeenth-century French West Indies.

13. Havana harbour in the aftermath of the British battle in 1762, during the Seven Years War, complete with sinking masts of defeated ships.

14. The taking of the French island of St Lucia by the British in 1778, during the American War of Independence. In addition to fighting the patriots in the thirteen colonies, Britain faced hostility from Spain, France, and the Dutch in the Caribbean.

15. Mr and Mrs Hill, as painted by Arthur Devis (c. 1750–51). Although little is known about the subjects, they represent the growing and aspirational middle-class consumer – complete with tea cups laid out for visitors, and of course, a sugar bowl.

16. James Gillray's 'Barbarities in the West Indies', which depicts an incident mentioned during the 1791 debate on the motion to abolish the slave trade.

rather than having to ship it to Cádiz first. By British standards this was hardly 'free' trade, but it was a significant change for the Spanish.

*

In the second half of the eighteenth century, war provided the inevitable background for the economic and social changes that arose from 'enlightened' government policies. But warfare was not the same as it used to be. Indeed, the next big conflict began not in Europe but in a rural North American outpost.

British and French settlers had moved into the valleys around the St Lawrence and Ohio rivers in the uncharted west of North America during the eighteenth century, triggering a number of skirmishes over the years, as both claimed land, and also encountered either hostility or help from the Native Americans. However, in the 1750s tension heightened as the French wanted British settlers to leave, and by 1754 British forces were involved. Led by a young General George Washington, they suffered an early defeat at Fort Necessity, Pennsylvania, where Washington was forced to surrender on 3 July that year. But that was not the end of the matter. It escalated into a conflict that raged for years and was further complicated by Britain and France making an official declaration of war in 1756. By that point, the war had pushed back across the Atlantic and south into the Caribbean, and was transformed into the Seven Years War. The fighting would spread still further, until it had reached nearly every corner of the globe, from Senegal to Bengal. In Europe it involved Prussia, Britain, and later Portugal, who were squared off against France, Austria, Russia, and later Spain. It was the first modern world war.

In 1759 Britain began to capture French territory in Canada and the Caribbean, scoring victories in Quebec and Guadeloupe. It also managed to seize Montreal in 1760. In that same year pamphlets began to circulate in Britain, asking which colonies should be retained when the war was over. In the first, *A Letter Addressed to Two Great Men* (ostensibly the Duke of Newcastle and William Pitt the Elder), the author argued it would not be long before France was 'reduced to the Necessity of suing for Peace'.[31] Reminding his readers of the extensive holdings France had in Canada, and of the proximity of the British North American colonies, he continued: 'In a Word, you must keep *Canada*, otherways you lay the Foundation of another War.' As to Guadeloupe, what need did Britain have of a sugar island 'when we have so many of our own'.

But the anonymous author of *Remarks on the Letter Addressed to Two Great Men* claimed that 'whilst ever we have *France* or any other Nation on our Borders, either in *Europe* or in *America*, we must, in the Nature of Things, have frequent Disputes and Wars with them'.[32] He declared that the West Indies was vital not only for its valuable sugar but also: 'Our *Caribee* Islands must be ever infinitely in greater Danger from *Guadaloupe*, than our *North American* Colonies can be from *Canada* circumscribed as it ought, and as it is presumed it will be. The *French* have a real Superiority in the *West Indies*, and they have once made it to be severely felt.'[33] As it transpired, French power in the Caribbean would be dealt a severe blow when, in 1762, the British captured Martinique, as well as St Lucia, St Vincent, and Grenada, Dominica already having fallen to an earlier attack in 1761. The balance of power was tipping in the West Indies.

Meanwhile, the French had convinced Spain's Charles III to sign another *pacte de famille* and in 1762 Spain entered the war on the side of France and Austria. Then Britain sent, in 1762, a fleet of 150 ships, including twenty-two ships of the line, and 15,000 men, to Havana, one of the biggest cities in the Caribbean, with a population of around 35,000.[34] Though it was dwarfed by a city such as London with around 740,000 people, it was considerably larger than the North American ports of Philadelphia, with 23,000 people, or New York, with 18,000. The fleet attacked in June 1762. The Spanish were caught off guard – they did not think the city, with its stern and solid El Morro fortress on Havana Bay, could be penetrated by any enemy. Instead, they had put more resources into reinforcing the fort in the southern port of Santiago de Cuba, where they thought an attack more likely, a plan complicated by outbreaks of fever and food shortages brought about by a particularly wet summer.[35] Troops in Havana did not fare well against the British, who by the end of the month had taken the city, as well as fourteen Spanish ships.[36] Buoyed by the victory, British ships in the Pacific set a course for Manila, which also fell. But the illness that had plagued the island spread quickly among the British troops in Cuba, and some 3,000 died; according to John McNeil, the number of British deaths from fever in Cuba was more than the number of deaths suffered by the British army in North America during the entire Seven Years War.[37]

This did not hinder British merchants, however, who soon changed the way business was conducted on the island. The British have been blamed for importing more slaves and moving the island toward intensive sugar production.[38] According to the Slave Voyages database, the number of Africans brought to Cuba in 1761 was 258, all of them carried on British ships. The following year it leapt to 1,289, and in 1763 it reached 2,342. Trees were cleared to make way for sugar cane just outside Havana, while other goods were now free of Spanish restrictions and trading in a wider market.[39]

*

The Seven Years War ended in 1763, and a settlement in the colonies was agreed under the Treaty of Paris. The pro-Guadeloupe pamphleteer would have been disappointed – France was allowed to retain that island, as well as Martinique and St Lucia. France was also granted possession of Gorée island in Senegal and Pondicherry and Chandernagor in India, all of which had been taken by the British. But in North America, France lost all its Canadian holdings bar the islands of St Pierre and Miquelon at the mouth of the Gulf of St Lawrence. It had also secretly ceded its vast Louisiana Territory to Spain under the Treaty of Fontainebleau in 1762, and relinquished any claims to land east of the Mississippi, including the Gulf of Mexico port of New Orleans. Britain returned Havana and Manila to Spain in exchange for its Florida territory. The British now controlled all of North America to the Mississippi, as well as what were called the 'ceded islands' of Dominica, Grenada, St Vincent and the Grenadines, and Tobago. In addition, they received territory along the Senegal river in Africa and were granted permission to log in the Honduras territory, as long as they did not build fortifications there.

Britain came away from the war in a dominant position, in Europe and overseas. Charles III of Spain, humiliated by the occupation of Havana, decided to take some of his Spanish silver and put it to work shoring up the defences in the Spanish West Indies. And in 1763, the Conde de Ricla and Field Marshal O'Reilly went to Cuba to implement these reforms. Ricla was appointed captain-general and governor, and the two men expanded the defences on the island. One of O'Reilly's tasks was to reorganize the militia to include free people of colour and blacks, creating a mulatto battalion and a black battalion of light infantry in Havana, and two more, one of which was mulatto (also known as *pardo*) in the eastern city of Santiago.[40] For their part, the creole elites, having had a taste of British commerce, now demanded freer trade, and the right to buy slaves from whomever they wanted. They wanted out of the strict mercantile world of Spain's economy, which many felt was strangling the island.[41]

The French, licking their wounds, turned to the coast of South America. The territory – today's Guyane, or French Guiana, then also known as 'Kourou' – had few settlers – only around 575 in 1763, while there were nearly 7,000 African slaves. France offered settlement – and land – to all comers, and, because they were keen to attract German settlers, known to be hardworking, they also offered religious tolerance.[42] Led by Étienne-François Turgot (whose brother would become French naval minister in 1774), some 17,000 people sailed from France to the colony between 1763 and 1764. Of the 17,000, 11,500 were from Alsace and the Rhineland.[43] They disembarked not on the mainland but on islets just off the shore.[44] By 1765, some 9,000 people had died, mostly of disease but also starvation. The survivors returned to France, spreading tropical diseases in places such as Rochefort and Saint-Jean-d'Angély, while some fled to the French West Indies islands, leaving a population in the colony of 1,178 in 1770. It was an unprecedented disaster.[45]

In a similar debacle, eight ships carrying some 1,200 settlers sailed into the new British Florida territory, though the majority of the passengers were not from Britain, but the British-controlled Balearic island of Minorca, off the coast of Spain. Others on the 1768 voyage included Greeks, Italians, and even some French. It was thought that southern Europeans would be better suited to Florida's tropical climate, but this was a mistake. Only two years later more than half the settlers in New Smyrna had died, and the rest were planning to decamp to Cuba, although that idea was derailed when the British speculator behind the scheme executed some of the people who were planning to leave. In the end, still more people died, and the settlement was eventually abandoned in 1777.[46]

*

The Seven Years War not only changed the political configuration of Europe, it wreaked havoc in many nations' treasuries, too. Despite Britain's victory, the Exchequer was short of money. The government thus levied a series of taxes – never a popular move at the best of times – which would prove to be a very poor decision. The British government had trouble coordinating taxes across the empire – one colony's preferential treatment was another's source of malcontent. This had been the case before the war in the form of the 1733 Molasses Act. British West Indian planters were angry that the colonists in North America were buying molasses – a key ingredient in making rum – from the French, who sold it for less. The planters on the islands complained that as a result the mainland colonists wanted currency in exchange for goods, not rum, sugar, or molasses, so they were forced to use their scarce money supplies.[47] The British government slapped a duty of sixpence per gallon on any foreign molasses sold in its colonies. People in the thirteen North American colonies were irritated, but few wanted to pay the tax and an illicit trade in cheaper French molasses sprang up.

Thirty-one years later, sugar was once again the subject of taxation, in the form of the Sugar Act of 1764, which lowered the tax on rum and molasses but increased the one on sugar. This time the colonists in North American were livid. To add insult to injury, the Stamp Act was rolled out the following year. The Act introduced a tax on printed matter, such as leaflets and newspapers. Unlike the northern colonies, the islands complied, and in the short time it was in force, some 78 per cent of its revenues came from the islands, while the colonists to the north mocked them for paying it.[48] The people of the thirteen colonies were angry that they had not voted for these taxes, and little of the legislation that followed would assuage them. The repressive Townshend Acts (1767) resulted in greater resistance among the colonists, who began to cry 'no taxation without representation'. The tension built, exacerbated by the killing of five colonists in Boston in 1770. However, one of the most symbolic acts of resistance arose not because of unfair taxes or wrongful deaths, but rather, the innocent tea leaf.

By the mid-eighteenth century tea from China had taken over the English-speaking world, but dealing with the Chinese, who controlled the market, was difficult. Tea had been known in the Arab world, and had appeared in Europe by the Renaissance, but it remained a scarce commodity in the West until the sea routes to the East became well established in the seventeenth century.[49] English traders in the East India Company (EIC) established a post in 1644 in Amoy, which lies on a tiny island in the Taiwan Strait – foreigners were not allowed on the mainland – and the Chinese continued to keep the English, and other Europeans, at bay. However, by 1713 the EIC had established a lucrative deal to set up a trading post in Canton, and pay for tea leaves with silver. In 1700, Britain imported fifty US tons of tea; one hundred years later it imported nearly 15,000 tons.[50] The government was happy, too; it taxed tea at 119 per cent. Tea was sold in Britain and resold by merchants to the colonies, or smuggled in by the Dutch, who had begun growing their own supplies in the East Indies. How much this cut into EIC profits is difficult to say, but by the 1770s the company was bankrupt. So Parliament passed the 1773 Tea Act, cutting the duty on tea and allowing a monopoly on sales to North America in order to help the EIC, which had warehouses full of unsold tea. As a result, the livelihood of American tea merchants was disrupted, yet again without input, much less a mandate, from the colonies. On 16 December 1773 a group of angry merchants attacked three tea ships in Boston harbour whose captains refused to leave without the duty being paid, and dumped the leaves of more than 300 tea chests overboard. The following year Parliament responded to this 'Boston Tea Party' with even more restrictions on trade, in the form of the Intolerable Acts, in 1774. The following year the opening shots of the American Revolution were fired in Lexington and Concord.

The West Indian islands received the news with mixed emotions. There were attempts from some of them to mediate between Britain and North America, but it came to nothing. There was some support on the islands for the colonists – indeed, copies of Thomas Paine's influential pamphlet *Common Sense* even reached Jamaica.[51] But the planters were too busy worrying how they were going to get enough food. The government passed a bill prohibiting any trade with the thirteen colonies. Given that the islands depended on them for staples, including corn, bread, and salt fish, many planters protested that the measures would lead not only to starvation among the slaves but, as a result, a possible uprising. By 1776 there were reports that slaves were indeed dying from starvation, and there were rebellions in Tobago,

St Vincent, and Jamaica. This last one particularly frightened the whites because it was led by island-born slaves, who were generally considered more loyal than their African counterparts. The weeks that followed were full of panic, arrests, and, eventually, seventeen executions.[52] The rebel leaders in North America meanwhile sanctioned the capture of British ships, so privateering once again disrupted trade throughout the Atlantic and Caribbean. The West Indian planters were quickly losing interest in the rebels' cause.

More problems would befall them: amid slave rebellions and food shortages came a hurricane in 1780 – thought to be one of the most destructive ever recorded.[53] The damage was so severe that Parliament voted to give Barbados £80,000 in aid, and £40,000 to Jamaica. Meanwhile, in North America, British generals were probably wishing that General George Washington had died of the smallpox he contracted while in Barbados in 1751 (assuming, of course, they knew of his visit). He had gone to the island as a nineteen-year-old, accompanying his half-brother, Lawrence, who was hoping the island's air would help alleviate his tuberculosis. During his time there, Washington lived on the edge of Bridgetown, not far from the military garrison, in a modest rented house. He explored the city and the James and Charles forts, and he also contracted smallpox and acquired an immunity that would later prove useful when he – unlike many of his troops – survived an epidemic. Disease was behind some of the vicissitudes of the war – while smallpox hurt the rebels, illness came to Washington's aid in Charleston in 1780, when British troops were felled by malaria, giving the colonists a much-needed boost. Even General Cornwallis became ill.[54]

As the fighting intensified, it became clear to Britain's enemies that it was the perfect opportunity to avenge some of the insults from the Seven Years War. By 1778 the sharp diplomacy of Benjamin Franklin had convinced the French to enter the war against Britain. Spain entered the conflict in 1779, claiming as justification Britain's refusal to abandon the Miskito territory under the terms of the 1763 treaty.[55] The Dutch would also join the fight.

Because all the rebels' allies had islands in the West Indies, it was easy to smuggle arms and ammunition to them. Some 90 per cent of all the gunpowder used in the first couple of years of fighting was estimated to have come from Caribbean islands, especially the Dutch ones.[56] Indeed, the tiny volcanic island of St Eustatius (also called Statia), which was just north of St Kitts, was not only the centre of the gunpowder trade, but it had long been a thriving free-trade port. At the beginning of the war, in 1775, a Scotswoman named Janet Schaw stopped over on the island on her way from her home in Scotland to North Carolina and she remarked that

> never did I meet with such variety; here was a merchant vending his goods in Dutch, another in French, a third in Spanish etc etc. They all wear the habit of their country, and the diversity is really amusing . . . From one end of the town of Eustatia to the other is a continued mart, where goods of the most different uses and qualities are displayed before the shop-doors. Here hang rich embroideries, painted silks, flowered Muslins, with all the Manu-factures of the Indies. Just by hang Sailor's Jackets, trousers, shoes, hats, etc. Next stall contains most exquisite silver plate, the most beautiful indeed I ever saw, and close by these iron-pots, kettles and shovels.[57]

In November 1776 a ship called the *Andrew Doria* arrived at the bustling port, sailing under what would have been to the Dutch an unfamiliar red-and-white striped flag with a Union Jack in the corner. The fort of St Eustatius, and the island's main town of Oranjestad, sit uphill from the port, giving the soldiers a good vantage point to see approaching ships. Despite the strange flag, they knew whose ship it was, and cannon fire rang out in recognition. In so doing, St Eustatius was the first island to recognize the United States. Unfortunately for the Dutch, the British soldiers on the Brimstone Hill garrison in St Kitts – which had a clear view to Statia – claimed to have seen every-thing, or at least heard the cannon fire. Events accelerated in 1778 when France entered the war, which meant that Martinique was no longer a 'neutral' port, and Statia increasingly began to fill the gap in the supply chain.[58] But the British knew what was taking place, and by 1780 Admiral Rodney was ordered to capture Statia and cut off the flow of goods and ammunition to the rebels. For Rodney, it was an easy victory – the garrison was outnumbered and the Dutch were quick to surrender. Other ships set off to capture St Maarten, Saba, Demerara and Essequibo (Guyana), and St Bart's. A 1781 letter to the colonial secretary, Lord George Germain, reports the 'capitulation of the Dutch Subjects of the Colonies of the Rivers of Berbice, Demerara

& Essquebo', which included the coffee, cocoa, cotton and sugar plantations whose value was estimated at £140,000, or around £14 million in today's money.[59]

Meanwhile, Rodney and some of his men remained on Statia to plunder. What happened next nearly ruined him. He took everything he could lay his hands on – even going so far as to rip the lining of the pockets of Jewish merchants he suspected of hiding money. He took goods from all the merchants, some of whom were British. Reports of his behaviour filtered back to England, where he was considered to have acted outside the customs of war. For Rodney, who had been heavily indebted in Paris and in Britain at the beginning of the Seven Years War, Statia was a means of recouping his losses. He was called back to England to answer for his actions, and while he was there the French Admiral de Grasse sailed from Martinique to Chesapeake Bay, strategically blocking British ships and helping to secure the rebels' decisive victory at Yorktown in October 1781.[60] The war in North America began to wind down at this point, but the French were not quite done with Britain.

De Grasse and his men then turned back on the West Indies with plans to take Jamaica. They started with an attack on St Kitts in 1782. From high on Brimstone Hill the troops in that fort would have seen the fleet advancing, and 350 members of the militia joined the regular soldiers in a five-week siege on the fort. While cannonballs flew, the soldiers there were unable to relay their situation to the British navy and eventually capitulated. French ships then hit the Guiana coast, taking the colonies Britain had seized. Some of the French ships were due to turn to Saint-Domingue to regroup and prepare for the attack on Jamaica. Rodney by this point had returned to the seas, and with luck and fortunate timing, he and his thirty-six ships of the line managed to intercept de Grasse's fleet of thirty-five ships near Les Saintes, a collection of rocky islets off the coast of Guadeloupe. On 12 April 1782 Rodney broke through a gap in the French line, and managed to win a decisive victory, even capturing de Grasse and his ship.[61] Now the war in the Caribbean was over. Rodney had left England a scoundrel, and returned a hero. There were celebrations of the victory, and he was given a peerage.

*

The West Indies were involved in the War of American Independence in other ways besides battle. Throughout the conflict, some 60,000 loyalists fearing for their safety left the thirteen colonies for other parts of the empire, taking 15,000 slaves with them. At the same time, around 20,000 slaves were willing to fight for the king and thus obtain their freedom.[62] Thousands of people went to Jamaica, as the white refugees thought they would fit well into another plantation society. And there were still fortunes to be had, or so some thought. Yet many of the uprooted loyalists could not gain a foothold in the often closed and interrelated island society, nor find any land, and so many pushed onwards. Some – with their slaves – went to the Turks islands and entered the salt trade. Many of the black loyalists faced a different journey, through Nova Scotia, London, and Sierra Leone.[63]

A few white loyalists tried their luck in Dominica, but by 1786 the governor was forced to ask the crown to help 'His Majesty's faithful American subjects, who have taken refuge in this Island' and who had failed to flourish. Petitioners such as Stephen Egan, Nicholas Warrington, Olive Young and Elizabeth Bryant were hopeful that the king would provide some sort of relief for their 'present distressed situation'.[64] Indeed, a letter from Alex Steward, president of the island's council, and Thomas Beech, speaker of its House of Assembly, recounted the disasters – which went far beyond the war – of recent times:

> The poverty of its Inhabitants, caused in a great Measure by the heavy Expences and Labor attendant on clearing and settling Land in standing Wood . . . and . . . by the Infertility of the Soil; Its [Dominica's] subsequent Capture by the Army of France; the Visitations of Providence in two dreadful Hurricanes in 1779 and 1780 and a Fire that consumed the Town of Roseau in 1781 added to the Rebellion of our Slaves which as this moment exists, are calamities that would have conquered the spirits of any other subjects.[65]

After Yorktown and the Battle of the Saintes, the conflict drew to a close. In 1783 the Treaties of Paris and Versailles once again settled the European disputes in the Caribbean and the Americas. Britain was forced to recognize the United States of America, though it kept hold of its Canadian colonies. France also returned Dominica, Grenada, Montserrat, Nevis, St Kitts, and St Vincent to the British, while keeping

Tobago and re-establishing its naval prowess in the region. Spain saw the return of the Mediterranean island of Minorca from the British, and the Florida territory. The treaty also forced Spain to recognize the boundaries of the Bayman settlements in Honduras – now between the Hondo and Belize rivers, with the New river as the western boundary. As for the Dutch, conflict continued for another year until it was ended by a treaty in 1784, which, in regard to the West Indies, returned to the Dutch all of their islands and coastal territory in South America.

On the north side of the crumbling and elegant Emancipation Square in Spanish Town, Jamaica,* a large white structure occupies the whole block, and overwhelms the more modest Georgian and Regency buildings that sit perpendicular to it. The structure is flanked by two-storey buildings, both of which have colonnades that meet at an elaborate six-sided pavilion in the centre. Set within it is a marble statue of a man dressed in a toga, shaded, cool and seemingly immune to the tropical sun which makes the white paint on the surrounding columns peel. It is not a Roman hero but Admiral George Rodney, and on the base of the plinth is an inscription commemorating the Battle of the Saintes.[66] The Jamaican assembly had voted to erect a memorial to the man who saved their island from French invasion and paid the English sculptor John Bacon around £30,000 for it. It is a strange, unlikely footnote in the history of a war over the northern colonies. But no island was simply an island – these worlds were bound together, and the formation of the United States owes a great deal to the fact that its allies all had colonies in such proximity. It also is a concrete reminder of how divergent the West Indian interests had become from those of the northern colonies.

The British islands, for their part, had felt some pain during the war – the increase in privateering had been costly and nature had been incredibly destructive. Yet afterwards, the sugar planters rallied, though they were still stifled by a restriction set in 1783 on trade with the United States, which permitted the US to export to the colonies but limited what the West Indies were permitted to send to the US, as well as stipulating that all goods should be carried by British ships. By the

---

* The square was known as Parade Square until fairly recently. Spanish Town was the capital of the island until 1872. When the island was under Spanish rule, this town was called St Jago de la Vega.

mid-1780s the British West Indies, however, were producing sugar worth around £4.2 million a year, more than the pre-war average of £3.3 million.[67] But life had not returned to normal – if there was such a thing in this period. Not only had yet another set of treaties altered the imperial dynamic in the Caribbean, the American War of Independence and the Enlightenment that inspired it brought forth new questions, and new ideas. While the founders of the US set out to establish equality, it only reflected their interests and worldview and did not extend to many of the people who lived there – the slaves. Before the end of the century, some of the West Indian slaves would return to the question of freedom, with profound consequences. In the meantime, in England and France, a fight was brewing over the slave trade.

*

In 1757 James Ramsay, a young Royal Navy surgeon, boarded the *Arundel* to take up his first post. While in the West Indies they intercepted a British slave ship, the *Swift*, where dysentery was killing the cargo. Ramsay was horrified – nothing in his medical training could have prepared him for the sight, smell, or sound of 100 Africans chained together, drowning in their own excreta, in the dark, dank hold of a ship. He was so distressed by what he had seen and so distracted that, upon returning to the *Arundel*, he fell and broke his leg, giving him a limp for the rest of his life and a physical scar to go with the emotional one. As a result of his injury, Ramsay could not continue his naval career, but he ended up returning to the Caribbean after being ordained as an Anglican priest. He worked as a minister and doctor in St Kitts, tending to the poor and also – as a plantation surgeon – to slaves hired by some plantations, and he married a planter's daughter, Rebecca Akers. But he soon began to speak out against slavery and the poor treatment of slaves, which caused him many problems on the small island. He returned to Britain, and around the time of the War of American Independence he was allowed to return to the navy as a chaplain, seeing action against the French off St Lucia in 1778, and Grenada and St Kitts in 1779, returning once again to Britain in 1781. Two years later he was introduced to a young Member of Parliament from Hull, William Wilberforce, who shared his concern about slavery. Around this time, Ramsay felt unable to stay silent about his experiences any longer, and he soon set a spark to the powder keg of the abolition debate.

An Essay on the Treatment and Conversion of African Slaves in the British Sugar Colonies – which at just under 300 pages was a weighty pamphlet – caused a public sensation when Ramsay published it in 1784. Drawing on his twenty years in the British West Indies, Ramsay told his readers how 'many are the restrictions, and severe are the punishments, to which slaves are subjected'.[68] Many readers would have been aware, that 'a horse, a cow, or a sheep, is much better protected . . . than a poor slave',[69] but he was able to give details of just how cruel their treatment was. He argued that it was imperative to treat the slaves better, pointing out, 'It is not an unusual thing on the same island to lose *in one year* out of such a number [180], *ten, twelve,* nay, as far as *twenty,* by fevers, fluxes, dropsies, the effect of too much work, and too little food and care.'

He also used a great deal of the book to focus on the conversion and 'improvement' of slaves, even citing their potential as consumers, arguing, 'Were their condition advanced, they would become . . . more valuable subjects . . . Instead of confining their demands, as at present, to a few coarse woollens . . . to a little grain, a few herrings, and salt-fish, they would open a new traffic in every branch of trade.' He argued slaves should have the Sabbath off and be given religious instruction, as well as gradual emancipation, and he outlined a plan to implement this. He mentioned the ongoing work of the Moravian missionaries in Antigua, Barbados, St Kitts, and Jamaica in the face of planter resistance, though they had made better progress in the Danish colonies. But in making the point that slaves needed to be put 'in possession of that humanity, which is pertinaciously disputed with them', he also countered racial ideas earlier expressed by Hume and others, arguing through his observations as a doctor that even if differences in skin colour 'mark a different race, they can in no respect determine their inferiority'.

Ramsay, unlike many whites at the time, thought the 'improvement' of slaves was possible because they were human. Many others were not so humane. Judged by modern standards, some of the notions about slaves and slavery that Ramsay was forced to address are, at times, shocking, especially the racist discourse in Europe and the islands which permeated Europeans and white colonialists with insidious ideas about Africans – ideas that were then used as justification for the slave trade.

As ever more tales of brutality and injustice reached the public, attitudes began to change. And five years after the publication of Ramsay's essay, in 1789, British audiences were the first to hear the story of slavery from an African himself, in Olaudah Equiano's account. People now not only heard of the horrors of the slave trade and the Middle Passage, but they did so from someone who had lived through it. At the end of his autobiography, Equiano wrote: 'I hope the slave trade will be abolished.'[70] It would not happen in his lifetime – he died in 1791 – but he died knowing that the fight was already well under way.

Even before the publication of Equiano's and Ramsay's books there had been a landmark legal decision, known as the Somerset Case. The lawyer Granville Sharp used the case of James Somerset, a slave kidnapped in London and placed aboard a ship bound for Jamaica, to argue for the abolition of slavery. Lord Chief Justice Lord Mansfield ruled on 22 June 1772 that 'no Master ever was allowed here to take a Slave by force to be sold abroad because he had deserted from his service or for any other Reason whatever'.[71] Somerset was not to be sent to Jamaica for re-enslavement. Setting foot on British soil would not make a slave free, as it did in France, but once in England, he could not be taken abroad as a slave. It was a significant victory. Yet it did nothing to affect (or dent) the slave trade: indeed, the number of Africans taken to the British islands had nearly doubled from 486,000 in the period 1715–50 to 875,000 between 1751 and 1790.[72]

In 1787 a group of abolitionists set up the Society for Effecting the Abolition of the Slave Trade, whose founding members included Sharp and campaigner Thomas Clarkson. In his 1788 *Essay on the Impolicy of the African Slave Trade*, Clarkson argued that '*free labour* can be made the medium through which the productions of their [Africans'] country may be collected', arguing that cane could be cut by free men as well as it could be cut by slaves.[73] Tobacco, rice, and indigo were now cultivated in Africa and offered other options for trade than slavery. But the abolitionists knew that the fight also had to be legislative. Wilberforce first introduced an Abolition Bill in the House of Commons in 1791, but it failed, as did a number of subsequent bills through the rest of the decade. The West Indian planters had built a powerful bloc by this point, and their interests extended to merchant houses, insurance brokers, and shipbuilders.

But the fight continued to gain momentum. In the same year as

Wilberforce's first bill, his fellow abolitionist William Fox published anonymously a pamphlet calling for a boycott of West Indian goods, declaring, 'The laws of our country may indeed prohibit us the sugar-cane, unless it be received through the medium of slavery. They may hold it to our lips, steeped in the blood of our fellow creatures, but they cannot compel us to accept the loathsome potion.'[74] He called on the British public to stop using sugar until it could be produced in a humane way that did not require slavery. He lashed out, charging that 'to purchase the commodity is to participate in the crime', and gave the modern consumer perhaps one of their earliest ethical conundrums. To him, sugar was not a staple but 'a luxury which habit alone can have rendered of importance'.

The West Indian lobby howled at such sentiments. Another anonymous pamphlet continued the war of words from the planters' side. Its author admitted it 'is not necessary to deny that such cruelties actually happened. They are, perhaps, too true. But it becomes us well to consider, before we judge of the whole by a few particular instances; instances, which have been selected with the greatest diligence; laid before us in one view; and we are required to form our opinion of the whole trade.'[75] The author then attempted to convince his readers that were the consumption of sugar to grind to a halt, 'the greatest part of the negroes, at present in the West-Indies, would be destroyed by famine', reminding them that the restrictions on trade during the War of American Independence had killed many slaves. He claimed that if sugar exports dropped, planters would simply turn to other crops. Abolition would damage the economy: 'it is no easy matter to estimate the numbers that, directly or indirectly, owe their daily bread to the sugar-trade . . . These have families, who depend on the price of their labour for support. The merchant that imports, the refiner that purifies, and the tradesman who distributes, this article, through the numerous branches of society, all owe their subsistence to this branch of commerce.' And while the author conceded that 'upon the whole, although it must be the earnest wish of every humane and feeling mind, that slavery should be abolished', he concluded with the warning that such an abolition could not happen 'without incurring greater evils than slavery itself'.

The question of abolition was not only preoccupying the British. In 1760 the French exported around 100,000 tons of sugar; by 1787 that had reached around 157,000 tons. Their slave imports across the islands rose from 8,438 Africans in 1760, taken mostly to Guadeloupe and Martinique, to 35,266 in 1787, taken mostly to Saint-Domingue.[76] But in 1788 Jacques-Pierre Brissot established the Society of the Friends of the Blacks (Société des amis des Noirs), using the British society as an example. Inevitably, just as the British planter class had done, so too did French planters organize themselves into an opposition, later known as the Club Massiac, to protect their interests. However, France was on the cusp of dramatic social change, the impact of which would have far-reaching implications for its West Indian islands.

*

The talk of liberty and equality circulating in France and its colonies was threatening to many people in Europe, not least the Spanish. Indeed, the governor of Santo Domingo, Joaquín García, after receiving intelligence from the French side of the island, was moved to write to Madrid, worrying, 'With those two words "liberty and equality" these people will do much damage.'[77] He would soon find out just how much.

By the time he wrote that letter in late 1790, the French Revolution had been under way for some time. The Bastille had been stormed more than a year earlier, on 14 July 1789, and six weeks later the revolutionaries had published their Declaration of the Rights of Man and Citizen, claiming 'men are born and remain free and equal in rights'.[78] More worrying to loyal Spaniards was the idea that 'the principle of all sovereignty resides essentially in the nation'. Republicanism was a frightening spectre, and sentiments challenging a king's divine right to rule caused shudders in Madrid. To ensure events in France did not inspire anyone close to home, Charles III's first minister, the Conde de Floridablanca, established a cordón sanitario around the peninsula, which tried to prevent French newspapers or pamphlets entering the ports and border regions with France. The Spanish Gazeta de Madrid was forbidden to mention events in France – a policy that was upheld for three years, only permitting a report of Louis XVI's execution in 1793. Even goods bearing revolutionary slogans or images, such as fans or stamps, were prohibited from entering the country.[79] Such policies were also extended to the colonies. Borders between France and Spain came under heavier surveillance in Europe and in Santo Domingo, and French nationals in Spanish territory were counted and monitored. Further south-east, in

Trinidad, which was still under Spanish control, the editor of the island's *Gazeta*, Juan Viloux, was arrested and subsequently banished for 'having copied and printed various articles of the foreign papers, relative to the actual revolution in France'.[80]

Back in Spain, there had been a harvest failure in 1788, and food protests were making the government nervous. Much of Spain's peasant population was illiterate and had no access to French propaganda, although they would have heard what was happening there. The population of the colonies, however, was another matter. Trouble was afoot, but the seeds had been planted long ago. One of Charles's major reforms had been to supplant creole officials with ones sent from Spain, as a means of wresting back control from people whose interests were growing ever more divergent from Spain's. This happened throughout the empire, and everywhere it was a source of discontent. But for the moment, this restlessness would only slowly stir, while creoles scrambled to hear the latest news.

For French Saint-Domingue, the reverberations were immediate, especially on the point of *égalité*. The question of equality was a fraught one for free people of colour. As with the American Declaration of Independence, which promised that 'all men are created equal', the French declarations were silent on the issue of non-white people. In the years running up to the Revolution, the large community of free people of colour in Saint-Domingue, as well as on the other islands, had seen what rights they had taken away.

The issue of racial mixing was born of and sustained by hypocrisy throughout the Caribbean, but especially in Saint-Domingue, where the wealth and status of free people of colour was a continual source of resentment for the white planters, as well as the poor whites. Yet it was the very white planters who propagated this either by marriage or more coercive means. Women suffered the worst, of course: many slaves were raped, and many free women saw no other option but to submit to various forms of concubinage. At the same time, the mulatto women of the island were famed throughout the Caribbean for their elegance and beauty – while also being denied equal rights. Mulatto indigo planter Julien Raimond, in his 1791 tract *Observations on the Origin and Progression of the White Colonists' Prejudice against Men of Colour*, explained:

Prejudice started around the middle of the colony's third age, and here is its origin. Just before the 1744 war, the colonies were so profitable that France paid more attention to them than ever before. Many Europeans crossed the sea, including large numbers of poor women who came to seek their fortunes. Mothers were frequently disappointed. Since these immigrant women brought no resources, many of the young men who came to the colony to get rich preferred to marry girls of colour, whose dowries included land and slaves they could use profitably. Such preferences began to inspire jealousy in white women.[81]

Indeed, one wealthy white creole, Moreau St Méry, wrote about this at length. St Méry was born in Martinique in 1750 and, like many men of his class, went to Paris to study. He returned and practised law, later becoming a judge, and publishing a multi-volume codification of the laws of the French Antilles. He also wrote an account of the island, in which he identifies at least eleven different possible combinations between black and white, claiming, 'Of all the combinations of whites and negroes, the mulatto is the one who derives the greatest physical advantages. Of all the blendings . . . it is he who draws the strongest constitution and the one best fitted to the climate of Saint-Domingue.'[82]

In the latter half of the eighteenth century, the lives of free people of colour were highly regulated, from having to provide proof of their free status to being deferential around whites. But their population was also rising; there were 6,897 people identified as free people of colour in the census of 1775, 10,427 in 1780, and 21,813 by 1788. The white population also rose, but not as much; from 20,438 people to 20,543, and finally 27,723, over the same period.[83] Given that the free coloured community was not only growing but well-off, court cases challenging the regulations restricting their lives soon followed. The French Revolution increased their urgency.

For the free mulatto Vincent Ogé, it was clear that it was in Paris, and not Port-au-Prince, where the real change needed to be sanctioned. He left the island and went first to London, where he met with the abolitionist Thomas Clarkson, and was able to raise money and credit that he would later put to use buying arms.[84] In a letter of 1790 he wrote that 'we will not remain under the yoke as we have for two centuries. The iron rod that has beaten us down is broken.'[85] From

London, Ogé travelled to Paris to argue the case for free people of colour. He told the National Assembly that as a taxpayer he deserved equal rights. Despite much heated debate, Ogé returned to Saint-Domingue with the same status with which he had arrived. He decided to take matters into his own hands and organized a revolt near the port town of Cap Français (also called Le Cap). It did not have quite the intended effect of inciting a mulatto rebellion, but instead galvanized the warring white factions to come together to fight the free people of colour.

Indeed, the white community, triggered by the French Revolution, had been arguing among itself, with the *grand blanc* planters, clergy, and administrators remaining royalists, and the *petit blanc* poor whites turning towards the revolutionaries. Ogé had, temporarily, united them. His rebellion suppressed, Ogé fled to the Spanish side of the island, where he was captured and extradited back to Saint-Domingue. Ogé had to be made an example of, and the French officials wasted little time putting him on trial and executing him – a shocking outcome to many in Paris who were following Ogé and his struggle. The planters had every reason to worry, though the Ogé incident focused their attention in the wrong place. The French Revolution was taking on a life of its own; not only was it increasingly difficult to maintain order in the capital, it was soon going to be well-nigh impossible in France's Caribbean colonies. Indeed, slaves in Martinique had heard a rumour that the king was going to free them, and they refused to work.[86] The colonial order was unravelling, especially in Saint-Domingue. Watching from Santo Domingo, in December 1790, Pedro Catani wrote to the Conde de Floridablanca in Madrid that 'in the neighbouring colony, according to the truthful news I have received, complete anarchy reigns'.[87] It would continue to do so for more than a decade.

Chapter Seven

HAITI, OR THE BEGINNING OF THE END

Francis Alexander Stanislaus, also known as the Baron de Wimpffen, called into Saint-Domingue in October 1788, having left Le Havre on 29 July. He intended to stop over en route to the Cape of Good Hope, but he ended up staying on the island for two years. His time there coincided with the dying days of the old regime, which he documents in detail. His account of this time of transition in Saint-Domingue takes the form of letters addressed to a friend, intended to be part of a larger work about the Cape but published separately because of the rising interest about events taking place on the island.

When he arrived that autumn, he was quick to observe the delicate contradictions that underpinned the colony, confessing 'Your colonies, such as they are, cannot exist without slavery. This is a frightful truth, I confess . . . You must then sanction slavery, or renounce the colonies: and as thirty thousand whites can only control 460,000 negroes by the force of opinion, (the sole guarantee of their existence) every thing which tends to weaken or destroy that opinion, is a crime against society.'[1] Yet he was not particularly impressed by what he saw of that society, certainly not by the wealthy planters, whose reputation for riches and indolence was known across Europe. Wimpffen thought them pretentious bores who 'scarcely ceased to speak of their negroes, their cotton, their sugar, and their coffee, ere they begin anew on their coffee, their sugar, their cotton, and their negroes!'[2]

For all the imagined luxury of life on the islands, the reality was far harsher. Indeed, a planter might live in a large house filled with mahogany furniture and Chinese porcelain, but the world around that house would have been rough-hewn, and most people who lived on the plantations were denied the most basic of goods, never mind any luxuries. The gilded existence that money could buy in Europe's capital cities was a world away from the islands where so much of that money was generated. This gap was quite evident to the baron, who observed that along the road to Port-au-Prince there seemed to be

> two kinds of plantations which we passed . . . one showed us only the picture of indolence in the last stage of wretchedness; and the other, that of the negligence and disorder of poverty, contrasted with the pretensions of opulence directed by the most execrable taste. Thus you would sometimes meet an elegant carriage drawn by horses, or mules of different colours, and of different sizes, with ropes for traces, covered with the most filthy housings, and driven by a postilion bedaubed with gold, and barefoot![3]

Once he arrived in the capital, the yawning gap between the display of wealth he thought he would see and the somewhat less opulent reality was clear. In his letters, he observed:

> Port-au-Prince! – When a person has been acquainted in France with colonists, and above all with Creole colonists, he cannot approach Port-au-Prince, now become the residence of the civil and military powers, the capital of the richest country on the face of the globe! the most fertile in delights! the throne of luxury! the center of voluptuousness! without experiencing that severe shivering, that pleasing and vague anxiety which precedes admiration, and prepares the soul for enthusiasm – To be brief; I entered between two rows of huts, jolting along a dusty track called a street, and searching in vain for Persepolis, amongst a chaotic mass of wooden barracks![4]

Like most writers and travellers of this period, Wimpffen also recounted tales of horrific abuses of power against slaves on the island. For instance, he wrote how 'a young lady, and one of the handsomest in the island, gave a grand dinner. Furious at seeing a dish of pastry brought to the table overdone, she ordered her negro cook to be seized, and *thrown into the oven, yet glowing with heat*.' Such accounts were commonplace, and such violence stitched into the fabric of everyday life. Outsiders like Wimpffen were shocked by these tales of abuse and excess, and he was taken aback that 'this infernal fiend whom public execration ought to drive with every mark of abhorrence from society . . . is followed, and admired – for she is rich and beautiful'.[5]

Wimpffen's observations of wider social interaction were similarly wary. Of the dances that took place between women of colour and white men, he remarked: 'These female mulattoes, who dance so exquisitely, and who have been painted to you in such seducing colours, are the most fervent priestesses of the American Venus. They have reduced voluptuousness to a kind of mechanical art, which they have carried to the highest point of perfection.'[6] Yet he was aware of the colour line and the paradoxes inherent in it, and in fact found 'the most shocking contradictions have no longer any thing striking in them'. He was thus not surprised to find that 'the colonist who would blush to work with his negress, does not blush to live with her in a state of intimacy'.[7] But by the spring of 1790, after travelling around the island and spending time on a coffee plantation, Wimpffen had had his fill. That July he embarked for the United States, observing, 'I found at Port-au-Prince, the two things which I expected: a vessel to take me to the United States, and minds excessively inflamed by the progress of the Revolution . . . I found the island attacked by the first symptoms of the political fever which preys upon you, and I leave it in the first convulsions of a delirium.'[8]

The ingrained violence, the sexual hypocrisy, and the delusions of grandeur could not last. Wimpffen correctly observed that Saint-Domingue could not exist without slavery. And it would not do so for much longer – by the following summer the world the baron had witnessed would be dying a bloody death.

*

The slaves on the island had been watching events unfold, and listening to the news and rumours of freedom. They had heard about the Revolution in France, and knew the poor and rich whites in the colony were now at odds with each other. And they were all too aware of the fate that had befallen Vincent Ogé. Now, they felt it was their turn. The slaves had begun to organize. The voodoo ceremonies that so many participated in made planning straightforward; they provided a cover as well as a chain of communication. At the helm was a priest called Boukman, who had been keeping up with the events of the past few years and was ready to lead the slaves into battle. The plan was to set the sugar fields and plantations of the north alight. However, eager slaves in Limbé rose up in August 1791, ahead of the planned signal. The French suppressed it quickly, and Boukman and the others realized they had no time to waste. On the night of 22 August 1791, the leaders met for a voodoo ceremony. Accounts differ, with some saying it took place on 14 August and that there was a blood sacrifice of a pig. Others say it was raining, and that there were prayers and drumming, and a blow on a conch shell to signal the beginning.[9] This time, however it began, the plantations did not stand a chance. Fire tore through the fields, white masters were murdered, and the cane burned. The details might vary about exactly what happened at what became known as the Bois Caïman voodoo ceremony in August 1791, but it was the moment when the slaves grasped at their freedom, the starting point of a battle which began that night and which would continue for thirteen bloody years.

The resulting conflict is generally called the Haitian Revolution, but a number of different struggles fall under that heading. The first phase lasted until around 1794, and in many ways was an extension of the republican struggle in France, though one that led to the abolition of slavery. The second, lasting until 1802, had three main elements: fighting the British, an internal civil war between black leaders, and a struggle to ensure that emancipation remained unchallenged. The third and final phase, which lasted two years, was a battle to secure the freedom of the former slaves, and ended in the establishment of Haiti.

However, in August 1791 such a prospect was a long way off. Earlier that year, in May, the National Assembly in Paris, having heard about the execution of Ogé, declared that free coloureds who had been born to free parents should be granted equality with whites. Despite the fact that this was only a small part of the freed population, the move was greeted with cries of protest by the whites in the colony. The island's white population was divided over the merits – or otherwise – of the French Revolution; poorer whites were broadly republican and the landowners royalist. After the storming of the Bastille, however, they all felt there had been little option to but seize control of the island from the remaining loyal colonial officials and royalist officers. Soon fighting broke out between whites and free coloureds in Port-au-Prince over the enforcement of the decree. Such distractions enabled the slaves to make their move that August, and only a few weeks later more than 1,000 plantations had been destroyed, burnt to the ground.

The fighting on the island continued into the following year, but the battle was in many ways for an area much greater than Saint-Domingue alone. Fear – one of the slaves' best weapons – was settling on the region like a heavy fog. Planters as far away as Bermuda, hundreds of miles to the east, were worried. There were more blacks than whites there, and even though the slave population – less than 5,000 – was far smaller than that of Saint-Domingue, the island's Council Chamber members were anxious and expressed their concern to the island's governor, Henry Hamilton, imploring him to secure regular military troops for the island, saying that:

> since the Dissemination of opinions respecting the lawfulness of Slavery through these Islands, as also the account of the Insurrections, Depredations and murders committed by Negroes of St Domingo, a very manifest alteration has taken place in the behaviour of the Negroes here, which together with their frequently assembling in large bodies in the night-time, have occasioned great apprehensions in many of the Principal Inhabitants respecting their own safety, as well as the safety of the Community.[10]

Unrest spread like a fever throughout the Caribbean, with island after island reporting incidents of rebellion or conspiracy. Such was the situation in Dominica in 1791. The island had only switched from French to British rule in 1783, and its Kalinago people had long made the rugged, mountainous interior a stronghold of resistance to European incursion. The island's planters were not helped by the fact that Dominica also sits between the French colonies of Guadeloupe and Martinique, which meant that the Revolution's ideas could not help but infiltrate the island. The island's governor, John Orde, noted in one letter that he heard that 'the slaves in Martinico [sic] have made further attempts at Liberty', but tried to play down the threat, observing that in Dominica the 'Situation of this Island is so peculiar both with respect to external and internal Circumstances.'[11]

On the night of 20 January 1791, a rebellion began in Dominica after rumours circulated that the planters were trying to suppress the news of a ruling allowing slaves more free time. Indeed, the slave leaders in Saint-Domingue had claimed that the king had freed them years before, based on rumours that had existed since the beginning of the French Revolution. During this period, rumour was a powerful force. And although events in Dominica took place before the slave uprising in Saint-Domingue began in August, people there would have been aware of the story of Vincent Ogé, of what had been happening in France, and the fighting already taking place on the French islands. Many slaves in Dominica decided not to work at all. A report into the event later described the slaves as being 'resolved *to take that Time themselves*, and that the Free People of Colour, who should refuse to assist them, should be put to Death'.[12] There were rumours that some of the slaves were planning to kill all the masters in a coordinated attack.[13] Nothing came of the alleged plot, and the unrest was soon suppressed, with one report claiming, 'The Slaves appear now perfectly dissuaded of their pretentions and expectations,' although this was, no doubt, what nervous officials wanted to believe.[14]

A free coloured man from Martinique, Jean Louis (also Jean Baptiste) Polinaire, was implicated as leader of the plot – apparently a Kalinago person had informed the authorities of the plan.[15] Polinaire and many other participants were rounded up and tried, and some were sentenced to death. Polinaire pleaded not guilty but to no avail. His punishment was to 'be there hanged by the neck and cut down alive, and that his Entrails be taken out and burnt before his Face, and his Head cutt off, and his Body divided into four Quarters, and His Head and Quarters disposed of at the King's pleasure'.[16] Like other alleged rebel leaders before him, he was made an example.

After August 1791, slave societies throughout the Caribbean became ever more anxious, with panicked planters fearing that any noise in the night might mean their cane fields were burning or that any shouts signalled the start of a rebellion. Rumours circulated, shifting shape as ships ferried tales of violence and bloodshed from port to port; indeed, the situation practically demanded the spread of misinformation. Some of the planters in Saint-Domingue looked at the brown smoke rising from their burning cane fields and decided the time had come to leave, looking to the nearest point of refuge, Santiago de Cuba, which lies just to the north-east of Saint-Domingue. But Spanish officials were wary; they did not trust the French planters and they had heard that an attack was being planned on Spanish Santo Domingo.[17] Meanwhile, amid the chaos, Africans were still being brought to the island: 44,572 in 1790, falling to 28,040 in 1791, and to 9,862 in 1792.[18] Some planters, especially the free people of colour in the south, continued to cultivate coffee and indigo. Fragments of the status quo persisted, but even these would soon crumble.

At about the same time, a young creole planter took up arms against the slaves. He left an anonymous account of his experience, in the form of letters, which was found among his family papers more than a century later.[19] In them, he describes his arrival from the frying pan of revolutionary Paris in 1791 to the fire of Saint-Domingue. He had little respite at his family's plantation in the north, near Caracol, before he found himself going into battle against the slaves. He recalls a dinner one night with fellow soldiers:

> We were eating heartily until the moment a cannonball passed through the window and carried away, right under our beards, the table and all the plates. The general, infuriated by this mishap, mounted his horse with food still in his mouth, and left camp with six hundred men . . . Two hours later one could not find a living Negro within a circle of two and half miles, and the roads were strewn with their bloody remains.[20]

The violence would only increase. There was bloodshed in France, too; 1793 began with the beheading of King Louis XVI. Revolution there once again whipped up conflict between France, Britain, and Spain. The French Revolutionary Wars, which began in February that year, at first saw Britain and Spain pitted against France. British troops in Jamaica quickly took advantage of the unrest in both Saint-Domingue and Europe, hoping to capture the valuable sugar colony. Britain also had an added pretext in that worried French royalist planters had asked planters in Jamaica to intercede on their behalf: they felt the British were fast becoming the only ones who would protect their interests.

Spain, however, was slower to get involved, initially opting only to add reinforcements around the border between the French and Spanish sides of Hispaniola. Like the British West Indies, the Spanish islands harnessed the manpower of free blacks and mulattos for use in the militias. In Cuba, these men accounted for a third of militia troops – 3,400 out of 11,667, divided into an infantry of *pardo* (free light-skinned people) and *moreno* (dark-skinned).[21] At first, the Spanish had no intention of getting dragged into Saint-Domingue's fight at all – indeed

Governor García was told to observe 'perfect neutrality'.[22] However, in Santo Domingo it soon became clear that perhaps the best option would instead be to bring in some of the leaders of the initial slave uprising organized by Boukman – who was later killed in battle – to help Spain's side. The Spanish promised these men their freedom and paid them for their service. They included Georges Biassou, Jean-François Papillon, Jean-Jacques Dessalines, and Toussaint Brèda, who had changed his surname to Louverture or L'Ouverture, meaning 'the opening'.[23] He had been born a slave, and working on the Brèda plantation in the sugar-rich northern plains of the island, where he was an overseer. By the time the conflict began, he had been free some twenty years, and is thought to have been the owner of at least one slave.[24]

The planters were getting increasingly nervous – they wanted to protect their wealth, which, after the destruction of the sugar cane, rested almost entirely in the slaves they owned. The need to leave the island became a priority. However, by 1793 edicts were passed throughout the surrounding territories to prevent people from travelling to neighbouring islands lest they spread insurrection. An official in Santiago de Cuba received a plea from a person recorded as José Corsi, who claimed to be from Genoa, and said he was a planter in Jeremias (Jérémie), a town on the southern peninsula of Saint-Domingue. Corsi feared for the loss of his farm, and wanted to bring his thirty slaves to Cuba. His wife, María Balenina, claimed to be from Santiago, where he said they had lived for twelve years before trying their luck in Saint-Domingue.[25] But he was only allowed to bring in their goods, and not their slaves. Indeed, the people of Cuba were not only following events with interest, but had been drawn into them, too. What was taking place in Saint-Domingue would also have profound ramifications for Cuba.

The Cuban planter Francisco de Arango y Parreño was not concerned about the fighting in Saint-Domingue, which he in fact saw as an opportunity to enter the sugar market. In his 1792 *Discurso sobre la agricultura de la Habana y medios de fomentarla* he wrote to the crown, claiming: 'The confusion and disorder that reigned in their [France's] colonies diminished their production and gave value to ours ... Today, in happier circumstances, because of the fatal increase in misfortune of our neighbour, we sell our sugar at an advantageous price; but tomorrow, what will be? Here is the real concern the island of Cuba should have.'[26]

He wanted the island to become the dominant producer. And two years later, in 1794, Arango and Ignacio Pedro Montalvo y Ambulodi, the Conde de Casa-Montalvo, in their eagerness to learn sugar techniques and better understand how the slave trade operated, took a voyage to Spain, Portugal, England, Barbados, and Jamaica. They were especially transfixed by Liverpool, then one of Europe's busiest ports. They also noted the role of the steam engine in industrial Britain, and realized it would be very useful at home (it was indeed used later in sugar cane processing).[27] Arango also wrote to his government contacts in Madrid to reassure them that a similar war between slaves and planters would not break out in Cuba. He cited large numbers of people of colour who were loyal to the king, the presence of a strong military garrison in Havana, and the better treatment of slaves: 'The French have treated them [slaves] like beasts and the Spanish like men.'[28] Soon there was official support for boosting sugar production, and organizations such as economic societies dedicated to improving agricultural techniques were established. In addition, refugee planters from Saint-Domingue brought their knowledge with them, and while the conflict there worsened, in Cuba slave imports rose, as did coffee and sugar exports. And so began the period historian Dale Tomich has called the 'second slavery'.[29]

Other slave owners fleeing Saint-Domingue were eager to go further afield, trying their luck in the United States, in port cities such as Philadelphia, Norfolk, Charlestown, or New Orleans, hoping they could bring their slaves with them. The first US president, George Washington, even donated $250 of his own money towards the relief effort for these refugees, in addition to the government funds and arms he gave the French in the early days of the uprising to help suppress the slaves.[30] But such generosity toward the fleeing planters would lessen over time. Restrictions soon grew with traffic from the island.[31] In 1793 the governor of the US state of South Carolina ordered all free blacks and coloured people from Saint-Domingue to leave within ten days; Georgia too forbade the entry of any West Indian slaves. Even Northern states were concerned, and in 1798 Philadelphia, Pennsylvania passed a decree prohibiting the entry of any more refugees.[32] That city was already home to a significant refugee population, which included Moreau St Méry, who had left Saint-Domingue in late 1793. Slaves and free people of colour, too, took the opportunity to leave.

Some of the slaves crossed to the Spanish side. Free people of colour, meanwhile, often tried to take their slaves to the US or Cuba but faced fierce restrictions. Planters on the other French islands grew increasingly worried. In April 1793, a similar battle had also begun in Guadeloupe. There was a slave uprising in Trois-Rivières, in the southern part of the island. The slaves killed twenty-three whites, justifying their actions by saying they were suppressing a royalist plot, and that they were on the side of the republic. They then joined forces with republicans and free people of colour.[33]

Meanwhile in Saint-Domingue, a new civil commissioner, Léger-Félicité Sonthonax, had arrived in September 1792, a few months after the National Assembly had granted equality to free people of colour. With the end of the monarchy in France in early 1793, the white population on the island was once again divided, and Sonthonax, who was a Jacobin, was swift to clear out any lingering royalists, promoting instead free people of colour.[34] Later the same year, the free people of colour were in positions of power, especially André Rigaud, a former goldsmith who now controlled the southern part of the island.

In June 1793, there was a slave attack on the wealthy port city of Le Cap in Saint-Domingue. The anonymous creole planter who had been battling the slaves claimed to have been there when the city was set on fire. By that point, his family's sugar cane had been burnt down, and the young man had decided to join some of the other refugees in the United States, arriving in Le Cap with plans to board a ship the following morning. But there was to be no rest that night:

> The creeping hours were hardly half run out when, all at once, horrible shrieks resounded in our ears; a great brightness lit the black skies. From the summit of the mountains down the roads to the plain, came immense hordes of Africans. They arrived with torches and knives and plunged into the city. From all sides flames were lifted as in a whirlwind and spread everywhere . . . I can still hear the whistling of bullets, the explosions of powder, the crumbling of houses.[35]

Sonthonax found himself in a quandary, exacerbated by the divisions among the whites, not least the naval attack on the city led by military governor François-Thomas Galbaud. He had abolitionist sympathies, but now faced a complicated situation in need of deft and pragmatic handling. Sonthonax decided to offer slaves in the north their freedom if they fought alongside the republican cause; this move proved so successful that slavery was in effect abolished on 29 August 1793. The policy spread across the island, and within a few months the blight of slavery had ended in the colony. It only remained to relay the decision to the National Assembly in France. When former slave Jean-Baptiste Belley, a free mulatto, Jean-Baptiste Mills, and a white clerk named Louis-Pierre Dufay arrived in February 1794 in the middle of the Terror to inform the National Convention – at that point under Jacobin control – that slavery had been abolished, there was little choice but to ratify it. Rather than an edict from Paris, abolition was won by the slaves of Saint-Domingue, and France could not ignore the implications. The early years of the battle had provoked many questions in the Caribbean and in Europe. Who was a citizen? Who was equal? Who was allowed to have liberty? Now, at least for the enslaved people of France's sugar colonies, the matter was settled.

The British, meanwhile, had every reason to try to preserve the slave regime on the island: not only because of its proximity to Jamaica, but also because Britain and France were again at war. Some 600 redcoats arrived in Jérémie on the southern coast of Saint-Domingue in September 1793. Soon Môle St Nicholas, a valuable port, fell to the British as well, and they continued to make gains in their first few months on the island.[36] Slavery persisted in the south under the free people of colour, and in the west, under the British, although plantations there were either burnt too, or the slaves simply stopped working in the fields.

When the news of slave emancipation reached Louverture, he quickly left Spanish military service and joined the French, as did Dessalines. Jean-François Papillon and Georges Biassou, however, stayed in Santo Domingo. In July 1794, Jean-François began to disregard General García's orders and massacred some 700 French colonists around Bayajá (known on the French side as Fort-Liberté) who were technically under the protection of the Spanish crown.[37] Dominican officers were horrified, and the events were quickly relayed back to Madrid. But they now found themselves in a dilemma – they were in no position to stop black soldiers from fighting on behalf of Spain, as they relied on their numbers, yet there was growing concern about how these generals were exercising their power.

British troops in the region also captured Guadeloupe, although

France soon took it back, and, later, Martinique, which they managed to hold on to for a little longer. But by this point much of the white population of Saint-Domingue had fled, with more than 10,000 people going to the United States. The majority, however, went to Cuba. Some 15,000 to 20,000 refugees landed there, while around 1,000 made their way through Santo Domingo and on to Mayagüez and San Juan in Puerto Rico. A few hundred went to Trinidad, and the rest scattered around the Caribbean region in places such as the coast of Venezuela.[38]

As Louverture began to make his mark in the French military, Spanish troops tried to push over their border and into the region around Le Cap. However, Spain did not have the forces to continue the fight for long, and in the 1795 Treaty of Basle the Spanish side of Hispaniola was ceded to France in exchange for peace between the two nations in the Pyrenees. One writer later described this as 'the oldest subjects of the Spanish crown, in the Western world, were thus bartered, like so many sheep'.[39] Spanish administration continued for a few years, but on that side of the island, too, an exodus began. Some of the 700 soldiers and their families were sent to Florida, others to Spain, Campeche, in New Spain, and Trujillo, on the Honduran coast, as well as Trinidad.[40] The 144 men and women who went to that island were met with immediate rejection. Although the island's population was still sparse, the whites were outnumbered by slaves, of which there were 8,944 – and the governor of Trinidad did not want any free people of colour or slaves settling there.[41]

Elsewhere in the Caribbean, much of 1795 was taken up with European troops suppressing revolts across the islands. Rebellions started in Grenada and St Vincent, while the maroons in Trelawny Parish, Jamaica, once again took up arms against the British.[42] Even in Curaçao, which did not have a large slave population, a revolt began in August after slaves there heard about the Netherlands' defeat at the hands of French forces and the subsequent establishment of the Batavian Republic that had taken place in January. Already aware of France's abolition of the slave trade, the slaves in Curaçao – led by Tula Rigaud and Bastiaan Carpata – refused to work. Some 2,000 people were involved, and it took a month for it to be put down; the Dutch showed little inclination to replicate French abolition.[43] The Dutch colony of Demerara, in South America, also experienced a revolt by slaves allied with maroons living in the jungle, though this, too, was suppressed.

The Spanish territories could not remain untouched either, and there were slave rebellions throughout. In the port of Coro, Venezuela, the uprising was led by a zambo, José Leonardo Chirino, who had often accompanied his master to Saint-Domingue, where he would have interacted with the slaves. In leading the uprising he demanded liberty for the slaves and declared the establishment of a republic, but it was quickly suppressed and around 170 people, including Chirino, were executed.[44]

In July, there was also an incident in Puerto del Príncipe in eastern Cuba. Led by two slaves named Romualdo and Joseph el Francés, 'the Frenchman', a group of slaves attacked the boss of the Cuatro Compañeros *hacienda*, Serapio Recio. They were later caught, and in the subsequent testimony it was asserted that 'they purported to destroy the town of Puerto del Príncipe, sack it, kill the caballeros, and want to do the same to all the whites', though they claimed they only wanted the freedom due to them, as Joseph declared, 'No one has a master now; we are all free.'[45] The Puerto del Príncipe leaders were later sent to Santo Domingo for trial, while the affair prompted the governor of the province to issue a decree forbidding anyone of colour from carrying arms.

Later in 1795, a Cuban mulatto by the name of Nicholás Morales agitated for change by invoking a recent royal order, the *gracias al sacar* of 10 February 1795, which allowed some non-whites to buy certain white privileges, basically permitting people to pay to move up the social hierarchy through public offices. Morales did not want to use the legislation to those ends; rather, he wanted to push for the eradication of certain taxes that harmed the poor and for more equal land distribution. He gathered about forty men in the eastern town of Bayamo to convince the governor of his case. That alone was cause for his arrest. In Puerto Rico, by October, rebellion had erupted in Aguadilla, though it was suppressed, and after that the island's governor, Ramón de Castro, instituted a number of measures to prevent propaganda or people from Saint-Domingue from entering the island.[46]

In an attempt to keep control of the island, officials unleashed a torrent of new rules, including orders to baptize *bozal* (African) slaves and instruct them in the Catholic faith, as well as give them Sundays off, while free blacks were not allowed to have altars for dances in their gatherings. Justices were to be vigilant about arresting prostitutes and 'suspicious' vagrants. *Pardos* and *morenos* were not allowed to use arms without clearly wearing a uniform, no one from the countryside was allowed to use a machete in the city, and everyone was banned from using a garrotte. There would be no singing or chanting in the streets or in houses after 11 p.m.; in fact, no one should be in the street at that time unless it was an urgent problem and he was carrying a lantern. No gunpowder was to be sold to a slave. No one could receive a slave inside their house, and taverns could not give slaves wine to take to their masters. Taverns and shops in the countryside could not buy goods from people of colour. But the whipping of slaves was still permitted.[47] Many of these rules had long been in place, but the need to reiterate or tighten them articulates an unspoken unease. Cuba's *cordón sanitario* may not have been strong, but a version of it was still in place.

In addition, a number of alleged conspiracies were uncovered across the region, and there are records of supposed plots from the Bahamas to Santo Domingo, and as far south as Trinidad, though no doubt there were others, too. Which were planned revolts and which were the imagination of skittish planters – or proven with 'evidence' obtained under torture – remains difficult to determine. Slave revolts took a variety of forms and had many causes. Some were born of mistreatment or local disputes, but by 1794 it was clear that many were spurred by the events in Saint-Domingue. Even when such revolts were not a direct result of what was happening on the island, they increasingly stemmed from a desire to be free, a wider understanding of liberty in the Americas, and the questioning of the right to keep slaves. It is not necessarily the case that *every* rebellion could be linked to events in Saint-Domingue, but it was certainly a time of great unrest, misinformation, and fear.[48]

In 1796, there was another realignment in Europe, as the second Treaty of San Ildefonso pitted Spain and France against Britain in the Revolutionary Wars. The fighting in Europe and the Caribbean continued as well. The British had put down the rebellion in Grenada and were trying to end their long-running battle against the Amerindians and maroons, known as 'Black Caribs', in St Vincent. In an echo of Columbus's 'Carib' and 'Taino' dichotomy, 'Black Caribs' were hostile to European incursion, while 'Red' or 'Yellow' Caribs were considered more amenable. The British had only taken control of the island from the French in 1763, and the intervening years were filled with hostilities and fraught negotiations between the Black Caribs and British officials, despite a treaty in 1773. Fighting resumed in 1795 and persisted for more than a year. In the end, British forces rounded up the rebels and sent 4,000 Black Caribs first to the isolated island of Baliceaux (one of the Grenadines) in 1796, and a year later, after many had died from disease, the surviving 2,000 or so were sent to the island of Roatán, in the Bay of Honduras.[49]

Meanwhile the British, after the Treaty of Basle, had redoubled their efforts in Saint-Domingue. They saw the ceding of its Spanish side to France as an opportunity to take control of the whole island; more troops were sent over from Britain and others put on standby in Jamaica. The plantations in the British-controlled south-west and north-west territories continued to produce coffee, while in the south, Rigaud was renting out plantations for cultivation, mostly under the control of free people of colour. Many ex-slaves were ordered to work on these plantations, triggering a number of local uprisings as a result of fears that slavery would be reinstituted. Around the same time, in 1795, the maroons in Trelawny Parish in the west of Jamaica resumed their long-running war against the British, which would last until the following year. There were suspicions underpinned by rumours that agents from Saint-Domingue were fomenting the unrest in Jamaica. However, this did not stop British involvement in Saint-Domingue, and more than 12,000 British troops had arrived by July 1796.[50] Louverture, for his part, was now fighting battles on many fronts – and not only against the British. He had also mounted a political campaign that, by 1797, had ousted Sonthonax and other French officials, and seen him consolidate his leadership in the north of the island. At the same time, Louverture and Rigaud came together for a final push to rid the island of the British, and by 1798 Britain could take little more. The British had lost around 15,000 of their 25,000 troops – many to malaria and yellow fever – and in August they surrendered.

Louverture also suppressed supposed plots to make the island independent, signalling to France that the island's stability depended on him, and not any of the other black leaders; he was rewarded with the title commander-in-chief. After the British defeat, Louverture faced one more problem: his erstwhile ally Rigaud. Louverture wanted to stem the power of Rigaud and other powerful mulattos, many of whom did not want black rule in the north. Within a year the two men were locked in a bitter struggle for power. Although what became known as the War of the Knives, or the War of the South, has been depicted as mulatto Rigaud versus black Louverture, the reality was that both had troops composed of ex-slaves, yet at the heart of the antagonism was a disagreement over where mulattos and blacks stood in the island's emerging hierarchy.[51] It was not just a conflict of colour, but also reflected the fact that Louverture had started life as a slave, and Rigaud had not. But by the end of 1799, after months of bloody fighting, Louverture had run Rigaud off the island, and now controlled the whole of Saint-Domingue.

Marcus Rainsford was an Irish-born soldier who had fought in the American Revolution, and later in the West Indies, spending time in Barbados and Jamaica. In 1799 he was sent to Martinique, and then was ordered to Jamaica, where he found his regiment had already set sail for England. To catch up with them, he boarded a ship from St Thomas, but they hit bad weather and were forced into Le Cap, Saint-Domingue, where he had an unexpected glimpse of the island during this turbulent time. He would later publish a short account of his adventure, *A Memoir of Transactions that Took Place in St. Domingo, in the Spring of 1799*. He describes Louverture, saying that 'the first object that excited our attention amidst thousands of People of Colour of every description, was the respectable Toussaint in familiar conversation with two private Brigands'.[52] He spent three weeks on the island, and claimed to have spotted the general many times, describing him as wearing 'a uniform, a kind of blue spencer, with a large red cape falling over his shoulders, and red cuffs, with eight rows of lace on his arms, and a pair of large gold epaulettes thrown back on his shoulders; a scarlet waistcoat, pantaloons and half-boots; a round hat with a red feather and a national cockade; and an extreme large sword is suspended from his side'. In the end, Louverture would save Rainsford's life.

Rainsford had attempted to leave the island again, but the Danish vessel he was travelling on sprang a leak, so they had to call into Fort Egalité (Fort Dauphine), about forty miles away. They hoisted Danish colours, which were neutral, yet less than a half-hour later he was arrested and 'informed that suspicions had arisen of my being a spy, and that my trial would be prompt and decisive', meaning he faced a possible death sentence. He was accused of being an English spy on a mission to reconnoitre the coast, and lacking any proof to refute this, he was sentenced to death. The ship's captain tried to plead that Rainsford was American, but to no avail. He languished in prison for a fortnight, and waited for Louverture to sign off on the execution, but instead 'that truly great man . . . ordered me to be released and suffered to proceed on my voyage', warning Rainsford that '"you must never return to this island, *without the proper passports*"'. Rainsford made his way to Martinique, and thence to Britain, where he published his memoir in 1802.[53]

*

The first year of the nineteenth century was a triumphant one for Louverture. He was now in charge of the whole colony.[54] At the same time, another general was asserting his order over the chaos of revolutionary France. Napoleon Bonaparte had made himself First Consul of France in 1799, and he had made Louverture commander-in-chief of the entire island of Saint-Domingue. But it did not take long for a relationship of mutual distrust to emerge. Bonaparte worried that Louverture was failing to follow his commands, and that he was perhaps attempting to lead the island towards independence, especially after Louverture decided to formally take charge of the Spanish side of the island. But even prior to that Louverture had negotiated secret commercial treaties with Britain and the US in spite of the fact that France was meant to be at war with Britain, and unofficially fighting the US in the Quasi War (1798–1800), which took place mostly at sea. He needed the food and goods the US provided and he also wanted to avoid the island being blockaded by the British.

On 6 January 1801 Governor García, who had remained in Santo Domingo despite the Spanish territory having been officially ceded six years earlier, received notice that the island would now be fully under French jurisdiction, and Louverture was prepared to use force to back up this edict. Louverture marched into the east, and a few days later announced 'with great satisfaction that I have taken possession of the Spanish Part of Saint Domingo in the name of the French Republic'.[55] Governor García had no choice but to submit, and a handover was arranged on 22 January.

Throughout the next few months, more Spanish creoles left Santo Domingo, mostly for other ports in Spain's empire. Two officials from the Real Hacienda who departed in February described 'a powerful reason to leave; the rain, the laments, the disorder of the changeover, the lack of help from the old government . . . and all the city in general full of terror and fright, waiting for sacking, death and violence'.[56]

García also left the island, and arrived in Maracaibo, Venezuela, in February on a Danish ship, along with his family and secretary Nicolás de Toledo. They were followed by ships bringing the 148 remaining soldiers of the Cantabria infantry.[57] But leaving proved difficult for many, partly due to British pirates sailing nearby and plundering them. Many people arrived at their destination completely impoverished and had to beg for charity. Such was the case for Pedro Sánchez Valverde, who had been a curate in towns such as Higüey and Santiago. He claimed he had tried to leave Santo Domingo in 1796 but that his application had been denied owing to the war with Britain, which made transport difficult to secure. In his letters to Maracaibo officials, whom he hoped would give him some money, he maintained he had done his share to help the fight of 'your Royal Arms against the negro Toussaint Louverture'. Now he was forced to draw on his loyalty to ask for help for himself and his family members, among them two women and five children, whom he claimed had lost everything to the English privateers, 'from their jewelry, and their only clothing . . . they are exposed now to begging'.[58] By the end of March 1801, 1,247 individuals, ten political and military corps, the Cantabria troops, 118 administrators, and 250 people without passports had arrived in the Venezuelan port.[59]

By July of that year, Louverture had drawn up a constitution for the whole of the island, now under his control, declaring 'there cannot exist slaves on this territory' and 'all men are born, live and die free and French'.[60] He had made it clear that the connection to France would continue; this was not quite a declaration of independence. It freed the slaves of the Spanish side of the island, who had continued to work under the previous system. Slavery in Santo Domingo had been on a much smaller scale than Saint-Domingue, reaching around 30,000 in this period, with many families having one or two slaves who lived with them, rather than the large plantations of the west of the island. Likewise, there was a significant community of free people of colour as well. There is scant evidence left about how these slaves and free people of colour on the Spanish side of the island reacted to Louverture's message of emancipation and equality; but many of the creoles with land or money were quick to leave rather than face rule under the French, and under the leadership of a former slave.

Louverture immediately tried to make that side of the island more productive, while simultaneously improving output in the war-weary west. Despite all that had happened in the years since 1791, by 1801 sugar exports had reached around 13 per cent of 1789 levels, coffee around 56 per cent, and even cotton hit 35 per cent.[61] This productivity was due to a considerable effort on the part of Louverture to encourage the now-free workers to remain on the plantations, convince the few white planters left to stay, and succeed in luring back some of the refugees who had left. In the east, however, he faced considerable challenges, not least that Dominicans had used land for grazing their cattle and made a livelihood selling the hides to the French; they were not necessarily committed to converting to plantation agriculture. Louverture considered Dominican land use 'backward' and instituted land reforms that involved changing the distribution, but these changes were met with anger.[62] This was a problem in the west of the island too, as many former slaves resented being forced to work on the plantations. In October 1801, frustrated workers, under the leadership of Louverture's nephew Moïse, rebelled. Louverture led its suppression along with his top lieutenants, Dessalines and Henri Christophe. Moïse was executed, along with many of the other participants.[63]

Bonaparte by this point was livid, and had had enough of the ex-slave who had declared himself governor-for-life and called himself 'the Bonaparte of Saint Domingue'.[64] He felt he was left with little option but to invade the island. Louverture, meanwhile, kept telling French officials he had no plans to make the island independent, but they offered little reassurance. On 31 December 1801 Bonaparte sent his brother-in-law, General Charles Leclerc, to Saint-Domingue with 10,000 troops and orders to undermine Louverture, return plantations to their former owners, and reinstitute slavery. Also on board was Louverture's old nemesis, André Rigaud. Louverture had suspected Bonaparte was going to take some sort of action and was ready. He had little faith in Napoleon, having heard that he was preparing to reinstitute slavery. By the time Britain had returned Martinique to France under the terms of the Treaty of Amiens (1802), it was clear that far from abolishing slavery there, Bonaparte was instead going to retain it, and, in addition, there were soon reports of Africans arriving in Guadeloupe again.

At first, Leclerc made rapid gains, with many generals surrendering, but Louverture, Christophe, and Dessalines continued to fight, and the war soon escalated. The casualties were high, and resources for Louverture and the others began to run out. By May all three surrendered, and waited for the summer – and the diseases – to come. But Louverture would not be on the island to watch yellow fever demolish French troops. Christophe and Dessalines later betrayed him to the French, alleging that he was plotting a rebellion. Louverture was kidnapped, and exiled to the French prison of Fort-de-Joux, in the mountains of the Jura, where he suffered through one freezing winter and died in April 1803. The news of his incarceration and later death soon spread around Europe, where many people had been following the press reports. Upon hearing of Louverture's capture, the English poet William Wordsworth was moved to pen a homage to the black general:

> TOUSSAINT, the most unhappy man of men!
> Whether the whistling Rustic tend his plough
> Within thy hearing, or thy head be now
> Pillowed in some deep dungeon's earless den;—
> O miserable Chieftain! where and when
> Wilt thou find patience? Yet die not; do thou
> Wear rather in thy bonds a cheerful brow:
> Though fallen thyself, never to rise again,
> Live, and take comfort. Thou hast left behind
> Powers that will work for thee; air, earth, and skies;
> There's not a breathing of the common wind
> That will forget thee; thou hast great allies;
> Thy friends are exultations, agonies,
> And love, and man's unconquerable mind.[65]

Louverture did, however, outlive Leclerc, who died of yellow fever in November 1802. Bonaparte sent General Rochambeau to finish the job, but, even without Louverture, it was going to be a battle. The fight had been reinvigorated by the news that the French were indeed going to reinstitute slavery in all their colonies. People left the plantations to take up arms. Nature aided them as French numbers continued to plummet owing to disease. To further complicate matters, hostilities resumed between Britain and France. Bonaparte could not afford to fight both enemies. British ships blockaded the harbour, and by the end of November 1803 Rochambeau relented. Dessalines had kept the slaves' freedom intact. France, for its part, had lost around 50,000 of the estimated 60,000 soldiers sent in total to the island.[66] Bonaparte decided to focus on the battles in Europe and sold France's Louisiana territory to the United States for $15 million. Saint-Domingue was gone, but France kept its other islands and continued to permit slavery in them.

Planters and officials in the neighbouring islands were horrified. There was no guarantee that the troubles in Saint-Domingue would not trigger rebellions elsewhere. The diaries of Lady Nugent, wife of George Nugent, the governor of Jamaica, reflect this anxiety.[67] In 1801–6 Maria Nugent's diary recounted this unsettled time in the Caribbean.[68] The tension is palpable in her 13 December 1803 entry, where she wrote: '—In the evening, many unpleasant and alarming reports, respecting the French prisoners on parole and the negroes in this town. One of the black men, a Dutch negro, had absented himself from prayers, and it was observed, by one of the staff, that he was seen making signs to one of the sentries, from a window. This, together with the rumours all day, of an understanding between the French prisoners and the free blacks, and their tampering with the negro slaves, was indeed most frightful.'[69]

On 1 January 1804 Dessalines, taking the indigenous name 'Ayti', meaning 'mountainous land', for the island, unveiled to the world the Republic of Haiti, and proclaimed: 'I have avenged America.'[70] This was followed by a radical constitution which declared, 'Slavery is forever abolished', and went a step further to say, 'All . . . Haytians shall hence forward be known only by the generic appellation of Blacks.'[71] At a stroke, Dessalines tried to end the long-running antagonism between the slaves and the free people of colour – now they were all free. While these were noble words on paper, in practice, the new country would soon fracture again along colour lines. Most of the pre-revolution white population of around 30,000 had fled, but those few who had stayed or those who had been lured back by Louverture, were not, however, to be made 'black'. Many were promptly massacred, though Dessalines did spare the lives of some who then too became 'black' Haitians. *The Times* of London carried a report on this final push against the planters: 'Captain Dodge, of the schooner *Mary-Ann* . . . states that on the 14th and 15th of May, a general massacre of all the remaining white inhabitants of Cape François took place . . . On the night of the 14th . . . these unfortunate people were strangled in their bed, by order of the Emperor; the blood-thirsty villains, not content with this, plunged their bayonets into their bodies.'[72]

What followed was a battle to control the new nation. Dessalines soon crowned himself emperor, which was not well received. He was killed by an assassin's bullet in 1806, and the country became even further divided. Black leader Henri Christophe took charge of the north, while the mulatto general Alexandre Pétion ruled over the south, and this compromise held for a while. But the struggle for freedom across the Caribbean would prove to be a much longer battle.

*

Although the abolition of the slave trade and the practice of slavery was most dramatic in Haiti, it was not the first instance of it. In 1792, while the British abolitionists were still struggling for a legislative victory, the Danish had decided to outlaw the trading of slaves, although this did not take effect until 1803, giving traders and planters a decade to arrange alternative means of income and labour. And, of course, it also meant that the trade increased in those years. Indeed, from 1782 to 1792 the Danish exported 13,231 Africans; this reached 21,782 from 1792 to 1802, while in the same periods the number of slaves brought to the Danish West Indies was 11,814 and 27,382, respectively.[73]

In 1807, the efforts of William Wilberforce and the thousands of abolitionists in Britain were finally successful – a bill was passed by 41 to 20 in the House of Lords, and 114 to 15 in the Commons to outlaw the slave trade, and the Slave Trade Act entered the statute books on 25 March 1807. Around the same time President Thomas Jefferson signed the Act Prohibiting Importation of Slaves, which took effect the following year. The Swedes and the Dutch were not long behind, with Sweden abolishing the trade in 1813, and the Dutch in 1814. France and Spain would take a while longer to sign up. Of course, the smuggling of slaves still persisted, but the official sanction by Britain, Denmark, Sweden, and the Netherlands had expired. And while the British were – and remain – rightly proud of their humanitarian leanings in stopping the trade, it seems to ignore the fact that the slaves of Saint-Domingue were the vanguard of true abolition. The Danes may have been the first to pass a bill, but the people of Saint-Domingue were the first to bring about not only the end of the trade to that island, but the first slave emancipation in the Americas. And although the slave trade had been abolished, the practice of slavery very much had not.

By the time Britain had passed the Slave Trade Act and Haiti had settled into its divisions, Cuba had experienced remarkable changes of its own, especially in the east of the island where some refugees from Saint-Domingue had settled near the cloud-topped mountains of the Sierra Maestra. In the east, the number of immigrants in Santiago de Cuba now totalled around 20,000, and they were transforming coffee-growing in that part of the island.[74] With its high mountains, the Sierra Maestra had just the right climate to nurture the growth of *cafetales*. Before the French arrived, production of coffee had not been more than a hundred tons a year, but by 1805 it had increased tenfold and was eventually thirtyfold.[75]

The French settlers in Santiago had their own neighbourhood, living in distinct single-storeyed houses with porches; they also had their own theatre, spoke their own language, and lived mostly within their own social world. There was tension between the settlers and Spanish creoles over differing ideas about the crown and the Church. The immigrants were often taunted with insults: the French were 'baptised in the water of rotten cod', to which the riposte often was 'Godoy's Spain', a reference to the unpopularity of the first minister.[76] By the summer of 1803, the governor of Santiago de Cuba, Sebastián Kindelán, codified the antagonism by restricting the actions of the French settlers. For instance *tumbas*, which were traditional dances held by the French and often attended by people of colour, were only allowed on festival days, and even then they had to finish by 8 p.m.[77]

Of course, immigrants were not limited to Santiago or coffee; others returned to sugar planting elsewhere on the island. In fact, they brought to Cuba improved techniques, a more modernized process, and, when possible, some capital to invest. Sugar exports averaged some 186,000 tonnes a year during the period 1802–6, compared with around 90,000 tonnes from 1792 to 1796.[78] But this state of affairs was not destined to last for long: European politics once again intervened in the Caribbean, and once again Bonaparte was to blame. In 1808 he installed his brother Joseph on the Spanish throne after convincing Charles IV to abdicate and forcing his heir, Ferdinand VII, into exile. This was the first domino to fall in a run of events that would not only lead to more war in Europe, but also end colonial rule in most of Spanish America. It also caused local difficulty in Cuba and the eastern portion of Hispaniola. Even Puerto Rico was affected. In August 1808 Governor Montes asked the island's planters to support the fight against Bonaparte, saying that although they lacked money, they should 'take the decision to put at the disposition of the *suprema junta* part of the fruits produced in your haciendas. Coffee in good condition, sugar, dye-wood, cotton, skins, are donations that can be placed in Spain'.[79]

In Santo Domingo, the reaction was even more dramatic. Upon hearing the news of Napoleon's invasion of Spain in 1808, Spanish creoles led by Juan Sánchez Ramírez launched a war against the French troops who were still nominally controlling the island. When Haiti split into north and south, it did not take the former Spanish part with it, and that area remained under the watch of a few French soldiers. No one knew what to do with it, except Dominicans, who wanted it returned to Spain.

Sánchez Ramírez was a wealthy Dominican who had fled to Puerto Rico in 1803 but came back in 1807 to resume his lucrative business exporting wood. He soon realized the other remaining Spanish creoles on the island felt as he did about French rule, and he knew he would have little problem rounding up men willing to fight to end the reign of Governor General Ferrand. Many wanted a return to Spanish rule, and now they had a reason. Ferrand was well aware what was afoot. He gave a speech in August 1808 imploring Dominicans to see their similarities to the French, saying 'you are already French, or, rather, French and Spanish together are one population of brothers and friends, whose only end is to defend the same interests, and profess the same spirit and sentiments'.[80] This did little to quell the sentiments of Sánchez Ramírez, who later wrote that the news of Joseph Bonaparte controlling the Indies – and especially his beloved Santo Domingo – had inspired him to take up arms: 'From that moment I could not shake from my imagination the idea of war . . . [it] produced in my spirit such rancour against [the French].'[81]

The fighting began in 1808, with Sánchez Ramírez and his 2,000 men invoking the deposed king in their battle cry of 'Viva Fernando VII!' After months of fighting, the loyalists managed a key victory in November, in the battle of Palo Hincado. Ferrand's pride was so wounded he killed himself after the defeat.[82] One of the few surviving French soldiers wrote in his memoirs that his general's head was 'presented on a spear to the English officials, who received with horror this bloody trophy of ingratitude and barbarity of those ferocious men'.[83] This would not stop the French, however, and General Barquier took over the fight. He resorted to enlisting Dominican slaves to fight against Sánchez Ramírez, though the Spanish creoles had also offered freedom to slaves if they fought alongside them.[84] In addition, Sánchez Ramírez had received reinforcements throughout the war in the form of free people of colour who wanted to fight, even including a *moreno* regiment.[85] The war continued into 1809, by which point the British had entered the conflict. Britain's ships provided a blockade which proved instrumental in the victory that was finally obtained in July of that year. Britain, for its efforts, was rewarded with a preferential commercial treaty.[86] When the news of the Dominican victory reached Santiago de Cuba, 'immediately they prepared a music concert, and everyone without distinction of class or person went out into the main streets until ten in the evening, singing praises . . .'[87] And what was left of the government in Spain thanked Sánchez Ramírez.

As Santo Domingo was embroiled in fighting against France, Cuba was waging its own battles with it as well. Indeed, the neighbouring United States thought the crisis in Spain would result in the secession of Cuba. The planters were nervous about what this would mean for their slaves. To US politicians, Napoleon seemed strong enough to take what he wanted, and with the fall of the Spanish crown, a carve-up of its colonies loomed. Cuba was the new pearl of the Caribbean, and with Havana only ninety miles from Spanish Florida, there was some hope that the United States could take both. To this end, former US president Thomas Jefferson wrote to his recently installed successor, James Madison, saying: 'I suppose the conquest of Spain will soon force a delicate question on you as to the Floridas and Cuba, which will offer themselves to you. Napoleon will certainly give his consent without difficulty to our receiving the Floridas, and with some difficulty Cuba.'[88]

Jefferson's optimism would go unrealized, as Spain proved more resistant to Napoleon than the US leaders had expected. However, the question of Cuba's annexation to the United States would recur at intervals throughout the rest of the century. The US had long been interested in the island – not only did it receive Cuban sugar but, more importantly, Cuba was a ready market for US exports. At the same time, the US was well aware of the similarities between Cuba and its Southern states, and how slavery could be extended there.

After Joseph Bonaparte was placed on the Spanish throne, Cuban officials set up a *junta de vigilancia*, which was an administrative body tasked with locating the French (or French creole) settlers on the island, and deporting them – with immediate effect. Those under suspicion were forced to profess their religion, why they were in Cuba, what they were doing, where they lived, and other information. Anyone officially deemed French was given seventeen days to leave Havana and twenty-five days to leave other locations.

One such settler family was that of Juan Bautista Peroden (probably Juan-Baptiste, as names were often Hispanicized), whose file in the Holguín *junta* records listed him as aged forty-six and a baker. Along with him was his wife, Tereza Origni, thirty-one; sons Enrique (Henri), six, and Carlos Victor, four; and daughters Angela Josefa, two, and Clara de Jesus, one month. They also had slaves Guillermo, twenty-four, Juan Bautista, seventeen, and Susana, twenty. Other members of their household included Victoria Origni, twenty-four, who was a seamstress, and Juan and Maria Michaela, aged two and four respectively. There were also *pardo* members, including washerwoman Maria Julia, fifty, and seamstresses Maria del Rosario, twenty, and Maria Magdalena, twenty-two. In the margin of their file, an official noted, 'The French Peroden, with his wife and the rest of his family here, in this city for five to six years have manifested conduct irreprehensible with the most distinguished of the city.'[89] Still, some 7,000 people like them were driven out – perhaps Peroden and his family were, too. This time, most of the refugees headed to French-speaking New Orleans, though Jefferson tried to stop them at first during his final days in office.[90] Like many southern slaveholders, he did not want slaves or people of colour associated with Haiti entering the US and he knew that this stream of people were not Cuban, but the residents of the former Saint-Domingue.

Of course, the Spanish were also well placed to take advantage of the fleeing French – the governor of Santiago, Sebastián Kindelán, bought fourteen slaves from a departing planter, including 'three negros *bozales* named Guillermo, Fulgencio, and Ambrosio'.[91] However, such an exodus was bound to be beset by logistical problems. In many cases the refugees had trouble getting out of the country within their allotted time. Many could not find buyers for their goods, leaving them no way to pay their passage, and in any case there was often a lack of ships.[92] Despite these difficulties, thousands streamed from Cuba throughout the summer of 1809. In a matter of months, some 6,060 people left Baracoa and Santiago; of these 1,887 were white, 2,060 were free people of colour and 2,113 slaves, indicating that the earlier regulations intended to keep people of colour out of the island perhaps had not been strictly observed.

These tumultuous years had given Cuba a handsome profit, not only from coffee, but also from sugar. At the beginning of the conflict in Saint-Domingue, Cuba had not been a major sugar competitor. In 1791 it produced only 16,731 tons (US) of sugar, compared with Jamaica's 60,900 and Saint-Domingue's 78,696.[93] But in the years that followed, the numbers began to rise. A German naturalist named Alexander von Humboldt had arrived on the island during this period of transition, and took a great interest in the sugar trade. During his travels all over Latin America, Humboldt had twice stayed in Cuba, for three months from December 1800, and again in March 1804. Humboldt brought an outsider's perspective and a scientist's eye for detail to the island. It was another twenty-two years before he wrote about what he saw in Cuba, but in the intervening period, he stayed in touch with his friends and tried to keep abreast of all the latest information, corresponding with the planter Francisco de Arango as part of this effort.

He noted that the greatest changes to the production of sugar cane happened between 1796 and 1800. He saw the connection between what had happened in Saint-Domingue and what followed in Cuba: 'First, mules were substituted for oxen, as motive power for the sugar mills; then water-power was introduced . . . having been used even by the first settlers in St. Domingo.'[94] Although he was not a planter, he took an interest in the rapid ascent of the sugar plantations. He even spent time poring over government trade statistics, often provided by Arango. He was fond of the city of Havana, where 'amidst a variety of soothing impressions, the European forgets the dangers that menace him in the populous cities of the Caribbean islands'.[95]

He noted the changes in land where 'civilization advances, and the soil, more stript of plants, scarcely offers any traces of its wild abundance'.[96] Alongside this, sugar exported in 1786 amounted, by his tally, to 63,274 cases, and based on records up to 1824, it hit a peak in 1823 of 300,211 cases.[97] The transformation was well under way. Humboldt pointed out that, by 1810, the population of Havana was 43,175, of which 18,365 were creoles, 14,510 enslaved, and 10,300 free, claiming that this was a doubling of the population of 1791.[98] Likewise the rest of the island 'furnishes the most striking contrasts in countries where slavery has taken such deep root'.[99] He placed this, however, alongside 'the whole of the English Islands' and calculated that out of a population of 776,500, 626,800 were enslaved, while in Cuba only 260,000 out of a population of 715,000 were. Like many Europeans, Humboldt thought Cuba should be capable of 'prudent and humane measures, [that] might procure the gradual abolition of slavery'. He would not see that in Cuba during his lifetime.

*

Meanwhile in Spain, a Cortes (national assembly) had been called in 1810, by the Regency government, which had set itself up in Cádiz. Deputies from Spain's American empire were invited to participate. The many officials throughout Spanish America were facing a grave problem – the question of legitimacy. There had been long-simmering tensions between the creoles and their interests, and those of the peninsular-born officials. With the lack of royal authority, sovereignty in this instance was transferred to the public, not the French.[100] The task at hand for the participants in Cádiz was now to craft a constitution.

They debated a range of issues, including the future of slavery. The effort to include the colonies, all of which sent representatives, may have been too little, too late. Yet there were more Spaniards in the colonies, at 16 million, than in Spain, with 10 million. There was also the question of who was a citizen.[101] There was wide agreement that indigenous people and mestizos (people who were part indigenous, part European) deserved to have their own representatives and some political voice, and so their citizenship was recognized, as there was a long legal history to their relationship with the Spaniards. The same could be said for slaves and free blacks, mulattos, and zambos, yet they would find themselves excluded. Just as there were legal frameworks for relations between Indians and the Spanish, so, too, were there ones for slave and free, including those that allowed slaves to buy their freedom. But it was not enough for them to be counted.

José Mejía Lequerica, a deputy from New Granada, made an impassioned plea for the inclusion of Americans of African origin, arguing, 'As plants are improved by grafting, so too are the mixed castes of America . . . Why should their blood be deemed impure?'[102] This particular speech, however, was omitted in session records from 1 October 1810, though it did appear in the periodical *El Observador*.[103] Despite the debate – much of which would attempt to make citizens out of people with African blood as well as stress the supposed racial harmony of the Americas – the real issue for Spain was that if all people of African descent were included, the number of Spanish representatives would have to be lower than the number granted to Americans, something the American delegates realized as well.[104] That being the case, black people in Spanish America would, in the end, be forced to forgo political representation.

Enslaved Africans, present and future, would further lose out during the abolition debates, which saw attempts to end the slave trade fail as well. This was the first significant articulation about slavery and its future in Spanish America, and it was long after the British and Danish had made their intentions clear. Liberal Spaniards wanted to push the country in new directions, and that included the suppression of the slave trade, as other nations had done. Abolition became a matter of debate in the Cortes, which roused the not inconsiderable anger of Cuba. The idea was initially proposed in April 1811 by Agustín de Argüelles, a Spaniard and one of the Cádiz *diputados*, who petitioned 'that the Congress declare this depraved traffic forever abolished'.[105] But the spectre of Saint-Domingue hung over the ensuing debate and the deputies became muddled about the abolition of the slave trade and the abolition of slavery. Mejía cautioned Argüelles, arguing that 'the abolition of the slave business requires much meditation and a steady hand, because to liberate at once an immense multitude of slaves, more than the bankrupting of their owners, would bring disgraceful consequences to the state'. But he went on to agree that no more slaves should be introduced to the colonies.[106] Argüelles re-entered the debate to clarify what he was proposing and said, 'the terms that have been conceded, manifest that they do not try to manumit the slaves of the American possessions, which is a matter that requires the greatest care, given the sad example of what befell Santo Domingo

[Saint-Domingue]'. The Cuban representative, Andrés de Jáuregui, weighed in, arguing that such an announcement would upset the 'tranquility' among races his island was enjoying, imploring them to remember 'the imprudent conduct of the National Assembly of France, and the sad, fatal results it produced'.[107] The case for the abolition of the slave trade was not without its supporters, but they would have a long wait ahead as slavery and the slave trade continued in Spanish America.

Around the time of the abolition debates in 1812, Puerto Rican representative Ramón Power wrote to his mother, Doña Josefa Giralt y Power, in San Juan, telling her about events in Cádiz. The letter sparked a series of events in Puerto Rico that nearly led to an uprising. Doña Josefa's slaves, Jacinto and Fermín, found out the contents of the letter, in which – drawing from the events at the Cortes – Power told her that 'if they [the Cortes] give liberty to the slaves, she would be the first in executing the law with hers'. On reading this, she began to cry and tore up the letter. It would not take long for her slaves to discover the source of her anguish, and relay the contents of her letter around the city.[108]

Cuba, too, would see related turbulence in 1812. A series of revolts in Havana, Puerto del Príncipe, Bayamo, and Holguín were discovered to be connected rather than being local disturbances on plantations. The trail eventually led to a free black man named José Antonio Aponte, an artisan who was also a sculptor and had been a captain in Havana's free black militia. His house was searched and a book was found, allegedly full of plans and drawings: sketches of military garrisons on the island, along with portraits of George Washington and, more significantly, Haitian leaders Louverture, Jean-François, Dessalines, and Christophe. This was enough for the authorities to blame Aponte, and he was hanged.[109]

The Havana planters won the argument during these debates in Cádiz, and Spain did not abolish slavery for many more decades on the island. Indeed, Cuba and, to a lesser extent, Puerto Rico would see slave imports rise throughout the decade. Between 1808 and 1814, the number of new slaves who disembarked in Cuba reached around 25,000 brought in on ships under Spanish, Portuguese, and US flags. Likewise, the port of Havana was growing alongside the burgeoning sugar and slave industries.[110] The British, for their part, now felt it was in their power to keep the seas free of slavery and began to send out naval squadrons to look for illegal slave ships.

In 1811 a Scottish traveller, J. B. Dunlop, arrived in Havana, where he observed that within a well-guarded city lay much diversion and a growing amount of wealth. He observed, 'Gambling seems to be a Vice to which all are passionately addicted, from the Government down to the most common individual.' He noted other aspects of Cuban life, including a thriving theatre scene, and fashionable resorts where *habaneros* went to be seen and to promenade.[111] Havana was an increasingly important commercial centre and, fuelled by agricultural wealth and trade, changing culturally and socially as well.

In 1814 Joseph Bonaparte was finally driven out of Spain, and the throne was returned to the Bourbons. The liberal reforms enshrined in the 1812 constitution – though abolition of the slave trade was not one of them – were ripped up by Ferdinand VII. Cuba and Puerto Rico were soon granted licences to allow Catholic settlers from other parts of the world to be given land to plant, but Ferdinand VII would not inherit the same empire his father left. From 1810 onwards, while the Cortes was debating the now-defunct constitution, angry creoles across Spanish America had been trying to push Spaniards out of positions of power, calling instead for the establishment of republics. There had been a number of plots and conspiracies, but the first serious blow was landed in New Spain by a priest, Miguel Hidalgo, who rang the church bell in the town of Dolores in October 1810 and started an uprising, known as *el grito de Dolores* – the cry of Dolores – calling for land reforms and equality. Hidalgo was caught and shot a few months later, but the door had been opened. Venezuelan rebels proclaimed independence in 1811, and others followed suit. The islands would be far more circumspect. Santo Domingo had only just returned ostensibly to Spanish rule, while Cuba and Puerto Rico, locked into a slave economy, were as yet unwilling to test the waters of independence.

Chapter Eight

CUBA AND THE CONTRADICTIONS
OF FREEDOM

By the time Ferdinand VII returned to the Spanish throne in 1814, the rebellions that had started from 1810 onwards had turned into wars for independence across Spanish America, stretching from New Spain (Mexico) to Argentina, pitting those who favoured independence against royalists. Independence was tied to a growing self-awareness and patriotism among creoles, who felt they had long suffered discrimination at the hands of the peninsular officials who ruled over them. In addition, the revolutions in the United States, France, and even Haiti also offered inspiration. But Spain's islands remained loyal throughout the tumultuous early decades of the nineteenth century. They were sustained by the contradictions embodied in Cuba and Puerto Rico's unspoken but acknowledged pact with Spain: in exchange for loyalty, they would receive protection from any slave rebellion or uprising, with the crown providing arms and soldiers to keep public order, should the need arise. Or so the thinking among white creoles went. They believed that if they made any attempt to gain their independence, there might be another Saint-Domingue. The events in Haiti had cast a long shadow.

For the time being, however, Cuba and Puerto Rico focused on their booming sugar trade. Both islands had received, as thanks for their loyalty, permission from the crown to allow Catholic settlers from Spain and elsewhere to come to the islands, and legislation had provided a number of incentives for them, including parcels of land, assistance in raising capital for agricultural development, and the abolition of some taxes on the 'trade and introduction of Negros in the island'.[1] Abolition of slavery, on the other hand, was a long way off. From 1804 to 1814, 43,982 Africans arrived in Cuba and 809 in Puerto Rico. Over the next six years to 1820, that number had jumped in Cuba to 101,809, while it dropped slightly, to 708, in Puerto Rico.[2] Although Puerto Rico would, like Cuba, turn to sugar and use slaves, it was on a smaller scale, and the numbers on that island did not rise in such a dramatic fashion. In addition, Puerto Rico had an established peasantry, people known as *jíbaros*, who often cultivated coffee in the mountains. Although their existence did not offset the arrival of African slaves, it did mean the labour dynamics on the island were somewhat different from those in Cuba. Overall, this influx of people – slaves and free immigrants – caused further demographic shifts on both islands. By 1827 Cuba had a white population of 311,051 people, 106,494 free people of colour, and 286,942 slaves, making whites about 44 per cent of the population.[3] By 1820, in Puerto Rico there were 102,432 whites, 106,460 free people of colour, and 21,730 slaves.[4] After the dramatic events in Saint-Domingue, there was a growing concern among officials and planters on these islands about the balance within the population between black, coloured and white, and slave and free.

Alongside the increase of slaves in Cuba, the number of sugar mills, or *ingenios*, rose from thirty-seven to ninety-three in the region around Matanzas alone; and going west from Havana, around Guanajay, the number rose from fifty-nine to one hundred and twenty-two during the same years of 1813 to 1817.[5] This was no doubt a factor in Matanzas being the site of the first rebellion of African-born slaves recorded in the nineteenth century. It took place in 1825, and involved around 200 people.[6] Before it was suppressed, some twenty-four estates were burnt down, and fifteen whites and forty-three blacks were killed.[7] And in the same year in Puerto Rico, in the sugar-producing region around Ponce a group of slaves were also arrested for plotting an uprising, though the overall organization of the plans was blamed on 'Haitian agents', confirming Spanish fears in Cuba and Puerto Rico that newly free Haitians would come to their islands and bring plans for inciting rebellion with them.[8]

In Europe, meanwhile, the defeat of Bonaparte in 1815 finally brought peace, while at the same time tilting the power balance in the Caribbean in Britain's favour again. The Congress of Vienna returned Martinique to France, but Britain kept Tobago and St Lucia, which it had captured from the French, and the Dutch territories of Demerara, Essequibo, and Berbice, which would later be merged into British Guiana. For the moment, the chaos was only at Spain's door.

*

The struggle among the Spanish colonies in Latin America was followed closely in the West Indies. Spain's loyal islands were by turns inspired and fearful about what was taking place in nearby Venezuela and New Spain. Plenty of people on the Spanish islands sympathized with the desire to get rid of costly, ineffectual, and restrictive Spanish rule, though not many were yet willing to take action themselves, fearful of the wider consequences. However, the people from one island did far more than simply watch. Haiti had been involved in the republican struggle almost from its inception.

On 2 February 1806 a ship named the *Leander* left New York and sailed towards Haiti carrying Francisco de Miranda, a Venezuelan who had fought in the French Revolution and now had plans to 'liberate' his homeland. Independent Haiti was thought to be a place where the necessary supplies for an uprising could be easily obtained. Indeed, the *Leander* was captained by Thomas Lewis, whose brother Jacob was well known in Haiti as a trader who could easily find guns and ammunition for anyone who expressed an interest.[9] Miranda spent the next six weeks in Haiti planning his expedition, but he never left the southern port of Jacmel.[10] Rumours had already reached Venezuela's shores, and the Spanish islands enlisted a spy to find out more. Madrid began to panic about the 'Haitian danger' and denounced Miranda's plans as a 'virus' – claiming they were part of a wider plot to unleash revolution in all the European colonies in the Americas.[11] Miranda, in the end, was unsuccessful: he instigated a number of expeditions – including one in 1811 – but he was ultimately captured and killed by the Spanish. With regard to the attack he launched from Haiti, however, Miranda would later deny the 'Haitian blacks' ever helped him, even though they were the earliest supporters of his enterprise.[12] But other rebels knew what had happened and continued to ask for help. A few years later, in 1813, Mexican rebel leader Ignacio López Rayón sent one of his colonels to Haiti to establish relations with and ask for assistance from the then leader of the northern part of Haiti, Henri Christophe, though apparently the mission failed. A few years after that, on 31 December 1815, the Venezuelan military leader and later 'liberator' of much of South America, Simón Bolívar, arrived in Port-au-Prince, seeking help from Alexandre Pétion, the southern president, who officially welcomed Bolívar on 2 January 1816.

Pétion was no doubt already aware of Bolívar, who had earlier been forced to flee his struggle in Venezuela for Jamaica, where he had spent the eight months prior to his arrival in Haiti. Bolívar had time while he was in the West Indies and in Haiti to observe and reflect on the situation in the Spanish islands, which left him perplexed. He wrote in his Jamaica 'Letter' of 1815 that 'Puerto Rico and Cuba . . . are the most tranquil possessions of the Spaniards, because they are not within range of contact with the Independents. But are not the people of those islands Americans? Are they not maltreated? Do they not desire a better life?'[13]

While he was in Haiti, he met Francisco Xavier Mina, who was fighting for the independence of Mexico. The two men spent some time together, though Bolívar did not join the Mina mission, as the latter had hoped.[14] Yet the presence of Mina in Haiti points to its ongoing role in aiding the Latin American fight for independence – a role for which it did not often receive due credit. Pétion was willing to help Bolívar with his struggle, though he was adamant that, in exchange, slavery must be abolished in the new republic that Bolívar was trying to establish. Pétion wrote to Bolívar, saying, 'you must be struck by how much I desire to see escape from the yoke of slavery those who still suffer from under it'.[15] Delivering on that promise, however, would give Bolívar more trouble than he anticipated. By March 1816, Bolívar had taken the 6,000 rifles, supplies, and money he had obtained in Haiti and returned to the conflict in Venezuela. By July he and his men landed at Margarita island, off the coast of Venezuela, and launched an attack at Ocumare, where he also issued a proclamation freeing the slaves. However, the operation failed and he was forced, as he later wrote, to 'return to the island of free men and place myself under the protection of the most generous republican leaders in the New World'.[16] He again set out from Haiti in December that year and this time his endeavour was more successful.[17] But when it came time to make good on the promise of emancipation, Bolívar offered the slaves freedom, but with a condition: they must enlist in his cause. He declared: 'There will be no more slaves in Venezuela, except those who wish to remain so. All those who prefer liberty to repose will take up arms to defend their sacred rights and they will be citizens.'[18] And although he freed his own slaves, other landowners were less eager to do so. Pro-slavery groups made sure the issue was not resolved as quickly as Bolívar, or indeed Pétion, would have liked, and slavery continued to be part of the political battle in South America for the following decade.

Around the same time, Spain once again lost Florida, its North American foothold. It had been traded to the British in 1763 after the Seven Years War in exchange for Havana, and won back again in 1783 under the Treaty of Paris that ended the War of American Independence. In the intervening years, US troops and settlers had been encroaching on the territory, and Spain did not have the will or the resources to defend it, especially when the majority of its empire was in revolt. The Spanish were also concerned that the US would start treading on its North American territory, which covered land all the way to the Pacific (from today's Texas to California). Spain and the US entered talks, and agreed that the US could have Florida in exchange for leaving the other North American territory alone. The treaty mapped out the boundaries, and the deal was made final in 1821. The treaty was finalized in the midst of a domestic political upheaval in Spain, a period known as the *trienio liberal* (1820–23). This was another attempt at reforms during which liberal politicians tried to reinstate the 1812 constitution in defiance of the king. The second bout of liberalism, however, did little to slow the disintegration of Spain's empire – already key territories had declared their independence, such as Mexico in 1821. The liberal period came to a violent end when Ferdinand VII decided to implement his royal sovereignty by force, with France invading in 1823 to restore him to the throne.

*

After the decisive republican victory in the Battle of Ayacucho (1824) in Peru, European nations, the United States, and even Russia began to put pressure on Spain to recognize the new Latin American republics, which Ferdinand VII resisted. With international recognition of the new nations stretching from Mexico to Argentina, Bolívar was eager to hold a congress for these republics in Panama (then part of Gran Colombia), sentiments he expressed in 1824 but that would not come to fruition until 1826. In the planning stages, however, they quickly turned into a diplomatic row. Bolívar's aims had widened to include the entire hemisphere, and he wanted to invite not only the United States, but also Haiti, which was a fellow republic. But as he soon found out, not all republics were equal.

In late November 1825 John Adams, the US president, received the invitation.[19] The secretary of state, Henry Clay, replied later that month, saying that the US would send representatives, but they would be observers rather than participants so that the United States could continue to consider its relationship with its neighbours as neutral. A few days later, Adams made a speech to Congress in which he told legislators about the forthcoming event.[20]

What Adams perhaps did not foresee was the great debate the news would generate in the House of Representatives, lasting throughout the first few months of 1826. When it reached the Senate, secret sessions were held to discuss the matter.[21] To defenders of slavery, the issue was clear: Haiti must not be recognized. The question resulted in months of political fighting. The Senate's Foreign Relations Committee was opposed to sending representatives to the Congress of Panama, though in the final vote in the Senate on 15 March it passed by 24 to 19, and the following month the House agreed to give the necessary appropriation with a vote of 134 to 60.[22]

The Congress of Panama convened on 22 June and sat until 15 July 1826, with delegates from Gran Colombia, Mexico, and the United Provinces (today's Guatemala, El Salvador, Nicaragua, Costa Rica, and Honduras). Representatives from Peru also attended, though there were none from Chile or Argentina. The US delegates, in the end, did not attend; one of the two representatives, Richard Anderson, had died on his way there, and the other, John Sergeant, finally arrived on 24 July, well after it had finished.[23] Clay had earlier sent them instructions on the Haiti question, saying, 'It will probably be proposed, as a fit subject of consideration for the powers represented at Panama, whether Hayti ought to be recognized by them as an independent State . . . The President is not prepared now to say that Hayti ought to be recognized as an independent sovereign power.'[24]

Haiti – eager for recognition of its statehood – never received an invitation.

*

Perched atop Haiti's Bonnet à l'Évêque mountain in the north, with rolling green hills below, sits the Citadelle La Ferrière, some 910m (3,000ft) above sea level. Far enough inland to see any invaders and high enough to have the tactical advantage from all sides, this fortress was built by an estimated 20,000 men beginning in 1806 and accelerated under the watchful eye of Henri Christophe, who, by 1811, had styled himself King Henri I of Haiti and was thorough about the creation of his kingdom: he also established an accompanying court and nobility, granting titles such as baron or duke to supporters, and he had a coat of arms designed for each title he bestowed. Pétion, for his part, had declared the south a republic.

While the republican battles were waging across Spanish America, Henri had been putting the final touches to the fortress, its thick walls, high ramparts, and hundreds of cannons finally complete in 1819. A few miles down the steep, winding road from the fortress was an elaborate structure near the village of Milot. This, too, had been the work of Christophe, or more accurately his thousands of labourers. He wanted a home to rival the palaces of Europe, and so, between 1807 and 1813, the palace of Sans-Souci (meaning 'without worry') was built. Indeed, he lavished money on it as if there were no worries; the palace was said to have the finest furnishings. Impressing Europeans was crucial to Christophe, and while in establishing a northern Haitian monarchy he bestowed titles, he was actually trying to bestow legitimacy on his fledgling nation. Pétion pursued a different course, giving his troops land and allowing a small-holder peasant society to develop in the south, while Christophe's plans relied on the continuation of plantations. The two men agreed only about fighting for the abolition of slavery, wherever they could. For Pétion this meant aiding republicans like Bolívar; for Christophe it was making alliances within the European abolitionist movement.

Christophe's plans were not cheap. The sugar produced under the final years of Louverture's governorship had dwindled to almost nothing, and Christophe was eager to turn this around. He did so by using a system he already knew: the plantation. So rather than dividing up all the land, he allowed some of his military chiefs and other allies to run large plantations. The difference was that they had to pay taxes and give a salary to their workers.[25]

To these ends, he introduced the Code Henri in 1812, which outlined laws and land use. That such a thing was produced by a former slave made him an object of admiration, if not curiosity as well, in Europe, and he corresponded with abolitionist Thomas Clarkson, who wrote in a letter to an acquaintance about the king of Haiti, that:

> we . . . have good reason to esteem his talents and his virtues, and to be assured that he will be ranked by posterity, not only among the best of kings, but among the benefactors of mankind. It must be confessed to be no ordinary task to civilize a barbarous people. That is, to bring them by degrees from ignorance to knowledge, or from slavery to rational freedom. Such however is the burden which Henry the 1st has imposed upon himself; and his success has been already so great as to leave no doubt that in a few years he will accomplish this glorious end.[26]

But Christophe also had a secret weapon in his campaign: good public relations. He had hired black American Prince Saunders, who had visited the island and was enthusiastic about its prospects. Born in 1775 in Lebanon, Connecticut, Saunders became a landowner and teacher in New England. He married the daughter of Paul Cuffee, a Massachusetts merchant who ran an early colonization scheme to take black Americans to Africa. Saunders helped Cuffee with the scheme and in 1815 accompanied him to England, where they were introduced to William Wilberforce, who convinced Saunders he ought to contact King Henri Christophe in Haiti.[27] Christophe was keen to have black people help him run his kingdom. The resentment between blacks and mulattos had continued, and Christophe was opposed to having a staff of lighter-skinned Haitians – one of the reasons for his antipathy towards Pétion, who had been educated in Paris and exemplified the supposed privilege of mulatto rule.[28]

Saunders and Christophe met in February 1816, and Saunders was then sent to England, where he published his *Haytian Papers*, in which he set the radical legislation of the kingdom of Haiti 'before the British people generally, in order to give them some more correct information with respect to the enlightened systems of policy, the pacific spirit, the altogether domestic views, and liberal principles of the Government'.[29] Indeed, Saunders had calculated that the abolitionist public would be receptive to the changes in Haiti. *Haytian Papers* included some of Christophe's correspondence from his time serving under Louverture and some letters from the period of the fight against Leclerc. Other sections included the 'narrative of the accession of their royal majesties to the Throne of Hayti', and an outline of the Code Henri.

When Saunders returned to the island in 1816 he brought with him two teachers charged with setting up schools, and Clarkson and Christophe exchanged letters about the importance of education in his kingdom. During his time under Christophe, Saunders also promoted the Anglican faith. He was sent again to England, where he mingled with some of the highest echelons of London society.[30] He later travelled to the United States and spoke in Boston around 1818 about Haiti as a destination for free black people, one of its advantages being its proximity, in contrast to the more distant African schemes such as the one his father-in-law had been organizing.[31] Saunders returned in 1820 to northern Haiti with the letters of eager migrants, enthralled by his descriptions and ready to try life on the island. He persuaded Christophe to pay $25,000 to bring black Americans to the northern Kingdom of Haiti, but the plan never materialized. Christophe suffered a stroke in August which left him paralysed physically as well as politically, and his enemies were quick to get out their knives. On 8 October 1820 he shot himself – some accounts say with a gold bullet, some say with silver – and died, and his wife and daughters fled into exile.

Jean-Pierre Boyer, a supporter and aide of Pétion, who lived in the southern Republic of Haiti, wanted to see the island reunited, and took the first step towards that goal by taking control of the south after Pétion died in 1818. After Christophe's death he sent troops into the north and the country was at last reunited. But the psychological scars would not easily heal. The years of division between Christophe and Pétion are, like the struggle between Louverture and Rigaud, often seen as black versus mulatto, but neither the dispute nor its ramifications are entirely clear. The historian Laurent Dubois has pointed out that their greatest difference was actually over land. Christophe believed that the country's prosperity depended upon the plantations, while Pétion parcelled out the former planters' land. And his successors continued to pursue that policy. In addition to questions over land distribution, Boyer also was concerned about foreign affairs, not least the possibility of Europeans invading the island. He was especially irritated that the ports on the Spanish side of the island were so easy to infiltrate. And there was also the ongoing annoyance of Saunders, who tried to press Boyer into continuing with the settlement plans, but was rebuffed and returned temporarily to the United States in July 1821.[32]

After the unification of Haiti under Boyer was complete, the Spanish governor, Sebastián Kindelán, was aware that the Haitian leader might have the east of the island in his sights. Kindelán had been an official in Santiago de Cuba, but had now come to Santo Domingo. He heard that an agent from Haiti named Dezir Dalmassi had been sent on a mission to lure black people living on the Spanish side of the island to Haiti, although the mission's real purpose often depended on who was speaking about it. By December of 1820 Dalmassi's mission extended well beyond the border area where there were reports of recruitment and plotting, and Kindelán's annoyance with Haiti began to grow.

Letters were exchanged, and Boyer calmly replied, 'If I had wanted to listen to the unfounded insinuations, to complaints, and I'll say it now, to disturb the Spanish part, I would have done it a long time ago . . . I desire no other titles than that of consoler and pacifier of the oppressed, and that my sword will never lead armies to bloody conquests.'[33] Kindelán was not reassured by this, and he wrote to Madrid to say so. He soon was dispatched again to Cuba, however, and so could only hear about the dramatic events that followed.

Santo Domingo's elites had finally had enough of Spain. The loyalism of 1808 had expired – the island had received little attention or support from Spain. Inspired by Bolívar, one creole, José Núñez de Cáceres, decided to declare the island's independence. His plan was to form an alliance with what was then known as Gran Colombia, a country set up by Bolívar, which lasted from 1819 to 1830, and comprised parts of modern-day Colombia, Venezuela, Panama, and Ecuador. With a cry of ¡Viva la patria, viva la independencia, viva la unión de Colombia! he tried to join this new republic.[34] The only hitch in the plan was that Bolívar was unable, or unwilling, to help him. The conspiracy was forced to turn in a different direction: towards Haiti. On 1 December 1821, it was declared that Santo Domingo would be the 'Estado independiente de la parte Española de Haiti', or the 'Independent state of Spanish Haiti', and with that the creole conspirators walked right into Boyer's hands. Although Boyer, like his predecessors, thought the Dominicans poor and backward, he wanted to secure the whole island. The Spanish creoles, left to themselves, might make a deal with a European power so there was a great deal of appeal to a unified island under his control.

At first Núñez de Cáceres tried to resist an actual unification, but Boyer had 12,000 troops; his fears of a French invasion meant the country had remained heavily militarized. By 9 February 1822, Boyer had consolidated power, as Louverture had done in 1801, but for Haiti rather than France. And, for the second time, slavery was abolished. More Spanish creoles left the island, while Boyer tried to reform the often informal and often baffling land tenure system on that side of the island, in order to cut back on cattle raising and encourage agriculture. He abolished commonly held land, and in doing so he was following in the overgrown footpath that Louverture had originally cut, and like Louverture he faced some resistance to change. Europe and the neighbouring islands watched these developments with interest, worried that this new leader might try to spread Haiti's emancipation through invasion. But by 1825 the island would face one more challenge – debt. France finally agreed to recognize Haiti, but at a price of 150 million francs, or around $30 million, an enormous sum of money at the time, and twice what the US had paid France for the Louisiana territory.[35] But no price was too high, and Boyer began to pay what he could.

Not long after Boyer had brought the island together, he was approached by an American minister, Loring Daniel Dewey. Dewey contacted Boyer to see if he would be amenable to receiving a few thousand African-American immigrants, and the president replied with enthusiasm, saying that 'I have prepared for the children of Africa, coming out of the United States, all that can assure them of an honourable existence in becoming citizens of the Haytien Republic.'[36] Boyer pledged land, and opportunity, and help with paying for the passage. Saunders by this point had reappeared, and though his relationship with Boyer was rocky at first, he eventually joined the government as attorney general, a post he held until his death in Port-au-Prince in 1839.[37]

That same year, John Candler left from Britain to work as a missionary in Jamaica. His ship called at Barbados, Martinique, Tortola, St Thomas, and Puerto Rico before sailing past Haiti. Candler noted that along the northern shore, there were no signs of life in the 'dark retreating bay' and it 'presented a picture of gloom and grandeur', piquing his interest.[38] Candler called at Cap Haïtien though only stayed

for a couple of hours, but he was sufficiently intrigued to return a year
later, arriving on 1 January 1841, the thirty-seventh anniversary of
independence. Candler was one of a small number of foreigners who
not only visited Haiti during this period but also wrote about it, and
though his impressions may be more hopeful than truthful – as a
missionary and abolitionist he might have been inclined towards optimism – they give some idea of the state of the island.

One of his most vivid accounts was of a night-time journey to
Sans-Souci, which took him out of the city and into the world of the
peasants, who were then, as now, the backbone of the nation. A few
miles out of the city he 'met a curious group of country people in
carts, and with horses and asses loaded with yams, plantains, and sweet
potatoes . . . they were bivouacking by fire-light, sipping coffee, and
waiting for the hour when the city gate should be thrown open . . . We
passed by the massive gateways of many deserted or neglected sugar
estates, where the mansions that once adorned them, are now crumbling and in ruins.'[39] Candler noted that Haitian peasants 'work to live,
as without some labour they cannot subsist; but they do not, and they
will not work hard to please anybody, and hence agriculture languishes,
and commerce is stationary'.[40] What he was witnessing was not lazy
labourers, a common post-emancipation charge against former slaves,
but an active resistance. By choosing whether or not to work, a choice
many of the surviving former slaves had not had until 1804, they were
asserting their personal autonomy.

Later in his trip, Candler had an audience with Boyer, observing
the general had 'the polish of France . . . During the interview of half
an hour, with which he kindly favored me, he made particular inquiries
after the venerable [Thomas] Clarkson; with whose character . . . he
was well-acquainted.'[41] His book also described the overall situation
on the island: that the number of troops in the standing army was
25,000; that Roman Catholicism was recognized by law, but there
was tolerance of other branches of Christianity, that the dominant
crop was coffee, with more than £800,000 worth exported – he
surmised that output was about 12 million pounds less than before
the revolution. Sugar, however, was almost non-existent. He also
mentioned the enormous debt Haiti owed France. By 1828, millions
of francs had been paid – in coffee or cash – but the balance was still

120 million francs.[42] Candler understood that such a vast sum had exhausted the treasury of the young republic.

*

In Cuba throughout the 1820s slavery continued and increasing numbers of slaves were brought to the island to work on its sugar plantations. The growth in the black population led the authorities to intensify the existing regime of surveillance on and oppression of all people of colour, while at the same time watching for incursions from their neighbours. The United States, for the moment, could also be added to this growing list of potential dangers. With Spain exhausted from trying to hold on to its other American colonies, Cuba was left vulnerable, to say nothing of the forces a popular uprising against the Spanish would unleash. John Quincy Adams, the US secretary of state at the time, was in no doubt about Cuba's value, writing in 1823:

> Such indeed are, between the interests of that island [Cuba] and of this country, the geographical, commercial, moral, and political relations, formed by nature, gathering in the process of time, and even now verging to maturity, that in looking forward to the probable course of events for the short period of half a century, it is scarcely possible to resist the conviction that the annexation of Cuba to our federal republic will be indispensable to the continuance and integrity of the Union itself. It is obvious however that for this event we are not yet prepared.[43]

Adams, like many people in Cuba, thought any attempt at independence on that island could trigger a race war, as it had done in Haiti, observing that 'were the population of the island of one blood and colour, there could be no doubt of hesitation with regard to the course which they would pursue' – that of independence.[44] These remarks were part of a wider political shift under way in the western hemisphere. The United States had grown increasingly exasperated with the ongoing European hostilities so near its own expanding empire, especially the Latin American republics fighting to free themselves from Spanish rule. In 1823 President James Monroe articulated this – later known as the 'Monroe Doctrine' – in his annual address to Congress saying, 'the American continents, by the free and independent condition which they have assumed and maintain, are henceforth not to be considered

as subjects for future colonisation by any European powers . . .'[45] Less
than a century into its own independence, the United States had been
quick to realize its regional power, and act upon it.

There were conspiracies in Cuba, and one particularly serious plot
had shaken the Spanish officials. Masonic associations had had an
important role in the organization of the American and French revolutions, and they played a part here, too. The Soles y Rayos de Bolívar
– the Suns and Rays of Bolivar – was uncovered around 1823. Many
of its members were sympathetic to independence, and the organizers
were the Colombian José Fernández Madrid, the Cuban José Francisco
Lemus, who had been in the service of the Colombian army, and the
Haitian Sévère Courtois, who had been an officer in the Colombian
navy. They wanted to establish the island as the Republic of Cuba-
nacán.[46] Lemus infiltrated Masonic groups and established a network
of supporters, ranging from free people of colour to members of the
creole elites frustrated with the restrictions of Spanish rule. Plans
spread through lodges up and down the island, from Matanzas to
Camagüey to Villa Clara. Lemus even started a rumour that the island
had been sold to the British. Soon after the latest Spanish captain-
general, Francisco Dionisio Vives, arrived in April 1823, he heard about
the conspiracy, including its plans to free any slaves who supported it.
He was quick to infiltrate the network and declare martial law 'to
contain the horrors with which this rebellion threatens'. Lemus was
arrested in August, and around 600 people were jailed.[47]

Although many creole elites had participated in the conspiracy,
others had been far more wary. On paper, Cuba was rich and powerful
enough to stand alone, like Mexico, or Peru. Yet, unlike those countries,
Cuba held hundreds of thousands (compared with tens of thousands,
if that) in human bondage, not to mention thousands of people of
colour who faced discrimination. The north of Haiti and the south of
Cuba were only a few hours' sail from each other. Sugar planters and
government officials had seen what had happened in Haiti in the
pursuit of liberty and racial equality, and, after the temporary loss of
a king and two liberal reformist eras, Cuba's wealthy conservative
regime continued to think that their 'colonial pact' was preferable.[48]

A little later, around the time of the Congress of Panama in early
1826, two Cuban conspirators, Francisco Agüero and Manuel Andrés
Sánchez, who had been in exile in Mexico, returned to Cuba to lead

another bid at independence. There had been rumours that troops from Colombia or Mexico were going to 'liberate' the island. With the congress as a distraction, the two men thought the timing was opportune. They were unsuccessful, imprisoned and later hanged.[49] The rumour mill kept churning, including a story that there was going to be an attack from Mexico on Manila, then a Spanish colony, to distract attention from attempts to free Cuba.[50] The United States was being watched as well, and, in a letter to the US minister to Mexico, the US secretary of state Henry Clay explained, 'The United States have no desire to aggrandize themselves by the acquisition of Cuba. And yet if that Island is to be made a dependence of any one of the American States, it is impossible not to allow that the law of its position proclaims that it should be attached to the United States.'[51]

In 1820 the British traveller Robert Jameson also spent time in Cuba, and upon his return he published an edited account of his trip. In it, he made his view on slavery very clear: 'The European farmer finds that the best manure is composed of the most offensive materials; – so does the West India planter – he spreads his fields with orphans and captives, and expects to find his harvests prosperous in proportion to the mass of misery he has heaped together.'[52] He believed that fear was the glue holding the island together, observing 'this mass of beings is forcibly conjoined – their bond of union is a *real chain*'.[53] Cuba was not alone in its continued use of slaves. The British, French, Danish and Dutch islands continued to use slave labour, but the British began to pressure France and Spain into agreements to stop transporting slaves, and although France passed a law in 1815 and Spain signed an agreement with Britain in 1820, neither enforced the legislation for decades. Indeed, Spain agreed to stop slaving only in the South Atlantic. As a result, for the next forty years, Britain would send anti-slaving squadrons to patrol the waters, claiming the right to stop and search any suspicious vessels.

Despite the British abolition of slave trading, in the early years after the bill was passed slaves could still be moved between colonies to satisfy planter claims of a labour shortage; between 1808 and 1812, some 7,500 slaves were transferred to Guiana, and 3,800 to Trinidad between 1813 and 1821.[54] This caused a controversy in the latter, because even though the British had taken Trinidad from Spain in 1797, they had not changed the legal system, which permitted slavery and the slave trade, but by 1810 that position had become untenable.[55] There was concern that should British law come into effect, and a legislative assembly be elected, they would want to continue slavery, whereas there was now an opportunity to stop it altogether in one colony. But it did not happen. In 1812 it was decided that all the slaves would have to be registered to stop smuggling. The results in 1813 showed that there were 25,717 slaves, with 8,633 being 'personal' and 17,084 on the plantations of Trinidad. This was a rise of 4,489 since the previous count in 1811, though there was confusion over the order and more than likely others were not counted.[56] The British-controlled Guiana territories, meanwhile, grew in total population from 31,000 colonial settlers in 1782 to 102,000 in 1812, while in the same period the colonial population of Suriname dropped from 60,000 to around 50,000. Meanwhile, before the slave trade ended, at least 123,694 Africans were imported to those colonies from 1782 to 1808.[57]

The struggle for freedom continued on the British islands, and there was a growing awareness that with the abolition of the slave trade, a corner had been turned for slaves, and pressure on the British islands and in London began to mount. In 1816 Barbados was gripped by a potentially explosive rebellion, surprising the planters because there had been no significant uprising on the island since 1702. It occurred on Easter Sunday 1816. It was well planned and it spread to seventy estates throughout the south-east of the island before being suppressed. One hundred and forty-four people were executed and 170 deported, and many others were punished.[58]

The rebellion arose following a misunderstanding over a bill aimed at changing slave conditions. The slaves thought they were to be emancipated by Parliament under the Imperial Registry Bill of 1815, which had been drafted in response to the confusion over slavery in Trinidad. It was backed by William Wilberforce, whose name was well known throughout the island. Planters were worried that the bill, which aimed to prevent smuggling by registering slaves to territory so they could not be moved, might pave the way for emancipation. When details of the legislation reached Barbados, they were transformed by word of mouth into an emancipation rumour.

During the unrest, some slaves thought soldiers from Haiti were going to arrive and help them fight the planters. Yet according to later testimony, many slaves were vague about this, some even referring to the island from which the soldiers were coming as 'Mingo' (short for Santo Domingo), rather than Haiti, a name that had been in use for more than a decade at this point.[59] Even so, that would have been of little reassurance to the nervous planters. It would be another fifteen years before more urgent action on slave emancipation would be taken, and the catalyst would come from the Caribbean rather than London. In September 1831, a plot on the island of Tortola was foiled in which the slaves had allegedly planned to murder the white men, take their vessels, and kidnap their wives, setting sail for Haiti.[60] A few months later, another plot was organized, which came to fruition before it could be uncovered. A slave named Sam Sharpe who lived near Montego Bay had a radical plan to obtain freedom for the slaves of Jamaica. Sharpe was also a leader in the Baptist Church. Like many others, he had heard white colonists discussing legislative matters in London pertaining to the improvement of conditions for slaves and their possible emancipation. This germ of information passed from person to person until a rumour grew that the slaves had been freed but that the planters were withholding the news. Sharpe decided that if slaves would just stop working until they were paid, the problem would be solved. If the planters relented and paid them, it meant they were no longer slaves, but free labourers. And if the rumours were true, then the military would protect them.

But it turned out the rumours were just that. However, Sharpe also had a back-up plan: an armed uprising. Two days after Christmas in 1831, slaves in the north-west parish of St James stopped working. Within the space of two weeks, thousands of slaves had begun to destroy sugar plantations and fields in what was later called the Baptist War (as well as the Christmas Rebellion). Whites and blacks alike were killed, and the military eventually stepped in to stop the fighting. Around 500 participants – including Sharpe – were executed. Some planters blamed the missionaries, and attacked their churches. The whole situation galvanized sentiment in London against the practice of slavery and in 1833 the Slavery Abolition Act was passed and came into force on 1 August 1834. But it was not instant liberty – the act provided a transition period of four years during which slaves were 'apprenticed' – they would work most of the week without pay and get a fraction of pay for the remainder of the time they worked. Planters, meanwhile, shared a compensation pot of £20 million.[61]

The Jewish-Jamaican artist Isaac Mendes Belisario had returned to the island around the time of emancipation, and his paintings and drawings provide a visual record of Jamaican life among the slaves during this period of transition. He had a particular interest in what he called the 'Christmas Amusements' – but, after the rebellion of 1831, this became a time of year loaded with wider significance. Christmas tradition had for decades involved people of colour dressing up in elaborate costumes, putting on symbolic masquerades, and playing musical instruments, including drum and fife. In 1837 Belisario published his three-part *Sketches of Character*, which were coloured lithographs intended for a wide audience. They depict black men in elaborate Jonkonnu (also, John Canoe) costumes, which could take on a variety of forms, such as a devil mask or a cow's head, and which merged African and European symbols and influences. One of Belisario's plates, 'Jaw Bone or House John-Canoe', shows a man in brightly striped trousers, and a red jacket with a face behind a white mask and a wig of long brown curls – though his hands remain black – holding a model of a plantation house on his head. In his collection there was also 'Queen or Maam of the Set Girls', an image of a black woman in a red-and-white striped dress, embellished with ribbons and roses, holding a whip. The costumes were meant to subvert the social hierarchy – black men dressed as European actors; black women called 'queens' wielding an overseer's whip. Through the apprenticeship period, whites became increasingly nervous about these subversive masquerades, worried that they might augur another violent uprising.[62] Belisario's landscape paintings, however, offer a vision of tranquillity and calm. His *View of Kelly's Estate* shows free workers peacefully tending to cattle, while other farm animals graze, with the plantation house in the distance, giving the impression of a smooth transition. But that was not necessarily the case – many former slaves stopped working on plantations and instead squatted on land and grew only what they needed to survive or could sell at the marketplace.

Apart from the growing awareness, especially after the Baptist War, that the slave regime was untenable, there was an economic element to the end of slavery. The cost of sugar production had risen sharply on the British islands. According to historian Selwyn Carrington, by 1787 the cost of producing a hundredweight of sugar was 75 per cent more than it had been fifty years earlier, and the price of slaves had risen by 140 per cent. And by 1806, the price paid in London for sugar was down 75 per cent on the 1793 price.[63] Abolition saw a decrease in the slave population too. The US market had no incentive to trade with the British islands after 1776 – and indeed were prohibited from so doing in the early years of independence – and had turned to Cuba instead. Planters were often heavily indebted, and some had to simply walk away from their plantations because they could no longer afford to run them. For instance, Jamaica's sugar exports throughout most of the nineteenth century were around 20,000 tons a year – down from a peak of nearly 100,000 tons in 1800.[64] Beet sugar by this point had also entered the European sugar market, and in Britain this, coupled with an end to protectionist tariffs, pushed Caribbean cane sugar further into decline. Sugar was also now imported from the Indian Ocean island of Mauritius, which Britain had taken from France during the Napoleonic Wars.

Britain was not alone in its decision to free its slaves, and from the 1830s onwards abolition slowly spread across the West Indies, and hundreds of thousands of people were emancipated. In some places there were changes in the law which allowed for a gradual emancipation based on birth, slowly giving rise to more free people of colour, for instance in the new republics of Venezuela and Colombia on the Caribbean coast. Laws enacted in 1821 banned the importation of slaves and decreed children would be born free, though they would have to work for their mothers' masters until they were eighteen years old without pay. While technically emancipation, it was hardly an unlimited freedom. However, the number of slaves along the Caribbean coast dropped from around 14,000 in 1770 to 6,827 by 1835.[65] Throughout this period, many people bought their freedom, and Caribbean port cities such as Cartagena had large numbers of free people of colour who, like their counterparts elsewhere on the islands, took up employment in a variety of important trades. During and after the wars of independence, this group, labelled generally as *pardos*, began to try to claim a stake in the societies that were taking shape. But there was much resistance from whites, and fears about free people of colour were often linked to Haiti. For instance, in the town of Mompox, near Cartagena, anonymous threats emerged in 1823, at a time of much political uncertainty, that whites would be chopped up with machetes, as had happened in Saint-Domingue. Other rumours emerged around the same time that Haitian agents were being sent to Venezuela to destabilize the regime, and two alleged plots to murder whites were uncovered.[66]

The end of slavery in the Danish islands was also not straightforward. The Danes abolished slavery in 1847, making all children born after 28 July of that year free but implementing a twelve-year grace period for all other slaves. On 3 July 1848, some 2,000 armed slaves in St Croix marched up to the fort in Frederiksted and demanded their immediate freedom. The officer on duty told them he could not permit that, so they began to attack.[67] They threatened to burn down the town if their demands were not met by that afternoon. When the governor general, Peter von Scholten, arrived on the scene, he granted their request 'to the amazement of the officers and citizens', as one contemporary account noted.[68] However, fires soon sprang up everywhere, and the unrest continued when it was revealed that the governor might have been lying. Two days later the authorities had arrested the leader, a slave named Buddoe, and others, who were shot. But many slaves refused to return to work until they had been given their freedom.

The other slave-owning European countries began to abolish the practice in the middle and later decades of the nineteenth century, as slavery was increasingly seen as out of step with the growing liberalism in Europe as exemplified by Britain's Reform Act 1832, or the numerous liberal revolutions in 1848. At the same time, rebellions such as that in Jamaica in 1831 made clear that slaves were aware of what was happening and willing to back up their demands for freedom with force. Sweden abolished slavery in 1847, France in 1848, and the Netherlands in 1863. The Central American nations (1824) and Mexico (1829) ended slavery earlier on, and were later joined by Colombia (1851), Venezuela (1854), and the other American republics. Spain, however, was still some way from joining them. Indeed, Cuba and the Caribbean spent the 1850s and 1860s grappling with US expansionists who wanted to bring slavery from the South into the islands.

*

By the 1840s the question of slavery in the US had reached a critical point. North Americans had expanded into western territories, especially after the US war against Mexico (1846–48), and others had gone south into northern Florida. The president from 1845 to 1849, James K. Polk, was a Southerner and an expansionist. Around this time, too, some in Cuba – often wealthy landowners who feared a slave uprising – were in favour of a closer alliance, if not direct annexation, to the United States. As a result, in 1848 Polk ordered an offer of $100 million – or around $3 billion today – to be made to Spain for the purchase of Cuba; Spain, after some deliberation, turned it down.[69]

Some expatriate Cubans tried to put the island's future into their own hands. One such was Narciso López. Born in Venezuela to a wealthy planter family, López had climbed the official ranks in Spain and Cuba. However, his fortunes turned and his career stalled, and he decided to join Cuba's growing anti-Spanish movement. In 1848 he moved to the US, where he could work on his plans to free Cuba from Spain. It proved to be a receptive environment – in the nineteenth century some seventy newspapers were published by Cuban exiles in the US, focusing on independence or annexation.[70] Other US newspapers jumped into the debate as well. For instance, the *Herald* pointed out how the 'agricultural and mineral wealth of Cuba were without precedent . . . notwithstanding . . . its inhabitants were wretched and impoverished to an indescribable degree, in consequence of the despotic and oppressively exacting character of its government'.[71] A rival paper, the *Sun,* called for the island to be a free republic and raised the 'free flag of Cuba' in front of its offices while a band of exiles and musicians marched through New York City.[72]

A rumour emerged from the 'Cuban *junta*' living in exile that the island would be liberated and annexed to the United States. This council was said to be enlisting agents from around the US, including Florida and New Orleans, in order to launch an invasion, which was to be led by López.[73] On 15 May 1850, 600 men under López's command left the Isla de Mujeres, off the coast of Cancún, and headed almost directly west of Cuba. But they sailed instead along the north coast, past Havana, landing in Cárdenas on the morning of 19 May. Spanish troops were not slow in arriving, and battle commenced. The rebels defeated the troops, hoisted the free flag of Cuba, and declared the town liberated. López unveiled a proclamation to 'Soldiers of the Liberating Expedition to Cuba!' promising the island would 'add another glorious Star to the banner which already waves, to the admiration of the whole world'.[74] Their next target was the sugar town of Matanzas, outside Havana. But López had one unforeseen problem: the locals were less receptive, probably because of the high number of sugar plantations in the area. Fearing that any change to Spanish rule might lead to a Haitian-style uprising, many chose the status quo. López's men were getting restless, coming to the uncomfortable realization that rumours of creole support for revolt were not quite true. They soon retreated to Key West, Florida.

To add to the drama, López was arrested in Savannah on 27 May and charged with leading an illegal expedition under the US Neutrality Act of 1818, though the charges were later dropped. He continued apace, travelling throughout the United States to raise money and support, and many Cubans wrote to him, reinvigorating his enthusiasm. For his next expedition, the plan was to target the town of Puerto del Príncipe (today's Camagüey), further south along the coast than Cárdenas, and inland. López had heard that there was an uprising in that region, and while he was preparing to move out on the steamer *Pampero*, with 400 men, he was informed that it was a full raging battle. In an effort to avoid Spanish troops, which he thought had been sent to stop the rebels, he decided to skip Puerto del Príncipe and go to Bahía Honda, near Havana, which turned out to be an unwise decision. López was forced to hide in the forest after some of his party were arrested and executed. He was finally caught – a coffee planter who took him and his starving men in for food and rest had betrayed them. Under the orders of Captain General José de la Concha, López was executed.

A few years later, in 1853, the United States, under President Franklin Pierce, once more tried to buy the island, offering $100 million, but was again refused.[75] By 1854, a communiqué between US diplomats had been leaked, claiming that if Spain did not want to sell the island, the United States had the right to seize it. This 'Ostend manifesto', as it became known, sparked a public outcry in the United States, inflaming tensions between the North and South, but the island was not taken. Many Cubans, for their part, were tired of propping up Spain's flagging economy through the high tariffs they were forced to pay. The planters and merchants were not making much money from the mother country anyway – the real fortunes came from trade with the United States. Throughout this period, there was growing public sentiment to press for independence whatever the consequences, but that battle was still some way off.

*

A small cemetery sits on the outskirts of the coastal Honduran town of Trujillo, behind a low, white wall. Tropical vegetation overruns old stone crosses, and vines hang from trees, above cracked gravestones. Amid the graves is one framed by a low, white rectangular iron fence, itself surrounded by a neat landscaping of purple and white flowers and small bushes. The plain tombstone bears only the words: 'William Walker, Fusilado, 12 Septiembre 1860'. William Walker, Shot by firing squad, 12 September 1860.

No one embodies the period of the short-lived wars known as 'filibusters' like Walker. The word filibuster comes from the pirate terminology of the seventeenth century, and in this more modern incarnation it described a type of land pirate, or an adventurer who takes what he wants by force, in this case claiming territory for the US but acting outside the auspices of official sanction.[76] Although the filibustering enterprise was linked with the question of Cuba, it could be found on the fringes of the expanding US empire, anywhere that national boundaries were thought to be open to interpretation. Although López, acting independently, was also considered a 'filibuster', many of the men who participated in these other adventures did not share his motivation to free Cuba; instead they pushed west. Some were adventurers seeking their fortunes, others were interested in expanding slavery. Indeed, Walker – nicknamed the 'grey-eyed man of destiny' – followed this trail to California. Walker was born in the state of Tennessee in 1824. By the 1840s he had given up life as a doctor in Nashville and, later, a journalist in New Orleans – where he wrote editorials attacking López's expeditions – to work at a newspaper in San Francisco during the California gold rush.[77] By 1854, he appeared to have changed his mind about the merits of filibustering, and he and around fifty men attacked the Sonora area of northern Mexico, where he proclaimed himself president of Lower California. It did not last long, and Mexican troops ran them out. But Walker had now acquired a taste for adventure.

While Walker was out west, the industrialist Cornelius Vanderbilt was working on a scheme for transoceanic steam travel.[78] The steam part was in place – ships were using the technology. But crossing from the Atlantic to the Pacific by ship was still not possible without going around South America. By 1848 France had been in talks with Nicaraguan leaders about building a canal, and indeed decades later they would start work on the famed Suez Canal project in Egypt. At that point nothing came of their plans. The gold rush in California changed the impetus. Thousands of impatient would-be miners wanted to make a quicker crossing, but for the time being they had to sail to Panama, cross by land, then sail up the Pacific coast to San Francisco. Vanderbilt knew that providing a way for shipping to cross the isthmus would be profitable, and a direct steamer could be a quicker route than going over land. After studying maps of the region, Vanderbilt decided to use the network of rivers leading in and out of Lake Nicaragua, and by 1851, after some fits and starts, a service was successfully running, cutting valuable time off the usual journey, which could take weeks. Around the same time, in 1850 construction had begun on a railway line across the isthmus by the US Panama Railroad Company. The work started at the peak of the wet season; the nightmarish logistics of such a project were unimaginable to its organizers. All the equipment had to be imported, as did willing workers. If disease did not kill them, the dangerous conditions did. Still, thousands of people signed up – Irish, Chinese and West Indian. By 1852 Jamaicans and other islanders had come to Panama to work on the railway, and many of them stayed, even after the forty-seven-mile track between Colón on the Caribbean and Panama City on the Pacific was finally opened for business in January 1855.

As gold prospectors looked west, Walker turned south. He had heard that a civil war was looming in Nicaragua between the incumbent conservative Legitimistas and the liberal Democraticos, and he was eager to intervene, setting off with sixty men in May 1855. Nicaragua had become independent in 1821 and, along with the other Central American republics, set up the United Provinces of Central America, a union that disbanded by 1838. Both parties wanted control of Vanderbilt's lucrative enterprise, and Walker too tried to double-cross the tycoon with a plan to seize the company. The sporadic and often confused conflict came to a decisive end at the then-capital, Granada, and by June 1856 Walker, with the support of the Democraticos, was the self-proclaimed president of the country. He made English an official language, issued bonds, scrapped duties, and confiscated property. Although slavery was still in force in the United States, it had been prohibited in Nicaragua. Walker was accused of reintroducing it when he reversed the 1838 ratification of this law, an action which, although it did not technically legalize slavery, gave the appearance to his southern US slaveholding supporters that the door was open – but this move also made him more enemies.[79] Walker was not president for long, as Costa Rica, El Salvador, Guatemala, and Honduras all opposed him, as did Vanderbilt – who procured soldiers of fortune to oust him after their dealings turned sour when Walker tried to seize Vanderbilt's company. He eventually surrendered and returned to the US in 1857, to a hero's welcome. His exploits and the breathless news reports about them had made him a celebrity – when he arrived in New York City later that year, his reception 'was like that of a conqueror . . . tens of thousands of citizens flocked to see the hero'.[80] Walker, however, could not stay away from the region, and he continued to intervene in Central American affairs, which ultimately cost him his life. An attempt to meddle in Honduran political affairs ended with his execution and burial in the quiet cemetery on the edge of Trujillo.

*

Eventually, the US had to face the issue of slavery on American soil, and the age of the filibusterer faded as the country marched toward its Civil War (1861–65). After the Union victory, some supporters and soldiers of the Confederacy hoped to continue the plantation system and considered schemes in the Caribbean. For instance, Charles Swett went to Belize, or British Honduras, in 1868. Although Britain had abolished slavery, it was eager to recruit settlers who were willing to try to re-establish plantations, albeit with free labour. For Southerners it was a way of getting out of the war-torn US and away from the progressive policies of the Reconstruction era.[81] Swett travelled from Warren County, Mississippi, to New Orleans and then onward by steamer in late December 1867. Aboard the vessel Swett found 'many gentlemen from Louisiana, Arkansas, Mississippi and from other Southern States, who, before the war were in affluent circum-stances . . . [who] now express their willingness to do, as far as they are able, whatever may be necessary to enable them to make a support for themselves'. They reached Belize on 5 January. Suffering biting sand flies, Swett and others journeyed into the hinterland, visiting a Miskito village. They also saw aspects of the mahogany trade, and went to Omoa and San Pedro Sula, in Honduran territory. At the end, Swett concluded that 'whatever the pecuniary condition of the people, we saw no one in Honduras, who left the United States, whose condition in that respect appeared enviable, and met but one person who had more money than he arrived there with'.[82] Even the warmer climate was little inducement: 'There can be no question that the "Eternal Summer" which prevails in Honduras will be monotonous to a degree that will prove anything but pleasant.' A return to the US beckoned. There were other such schemes, but few Southerners opted for a life on a tropical plantation.

Britain's neglected Central American coastal territory had, however, gained a new colonial lease in 1840 when the territory's superintendent, Colonel Alexander McDonald, proclaimed that the stretch of land along the coast was officially under British control. Placed under pressure by the new Central American republics, Britain was forced to make its relationship to the territory – and its people – clear.[83] Its colonists had profited from the mahogany trade, but fortunes were fluctuating – 13,719,075 feet of the wood was shipped in 1846, but by 1878 this had dropped to 3,146,582 feet.[84] By 1862 the territory was formally declared a colony under the jurisdiction of Jamaica. But by 1881 only 27,452 people were living on the sliver of land – and they were not necessarily British subjects. As one contemporary account of the colony noted,

> Representatives of every nation under the sun are to be found in this peculiar little colony. The phlegmatic German, the volatile Frenchman, the Belgian cross between these two, the morose but imperturbable European Spaniard, contrasting with his colonial counterpart, the hot-blooded Italian, the Swiss, Dane, Swede and Norwegian, occasionally a Russian Finn or a Polander Jew, and the three varieties of the insular-minded Briton, all preserving their national traits . . . The East sends its . . . delicate-featured Hindoo, and 'heathen Chinee,' . . . Maya Indians . . . Waikas and Caribs are indigenous . . . and then there is every shade of colour . . . from the coal-black cicatrized Eboe or Mandingo from Guinea . . . through all the variations of and gradations of mixed descent.[85]

There was growing European settlement further along the coast as well – in 1846 Germans had arrived in Bluefields. The export of bananas began, and Jacob Weinberger set up the Bluefields Steamship Company in 1890. It took tropical produce to the east coast of the United States, as well as nearby New Orleans. Meanwhile, the Miskitos were cautious about their alliance with new republics that had replaced Spanish control, and it continued to remain in the British interest to keep their territory separate, until it became politically expedient to make the Miskito territory a protectorate in 1844.[86]

*

In eastern Haiti, the Spanish creoles were continuing to chafe under Boyer's rule. One Dominican, Juan Pablo Duarte, had organized a secret society called La Trinitaria to plot a path to independence. It was aided by the unexpected ousting of Boyer. He had managed to hold on to power for twenty-five years, but there had been growing discontent at his land reforms – he had continued to distribute smallholdings in the west – coupled with the economic strain of paying French reparations and eventually he was brought down by an opposing faction.

Duarte and his men struck in 1843, and by February the following year they had established the Dominican Republic. But poor relations continued to stalk the two sides of the island, tensions that were exacerbated by the arrival of the Haitian ruler Faustin-Élie Soulouque. At first he was simply president but, like Henri Christophe before him, he aspired to higher titles and crowned himself Emperor Faustin I in 1849. He was also eager to control the whole island and launched numerous invasions to return the Dominican Republic to Haitian control. But he was not popular with his subjects, and Soulouque was driven out by 1859, when he fled to Jamaica.

Novelist Anthony Trollope was in Kingston at the time and recounted the emperor's fall, which he thought was partly triggered by his treatment of his troops. They were tired of the constant fighting and began to resist, so Soulouque punished them severely. However, as Trollope pointed out, 'he had not exactly chosen a bed of roses for himself in coming to Jamaica . . . at Kingston there were many Haytians, who had either been banished by Soulouque . . . or had run from him as he was now running from his subjects'.[87] According to Trollope, the refugees followed and surrounded the carriages carrying the emperor, his wife, and daughter, and also shouted loudly in celebration across from their lodgings for three days.[88]

Even with Soulouque gone, problems persisted in the fledgling Dominican Republic. There was an ongoing rivalry for power between Buenaventura Báez and Pedro Santana. While the latter was in power, he annexed the republic to Spain in 1861, ostensibly to protect it from further invasion from Haiti. There was an outcry from the United States, which considered Spain's presence a violation of the Monroe Doctrine, but it was too preoccupied with its own civil war to take action. This time the annexation was not popular with Dominicans either, and in 1863 another war of independence was launched. Spain annulled the annexation in 1865, and the republic returned. However, by the end of the decade, the US, under President Ulysses Grant, would try to purchase the island to become the thirty-eighth state of the US, a plan that had been circulating for some years and gained the support of prominent abolitionists, reformers, and African-Americans; it was also considered to be a strategic place for a naval base. Indeed, in the 1820s, during Haitian rule, some African-Americans from Philadelphia had settled in Samaná Bay on the eastern coast. But in the end, the plans were not successful.[89]

Despite the ongoing rhetoric from the Dominicans about the Haitian threat, around the same time Haiti was again being touted as a destination for free blacks in the United States who wanted to live away from the racism of that country. A *Guide to Hayti* in 1861, edited by abolitionist James Redpath, brought together a collection of articles to entice possible settlers. Redpath had sailed to Haiti to have a look at the country, arriving in January 1859, just in time to see the overthrow of Soulouque, though such unrest did not seem to give him pause about the viability of his vision. Redpath stayed on the island for a couple of months. The *Guide* included a foreword by the then-president Fabre Geffrard, who wrote, 'Hayti is the common country of the black race . . . Listen, then, all ye negroes and mulattoes who, in the vast Continent of America, suffer from the prejudices of caste. The Republic calls you; she invites you to bring to her your arms and your minds.'[90] The scheme was subscribed to, and in Boston there was even a 'Haytian Bureau of Emigration'. Redpath returned twice more, once to visit the later settlement of American blacks at L'Arcahaie. Passage cost $18, and settlers were given three years to pay it back.[91] And in 1862 – after the secession of the Southern states – the United States finally gave Haiti diplomatic recognition. By this point, however, Haiti was governed by Fabre Geffrard, a general of Soulouque's who reduced the size of the army and channelled power back to lighter-skinned elites. But at the same time, like other black leaders before him, he was eager for African-Americans to settle on the island, and offered to cover travel costs and give them credit to purchase land.[92] The following year, some 453 freed African-Americans arrived on the Île à Vache, a small island off the south coast of Haiti, to start a settlement, but it failed within months, much to the disappointment of US President Abraham Lincoln, and a relief effort brought the remaining 300 or so who had not died from disease or starvation back to the US.[93]

*

The British, meanwhile, had turned away from the West Indies. Slavery had ended, and Cuba had become the dominant sugar producer, though the British islands continued to produce a small quantity. Compared with elsewhere in the empire, the Americas seemed of less interest. Britain now focused on other parts of its realm; its rule had been secured in much of India, and settlements as far away as Australia and New Zealand were growing fast.

Less straightforward was the question of China. Britain had long wanted better access to the many luxury goods, and not least of all tea, that seemed hidden from Western view. Indeed, China had kept outsiders at the door quite literally. It stood firm against foreign incursion, forcing traders into island ports far away from the mainland. A 1793 British delegation led by George Macartney tried but failed to secure more open trade with China; whereas Britain and the East India Company had made trading inroads with Indian kingdoms, they were always forced on to the back foot by the Chinese.

Tea, ostensibly, was their concern. George Staunton, a member of the Macartney delegation who wrote an account of the trip, noted that tea was 'one of the chief articles of import from China, and not to be had elsewhere', and had 'become a necessary of life in most of the ranks of society in England'.[94] Tea consumption had risen fourfold in less than a century.[95] Staunton described the trading stations, or factories, as 'situated in a line along the river, outside the walls of the city, each with its national flag flying over it . . . The neighbourhood of the foreign factories is filled with storehouses for the reception of European goods.'[96] It was not quite so straightforward. Merchants near Canton and assorted bureaucrats controlled the trade, and Europeans had little say in the matter.

Over the intervening decades the commodities Britain and China exchanged had significantly altered, prompted by a number of factors: the decline of Spanish America, the Chinese need for silver, and the British love of tea. By the 1820s, silver supplies were not nearly as plentiful as they had been a hundred years earlier, much less two hundred. Many mines had been depleted, and the wars in Latin America during the 1820s had also disrupted the silver supply from the remaining mining sites in Mexico. China wanted little other than silver in payment for its silks and tea, and Britain could only provide so much. Then it occurred to British traders there might be something equally valuable they could exchange with the Chinese: opium.

Opium, the seductive nectar of the poppy, was not grown in China, though the country had a long association with it. Rather, it came from the fields of Bengal, which by this point were owned by the East India Company, which oversaw its growing and processing. From there it was taken to market and sold to merchants, at which point the EIC took its money and bowed out.[97] When this began to happen on a much larger scale in the 1820s, opium had already been around a long time. Like sugar, its initial use was mostly medicinal. But as tobacco smoking conquered the globe in the late 1600s some enterprising thinkers began to put the two elements together and, by the early 1700s, tobacco leaves soaked in opium syrup were often found on Portuguese ships arriving from Java.[98]

From there, opium's popularity grew, and it became another tropical luxury. And with the introduction of elaborate jade or ivory pipes, the tobacco could be done away with altogether.[99] By the start of the nineteenth century – and despite attempts by emperors to ban it – China was hooked. The EIC shipped on average 4,000 chests of processed opium a year between 1800 and 1818, and by 1831 the figure had reached 20,000 chests.[100] When the EIC sold the chests at auction, it was paid in silver, which in turn was used to buy the tea, silks, and other goods to be exported back to Britain. It was a tidy system, but one that could not last, not least because successive emperors were concerned about this national addiction, and the effect on the trade balance. Edward Brown, a British sailor who claimed to have been held in captivity by Chinese pirates in 1857, wrote that his captors thought opium 'was an excellent thing, and . . . that there was only one reason against using it, and that was the expense, which kept the Chinese very poor; and that their animosity towards the English was owing to their considering the price charged for it as extortionate in the extreme'.[101]

Despite the popularity of the drug, British traders were resentful of the means by which they had to sell it, and wanted to cut out the middleman. They wanted to free the trade and make it legitimate. Eventually there was a stand-off over the seizure of an opium shipment, and, for Britain, it was the perfect pretext for war. The Opium Wars began in 1839, with the first lasting until 1842 and the second fought from 1856 to 1860. At the end of the first round of battle, the two nations signed the Treaty of Nanjing, which granted Britain the right to establish five treaty ports, and China also ceded Hong Kong, a concession that would endure, despite later unrest and diplomatic quibbles, until the late twentieth century. While this war and the opium trade had many implications for China and Britain, it also would soon have some significant ones for the Caribbean.

*

Meanwhile, the 1840s and 1850s had brought a new wave of people to Caribbean shores. In the wake of abolition, there had been a shortage of labour on some islands. For instance, in Trinidad, the abolition of slavery had been met with mirth; former slaves thought the apprenticeship stipulation was some sort of hoax dreamt up by the governor and plantation owners. On 1 August 1834, they protested in front of the house of Governor Sir George Hill and he called in troops to suppress them.[102] With the slave population already having fallen by 32 per cent between 1816 and 1834, plantation owners struggled to keep workers in the field, and the island's government had to enact vagrancy laws and other similar legislation.[103] But such measures were no match for freedom, and the freed slaves began to squat on the land.

The first attempt to fill this shortfall was to bring migrant workers from other islands; some 10,300 people came from Grenada, St Kitts, Nevis, and Montserrat by 1846, and even 1,300 free blacks came from the United States.[104] Free workers still faced indignities and oppression: pass systems were instituted, meaning workers could be arrested if they did not have permission to be off the plantation. Such draconian measures were intended to keep people working the land, but they often failed. As in Trinidad, people elsewhere were squatting, provisioning for themselves, and staying away from the plantations. The simple wooden 'chattel houses' that popped up in Barbados could be disassembled and hastily moved when their owners were chased off the land on which they were squatting.[105] An idea soon dawned that perhaps the answer to the labour shortage lay in the British empire: bring in Indians and Chinese. A pamphlet written by Thomas Hancock, who claimed to be from the West Indies, was published in London in 1840 and laid out 'a few plain facts'. Hancock argued that the British colonies had suffered since emancipation and that without assistance 'the commercial intercourse they have hitherto maintained with the mother-country will be destroyed . . . already have the crops fall[en] off one-half . . . Many estates in Demerara have, moreover, been abandoned'.[106] His answer was for the government to encourage and permit free immigrant workers from all over the world to come to the colonies, especially Guiana, arguing that such action 'can alone save this fine colony [Guiana] from impending ruin; while, by conducing to a more general and productive cultivation, it affords the only chance of rendering slave labour unprofitable'.[107] The first shipload of Indian labourers arrived in Trinidad on the *Fatel Razack* in May 1845.

The journey from India was long, cramped, and often dangerous – and no doubt more horrible than anything an unsuspecting worker might have been told. Captain Swinton's ship, the *Salsette*, made one such unfortunate trip. He had a contract to bring labourers from India to Trinidad, and his wife was on board as well. Drawing on her journal – and her husband's – she later published an account of the voyage, which began on 17 March 1858. Over its duration, 120 Indian labourers of the 324 on board died of illness. This was, as the anonymous introduction points out, due to no fault of the captain or his wife, who worked as nurse on board 'like another Florence Nightingale'.[108] (In fact, Swinton, who wanted to protect his reputation, ordered a medical investigation into the causes of the deaths, and was later absolved of any wrongdoing.)

The journal seems to record a death every day: 'April 2nd. A Coolie, twenty-one years old, died . . . 3rd. An infant died who lost its mother . . . 4th . . . An infant died, and a girl twelve years old . . .' When the ship arrived on 2 July in Trinidad, a doctor and the harbour-master came aboard and 'thought the Coolies a miserable set . . . and they were surprised at such people being sent'. At the end of the book, Mrs Swinton argued, 'The manner in which the Coolies are collected together in Calcutta is from native travellers being sent out into the country and villages, to induce them to emigrate by fine promises. These travellers bring in the scum of the villages as well as some desirable emigrants. They should be kept at least a month at the depôt, to get them into a fit state to bear a three months' voyage.' Life in Trinidad held few great rewards after such a voyage, and she observed that 'many of them cried bitterly on leaving the ship . . . They made the best appearance they could when the planters came to select them. (It looks very like slavery.) They were put into boats in sixes and sevens like cattle, and sent to their different destinations.' In the end, every death cost the ship's owner £13, so the voyage represented a loss of some £1,500.

Ships continued to arrive from the ports of Calcutta, Madras, and Bombay in Jamaica, British Guiana, and Trinidad.[109] From 1838 to 1918, some 143,900 Indians – mostly from the Bihar and Uttar Pradesh provinces – went to Trinidad, 238,900 to Guiana, 46,800 to other British islands. The Dutch too used workers from the East. The Dutch had also instituted an 'apprenticeship' period when ending slavery in their colonies, and contract labourers were brought in. British Indian workers – known then and now as Hindustani – were initially taken to the Dutch colony.[110] Later, between 1890 and 1939, around 33,000 Javanese arrived in Suriname from Dutch Java.[111] Unlike the African slaves who preceded them in the cane fields, Indian and Javanese workers were not stripped of their heritage, but rather encouraged to live in close communities and preserve their traditions, partly because plantation owners wanted to keep them isolated and underpaid.

Of the Chinese workers arriving in the West Indies between 1852 and the 1880s, around 13,500 went to Guiana, 2,600 to Trinidad, and 1,700 to other British islands. The Chinese were also sent to Cuba, which was struggling to obtain enough labour to meet the rising sugar demand, despite its ongoing slave importations, and some 124,800 workers went there.* In general, these migrants were poor, and they received a contract for around five years of indenture, and then a passage back, or, later on, land grants.[112] What these contracts also

---

* A further 90,000 Chinese went to Peru, which had abolished slavery in 1854, to cut cane along the coast.

meant was that wages could continue to be fixed quite low. The labourer
arrived to find that there was to be little money to spare under the
terms of his contract after the costs of living were deducted from his
pay. It was hardly better than enslavement. There were various social
restrictions as well. For instance, even though the Chinese in Cuba
were classified as 'white', their contracts on that island meant they
were more or less not free, and treated as such.[113] Most of the time
they were not allowed to bring women, or to be in contact with any
on the island. An 1868 census listed 30,591 Chinese men, only 237 of
whom were married, and there were only sixteen women present.[114]

Trinidad was one of the largest recipients of Indian labour in the
West Indies. The island had languished in the past, and the influx of
workers was considered by some, both in London and on the island,
as a means of improving productivity. Even by the end of the century,
after tens of thousands of Indians had arrived, there was ongoing
discussion about the merits of such a scheme. Some argued there was
no spare labour in the rest of the British islands, and that during cultivation season 'the sugar estates cannot secure the necessary labour',
which was detrimental to the industry.[115] Opponents of Indian immigration argued that these workers were paid far less than islanders,
depressing wages, though proponents maintained that the sugar
industry simply could not afford to pay any more.[116] There was a
cultural element as well, as one pamphlet argued:

> But says the objector, you have flooded the country with hordes
> of barbarians, Pagans, and Mahomedans. Comparisons are
> proverbially odious. We will therefor avoid them by enumerating
> what we believe to be some of the acknowledged virtues and vices
> of the East Indian. He is sober, industrious, thrift[y] and provident.
> He is kind to animals, and children, and to his wife except in cases
> of jealousy when he is apt to resort to extreme measures. He is
> the heir of an ancient civilization and literature, and generally
> respects both himself and his fellow men.[117]

The Chinese, Javanese, and Indians brought their traditions and
culture with them, which soon became woven into the fabric of the
Caribbean. Muslims had been in the Caribbean since the earliest European arrivals – often in the guise of forced *morisco* converts – but now,
both Sunni and Shia sects as well as Hindus from India were arriving

in significant numbers. Hindu temples joined churches in Trinidad and Guiana, new words emerged, and island palates developed a taste for different foods. The Indians also brought with them a medicinal herb that would later become very much associated with the Caribbean: *ganja*, or cannabis.[118] Immigration, however, was not limited to people from India, Java or China. Other groups had come to Guiana and Trinidad to try their luck, such as Madeirans, whose island was still – and would continue to be – under Portuguese rule. Also 'Syrians', a catch-all term that included people actually from Syria, Lebanese Christians, who also had a significant diaspora around the ports of Latin America, and other Middle Eastern people. They were often merchants and were met with acquiescence at some times and hostility at others – especially when members of their community grew rich.

*

By the 1860s, the labour landscape in the British Caribbean had shifted significantly. Not all former slaves refused to work, but the number of people brought to the islands goes some way to illustrating the extent of the shortfall. The meaning of freedom was still to be clarified, a process that would continue throughout the decades that followed, especially with regard to what was considered acceptable treatment of the former slaves and people of colour.

Post-emancipation societies struggled, but now workers, rather than slaves, spoke out. At the same time, people of colour protested or went on strike over pay or working conditions. There were other political changes as well. In Dominica in 1832, for instance, there had been a Brown Privilege Bill, which permitted coloured members to be elected to the House of Assembly. Within six years there would be a non-white majority, known as the 'Mulatto Ascendancy', which controlled the island legislature until 1863, after which the crown appointed its own members and made the island a crown colony in 1865.[119]

In that same year, Jamaica was marked by one of the most shocking displays of the contradictions of emancipation. In St Thomas Parish, in the south-east of the island, people were struggling to survive, despite being free. Sugar plantations paid such low wages that a person could barely live on them, if there was work at all. People with land could grow provisions to supplement their diet, or to sell, but those without land were forced to squat. There had been ongoing disputes over these issues in this part of the island. Many cases about land were coming before the magistrates; one, involving what angry peasants saw as an unfair fine, tipped them into action. Fights broke out with the police, and arrests were made in early October 1865.

A few days later, one of the community leaders, Baptist deacon Paul Bogle, led a protest march. It quickly turned violent, and spread beyond the town. The governor at the time was Edward Eyre, who had been held in high regard when he arrived in the West Indies in 1864, but who did not prove popular. His response to the protest only fuelled the islanders' dislike, and it nearly cost him his professional reputation in London. The suppression of the unrest in Morant Bay harked back to the sort of punishments meted out under slavery: nearly 500 people were killed, even more flogged, houses burnt down, and martial law declared. Not only did Eyre order Bogle's execution, but he ordered the court martial of businessman and politician George William Gordon, charging him with 'complicity'. Gordon was tried without due process and executed, even though he had been in Kingston when the protests started.

When news of this reached London there were immediate calls for an official inquiry, which was commissioned in December. Eyre maintained that he was keeping order and had taken necessary actions to prevent a race riot. The events also prompted intense public debate between the British intellectuals John Stuart Mill and Thomas Carlyle. Mill set up the Jamaica Committee to secure Eyre's prosecution – and was backed by thinkers such as Charles Darwin and Herbert Spencer. Carlyle defended the governor, convincing Charles Dickens and Alfred Tennyson, among others, of the injustice of Eyre's case. As for Eyre, he told the committee that the rioters were 'determined to make Jamaica a second Haiti'.[120] His case was apparently persuasive; he never faced any punishment for his actions.

*

By the second half of the nineteenth century, despite the collapse of Saint-Domingue and some rearrangement of the industry, sugar output in the Caribbean was still ten times greater than it had been in 1700. Although the British colonies had declined, Cuba had not.[121] That island was leading the producers, and Spain soon grew to depend on Cuban revenues, having lost all its mines. Fernando VII died in 1833, which triggered a succession crisis and cycles of civil war – known as the Carlist Wars – that forced an already underdeveloped Spain further behind its European rivals. It also lagged, in many respects, behind the wealth and productiveness of Cuba. Cuba and Puerto Rico were also an important market for Spanish exports; the value of imports from Spain had been 2,858,792 pesos in 1826 and rose to 4,739,776 pesos by 1830. The growing wealth of Cuban planters meant that they had capital to invest in Spain, and the money went into enterprises such as banking, Catalan cotton, and some manufacturing.[122] The real trading partner for Cuba, however, was the United States. Cuban exports there were worth 4,107,449 pesos, while the island absorbed around 6 million pesos a year in imports from the United States in 1826 to 1830.[123] This continued to grow: by 1856–65 the mean annual value of sugar output for Cuba was pushing almost $70 million, or around $1.9 billion in today's money.[124]

As early as the 1820s, Havana was the biggest, brashest city in the Caribbean, as sugar wealth flowed through Cuba's ports. The houses grew larger, the carriages grander. Robert Jameson noted that some slave owners had 'no less than sixty household slaves'. He also was impressed by the popularity of gambling and the pursuit of finery:

> This vice [gambling] and an immoderate love of dress are the bane of the labouring class. You would smile to see groups of black females with silk stockings, satten [sic] shoes, muslin gowns, French shawls, gold ear-rings and flowers in their woollen head-dress, gallanted by black beaux, with white beaver hats, English coats and gold-headed canes, all smoking in concert like their superiors. These are your washerwomen and cobblers, festival-izing on a 'dias de los cruces,' or a church holiday. The next day you will have them at your door with some article of this finery, which they are seeking a sale for, to pay for the day's subsistence![125]

But by 1859, Anthony Trollope described Havana's streets as 'narrow, dirty, and foul . . . there is nothing to justify the praises with which the Havana is generally mentioned', though for him it was redeemed by the Paseo, a long, wide, tree-lined boulevard: 'It is for their hour on the Paseo that the ladies dress themselves, and the gentlemen prepare their jewelry.'[126] The evening strolls, the dressing up, the gambling, and the slavery would continue until the end of the nineteenth century. But so, too, would fear and repression. Through the 1830s until the 1860s, 385,949 Africans – many from the Bight of Biafra and West Central Africa – arrived in Cuba, and 10,253 in Puerto Rico.[127] The numbers were such that, in the 1840s, there were concerns that, should the island become independent, the abolition of slavery would lead to the 'Africanisation of Cuba' and a race war, concerns that reached their peak during the brutal suppression of the *Escalera* conspiracy. In officials' panicked imagination, this alleged plot involved African and creole slaves, free people of colour, and even British abolitionists. In June 1844, the supposed ringleaders were shot, and a long-running campaign of violence and repression followed. *La escalera* is Spanish for ladder, to which those accused of participating were tied while they were lashed as a punishment. The fear of rebellion persisted.

At the same time, the British continued their anti-slaving patrols, trying to end the trade to Cuba. The *emancipados*, Africans 'rescued' by the British navy, however, posed another problem. Rather than being returned to Africa, they were given papers and allowed to live in Cuba.[128] But although their certificates of emancipation made them free, they were often denied the chance to find their own place in society and instead were employed on seven-year contracts in 'public works'.[129] And despite Britain's effort at sea to abolish Cuba's slave trade, on land, Britons continued to consume the island's sugar. In 1846 the British government placed the same duties on all sugar producers, which was disastrous for British West Indian planters because the small islands could no longer compete with Cuba and Brazil. The sweet tooth of Britain thus became sated on Cuban sugar, as imports grew in volume from around 22 million pounds in 1845 to 183 million pounds in 1859.[130]

*

The Iberian nations were the first to bring slavery to the New World and the last to end it. Portugal signed an agreement with Britain around 1815 which stipulated it would only use slaves south of the equator, but it did not abolish the trade until 1836, and even then there was a lot of smuggling. Brazil, which had been independent since 1822, only banned the slave trade in 1850, and, in 1888 was the last territory in the Americas to abolish slavery.

Spain proved similarly stubborn, but by 1864 the Sociedad

Abolicionista Española had been established, and the trade was officially ended in 1867, despite pledges to Britain to stop it earlier. It had already tapered off, with many planters no longer seeing slave labour as cost-effective. Plantation life was changing: the owners who could afford it had modernized their sugar mills, bringing in steam power. There was also better infrastructure, such as railways and steamships, and so the cost of transporting cane came down as well.[131] Finding a reliable source of labour was still a concern, however, and it was around this point that the island turned to the Chinese. By the 1860s, the number of slaves had declined significantly: some 26,290 Africans had been brought to Cuba in 1859, but by 1866 that number had fallen to 722.[132] At the same time, there was another major demographic shift under way; immigrants from Spain were coming to the prosperous island. By the 1860s the percentage of the population who were enslaved had dropped as well, to around 27 per cent, down from 44 per cent a couple of decades earlier. The increase in white settlers meant that for the first time in decades there were more whites than people of colour on the island. The abolition of slavery in Puerto Rico and Cuba was a longer process. In 1870, 'free womb' legislation, known as the Moret Law, was enacted in Cuba and Puerto Rico, which meant children born to slaves after that date were free. But there was an inevitable catch – the child had to serve their mother's owner until he or she turned eighteen. The owner, according to the law, could not separate the child from the mother until the age of fourteen. The law also freed slaves older than sixty. Inevitably, the law was met with protest, and some people flouted it. But the momentum and the will were now there to end slavery. It stopped in Puerto Rico in 1874, but in Cuba, an apprenticeship system – *patronato* – was set up, though many also ignored it, and abolition finally came in 1886.

A combination of factors now created the conditions for more talk of independence. The US Civil War and subsequent abolition of slavery in North America was a strong indication that the slave regime in Cuba would not be tenable for much longer. Fears of a Haitian-style race war had started to fade. And in Spain, the Carlist Wars which raged throughout the nineteenth century drained the coffers and distracted the government. By 1868 Queen Isabella II was deposed and fled the country. That same year, the opening salvos of independence were fired in both Cuba and Puerto Rico. One crucial development had also helped to bring this about. People in both islands were ready to fight for their independence. In September 1868, people in the inland Puerto Rican town of Lares organized an armed uprising. Known as the *grito de Lares* – the cry of Lares – it was a short-lived rebellion, and within a few weeks it had been suppressed. But Cuba was not long to follow. In 1868 Carlos Manuel de Céspedes echoed what happened in Puerto Rico with the *grito de Yara* in October. Unlike Puerto Rico, however, Cuba's rebellion turned into a long-running conflict, known as the Ten Years War. Although it was mostly started by disgruntled elites, over time the movement broadened in class and race and soon included people like the mulatto Antonio Maceo, who became one of the top commanders. And although the Ten Years War ended in defeat for the rebels, it brought together many factions on the island in the cause of independence.[133] It was followed in 1879–80 by another short-lived uprising known as the Little War.

Around the same time in New York, José Martí was making new plans. The world of the Cuban exiles in the US that had supported figures like Narciso López some thirty years earlier had grown stronger and more vocal. Martí was already well known as a poet and writer whose fierce criticism of the Spanish regime in Cuba meant he had spent much of his life in exile. After the Ten Years War, rebel leaders such as Maceo and Máximo Gómez, a Dominican who had supported Cuba's efforts and later led troops as a major general, also had little option but to leave. Martí was in contact with them while at the same time raising money among Cuban exiles in the United States, especially the large community of tobacco workers in Florida. In 1892 he set up the Partido Revolucionario Cubano (PRC) – the Cuban Revolutionary Party. He persuaded Goméz and Maceo to come out of exile and try again. Martí made a point of including Cubans from all backgrounds and, importantly, of all hues. 'A Cuban is more than mulatto, black or white,' he wrote in an 1893 newspaper article. 'Dying for Cuba on the battlefield, the souls of both Negroes and white men have risen together.'[134]

The following year, 1894, while Martí and his men continued to organize, the US introduced the Wilson-Gorman Tariff Act, which imposed a 40 per cent duty on imported sugar, eradicating any trade advantage Cuba had with the US; Spain, in response, dropped its preferential concessions and reinstated tariffs, and the island was soon shut out of its formerly lucrative market. Exports plummeted, from 800,000 tons in 1895 to around 225,000 tons the following year.[135] With the island plunged into economic chaos, public anger grew against the Spanish policy, and Martí knew that the moment to strike was imminent. The US offered further incentive to get the rebellion under way when in January 1895 it confiscated three ships containing valuable military equipment, alerting the Spanish that another rebellion might be in the making. In February the plan was put into action: on the 24th there were a number of uprisings all over the island, from villages in the east to Havana in the west – the Cuban War of Independence had begun. By April Martí was on the island, but the following month he was dead: killed by the Spanish during a battle at Dos Ríos. Gómez and Maceo continued the fight, though Maceo too was killed in 1896.

As a result, the United States now began to focus more intently upon Cuba. Some felt that Spain would best protect US interests while others believed that Cubans had the right to independence, and that Spanish interference contravened the Monroe Doctrine. Despite concerns about both its citizens and its commercial interests on the island, the US did not officially take action until it sent the battleship *Maine* from Key West to Havana in January 1898. But on 15 February the ship was blown up in Havana harbour, killing 260 members of the crew. By April the US had been drawn into the conflict, declaring war on Spain, but by July, Spain was suing for peace. The armed conflict had been brief. In Cuba it had initially involved US ships blockading the harbours and attacking fortifications to aid the rebels. However, US troops had landed in June – including the famed 'Rough Riders' cavalry unit led by future US President Theodore Roosevelt. San Juan in Puerto Rico had been bombarded as well, but troops did not arrive on that island until the peace agreement had started. By the end of 1898 the US had won control of Puerto Rico and paid $20 million for the Philippines, which had also engaged in a revolt with American backing, in 1896 (though later it would have to fight the US for its independence). And Cuba was now nominally independent. All this took place with only three months of fighting – 'a splendid little war', as US secretary of state John Hay described it. But the involvement of the US in Cuba did not bode well, and it was something Martí had vehemently opposed when he was organizing the struggle. In 1889 he had written in a letter to Gonzalo de Quesada, who was also involved in the independence struggle, regarding the possibility of US assistance: 'And once the United States is in Cuba, who will drive it out?'[136]

*

The nineteenth century closed on an uncertain note. The Spanish–American war, coupled with the earlier wars for independence in Latin America, meant Spain no longer had any territories, much less power, in the Caribbean. France, Britain, the Netherlands, and Denmark persisted in keeping colonies, though many of their former sugar islands had been damaged by the continued strength of Cuban sugar, as well as by competition from Brazil. In addition, the century had been peppered with natural disasters such as hurricanes and earth-quakes, although unlike the century that preceded it, there were far fewer wars. The real battle had been over the continuation of slavery, and it had been won by the slaves.

But as the twentieth century began, most of the governing class on the islands had yet to fully come to terms with emancipation and what it meant. The spectre of Haiti may have faded, but for the people of colour, the memory of events in Morant Bay stalked their hard-won freedom. Outside Cuba, economic fortunes declined, and life became more difficult, if, albeit slowly, more just. The world of the opulent planter had been torched by the events in Haiti, even if that fire took a while to spread around the islands. Those days were gone. Now there was freedom, but there was little even-handedness in how it was meted out. Slavery was gone, but its inequalities remained.

Chapter Nine

BANANA WARS AND
GLOBAL BATTLES

When Ellery Scott and Charles Thompson arrived in New York aboard the *Korona*, they brought tales of raining fire and ash, as if they had dropped anchor in hell's harbour. The first officer and assistant purser had been on a voyage to St Pierre, Martinique, not on the *Korona*, but its sister ship the *Roraima*, which had tied up in St Pierre on the morning of 8 May 1902. The crew had just finished breakfast when, in the space of a few minutes, the ship was consumed by burning lava rocks raining down from the exploding summit of Mount Pelée 1,400m (4,600ft) above.[1] People in the West Indies, accustomed to and stoic in the face of regular natural disasters such as hurricanes and earthquakes, were not prepared for this. Although most of the Leeward Islands are volcanic formations, eruptions are rare. But the scale and the fury of Martinique's Mount Pelée, woken from a long slumber, took not only the island, but the world, by surprise. Locals in St Pierre had noticed strange things in Pelée for about a week – rumblings, small eruptions, a bit of smoke – but they had died down and people went about their usual business. Scott said he heard a 'noise like a million thunders all at once – and then a rain of fire and mud and sulphur . . . We choked and shrieked and lost our mind for the time being.'[2] The captain and his men tried to leave the harbour as quickly as possible but were surrounded by flames. Scott saw his captain on fire, 'writhing in pain', and the others rushed into the fo'c'sle and buried themselves in blankets for protection.[3] After the initial blast from the volcano, the men began to assess the state of the ship, finding it heavily damaged. They were rescued that afternoon by a French cruiser, and in the end out of the original sixty-eight passengers and crew on board the *Roraima* only sixteen survived.[4]

Captain Carey of the *Korona*, which later took the survivors to New York, was in Barbados harbour around the same time. He claimed to have to heard a series of explosions 'which sounded like a man-of-war firing heavy guns'.[5] About half an hour later, ash rained down. This was on 7 May, and the source was St Vincent – which sits about 160km (100 miles) west of Barbados and about the same distance south of Martinique – where the La Soufrière volcano had erupted. People in the town had also been feeling tremors and even seen lava flowing from the 1,200m (4,000ft) mountain for a few days; some might have been old enough to have heard stories about its eruption in 1812. Both eruptions were devastating, but the one in Martinique especially so. Known as the 'Paris of the Antilles', it had been reduced to ashes, and most of its 30,000 people were smothered or burnt to death while trying to flee.

It was a dramatic and terrifying start to a century whose course in the region would be shaped not only by natural events, but by the growing might of the neighbouring United States. The US was showing the extent of its force with attempts to assert its self-proclaimed hemispheric authority. It still wanted to keep Europeans at bay, so, for instance, when British and German warships blockaded the Venezuelan coast in 1902 in an attempt to recover some debts, the United States threatened to go to war, leaving the Europeans little choice but to limp back across the Atlantic. Germany, however, was keen to expand its overseas empire, by adding a yet-to-be-determined sliver of the Caribbean to its African territory and Micronesian islands. There was talk of setting up naval stations for German ships in St Thomas or Curaçao, though no action was ever taken.[6] Still, the United States viewed European ships in its waters as being a bit too close for comfort.

A few years later, in 1904, European creditors once again came calling, this time to the Dominican Republic, which could not pay its debts. And the United States was again irritated by the possibility of European powers encroaching on free territories in the Americas. As a result, it was 'invited' by the government to administer the Dominican customs department, and by 1911 the republic was solvent. More importantly, perhaps, it opened the door to further US intervention.

This was all part of a larger adjustment of the political tectonic plates in the Caribbean. European interest was crumbling away, replaced by the United States. All the island nations, with the exception of Cuba, the Dominican Republic, Puerto Rico and Haiti, were still under European control, but the powers in Europe were distracted by their march south to Africa, embodied and outlined in the Berlin Conference of 1884, which codified the infamous 'scramble for Africa' in which European nations literally mapped out their claims to the continent. All the major nations took part, and even some of the minor ones. In the years that followed, Portugal, Britain, Spain, Germany, Italy, and even Belgium claimed colonies. The Dutch, meanwhile, had focused more energy on Indonesia, though other European powers, including Britain and France, also had a presence throughout southeast Asia, and Britain of course had its empire in India as well. Natural resources flowed from colonies to capital cities, and more highly prized commodities like rubber obscured the traditional Caribbean produce. Men no longer went to the islands to seek their fortunes; instead, the islands attracted US corporations seeking profit.

Unlike the European powers, however, the United States was poised to make the most of Cuba and Puerto Rico, economically and politically. It brought a different worldview to the Caribbean, as its firms settled in. The managers often did not speak anything other than English; they lived in compounds and did little to integrate. They were there to do business and get out when it was done. At the same time, their interests were protected by the might of the United States. This nascent colonialism affected the development of every island – and the US itself – for decades. The United States had gone into the war against Spain in 1898 as a strong nation, but came out a fledgling empire. While the statuses of Puerto Rico and the Philippines were established in a clearer, colonial sense, the ever-prized island of Cuba was to be independent, although that independence was initially limited; the US occupied Cuba until 1903. In 1901 the Platt Amendment, which was later adopted into the island's constitution of 1902, gave the US the 'right to intervene for the preservation of Cuban independence' and establish a military presence, including a base at Guantánamo Bay.[7] Many Cubans, no matter how eager for their island's independence, opposed such measures, but the island's first president, Tomás Estrada Palma, had not only lived in the United States but was Washington's preferred candidate. This pattern of US influence was replicated across the region for decades. And the Roosevelt Corollary, initially part of President Theodore Roosevelt's State of the Union address in 1904, shaped US policy regarding the Caribbean throughout this period. In the speech, Roosevelt, who was president from 1901 to 1909, invoked the policy of his predecessor, William McKinley, saying, 'in the Western Hemisphere the adherence of the United States to the Monroe Doctrine may force the United States, however reluctantly . . . to the exercise of an international police power', adding:

> If every country washed by the Caribbean Sea would show the progress in stable and just civilization which with the aid of the Platt amendment Cuba has shown since our troops left the island, and which so many of the republics in both Americas are constantly and brilliantly showing, all question of interference by this Nation with their affairs would be at an end. Our interests and those of our southern neighbors are in reality identical.[8]

But of course, their interests were anything but identical, something West Indians already knew.

*

Sugar continued to be an important crop for the Caribbean, but beet sugar from Europe and the US was already providing West Indian producers with stiff competition. Extracted from the root vegetable, beet sugar was first used by Europeans during the Napoleonic Wars – Bonaparte was eager for it to flourish as an alternative to easily blockaded West Indian sugar. By 1900, some 65 per cent of sugar sold worldwide came from beet farms in Europe and North America. But this was short-lived, because technological developments and European expansion in Asia meant tropical cane once again became both cost-effective and competitive. By 1930, cane had rebounded to take the majority – 62 per cent – of the market.[9] Although Cuba was the dominant producer, Jamaica, the Dominican Republic, Puerto Rico, St Croix, St Kitts, Antigua, Guadeloupe, Martinique, Barbados, and Trinidad still had cane fields.[10] Sugar production would be complicated throughout the 1920s and 1930s by a variety of treaties with a number of intended outcomes, ranging from stimulating growth to restricting it; or adding duties to taking away bounties. This left planters at the mercy of the markets and international diplomacy.

It was the Spanish-speaking islands which enjoyed the most

significant expansion in sugar production in these years. The combined sugar output of the Dominican Republic, Cuba, and Puerto Rico in 1900 was 433,000 tons (US), rising to 1,127,000 tons (US) in 1902, and 5,033,000 in 1919.[11] This time, however, it was the North American sweet tooth, rather than the British, which was fuelling much of the demand – in 1900 the average per capita sugar consumption in the US was 65.2lb, in 1930 it was 109.6lb.[12]

When the conflict between the US, Spain and Cuba ended in 1898, the sugar fields of that island were in ruins, as many plantations had been torched during the Cuban War of Independence. US investors were quick to start replanting and to pour money into sugar mills on the island. And although the US began to pull out its troops from Cuba in 1902 and President Estrada Palma had taken office, American finger-prints were still all over the island's affairs. Cuban sugar received a preferential trade deal with the US, while at the same time, US firms continued to buy up land on the island. The US also intervened in diplomatic spheres, such as meddling in Cuba's attempt to negotiate a trade deal with Britain in 1905.[13] Political life was unstable and violent in these early years, and when Estrada Palma faced a rebellion in 1906, he turned to the US for help and then resigned. The US once again took Cuba under its control and sent in the secretary of war and future president William Howard Taft as governor. Taft arrived in 1906 but was soon replaced by Charles Magoon. Following a presidential election at the end of 1908, José Miguel Gómez took office in January 1909 and sovereign government was resumed. But the turbulence continued. In 1912 there was a brief but significant suppression of Afro-Cubans who were trying to establish a political voice. Many were veterans of the Cuban War of Independence, and had fought for their nation's freedom alongside whites. One of these veterans, Pedro Ivonnet, was not only a descendant of refugees from the Haitian Revolution, but also a founding member of a new political party, the Partido Independiente de Color, the first black political party in the western hemisphere, established in 1908.[14] Many thought the party was the first step to black domination of the island – echoes of the earlier La Escalera conspiracy and an expression of Cuba's long history of fears of race war – although Afro-Cubans were thought to comprise about 30 per cent of the population. The party wanted more opportunities for people of colour and an end to racial discrimination, a tall order on an island where many whites bought into 'scientific' notions of race, popular at the time in the US and Europe, that put whites at the top of a racial hierarchy, with blacks firmly at the bottom. This same pseudo-science was used to justify the European occupation of most of Africa, and also kept African-Americans oppressed in the southern United States. Frustrated, Ivonnet and his men eventually staged an armed protest, which was suppressed by people they had probably fought alongside less than a decade before. The US warned Cuba to stop the rebellion, and President Gómez sent out the army. Ivonnet was killed on 18 July 1912, and the party disbanded, but not before another 2,000 to 5,000 rebels were killed.[15]

Although events in Cuba were particularly dramatic, there was unrest more widely across the region, as sugar workers disputed their low wages and the exploitative nature of their contracts – and such demonstrations were often brutally suppressed. In Suriname, in 1902, twenty-four workers were killed – and their bodies dumped in a mass grave – over a wage dispute at the Marienburg sugar factory. In 1905 there were riots against unfairly low wages in the sugar estates in Demerara, spreading from the cane cutters in the fields to the dockside stevedores in the capital of Georgetown, and later even to tram conductors. The tensions there came to a head around 30 November, when there was a large public demonstration. The momentum was lost though, as the need for a daily wage forced people back to work. But it brought to the attention of the authorities not only the issue of pay, but the often horrendous living conditions of the working poor: lack of sanitation, overcrowding, and disease. There was anger, too, at the lack of will to help eradicate these problems.[16] A few years later, in March 1913, fifteen Indian workers were killed on the Rose Hall plantation after a protest over a promised holiday.[17]

*

Even as late as 1900, the dream of an easy journey from the Atlantic to the Pacific by ship remained unfulfilled although there was now a railway line across the isthmus of Panama. The US had toyed with plans for a waterway in Panama, and also Nicaragua. But it was the French who resumed work on the project. Buoyed by the success of his Suez Canal project in Egypt, Ferdinand de Lesseps decided that a similar project in the Americas would be straightforward. His plans, however, were met with anger by the US. Lesseps managed eventually to obtain a concession from wary Colombia, of which Panama was then part. The US had earlier been in talks with Colombia for a similar project, but it came to nothing. When news of the Frenchman's arrangement reached Washington, however, the European incursion was deemed to be a threat to national security. President Rutherford B. Hayes told the Senate in the spring of 1880 that 'the policy of this country is a canal under American control', declaring: 'The United States can not consent to the surrender of this control to any European power or to any combination of European powers.'[18] When Hayes's time in office ended in 1881, the US had done nothing to stop Lesseps, who had also raised money to start the project, which he did in the same year. But the French engineer was no match for the forces of the natural world, and while thousands had died laying track for the railroad, thousands more would die in the near-Sisyphean task of trying to dig a canal across the isthmus. The flat, arid entrance to the Red Sea was far more hospitable to construction than the tropical lushness of Panama with its torrential rain, constant mudslides, and yellow-fever-laden mosquitoes. The project went bankrupt and ground to a halt in 1889.

Still, the dream would not die. By the turn of the century there were murmurs in the corridors of the US Congress about picking up where the French had left off. Some politicians opposed a scheme so far to the south, preferring one closer to the United States, in Nicaragua or Costa Rica. After the eruption of Mount Pelée, however, minds were changed by the realization that both of those countries were also highly volcanic, which could put a future canal at risk. Besides, the French had left behind a great deal of construction material from their failed effort in Panama.[19] In 1902 the US purchased the French assets for $40 million, but still needed permission from the Colombian government. The Hay–Herrán Treaty, in which the US agreed to pay Colombia $10 million for a ninety-nine-year lease and $250,000 a year in rent, was signed by both sides. Yet its ratification was immediately a point of contention with Colombian legislators, only too aware that they were receiving far less for their land than France had been given for its rusted equipment. They unanimously refused to ratify the treaty, with a vote of 24 to 0.[20]

Angrily, the United States searched for someone to lead separatist Panamanians in a 'revolution', the first major incident in a long line of such interference in Central America. The US found Manuel Amador Guerrero, who later became Panama's first president. By 3 November

1903, thanks to US battleships in the harbour and a rail company that refused to transport Colombian troops, the Republic of Panama was proclaimed and soon after recognized by the United States. Before November was over, a new contract had been signed that gave the United States what it wanted: control of the zone around the canal at a bargain price.

The attraction of a job on the canal project was obvious to people living on islands with flagging sugar industries and little employment. The wages seemed good, and contracts often included promises of room and board. Thousands of British West Indians signed up, and in the decade during which the canal was built, from 1904 to 1914, around 40,000 people came from Jamaica and Barbados alone to seek employment.[21] In the case of Barbados, the Panama Canal Agency set up a recruiting office in Bridgetown in 1905 and three years later some 10,000 men had left on ships destined for Colón, on the Caribbean coast. Census data shows the population dipped in Barbados in 1921 to 156,312 from 171,983 ten years earlier.[22] Other groups arrived in Panama as well, including people from the southern Mediterranean. Around 12,000 arrived between 1906 and 1908, though they demanded – and received – higher wages, and many were susceptible to yellow fever. But like the previous projects, the work was difficult and the dangers many, and the letters back home were not glowing. The work often demanded body and soul – taming the fetid, rainy, disease-ridden jungle was a daunting task. Soon the Europeans stopped arriving in such significant numbers.

The West Indians continued to come, though, and were not limited to those from British islands. People from the French colonies went over, too; in 1905 one ship carried 664 Martinicans to Panama, but by the time they docked, around 140 of them refused to disembark because of rumours they had heard: 'it had been reported to them that the Canal labourers are badly treated on the Isthmus'. The police were called in, and about fifty of the resisters jumped overboard, though all were rescued except one man, who drowned.[23]

It was not only men who went over or worked on the canal. West Indians were keen to perpetuate their own culture and women often went, too, to cook, or to tend their families – some male workers would only come on the condition they could bring their wives and children with them. In 1906, US overseers were concerned that a group of about

280 women from Martinique had been brought to the Canal Zone 'for immoral purposes', though police surveillance later found them to be 'industrious, peaceable, honest and up to the standing of morality of the women of their class in the West Indies'.[24]

The harsh working conditions on the canal coupled with poor pay inevitably led to anger and resentment. The British consul in Panama, Claude Mallet, explained in a letter to the foreign secretary, the Marquess of Lansdowne, that the root cause of one violent episode was that Jamaican workers were promised good food and accommodation in addition to a wage of $14 in US gold a month. But when they arrived they found the reality did not match up. Black workers were paid in silver coins, and white bosses were paid in gold. The incident in question took place on 27 April 1905, when the workmen filed into the cafeteria for breakfast as usual but 'there was so much disorder and delay that many of the workmen had finished when others were just commencing to eat, with the result that, on the order being given at 12.30 p.m. to return to work, those who had not breakfasted refused to leave the barracks'. According to Mallet there were conflicting reports, but what actually transpired was that a policeman upset a worker, who was struck when he protested against his treatment. Once the police had left the building a stone hit another officer. Soon bayonets were out, shots were fired, and some workers ran to the protection of the Canal Administration building on Cathedral Square to complain. Twenty-one Jamaicans had been injured in the incident, which the consul called a 'savage exhibition of armed violence against British subjects in the employment of the American Government' that had 'caused a feeling of profound indignation among all ranks'.[25]

Overseers and managers from the United States also often brought the prejudices of its racist system with them. In another letter to the Foreign Office, Mallet explained that 'I must inform your Lordship that the majority of Americans here – I refer particularly to those who hold subordinate positions – exhibit an extraordinary contempt for the Jamaican negro.'[26] In 1906, the chief engineer on the project, John Stevens, told a US Senate committee that 'the islands negro is a peculiar being. The majority of them, you know, can not see very far ahead'. He argued that if the workers got paid a higher daily wage, it would stop them turning up the next day for work – they would live off the money until it ran out, and then go back to work – to which Senator

John Tyler Morgan, from Alabama, replied, 'The South is full of object lessons of exactly that character with our own negroes . . . They will work two days in the week and live the balance of it in idleness.'[27] Stevens said that 'the average American negro laborer I have seen and had around me on railways is worth at least two of the island negroes'.[28] Such were the attitudes towards the men working on the canal. Still, for some West Indians it was worth the discomfort and humiliation. Barbadians, for instance, brought back more than £80,000 to the island in 1910 alone. Many people wanted to use their money to buy land and soon the island was beset by inflated prices.[29] Others returned to Jamaica, where they were known as the 'Colon men', and flashed their earnings around town.[30] The canal's opening in 1914 heralded a return to the economic uncertainty of island life for thousands. Others, however, stayed on in Panama – by now many had families there – hoping more work would turn up.

Today, watching a ship go through the Miraflores locks in Panama is a marvel: electric towing engines move the enormous tankers like ants carrying a watermelon. There is barely a centimetre to spare, as the 33.5m (110ft) width of the lock is only just wider than the ships. After that set of locks, ships are back at sea level and the Pacific beckons. If one is coming the other way, the majority of the fifty miles still lie ahead, a journey that stretches into eight or more hours. It took big dreams, false starts, $400 million and thousands of lives, but some four hundred years after the Spanish conquistador Vasco Núñez de Balboa became the first European to cross the isthmus of Panama, the marine link between East and West was complete.

*

In 1923, thousands of Americans danced to the hit tune 'Yes, We Have No Bananas', a novelty song based on the nation's growing love for the fruit. Imports had boomed from a wholesale value of $250,000 in 1871 to $12.4 million by 1911.[31] Many varieties of banana – and of plantain – are thought to have travelled, much like sugar, from the New Guinea region during the sixteenth century. To thrive, the banana plant needs a steady climate and lots of rain, and it took root in the western tropics as well as it had in the east. For decades, plantain, which generally needs to be cooked before it can be eaten, was a staple of the slave diet. The sweeter banana could be peeled and eaten on the spot, but the dreaded Panama disease often wiped out the crop, leaving little for the banana boats to take from Central America, Cuba, and Jamaica to eager American consumers: 'Yes, We Have No Bananas' was thought to be inspired by one such shortage. Soon, though, disease-resistant varieties were developed and trade with the US was brisk.

By the late nineteenth century, vessels had been calling in to Central America for some time, buying bananas from the Garífuna (black and mestizo descendants of the black Caribs), who had long lived on the coast, and taking the fruit to the United States; by the 1880s it had become clear that there was a great deal of money to be made from this simple food.[32] It was thought to be exotic, as were the magical banana boats that arrived at cold US ports from trips to the tropics. A *New York Times* article in 1882 described the scene of a boat unloading at Pier No. 14 in the East River: 'Stout-looking young fellows in checkered jumpers are passing up the fruit from the hatches, while women with baskets, sailors and idlers of all descriptions swarm the deck from the stem to the stern of each vessel. The hatches have just been removed from one of the schooners, and a fresh, delicious smell from the fruit pervades the air.'[33]

There were similar scenes in the Caribbean, as one woman who visited the Caribbean port of Puerto Barrios, Guatemala, in the 1940s, observed:

> Burly Negroes and short, squat Indians, stripped down to 'drudgin' clo's,' shout happily among themselves in a rhythmic chant: 'Lif', mon, lif', lif', lif' mon, lif' mon.' They bear huge banana bunches effortlessly on their shoulders, their magnificent torsos gleaming like polished satin. The banana loader runs up and down in an endless chain, like a Coney Island ferris wheel. It deposits the bananas carefully on the deck floor. The bananas will be taken down below and packed most painstakingly in refrigerated holds.[34]

Soon the small US importers banded together, or were bought out, and United Fruit – a Boston firm – emerged as the market leader.[35] United Fruit began setting up plantations along the Caribbean coast of Central America. It also opened operations in Cuba, around 1902, when US capital began to flow into the island, establishing banana and sugar plantations. United Fruit was no ordinary company. It soon came to represent the long arm of US interests and got into a number of diplomatic scrapes in Central America; many Spanish speakers called it *el pulpo*, the octopus. This was the second tier of growing US imperialism. Ostensibly, firms such as United Fruit were part of a commerce-driven informal empire, meaning that a power like the US used trade as a means to extend influence, rather than imposing control on another nation. If trade interests were threatened, there would be gunboats to smooth over any dispute. The British empire had long been extending itself through the 'imperialism' of free trade.[36] Likewise, the US was soon to find that while such a concept might seem cheap and easy, the reality of informal empire would be messy and costly. It did not take long before the United States was intervening on a military and political level in the name of 'protecting' its interests, complicating its relationship with the Caribbean basin as the lines between business and government blurred.

United Fruit was canny in manipulating its workers as well. Its relationship with Central America was difficult. It tried to push small banana growers off their land, or put them in a very unprofitable position where the grower ended up in debt to the company, the result of which was a great deal of hostility directed at United Fruit. Many of the company's managers did not speak Spanish, which often compounded the problem. As a result, the company was eager to hire West Indians from the British islands, which it did in significant numbers throughout its holdings in Central America and Cuba. And they were more than willing to work for the company, as labour prospects in the islands were either scarce or the work was badly paid. In the first couple of decades of the twentieth century, British West Indians, and later Haitians, found work in Cuba, believed to be one of the most prosperous islands, and some 217,000 Haitians and Jamaicans emigrated there between 1910 and 1929.[37] Literate English-speaking Jamaicans were often given jobs as electricians or stevedores, rather than cane cutters and banana pickers, while women often served as domestic help for the overseers and managers. By the early 1930s there were some 65,000 British West Indians in Cuba, with 25,000 working as domestic help and 15,000 in skilled trades.[38] Meanwhile, the often illiterate, Kreyol-speaking Haitians were sent to the cane fields. However, their poor treatment was reported back to Haiti, and the government issued a decree in July 1928 that prohibited travel to Cuba to find work.[39]

British West Indians also became a significant part of the workforce in Central America, where there were constant tensions between the Hispanic locals and the immigrants – tensions that played into the hands of United Fruit. One US visitor remarked, 'One learns that although there are many, many Negroes in Puerto Barrios [Guatemala], they are seen only in such seaport towns. They are exceedingly unpopular in the country.'[40] But, of course, such antagonism meant that it was unlikely that the two sides would unite in any sort of industrial action, keeping the workforce compliant at a time when exports were rising exponentially. In 1913 United Fruit had taken the lead in the global market, having shipped some 11 million stems of bananas.[41]

By 1927, a significant British West Indian community had developed on Central America's Caribbean coast, and in Port Limón, Costa Rica, alone there were 20,000 black workers, making up 55 per cent of the population.[42] Yet growing nationalism and racism in Costa Rica, Honduras, and Guatemala imperilled this community. Many of the Central American nations' leaders were compliant with United Fruit's requests, but this also extended to banana plantations further south. In an infamous incident in 1928, the Colombian army was sent in to suppress striking banana workers in the town of Ciénaga, in the Magdalena region, near the Caribbean Sea. The army opened fire on the protesters, though the number killed has never been established, and estimates range from nine to 3,000.

In addition, many Latin American countries were further transforming or solidifying their national and international identities, and blackness was not to be part of them for some time. In some parts of Central America, nationalism instead looked towards their Spanish heritage, and whiteness, or even the Mayan past. But this utterly failed to acknowledge the changing dynamics of the present – not least that many black workers had families with Central American women – another factor feeding the antagonism between Central Americans and British West Indians. Not all West Indians had to go to Central or South America. The banana trade came to some of the islands as well. For instance, in Jamaica, there were some plantations, but they were small. Local growers there not tied into United Fruit had a guaranteed 75 per cent of the market in Britain because the Fyffes export company tried to keep that US firm out of operations on the island.[43]

*

In 1910 a young Jamaican left the island, like so many others, to work for United Fruit in Port Limón. Around the time Marcus Garvey arrived in Costa Rica to take up a position as a timekeeper, there had been a dispute between the British West Indian workers and the United Fruit managers. The Costa Rican government had put a 2 cent per stem tax on exports, and United Fruit passed that loss on to its workers, cutting pay from 85 cents to 75 cents a day. If that were not enough, the Jamaican workers wanted 1 August off to celebrate Emancipation Day, marking the anniversary of the abolition of slavery, and United Fruit's response was to select 600 of the unionized members and lock them out of the plantation for good. The firm then sent recruiters to St Kitts to find more willing workers after they were unable to secure enough Costa Ricans to fill the posts. They succeeded, but the Kittians were none too happy to discover when they arrived that they were being paid 10 cents less than the other West Indian labourers.[44] By November, the Kitts workers were also protesting, though United Fruit and the authorities in Costa Rica brought the matter to an end before December was out.

The following year, the politically minded Garvey wasted little time in setting up a bilingual newspaper, the *Nation/La Nación*, which rivalled – and rankled with – the local *Times*. The *Nation* was not long-lived – its press caught fire – and no copies remain. But Garvey was quick to catch the eye of the authorities, and his fellow workers. One item in the *Times* noted, after the destruction of Garvey's press, that 'News reaches Siquirres [a nearby town] that Marcus Aurelius Garvey is dead and buried. Poor fellow! He was killed from the stench of his own rubbish-heap.'[45]

Garvey would go on from this inauspicious start to become one of the most influential black thinkers of his time, though his fortunes would rise and fall in epic swells. Garvey left Limón in 1911 for Panama, and attempted to set up a newspaper in Bocas del Toro, where many British West Indian canal workers lived, but he was dogged by ill health and eventually returned to Jamaica. He went to England, arriving in 1912, and returned again to Jamaica in 1914. That same year, he set up the Universal Negro Improvement Association and African Communities (Imperial) League (UNIA) to promote black unity. The organization was social in nature, offering debates and literary events, to foster further education and self-improvement.

Although the majority of Jamaicans shared an African heritage, there was a distinct order of precedence, with lighter-skinned people at the top, and darker at the bottom. The darker a person was, the more difficult it was for them to succeed. The idea that light-skinned coloured people should unite with darker ones, under the banner of a 'Universal Negro' – i.e. black – heritage was not going to gain the support of the light-skinned middle classes, despite Garvey's efforts, and he faced continual criticism and attacks in the press.[46]

Frustrated, he left the island again, this time for New York. Harlem, home to both a large African-American community as well as many Jamaicans and West Indians, proved more fertile ground for his vision. Soon Garvey had built UNIA into a large movement, launched the *Negro World* newspaper, and later sold shares in a shipping line, Black Star Line, meant to rival the elegant White Star Line. He also devised a scheme to reignite the African-American settlement of Liberia, which had been colonized by freed blacks around a century earlier, in 1820, after the American Colonization Society bought land on the west coast of Africa. He was soon in negotiations with the Liberian government and started to raise money for the plan. UNIA branches sprang up across the United States, and Garvey was often on the move making speeches. He even returned to Central America in 1921, though he had to reassure United Fruit and the authorities that he was not there to cause trouble.[47] More UNIA branches popped up in his wake: there were fifty-two UNIA branches among British West Indians in Cuba, forty-seven in Panama, twenty-three in Costa Rica, eight in Honduras, and three in Guatemala.[48]

Garvey very quickly appeared on the radar of both the British and the US authorities, who found him a worrying presence. Indeed, Robert Lansing, the US secretary of state during this period, warned that Garvey's actions 'might repeat the French experience in Haiti' if he were not stopped.[49] And a confidential monthly review of 'revolutionary movements' given to the British Cabinet in 1921 claimed that 'unfortunately trade and labour unions among the coloured employees are becoming much better organized, and agitators of Marcus Garvey type [sic], who thunder against White rule and preach the doctrine of self-determination . . . are becoming factors to be reckoned with'.[50] But even before that, riots in Washington and Chicago in 1919 had been significant enough to cause concern in London. One secret 1919 Home Office report, 'Unrest Among the Negroes', claimed, 'It now seems clear that the riots were not the sporadic outcome of race prejudice, but the first fruits of the doctrine of socialistic equality preached by agitators to negro audiences throughout the country.'[51] The report discussed recent disturbances in British Honduras and Jamaica, concluding that they were caused by anger over work assignments. But it noted 'it is certain that the various negro organizations in the United States will not leave the British Colonies alone', naming black publications and prominent organizers, including Garvey.

Within a few years, the US was prepared to take more drastic measures, and in 1923 Garvey was charged with the federal offence of mail fraud. He was imprisoned for three months. By this point UNIA was faltering – there were bills overdue, and Garvey's back-to-Africa plans with Liberia had hit the buffers. He was arrested again in 1925, and upon his release from prison in 1927 he returned to England, and then Jamaica, where he was this time embraced. By 1929 he had set up the island's first political party, the People's Political Party, but he soon had trouble with the authorities, and served a brief prison sentence. His popularity at home began to wane.

In the years that followed, he took stances that were often at odds with black West Indian and African-American popular opinion – there were strikes he did not support, his views on returning to Africa rankled with prominent black American leaders, and supporters found his views on Ethiopia's Haile Selassie confusing. Garvey had earlier championed the leader of Ethiopia, the Ras Tafari, as the spiritual messiah for black people. But Italy's invasion of Ethiopia in 1935, and Selassie's subsequent departure during the battle, were, to Garvey, occasion for criticism. But many saw this war as a rallying point uniting blacks throughout the world, and Garvey's disapproval of Selassie lost him even more followers. By 1935, and living in London, Garvey found himself vocally opposed and socially ostracized by a younger generation of Caribbean intellectuals, such as Trinidadians George Padmore and C. L. R. James.[52] And after his death in 1940, his influence declined still further. But his call for black pride and unity did not languish long; later generations would find a new appreciation for his message.

*

When the First World War began in 1914, many people in the British Caribbean were willing to put aside ill will and resentments towards the mother country. The British West Indies Regiment (BWIR) was formed in 1915. There was much initial enthusiasm as men enlisted, some out of a sense of patriotism, others for pay, and others from more political motivations, hoping a good war might lead to reforms; in the end the regiment boasted more than 15,600 men. However, in March 1916, a ship carrying recruits to Britain was attacked at sea, forcing it to divert to Halifax, Nova Scotia. The ship and the men on board were ill-prepared for the remnants of a Canadian winter, and soon some suffered such severe frostbite that deaths and amputations followed. When news of this circulated back to the islands, potential recruits were more wary about signing up. And if the Halifax incident did not dissuade young men on the islands, then reports from friends and family in the battles might have. As it turned out, many BWIR soldiers ended up far from the front lines, and were put to work digging cable trenches and even cleaning latrines. In the face of global battle, some West Indian soldiers were reduced to little more than orderlies.[53]

Although some in the British high command thought that black colonial subjects could not be given the task of killing white Europeans, many battalions of the BWIR did see action on the Western Front. Two battalions were also sent to fronts in Palestine and Jordan, and many others were put to work behind the scenes. Towards the end of the war, when British soldiers were to receive pay rises of around 50 per cent, BWIR troops would get nothing because they were considered 'natives'.[54] This led to a rebellion among the members of the 9th Battalion, who attacked their white officers and protested against the blatant discrimination. After some soldiers refused to do any more work, the War Office decided to disband the entire regiment. A few of the men organized a secret group known as the Caribbean League, but it was later betrayed to officers. Some of those involved went to prison, and one was even executed by firing squad.[55] By the war's end, 1,256 West Indians had been killed, and 697 wounded.

The British troops were not, however, the only West Indians to join the war effort. French subjects in Guadeloupe did as well, with some 1,470 being killed in Europe, out of 11,021 who were mobilized.[56] For its part, the United States tried to shore up security around what it considered its zone of influence during the war's early years. US interest in keeping Germany out of the Caribbean led to the purchase in 1917 of the Danish Virgin Islands at around the time America entered the conflict in Europe. The US paid $25 million for the islands of St Thomas, St Croix, and St John's, whose combined population was about 27,000 people. When the US sent inspectors to see what they had bought, the report was not encouraging. It said the islands faced problems that required 'the most elementary improvement of the present conditions . . . with particular reference to sanitation, hygiene, public morality, finances, etc.', which it considered to be 'so many and so grave'.[57] The outright purchase of the island was not seen by its neighbours as a necessarily positive move to ensure the safety of the Caribbean, but rather as a continued imperial advance. However, Virgin Islanders were hopeful that US rule would bring social reform, jobs, and universal suffrage, but they were not even given citizenship until 1927. Puerto Ricans had received theirs a decade earlier, under the Jones–Shafroth Act of 2 March 1917, which also made these new citizens eligible to be drafted into the military – fortunate timing given that the US was about to enter the First World War the following month.

The US purchase of the islands continued to annoy well past the end of the war, giving rise to an anxiety that the United States could simply buy up whatever islands it wanted. A critical editorial in a 1933 copy of the Jamaica *Daily Gleaner* warranted enough attention from a US official to be clipped and sent to Washington.[58] The piece reported that rumours had started in London, at the annual West Indies service at St Andrew's Church, claiming that the United States might take some of the island in repayment for British war debt. It cited the 'fervent protestation which Denmark made years ago that the Virgin Islands . . . would remain part and parcel of Danish Sovereignty, the Government . . . sold those colonies to America. Britain might do the same thing, the preacher hinted.' The editorial raged that 'Some individuals, including Senators, think that the Caribbean Sea should become an American Lake' because it would strengthen the US position in Panama and the region. The editorial pointed out, however, that the British government had no intention of letting this happen, and that the colonies were not for sale. And, it warned, 'it is well that public opinion in the British West Indies should maintain a solid front against such vapourings . . . The difference between British and American administrations is as wide as east is from the west. The British West Indies prefer to remain within the Empire than to share the fate of the Virgin Islands, whose inhabitants are in the welter of poverty.'

*

The adage 'when America sneezes, the rest of the world catches cold' seemed particularly apposite after the Wall Street crash of 1929. The

West Indian islands that remained beholden to sugar were especially susceptible, as prices for the commodity plummeted. This had been preceded, inevitably, by a boom. During the First World War there had been demand for sugar bolstered by the collapse of European beet because of the fighting. In Cuba, the price for sugar in 1912 was 1.95 cents per pound; by 1920 it had reached 23 cents per pound. At the same time, US investors were putting money in, and everyone was scrambling to buy land, while also trying to pay workers as little as possible on the island.[59] With the onset of the financial crisis, however, the US turned inward and implemented tariff protection for its own beet sugar producers, pushing out Cuban imports.[60] Sugar prices on the island dropped from $2.17 a pound in 1928 to $0.57 by 1932,[61] and Cuban production dropped from 4.67 million US tons in 1930 to 2 million US tons only three years later.[62] The decade that followed would be one of hardship for many throughout the Caribbean, even those no longer involved in sugar production. The knock-on effect would depress wages and standards of living throughout the region.

Around the same time, West Indians across the islands were beginning to organize into labour unions. Trinidad had a Workingmen's Association dating back to 1897, and by 1920 it had about 6,000 members. Other islands followed suit, often after a period of unrest or a strike.[63] The Caribbean and Central America had a combustible mix during this time: low wages, physically demanding labour, living conditions that did not match the contracts offered, and the antipathy of the often foreign, mostly US-owned companies who saw West Indian labourers as cheap and expendable. In the British West Indies, according to historian Nigel Bolland, there was an important additional factor: the angry demobilized West Indian soldier.[64] After their bad experiences during the war, there was a growing awareness of the persistent discrimination against West Indians, almost as if the islands and their inhabitants were preserved in social aspic. Also, throughout the 1920s and 1930s, many British West Indians had been out into the world searching for work, and they brought back an awareness of their place in it. Events in Russia had captivated many Caribbean people, who were interested in what communism could bring to the very unequal world of the islands. On a more local level, there was also a mounting anger within many of the colonies that so little was being done to help alleviate the dire poverty and poor living conditions of so many people. Protests and strikes erupted in the 1930s across Cuba, Jamaica, Trinidad, Puerto Rico, Suriname, British Honduras, St Kitts, St Vincent, Lucia, Barbados, Antigua, and Guiana.

There had been industrial action in the preceding decade with strikes in Trinidad, St Lucia, British Honduras, and the Bahamas; but the ones that followed were not only fiercer but also infused with a piquancy for the people of the British West Indies.[65] Of course the unrest coincided with the Great Depression, but the 1930s also marked the centenary of abolition (the apprenticeship period of slavery ended in 1838). Despite his declining popularity, the work of Marcus Garvey continued to influence many, and there was a growing anger at the discrimination that so many people of colour faced abroad and at home.

Despite the vocal unrest by labourers in Trinidad and some of the larger islands, it was British Honduras that lit the fuse that set off a damaging series of strikes in Britain's colonies. On 10 September 1931 a hurricane hit British Honduras, killing around 1,000 people. The damage further slowed the already sluggish timber trade – then the mainstay of the economy. Most woodcutters were out of work, and there was little other employment. At the same time, the colonial government was slow to distribute disaster relief, which, when it did come, was in the form of public-works jobs such as rock-breaking or being forced to queue for a small ration of rice. By 1934, Hondurans took to the streets to protest at the woeful conditions, the demonstrations accelerated under the leadership of Antonio Soberanis Gómez, who set up the Labourers and Unemployed Association (LUA). Trade unions were illegal in many colonies, but Soberanis Gómez still managed to lead a series of strikes from autumn 1934 into the following year.[66]

By the end of 1935 there had been strikes or protests in St Kitts, Trinidad, St Vincent, St Lucia and British Guiana, causing a US observer to conclude there was a 'definite racial consciousness on the part of the negroes of the West Indies . . . an emergence in the black man of a "will to power" as expressed through labour agitation', though in a hint of what lay ahead, the American also felt there was a 'suspected presence of organized agitation throughout the Leeward and Windward Islands which is most likely of Communistic or Soviet origin'.[67]

Meanwhile, in Panama, many of the men who went out to work on the canal or the earlier railway had decided to stay, despite the hard work and bad conditions. In 1930 the black population in Panama, including the Canal Zone, was estimated to be between 50,000 and 90,000 people, making it a sizeable community.[68] The question of British West Indians in Panama was complicated: many of these labourers had illegitimate children with local or West Indian women, which meant that these offspring would not qualify for British citizenship. Panamanian authorities were also concerned about them, although the British legation considered them to be 'a purely Panamanian problem'. The legation's report went on, 'not only do they and their offspring make up a numerous category, but they are increasing rapidly . . . in years to come it may not improbably happen that the population of the Republic is in danger of becoming West Indian racially to a predominating extent and, unless miscegenation occurs on a large scale, there may be reason to fear a clash one day'.[69]

The question of what to do with the West Indian community kept flaring up, usually prompted by corresponding swings in employment, and surges of Panamanian nationalism. By the 1930s, Panama tried to prohibit foreign workers. One British dispatch claimed a West Indian informant said 'the Panamanian trades unions are deliberately trying to oust alien labour from the local market, with the sinister design of instituting a general strike'.[70] The island governors took the matter seriously, not least because they did not feel they had the resources to cope with a large unemployed population looking to return home. One 1933 dispatch to Barbados explained that 'the continued economic depression in Panama has drawn attention more than ever to the problem presented by the many coloured West Indians unemployed in this country. The question has been taken up by both the Government and the press – in the case of some newspapers with an animosity and in a spirit of racial antagonism which are very regrettable.'[71] But by this point, many West Indians had no intention of leaving Panama.

The combination of poor living and working conditions, the change in political climate brought about by events in Russia, the rise in the cost of imported foodstuffs, and the lack of opportunity were a potent combination across the region. Strikes broke out over varying mixtures of these global and local elements. One St Lucia official complained in a letter to Barbados that the root of recent disturbances on St Vincent was the 'bitter black v. white feeling arising from this Italy-Ethiopian [c.1935] war, which has been carefully worked up by the worst type of local agitator'.[72] There was a riot in Kingstown, the capital of St Vincent, in October 1935 when a mob of about 300 people tried to break into the Legislative Council building, an action accompanied by looting. Shops owned by merchants of European descent, especially the Portuguese, were targeted. This was partly because the unrest started in the first place over a rumour that shopkeepers were going to raise their prices. Indeed, a bill that was said to approve the measure was about to have its second reading in the assembly on the day of the riot – which is why members of the public went there to protest against its implementation.[73] A confidential US intelligence report laid the blame for the demonstration on unemployment, low pay, and 'racial antagonism' brought about by the Italian–Ethiopian conflict, as the Windward Island governor also claimed. However, the US observer felt the real threat was the 'agitation among the labouring classes' and the circulation of 'subversive propaganda'.[74]

A few weeks later, on 4 November 1935, workers in St Lucia who unloaded coal went on strike, calling for better pay. There had been an earlier strike on Buckley's Estate over the fact that wages for cane-cutters had dropped from 11d per ton of cane in 1932 to 8d per ton, and they wanted it restored to the previous level.[75]

In the same year, some 300 unemployed Jamaicans marched on the offices of the mayor of Kingston, calling for work and financial assistance. The US consul on the island was dismissive, noting in a memo that a mule that had been hit by a truck and needed to be shot at the same time 'created more excitement than did the riot of the unemployed'.[76] The British officials could ill afford to be so blasé. Many were perplexed and did not know what to do with so many unemployed and angry people. They were not willing to consider forcing employers to pay more, and they were usually quick to call for troops to suppress trouble. Some thought colonial resettlement might be an option, such as sending islanders to Guiana, where cane fields needed labour. The governor of British Guiana noted the lack of fellow West Indians, pointing out to the governor of Barbados that 'it appeared that some of your people had the impression that British Guiana is a feverish swamp where Barbadians could not risk their lives'.[77] He thought people from the islands could work in the fields during the harvest season, as they were doing in Cuba and the Dominican Republic, but such a plan failed to materialize.

Even Barbados, which did not have the same record of rioting as the other islands, had unrest in July 1937 over continued unemployment. The island still relied on sugar for much of its income, and the price had been badly hit by the depression as well. Prices fetched in London plummeted from the 1923 level of 26 shillings per hundredweight to 5 shillings by 1934, with wages hovering around a shilling a day, scarcely enough to subsist on.[78] A few years later, the governor of Barbados, E. J. Waddington, set out his position on the emigration of workers, saying – and echoing earlier arguments in favour of a mobile workforce – that there were '20,000 in excess of that which the Island can adequately support', with the island's population at that point around 200,000; but in 1921, when it was 156,000, there was no labour shortage.[79] Waddington claimed emigration was the only 'practical solution' and he was looking to move at least 400 people to St Lucia. He actually felt that sparsely populated British Guiana and British Honduras were the only 'possible outlets' for large-scale resettlement, but St Lucia, being closer to Barbados, would likely appeal to more volunteers.[80]

Likewise, there was unrest in the Bahamas, which had enjoyed a boom during America's prohibition era. Between 1919 and 1933, rum-runners smuggled illicit alcohol into the US, while thirsty visitors arrived to drink legally. This helped to stimulate trade in the Bahamas, partly because of its proximity to the US, with the islands operating as liquor depots, as well as selling their own rum. But with the repeal of the Eighteenth Amendment in 1933, the party was over, and there were no other similar means of income. The salt industry provided what little work there was, yet the pay was a pittance. In 1937, a protest started at the saltworks on the southern island of Great Inagua.[81] In Trinidad, too, in this period, protests erupted from the sugar fields to the docks to the oil industry, which had begun in 1912. Now oil workers went on strike for better wages and when the police attempted to arrest the strike's leader, Tubal Uriah 'Buzz' Butler, riots broke out and other groups of workers joined the strike. By 22 June the island was paralysed. The governor called in two warships and mobilized troops to suppress the unrest surrounding the walkouts. By the time order was re-established, fourteen strikers were dead, fifty-nine were injured, and dozens more were imprisoned.

Meanwhile, in Jamaica, unrest continued as sugar and banana

workers demanded more pay. Strikes and riots peppered the intervening years, but it was a strike in 1938 that brought the condition of the workers in the West Indies to the attention of the British government. On 1 May employees of Tate & Lyle sugar producers went on strike over the low wages on the Frome estate in the south-west of the island in Westmoreland Parish. One labourer, Alfred Francis, told the *Daily Gleaner*: 'It is impossible for us to live on the wage we have been paid; the amount received is no fair reward for the work we are called upon to do.' The company had said it would pay four or five shillings per day for work, and for such a wage many people came from all over the island in the hope of securing employment. But, like Francis, they often only got a bit of work here or there. He secured only two days' work the first week, and only one the following week.[82] This unrest turned violent the next day when the police opened fire on the strikers, while eighty acres of sugar cane burnt to the ground. That morning, men and women were chanting their demands for 'a dollar a day' in pay (about five shillings).[83] One breathless journalist on the scene wrote that the 'strikers are running around arming themselves with anything they can lay their hands on – pieces of wood . . . iron pipes, old iron axles . . . The mob has got clean out of hand – they are a raging torrent of violence.'[84] Like all the other strikes and associated riots, it was suppressed with violence. But reports were not limited to the Jamaican press, and the colonial secretary, William Ormsby-Gore, was soon forced to explain to the House of Commons what had happened, after which a commission was named to investigate the causes of the riot. His successor, Malcolm MacDonald, told the Cabinet that these events were 'ultimately . . . due to economic causes', though he also blamed the unrest on other underlying problems, especially 'a good deal of racial feeling between coloured and white people, which had been much stimulated by events in Abyssinia and had now become serious'.[85] The unrest was not confined to the fields. Disturbances spread through the streets and docks, with stevedores striking on 19 May 1938. A report compiled by the US consul on the island described events in Kingston on 23 May:

> It spread with startling speed. Before eight o'clock in the morning crowds of rioters took possession of the streets. All stores and offices were closed. Factories were invaded and the workmen forced to leave. Tramways ceased running. Sanitary workers of the civic

corporation joined the movement and the crowds littered the streets with garbage and refuse. Telephone service was impaired. Electric current and water supply alone continued their service.[86]

In most of the islands, the workers who organized were black people; this continued to be the case in Trinidad and Guiana, even though a significant proportion of labourers were Indian. Indeed, Indian workers in Guiana had plenty of reason to go on the march. In 1935 a black cane-cutter could earn $1.39 per day while an Indian would only get $1.05 for the same job. Wages on average were $112 a year for black workers, and $98 for Indian.[87] Although there was some Indian participation early on in Trinidad and Guiana, long-standing resentments lingered, and the two groups failed to mobilize, a fissure that would later turn into a serious political gulf. Guiana too had a number of disputes in the late 1930s.

These strikes, and the unions that followed in their wake, would prove to be a crucial step on the road to independence. The more Britain seemed powerless to alleviate poverty, the more people thought about other options, including the end of colonial rule. The development of trade unions allowed for the construction of the necessary infrastructure, namely political parties. In Jamaica, lawyer Alexander Bustamante set up the Bustamante Industrial Trade Union in 1938, and he would later become Jamaica's first prime minister. Many of the leaders and lawyers from this period would not simply return to work after the strikes but go on to help forge independent islands. At the same time the government in London realized that matters had got out of hand. Concerned about claims of woeful living conditions and wages, a commission headed by Walter Guinness, Lord Moyne, was set up in 1938 to investigate. The group lost little time setting off for the West Indies. The strikers had put the islands back on the imperial map.

*

Cuba, too, was unsettled in this period; in 1933 there had been a well-supported general strike in Havana, and other cities followed suit, during the dictatorship of Gerardo Machado y Morales. The workers who made up a large part of the strike were in the sugar business, and during this period they seized mills and halted operations. There were also attacks on black workers – including Afro-Cubans, as they continued to be seen as a potential source of destabilization. During the sugar boom, Jamaicans and Haitians had been brought in as a cheaper source of labour, but with the onset of the economic downturn, hostilities were brewing. The United States, coping with the depression, had repatriated its workers, with Puerto Ricans and Virgin Islanders sent back in 1931–2, and Jamaicans were brought back around 1930–33. These outside labourers – *braceros* – were also seen as a threat to Cubans' growing national identity, or *Cubanidad*.[88] Distrust of blacks on the island – the events of the Partido Independiente de Color in 1912 lingered in public memory – and racism more generally continued to permeate the official mentality, and underpinned the attacks on blacks in the 1930s. Unrest against Machado was met with further violence and repression, until he could no longer control the situation, and by the end of 1933 he had left Cuba for the Bahamas, allegedly with seven bags of gold.[89] A parade of provisional presidents followed. Carlos Céspedes was sworn into office in 1933, but the army rose up against him. He was replaced by the favourite of the highly politicized students, Ramón Grau San Martín, but his tenure only lasted four months. Strikes, unrest, and short-lived presidents followed. However, by 1935 Rubén Fulgencio Batista Zaldivar, the son of a cane-cutter who had worked his way up through the army and had been involved in the rebellion against Céspedes, became the power behind the office of president. A number of puppet presidents were installed, and army suppression began to bring an end to the strikes. Some reforms were implemented, including the official recognition of the Communist Party in 1938. In 1940 a new constitution was brought into force, and Batista and Grau San Martín faced off in an election in the same year, with Batista emerging the victor.

*

At the beginning of the twentieth century, the two sides of Hispaniola were once again forced into a strange alignment by external pressures. It was, this time, not the competing interests of France or Spain causing the problem, but the United States: Haiti and the Dominican Republic both found themselves under occupation by US Marines at roughly the same time. Haiti was first, in July 1915. Independent for more than a century, Haiti now faced the military presence and paternalistic attitude of this unwelcome intruder, which would last for nearly twenty years.

US troops had, since 1900, made brief landings many times in the name of protecting US interests.[90] And although Haitian politics remained complex, and often baffling to outsiders, this did not stop the creep of US capital into the island. The political chaos accelerated around 1900; there were seven presidents in the five years leading up to 1915, six of whom were killed by their opponents.[91] The most gruesome was an angry mob's dismembering President Vilbrun Guillaume Sam in July 1915. Soon after this incident, President Woodrow Wilson used the political unrest as a pretext to send troops to the island to protect US interests – and he sent the marines without a vote from Congress. US firms had become involved with infrastructure projects, including electricity and railways. Given the outbreak of the First World War, he was also concerned by the threat of possible German influence on the island – there were communities of German merchants in the ports who had come over throughout the nineteenth century. When the US arrived, it not only established a military presence but also took control of the customs houses to get the country's debt under control, as it had done in the Dominican Republic in 1905.[92] Prior to the official military occupation, in December 1914 troops had entered the National Bank and taken $500,000 worth of gold – or at today's value $11 million – and loaded it onto the USS *Machias*. The US claimed it was to pay Haitian debts to US banks, and no one on the island had stopped the marines.[93]

Not long after the marines' arrival in 1915, an acquiescent president, Philippe Sudre Dartiguenave, was installed in office, and a treaty between the two nations was soon ratified. The US secretary of state Robert Lansing was uncomfortable about the arrangement, and wrote to President Wilson, criticizing this 'high handed' behaviour while also resigning himself to the mission to 'cure the anarchy and disorder that prevails in that Republic'.[94]

The marines reformed the Haitian military, setting up the gendarmerie in their own image.[95] They also set about building roads and bridges and installing telephone lines to make the infrastructure more amenable to commerce: Haiti had too many natural resources for the US to let them lie dormant. The works went ahead using forced labour – the conditions were near-enslavement. But many Haitians were reluctant to accept this fate and were quick to organize opposition. There had been mounting hostility to the US prior to the invasion as peasants were pushed off their land to make way for the US project to build a rail line.[96] It did not take long for there to be clashes between the troops and a group of peasant fighters known as the *cacos* in the north of the island. As a result the US declared martial law.[97] Resistance leaders Charlemagne Péralte and Benoît Batraville continued to rally their supporters against the US soldiers. They were killed in 1919 and 1920 respectively, and the fighting carried on, though many peasants were either killed or saw their homes burnt down. By this point the occupation had attracted public criticism both in the United States and overseas, as reports of marine abuses and the attacks on Haitians were relayed by missionaries and visitors. The occupation even became an issue in the 1920 presidential election.[98] The fighting was mostly suppressed from 1922 to 1929, and the occupation continued. However, the economic troubles triggered by the Great Depression led to strikes in Haiti involving students and other sectors of society as many people plunged into poverty. In 1930, one visitor to the island gave a grim diagnosis of Haiti's condition:

> I have said the country was poor; miserable would be more appropriate a term . . . The directing class having naught but contempt for the negro (they being mulattres) have done nothing to instil ambition in him [the peasant]. All they have done once every two years or so is to drive him out of his fields by means of armed forced and take part in a revolution of one general against another.[99]

The labour unrest culminated in a skirmish in Aux Cayes, in the south of the island. The marines fired on an angry mob, and twelve people were killed.[100] International pressure to end the occupation intensified, and in the United States the Forbes Commission, established to review the occupation, recommended the withdrawal of troops. By 1934 US troops had left, but the scars would take longer to fade. The previous year the new American president, Franklin D. Roosevelt, articulated what became known as the 'good neighbour' policy begun by his predecessor, Herbert Hoover. This was an attempt to buffer the growing anti-Americanism among the US's neighbours. On a practical level, it included the withdrawal of troops from Haiti and less willingness to intervene militarily, at least for a while.

Some marines – and there were many from the southern US, which was racially segregated at the time – wrote about their time in Haiti, and a few published books. With titles like Captain John Houston Craige's *Cannibal Cousins* or Faustin Wirkus's *The White King of La Gonave: The True Story of the Sergeant of Marines Who Was Crowned King on a Voodoo Island*, the contents often exploited long-held stereotypes about the island.[101] Despite all the controversy about the occupation, the United States still managed to oversee Haiti's economic affairs until 1942.[102]

The Dominican Republic, also convulsed by long-running power struggles, was not far behind Haiti in seeing the arrival of the marines. The twentieth century had not started well – in 1899, the dictator General Ulises Heureaux was assassinated and Ramón Cáceres eventually took power until he, too, was assassinated in 1911. From that point, as in Haiti, there was a succession of presidents, none of whom lasted long. In 1915 President Wilson, in an echo of what had happened to customs revenue on the island in 1905, demanded that the island turn over its customs money to the United States once again. This time, the idea was met with fierce resistance and voted down. The following year the marines arrived. With the US unable to find a suitable puppet president, martial law was declared, and the soldiers put locals to work on infrastructure projects. One US objective was to divorce political office and military control on the island, so, as in Haiti, the marines trained a military force, the Guardia Nacional, to patrol the border and repress political insurgents, among other duties.[103] By 1920, the continued occupation of the Dominican Republic surfaced as an issue in the US presidential election. As that part of the island was more stable, marines were given their leaving orders in 1924. However, the United States was not so quick to relinquish customs control there either, and that stayed under its authority until 1940.

During the occupation, a young working-class Dominican named Rafael Leónidas Trujillo Molina enlisted in the Guardia Nacional and was quick to move up the ranks before the United States left the island. He proved himself to be a shrewd and ruthless political operator as well, and by 1930 he was able to rig an election and win the presidency, neatly combining the nation's political affairs with its military once again. His fraud was obvious: there were more votes counted than there were eligible voters.[104] The island then sank into thirty years of dictatorship. Trujillo quickly made his mark, changing the fifteenth-century name of the capital, Santo Domingo, to the more modern – and vainglorious – Ciudad Trujillo (Trujillo City) in 1936; but this was the least of his offences. His regime was marked by violence, corruption, and brutality.

Migrant labourers from Haiti had been coming to the north-west of Santo Domingo, along the border, to work in the cane fields for decades. Some even arrived during the period of mutual occupation, when US investors were opening new sugar estates. The border area had long been fluid – a century of Dominican independence still had not passed. People lived together with little problem, intermarried, and spoke Spanish and Kreyol. But Trujillo, like some of his fellow presidents in Central America, was obsessed with rooting national identity in a white, Hispanic heritage that was very much out of step with demographic reality. For Trujillo, staring into a sea of mulatto faces wherever he went on the island, this was clearly an enormous leap of the imagination. As in Central America, the Dominican leader also wanted to ignore the island's African – let alone its Haitian – past. In the 1808 war the creoles fought to have the island returned to Spanish rule, rather than take up the revolutionary struggle with the Haitians. There had been lingering resentment during the period of Haitian rule that had come before independence, yet both sides of the island shared a common African heritage. The relationship between the two was a knot of contradiction. While Haitians often embraced their African roots, as was reflected by their religious practices and other cultural manifestations, many Dominicans generally looked to Spain for their heritage, not to Haiti and certainly not to Africa.

In August 1937 Trujillo decided to make a tour of the border region, often using horses to reach more remote areas and talking to people of all backgrounds, giving no indication of what was to come. On 2 October 1937, he made a speech in the border town of Dajabón, in which he proclaimed:

> For some months, I have travelled and traversed the frontier . . . I have seen, investigated, and inquired about the needs of the population. To the Dominicans who were complaining of the depredations by Haitians living among them, thefts of cattle, provisions, fruits, etc., and were thus prevented from enjoying in peace the products of their labor, I have responded, 'I will fix this.' And we have already begun to remedy the situation.[105]

His remedy was a massacre. He sent troops to the north-west frontier and the Cibao region, with instructions to kill any 'Haitians' living there. He also ordered the checkpoint at the border closed, in effect trapping thousands of people trying to leave. The killings began on 3 October. Many trying to flee to safety had to cross the Massacre river, named for a battle between Spanish troops and buccaneers in 1728. Now, it was again the site of violence and bloodshed. But the soldiers under orders to kill had a problem: how to identify who was Haitian and who was not? They turned to an old trick, first implemented when Trujillo had imposed an 'immigrant tax' on Haitians. They asked them to say the word *perejil*, which means parsley, or *tijera*, which means scissors. The theory was that Haitians could be identified by their supposed inability to pronounce the 'r' in the way a native Spanish speaker would.

With the targets now identified, the troops followed orders to bayonet, hack with a machete, or simply club Haitians to death – bullets would have revealed that guns belonging to the army had done the killing, but machetes could in theory obscure the identity of the killers because most people in the countryside had at least one.[106] Not for nothing is the ensuing slaughter called *el Corte*, the cutting, or – in a more macabre translation – the harvest. Haitians call it *kout kouto-a*, the stabbing.[107] Trujillo later justified the killings on the grounds that Haitians had been 'invading' the Dominican Republic.

By 8 October, it was over. After the deaths of an estimated 25,000 Haitians Trujillo was, momentarily, satisfied. Tens of thousands more were thought to have fled to safety. A US delegation on the island at the time noted that the 'Dajabón side is absolutely devoid of Haitians'.[108] Trujillo ordered a similar massacre the following spring in the more sparsely populated southern border region, and hundreds were killed or displaced there as well. Trujillo was later pressured into accepting an indemnity to Haiti of $750,000 (of which only $250,000 was ever paid). However, the wording of the deal, which was signed in Washington, DC on 31 December 1938, ensured that the Dominican government recognized 'no responsibility whatsoever' for the murders.[109]

And no one who witnessed the signing would have been aware that Trujillo's grandmother was a Haitian.

Chapter Ten

THE ROAD TO INDEPENDENCE

The labour unrest in the British Caribbean had become a serious cause for concern in the 1930s, and so, in 1938, the West India Royal Commission was set up, headed by Lord Moyne. Commission members went to the islands to examine living standards, and when they returned to England and published their report, the results did not please the government, and the timing was terrible. The colonial secretary Malcolm MacDonald, even wondered about the wisdom of publishing the report because it revealed 'deplorable standards of health and housing, and in social conditions generally, among the working population in the West Indies'. He and others were afraid that the findings would prompt more unrest across the islands. Yet withholding it might cause problems, too; the islanders knew the investigation had taken place. In addition, MacDonald was concerned that such a critical report could 'be fastened on by our enemies, who would make the fullest use of the strong criticisms'.[1] The prime minister, Neville Chamberlain, agreed, convinced it could inflict 'serious damage on our war effort' not only in Germany, where it could be taken advantage of and used in propaganda, but also in the US, which was 'at the present time very much on the look-out for items of information that were damaging to the British cause'.[2] However, at a meeting a few weeks later, it was decided that a summary could safely be published, as well as some of the commission's recommendations. This was intended to give island governors the freedom to implement some improvements and thus stifle any possible anger or unrest on the islands.[3] But it was not until 1945 that the report was published in full,[4] and even then, some sections on housing and the often difficult conditions for women were edited out.[5]

The United States soon found out about the report. The colonial government of India had been notified about the Moyne Commission's findings and the US consul general in India in turn notified Washington. According to the report, some 300,000 East Indians in Trinidad, Guiana, and Jamaica lived in conditions 'said to be sufficiently distressing to require the attention of the Government of India' and the idea of repatriation was being considered.[6] But it was thought that because 'they have no knowledge of life in India, repatriation . . . would amount simply to translation from depression to destitution'. Most of them still worked on sugar estates, which were facing a severe downturn, especially for the 18,000 who lived in Jamaica where conditions were the worst, and where Indians faced much resentment from other workers: 'the Indians have suffered most and the report described them in Jamaica as a people depressed, illiterate and friendless, deplorably housed and appallingly underfed'.[7]

One of the recommendations was the establishment of a West Indian Welfare Fund with an annual grant of £1,000,000 for twenty years, aimed at the 'general improvement of education, the health services, housing and slum clearance, the creation of labour departments, the provision of social welfare facilities, and land settlement'.[8] A subsequent Colonial Development and Welfare Act of 1940 allotted around 60 per cent of available funding to the island colonies.[9] But more importantly, the report showed the British government that workers in the West Indies were not rioting for the sake of it, or to cause trouble. The conditions in which they lived and worked were often appalling, and their demands were warranted. But then again, their poverty was not recent. The former British prime minister David Lloyd George had once called the islands 'the slums of the empire'.

The Second World War did not put an end to labour strife in the British islands. In 1944, for example, there was increasing unrest in Barbados.[10] During the war, thousands of Barbadians were working in the United States, where they earned up to $5 a day. Workers on the island made, if they were lucky, the equivalent of around $1 a day; they were well aware of the pay discrepancies. The island's governor noted that although 1,800 Barbadians had left for the United States, there had been continued restlessness and complaints from planters that they could not find workers because the pay on the island continued to be so low.[11] A short time later, he received a telegram from the colonial secretary, reporting that the sugar price was predicted to rise, and pointing out that, 'It might, however, make a good deal of political difference if the appearance of the employers yielding to threats was avoided by anticipating the demands of the labour representatives by a specific offer of increased wages as soon as the price is announced.'[12] For the Barbadians in the United States, the situation, while financially better, came with its own challenges. A report from Barbados to the colonial secretary at the end of 1944 noted that '340 labourers were repatriated from the United States of America. The majority of these were not prepared to renew their contracts . . . From reports which I have received it seems that many of them disliked the conditions . . . particularly in the southern states; they complained of the quality of food and the rough treatment they received.'[13]

*

The West Indies were drawn into the Second World War almost from the outset. German U-boats had been quick to attack in the Atlantic and the Caribbean, disrupting the movement of oil and other necessary supplies and putting passenger ships at risk. With the fall of Holland in 1940, British and French forces from Jamaica and Martinique immediately occupied Aruba and Curaçao to ensure they did not fall into German hands. Aruba was particularly important because it was refining the oil discovered offshore from Venezuela and could process in excess of 250,000 barrels of crude a day.[14] In September that year, a deal was struck in which the United States gave fifty destroyers to Britain in exchange for the right to set up bases on ninety-nine-year, rent-free leases in British territory in the region, including Trinidad, Bermuda, Guiana, Antigua, and St Lucia.

The establishment of the Chaguaramas base for navy destroyers was contentious from the beginning. On the north-west tip of Trinidad, the bay had long been a popular bathing beach, but with the arrival of US soldiers it was suddenly off-limits. Even more distressing were the eviction notices served to local people, who were given three months to leave their homes before the base was extended and cordoned off by the navy. There was also an air force base on the island; soon, US soldiers were everywhere. The young narrator of V. S. Naipaul's novel *Miguel Street* offers a glimpse of this world:

The Americans were crawling all over Port of Spain in those days, making the city really hot. Children didn't take long to find out that they were easy people, always ready to give with both hands. Hat began working a small racket. He had five of us going all over the district begging for chewing gum and chocolate. For every packet of chewing gum we gave him we got a cent. Sometimes I made as much as twelve cents in a day.[15]

The Yankees brought money with them, but Trinidad, while it had oil, continued to suffer a great deal of poverty, which was exacerbated by the erratic arrival of provisions and the ongoing wartime austerity. The soldiers, on the other hand, had money to burn. Some Trinidadians took jobs on the base, including work as musicians, while others looked at the Yankees' wealth and decided to try their luck in the United States. Others resented the soldiers, who enjoyed the company of the island's women and drank those rum and Coca-Colas, and indeed this particular drink – or at least a song about it – became the centre of a legal battle. US comedian Morey Amsterdam was impressed by what he was hearing in Trinidad. On the island as part of a United Service Organizations mission in 1943 to entertain troops stationed there, Amsterdam was particularly taken by a sharp calypso song originally sung by Lord Invader (Rupert Grant). Calypso music was more than a type of 'folk' tradition in Trinidad, it was a creative avenue to express social commentary in a double-edged, often humorous way. Lord Invader had adapted an old melody by composer Lionel Belasco, 'L'Année Passée', and given it contemporary lyrics in a calypso called 'Rum and Coca-Cola':

> When the Yankees first went to Trinidad
> Some of the young girls were more than glad
> They said that the Yankees treat them nice
> And they give them a better price
> They buy rum and Coca-Cola
> Went down to Point Cumana
> Both mothers and daughters
> Working for the Yankee dollar.

It was a barbed commentary on the relationship between US soldiers and local women, and the melody, combined with Lord

Invader's skill and prominence, made it an island hit. Amsterdam thought a version without the prostitution references might do well back in the United States. When he returned, he set to work and in 1944 had scripted a version for Jeri Sullavan to sing in the Versailles nightclub in New York City. It was a sensation.[16] Soon a version of the song was given to the popular Andrews Sisters trio, who scored a US Top 10 hit in 1943 with a cleaned-up version of it, singing:

> If you ever go down Trinidad
> They make you feel so very glad
> Calypso sing and make up rhyme
> Guarantee you one real good fine time
> Drinkin' rum and Coca-Cola
> Go down Point Cumana
> Both mother and daughter
> Workin' for the Yankee dollar.

This version credited Amsterdam with the music and lyrics. A short time later, New York lawyer Louis Nizer received a call from one of his former expert witnesses, musician Maurice Baron, who was upset about the Andrews Sisters song. He knew that melody better than most people – it had been included in a collection of music he had compiled, called *Calypso Songs of the West Indies* – and that the composer was Lionel Belasco, not Morey Amsterdam. Nizer took the case and later recounted how, in preparation for their prosecution, 'for three years, we followed trails from African Stick Songs to Spanish *pensamientos*, from Mexican and Indian melodies to King Ja-Ja of Barbados'.[17] They brought Belasco to New York and tracked down some of his childhood friends who remembered the original 1906 melody. Lord Invader also came to New York, and in 1947 Nizer went to trial. There were twenty-eight witnesses and the trial lasted eleven days; each note was dissected with care in the courtroom. The case did not contest the lyrical content – the suit was over the rights to the music – but there was no mistaking the similarity there either. Amsterdam claimed to have never heard Belasco's composition, saying he picked up the song from US soldiers who were singing it on the island, though he had previously said in an interview that he 'imported the song'.[18] The judge ruled in favour of Baron and the calypsonians, a decision confirmed by an appeal court ruling. This courtroom drama may be just a footnote in the rich musical history of Trinidad, but it also gives a flavour of what the island experienced when its neighbours came to visit during the war.

*

With the fall of France in June 1940, the French islands became a growing concern. There were French cruisers stationed off Martinique, and Vichy France had been clamping down on any resistance in its territories. Admiral Georges Robert arrived in Martinique with a shipload of gold sent for safe-keeping and put the islands, for the moment, under the control of Marshal Pétain's Vichy regime. One of their initial efforts included destroying a monument to the First World War in the Guadeloupian village of Trois-Rivières, a potent reminder of Free France.[19] Initially, Roosevelt was eager to keep the island neutral and not to violate the 'no transfer' agreement, which meant colonies could not pass from one European power to another. If they complied, the United States was willing to allow the shipment of consumer goods. However, after it entered the war in December 1941, it became more active in the Caribbean, taking over from the British troops in Curaçao the following year and pressuring other islands to stop trading with the French colonies. US troops also occupied Suriname to protect the bauxite mines and the exports so crucial in the production of aluminium.[20] Over the course of the summer of 1943, the Free French movement gained momentum in French Guiana, Guadeloupe, and Martinique, calming Allied fears about the territories.[21] However, it caused the British a bit of a problem. Many members of the resistance were eager to escape to nearby British territories, particularly Dominica. Not only does the island lie between Guadeloupe and Martinique, but its own past as a French colony meant it retained some of the culture and language, and around 5,000 refugees from the French islands went there. As a War Office report from 1943 observed, 'Those escaping from Martinique and Guadeloupe cross the channels, separating these islands from Dominica, in small fishing boats . . . They pay the fishermen to take them across, or steal the boats. Many, however, are drowned in attempting to cross.'[22]

Dominica could ill afford such an influx of people and tried to force them to leave. A War Office dispatch from 1943 noted that on 21 July, 1,221 people were evacuated from Dominica, and the following day another 1,229, but that still left '410 males, 431 females, and 161 children' in Roseau and Portsmouth, the capital and main town.[23] The swelling population was unsustainable. A report on the situation in Dominica in May 1943 noted 'a certain antagonistic feeling between the local population and the Fighting French', the cause of which was in the most part lack of food:

> Certain commodities are scarce, others, termed luxuries, have been prohibited. These the Dominican can put up with, but when he sees the Fighting French, who to him appear no better than he is, getting well fed with farine, vegetables and ground provision, while he goes short and, furthermore getting clothed, housed and given 5/- a week pocket money, he naturally harbours a grudge.[24]

The situation was even worse on the French islands, as refugees reported that Vichy supporters, including whites, planters, and the Catholic Church, had better access to increasingly scarce food supplies. In Guadeloupe the lack of provisions caused violent demonstrations and crowds were fired upon.[25] But the resistance grew, and the Free French were, apart from a few whites, mostly people of colour. After the war, a squat, stone obelisk-like monument was erected in Roseau, with a marble plaque bearing crossed flags of Britain and France, saying in both languages: 'Glory to the French who lost their lives in the years of Resistance, 1941–1945'.

*

The only thing young Hans Stecher knew about Trinidad was what he saw on the postage stamp from the island that he had in his collection. Little did he imagine he would soon be leaving Vienna for Trinidad's shores. The island opened its doors to a small influx of refugees, of whom Stecher is the last survivor; he is now affectionately known locally as the 'Calypso Jew'. His family was able to come to the island because of its relaxed immigration laws at the time. No visa was required: 'All you needed was to make a security deposit, either before or at the time of entry, of 50 British pounds, to ensure that the immigrant would not become a public charge, and it was refundable after one year.'[26]

The Stechers arrived in Port of Spain on 13 October 1938, and there were no other Austrian or German Jews that they knew of, bar the Strumwassers, who had a dry goods shop there. Three years later, in 1941, there was an influx of refugees when the ship *The Winnipeg*, flying the Vichy flag, left the south of France bound for Santo Domingo. It was intercepted by a Dutch torpedo boat in the Caribbean, and its passengers were taken to Trinidad.

The British government was wary of 'enemy aliens', concerned that some refugees were actually spies. As a result, all German and Austrian passport-holders on the island were interned. Stecher remembers the internment camp as being 'surrounded by a tall barbed wire fence with sentry towers and search lights in the corner'. Children were allowed to go to school, while adults dug ditches, took classes, and kept small garden plots. Even upon their release at the end of the war, there was still a measure of restriction. The refugees had to check in daily with the police, were forbidden to drive, and could not leave the city without police permission.[27]

The West Indies did not see an influx of refugees on the same scale as some other countries, notably the United States, but a significant number came and were scattered about the islands. Some people fleeing Europe tried to get to Cuba – indeed, that island had earlier seen the arrival of many republicans escaping the Spanish Civil War – while the Dominican Republic, in an effort to counter the negative image that prevailed after the 1937 massacre, openly welcomed Jewish refugees. Behind the seemingly generous offer lay Trujillo's desire to continue to 'whiten' the country by bringing in these settlers. Between 600 and 700 Jews took up the offer, settling in the town of Sosúa, on the north coast of the island. Many did not stay long, opting instead to get visas for the US, but a small group of Jewish families continues to live in the town today.

*

After the Second World War, Britain was exhausted – bankrupt and bomb-scarred, its commodities still on rations. The interaction between the US and the Caribbean in the Second World War, and its role in Europe's victory, left no doubt in the minds of people across the region. Its corporate interests, exemplified by the banana plantations and sugar refineries, coupled with its military prowess ensured that the United States was the true power in the region, a realization that was met with mixed feelings. One result was to add fuel to the growing fire for independence in the West Indies. It was clear that Europe had taken a heavy blow in this war. The sun seemed to be setting on European imperial powers, while the might of the United States was rising. For Britain, the expense of global dominions, especially in the face of growing resistance to colonial rule, meant that its empire slowly began to unravel, first with the independence of India in 1947, and later with the African colony of Ghana in 1957, events watched with great interest in the Caribbean. Reforms had followed the unrest in the late 1930s, with more islands granted suffrage and new political parties also gaining legitimacy throughout the 1940s. However, the war's end brought an enormous shift, and men and women from the islands answered Britain's call for help in rebuilding. In 1948 the *Empire Windrush* arrived at Tilbury Docks in Essex with 492 passengers eager to work hard in the jobs they had been promised. But what they found in the 'mother country' was often racism and poverty, and it shattered their ideas that they were British – instead, they were treated as outsiders. White Londoners would stop and stare at the new arrivals, many of whom were among the thousands of West Indians who had fought for Britain during the Second World War, while landlords often refused to rent to black people, who were frequently forced to pay exorbitant rents for substandard housing. Trinidad calypsonian Lord Kitchener (Aldwyn Roberts), who came over on the *Windrush* – and was filmed for a Pathé news reel singing 'London Is the Place for Me' – summed up many of the frustrations of living in England in another song, 'My Landlady':*

> No chair, no table, the convenience is terrible
> And on the other part no hot water to take a bath
> And then you sleep like a rabbit
> Under the sheet with half of a blanket
> And she has the audacity
> To tell me I'm living in luxury.

The hostile reception helped to further develop a West Indian consciousness that wanted a future without British rule. But it also marked a new phase for the Caribbean diaspora. Islanders began to realize that they brought something different to the metropolis.

---

* The calypso CDs reissued under the series title 'London is the Place For Me', the first of which includes this track, are an audible history of the immigrant's struggle in Britain.

Whatever it meant to be Jamaican, or Barbadian, or Dominican was being figured out on both sides of the Atlantic. The West Indians who moved abroad became as much a part of the independence process as the people who stayed, their identities still intertwined with the islands where they had lived. And while many thousands of people who went to Britain in that period only meant to stay for a short time, a significant number – despite all the frustrations – found themselves in Britain decades later. Although the hostility was directed at most West Indians because of their colour, even white creoles faced the difficulties of being foreign in Britain then. Dominican writer Jean Rhys's novel *Voyage in the Dark* follows young white West Indian Anna to London, where she works as a showgirl. At one point, during a conversation, a friend says of Anna: 'She was born in the West Indies or somewhere, weren't you kid? The girls call her the Hottentot. Isn't it a shame?'[28] But her life quickly falls apart and she ends up living on the fringes, in a life of quasi-prostitution. Race was not necessarily a guarantee of fortune in the mother country.

Of course, West Indians had gone to England prior to *Windrush*, but on a smaller scale. There was no institute for higher education in the British West Indies until 1948; many upper- and middle-class students left the islands to finish their education in Britain. One such person was the future prime minister of Trinidad, Eric Williams. Although he arrived in England to take up a scholarship seventeen years before *Windrush* and the large-scale immigration that followed, he experienced first hand the contradictions in Britain that would later afflict other West Indians. After taking his first degree, he stayed on at Oxford, though British racism chafed, and despite the brilliance of his doctoral thesis no English publisher would consider it. It formed the basis for his ground-breaking book *Capitalism and Slavery*, which ignited a debate that continues to smoulder.[29] The British found Williams's arguments objectionable, despite his meticulous research into the economic aspects of the end of slavery, chiefly his suggestion that the abolition of slavery was driven by something other than the noble sentiment of the British people. While the idea that something as complex as the abolition of slavery might have a number of different causes may seem a reasonable position now, in the dying embers of the British Empire it did not sit well with historians, many of whom could see little point in studying the West Indian colonies in the first place. Williams, however, had the colonial perspective. He made a connection between the profits from the brutal regime of Caribbean slavery and the development of the Industrial Revolution in Britain, and then claimed it was market economics – and not enlightened humanitarianism – that had ended slavery. The development of 'mature capitalism' fostered by the slave regime also spelt its end, and it happened in three phases: the end of the slave trade, the end of slavery, and in 1846 the end of preferential sugar duties for British West Indian producers. The system had become unprofitable, and it was economic self-interest that led to slave emancipation, Williams argued: 'The rise and fall of mercantilism is the rise and fall of slavery.'[30] The debate that was ignited over what became known as the 'Williams thesis' continues to the present day.[31]

In 1939 he took up a post at Howard University, in Washington, DC, which then was a higher education institution for African-Americans, and he was able to find an eager publisher in the US for his book, which came out in 1944. Despite his success in academia, Williams returned to Trinidad in 1948. He initially took a post at the Caribbean Commission, a body established during the war, but he soon left to begin his political career, setting up the People's National Movement in January 1956.[32] Williams endeared himself to the public through a series of lectures in Woodford Square, a park in the heart of Port of Spain that affectionately became known as the University of Woodford Square. The elegant plaza, with its fountain, benches, and leafy shade, was large enough for the public to gather, and they did. As the Barbadian writer George Lamming later noted, Williams 'turned . . . the history of the Caribbean, into gossip so that the story of a people's predicament seemed no longer the infinite barren track of documents, dates and texts . . . His lectures retained always the character of a whisper which everyone was allowed to hear.'[33] Trinidad's black and Indian communities would remain deeply divided despite Williams's popular touch and a stronger economy boosted by oil revenues. Still, Williams would not only guide Trinidad and Tobago to independence in 1962, but would remain in office until his death in 1981, and his party stayed in power until 1986.

There were many talented men in the British Caribbean who, like Williams, had been educated in England and whose charisma dominated island political life from the 1950s onwards. In Jamaica there was Norman Manley, a cousin of union and political-party organizer

Alexander Bustamante. Manley was a lawyer who studied at Oxford, and in 1938 he was one of the founders, along with Bustamante, of the People's National Party. However, by 1943 the cousins had fallen out and Bustamante set up the Jamaica Labour Party. The pair would dominate the island's political life for the next three decades. In Barbados Grantley Adams returned after studying at Oxford and became a lawyer, involving himself in island politics during the strikes of the 1930s. He set up the Barbados Labour Party (BLP) in 1938, though by 1955 the island had a schism, and Errol Barrow left the BLP to found the Democratic Labour Party. In the smaller islands, the political leaders often came from more diverse backgrounds, but certain parties managed to hold power for similarly long periods, such as the St Kitts-Nevis-Anguilla Labour Party (in power from 1946 until 1980) or the Antigua Labour Party, which kept Vere Cornwall Bird in office as its leader and later prime minister from 1983 until his resignation in 1994.

This was still to come. In 1947 there was a conference in Montego Bay, Jamaica, to discuss federation, an idea that had been mooted for decades – previous Colonial Office regimes had tried to group together some of the smaller islands to cut costs. There were political representatives, as well as those from the planter class and trade union leaders at the meeting. While most of the colonies agreed to the proposals for federation, three rejected them: Guiana, British Honduras (Belize), and the British Virgin Islands. The plans moved at a glacial pace, and it was not until 1958 that the West Indies Federation was set up; its members were Jamaica, Trinidad and Tobago, Barbados, Grenada, St Kitts-Nevis-Anguilla,* St Vincent and the Grenadines, the Turks and Caicos, Antigua and Barbuda, St Lucia, Dominica, and Montserrat. Grantley Adams was appointed the federation's prime minister. He was to have a Cabinet and there were to be elections for a House of Representatives of forty-five members, as well as a British governor-general who appointed a nineteen-member Senate, and the federal capital was in Trinidad. It did not take long for the cracks to appear. It had been initially agreed there would be no federal taxation for the first five years, but there was little consensus over other matters. Tax and customs, as well as inter-island migration, were some of the many issues the islands could not agree upon. In addition, the larger islands

---

* At the time these islands were administered together.

of Jamaica and Trinidad had far bigger economies, with a booming bauxite industry in the former and oil in the latter, and no interest in subsidizing the smaller islands. Adams tried to maintain enthusiasm in the federation, but in 1961 Jamaicans – who were very divided about membership – were given a referendum on the matter, and 54 per cent of voters wanted to opt out. In Trinidad, Eric Williams said that it would be impossible for the organization to go on, and by May 1962 it was disbanded. The body had been set up to allow for the transition of the islands to a form of independence, and so British officials had little option but to honour the result in Jamaica by allowing it to become independent. The federation's demise left unsolved the question of what, if anything, would replace it. Officials in London had wanted Jamaica and Trinidad to shoulder the fiscal burden of the smaller islands. In addition, government officials were nervous: there was general political anxiety encompassing both the spread of communism and black–white relations in former colonies as well as in Britain. There were fears that some of the island leaders would not be able to oversee an orderly transition nor keep an independent state under control, and that independence would lead to even more immigration from the islands to Britain.[34]

Later that year, Jamaica and Trinidad and Tobago were granted their independence and membership of the Commonwealth. Jamaica was first, on 6 August 1962, under the leadership of Bustamante. The celebrations were extensive. Princess Margaret, Queen Elizabeth II's sister, and her husband the Earl of Snowdon were sent to preside over the ceremony. Also in attendance was the US vice-president, Lyndon Johnson. A ministry paper set out the planned celebrations in minute detail, even down to commercial memorabilia. Item 36 in the plans said: 'Government has approved the award of silver spoons suitably embossed and engraved to all children born in recognized institutions on that day as well as to all others whose births can be properly certified and authenticated.'[35] The estimated cost of the celebrations was around £250,000; outlined expenditure included £50,650 for the hosting of international delegates and £78,000 for 'islandwide treats, souvenirs, flags, etc.' for 450,000 children aged four to fourteen.[36]

The 2 August edition of the *Daily Gleaner* brimmed with enthusiasm. In addition to the excited reporting, advertisers lost little time in using the events to their advantage, with exhortations to 'Invest in

Independent Jamaica. Buy National Savings Bonds', or a few pages later, to take up an offer from Shell petrol stations for a 'Free wash or engine clean plus souvenir independence cloth duster'.[37] An advertisement on 5 August, the day before the official ceremonies, beseeched housewives to 'Be Independent of Housework! Yes! You can celebrate your independence from housework – with Hoover.'[38] In the same edition, a colour page was devoted to explaining the new symbols for the country, such as the national fruit (the ackee) and bird (swallow-tail humming-bird, also known as the doctor bird), as well as the island's national motto, 'Out of many, one people'.[39]

This phrase caught the attention of the US civil rights activist Martin Luther King, Jr, who, a few years later, included it in his 'American Dream' speech, which he delivered at a church in Atlanta, Georgia, on 4 July 1965. Although it was perhaps easy to get caught up in the optimism of the time and overlook the stark inequalities of the island, as well as the colour hierarchy, there was much to capture King's imagination – Jamaica might well have looked a great deal more equal than the southern states of the US:

> The other day Mrs. King and I spent about ten days down in Jamaica . . . And over and over again I was impressed by one thing. Here you have people from many national backgrounds: Chinese, Indians, so-called Negroes, and you can just go down the line, Europeans, European and people from many, many nations. Do you know they all live there and they have a motto in Jamaica, 'Out of many people, one people'? And they say, 'Here in Jamaica we are not Chinese, we are not Japanese, we are not Indians, we are not Negroes, we are not Englishmen, we are not Canadians. But we are all one big family of Jamaicans.' One day, here in America, I hope that we will see this and we will become one big family of Americans.[40]

Trinidad was next, with its independence granted on 31 August 1962. Barbados followed on 30 November 1966, under the political leadership of Errol Barrow. That island, like the two before it, had a large celebration, and the festivities included 'street dancing' and a historical pageant.[41] The smaller islands, however, were – for the time being – put into an associated state with Britain, though they would later opt for full independence, with Grenada peeling away in 1974,

Dominica in 1978, St Lucia and St Vincent in 1979, and Antigua and Barbuda in 1981. The Bahamas, which had not participated in the earlier federation, secured its independence in 1973, while Montserrat, the British Virgin Islands, the Cayman Islands, and the Turks and Caicos remained British dependencies.

The independence of St Kitts, Nevis, and Anguilla was slightly more complicated than the others. The three had been put together in 1967 as St Kitts-Nevis-Anguilla, much to the resentment of the latter. St Kitts and Nevis are so close they almost touch, while Anguilla lies further out, separated from the other two by French St Bart's and Dutch/French St Martin. Anguilla seceded from that union in the same year, kicking out the Kitts police – all fifteen of them – stationed on the island and calling for independence.

It was not an ideal situation, but when William Whitlock, then a Foreign Office minister, arrived in Anguilla, which measures 26km (16 miles) by 5km (3 miles), to discuss its future in 1969 he could not have imagined that he would be there only a few hours before being ejected from the island at gunpoint. His visit began quite normally. Whitlock was met by about 500 people at the airport. From the airport he went to lunch at the home of a retired colonial, Henry Howard. It was just after lunch, when Whitlock's delegation was preparing to depart, that armed Anguillians appeared and the visitors were told they would have to stay there until Ronald Webster, who was said to be leading the separatist movement, returned. Webster had made it known that he thought the proposals Whitlock had brought with him were a 'trick' to force Anguilla to return to its association with St Kitts and Nevis. Whitlock's demands to talk to Webster in person were met with rifle shots as a reply. By now very alarmed, Whitlock and the rest of the delegation wasted no time returning to the airport.[42]

Not long after Whitlock got back to Britain, the 16th Parachute Brigade was sent to the island as part of a force of some 300 soldiers – an operation later dubbed by the press as the 'Bay of Piglets'. They dropped leaflets 'appealing to the 6,000 islanders to cooperate in restoring peace and stability'.[43] There was some local protest, and foreigners living on the island were questioned, including a Florida businessman. Rumours were rife that the island was under the control of a 'Mafia-type organization that represented American interests'.[44]

A London *Times* editorial was more pragmatic, chiding that 'Britain's original mistake lay in trying to parcel together three incompatible islands; it should have been foreseen that Anguilla would chafe under the rule of St Kitts.'[45] In the end, Anguilla remained under British control as an associated state, and later an overseas territory. St Kitts and Nevis stuck together, and were granted their independence in 1983.

There was an effort to keep a form of trade links between all the English-speaking islands, and a body named the Caribbean Free Trade Association (CARIFTA) was set up for the purpose. By 1973 it had been extended and renamed the Caribbean Community (CARICOM), an organization that continues to deal with trade issues today. Although the decades from 1950 to 1980 were politically tense and complicated, the result was independence for the former British islands. However, the path for two of the colonies that had stayed out of the West Indian Federation – British Honduras and Guiana – was strewn with international boundary disputes and US interference.

*

A telegram dispatched on 28 April 1933 from the governor of British Guiana to his counterpart in Barbados was blunt: 'Have you any information Communist Agents to ferment labour troubles. Shall be glad if you will keep me in touch with such movements if any suspected persons likely to visit this Colony.'[46] Although the context of such a message fits with the larger concerns of the strike-ridden 1930s, it articulates an anxiety that would cause the political life of Guiana to be turned on its head twenty years later.

Having opted out of the West Indian Federation, Guiana's fortunes in the 1950s and 1960s followed their own long and troubled path. In 1950 a dentist of Indian origin named Cheddi Jagan and a black lawyer named Forbes Burnham established Guiana's first political party, the People's Progressive Party (PPP). A few years later, on 27 April 1953, elections were held and to the surprise of many, the PPP took eighteen out of twenty-four possible seats and 51 per cent of the vote in the House of Assembly, with the party representing a mix of black and Indian voters.

A few months later, the British government suspended the new constitution under which the election had taken place and threw the PPP ministers out of office. Jagan was suspected of being a Communist, and it was rumoured that if he were to be the first prime minister of an independent Guiana the US feared that he would align the country with the Soviets. Given that Guiana is far closer to the US than to the USSR, policy-makers in Washington did not want another Cold War satellite in their backyard.[47] This was a sensitive time in the United States, where any even vaguely liberal policy could be taken out of context and twisted into the shape of a hammer and sickle, especially if it had anything to do with land reform or the nationalization of industry. And indeed, in agricultural Guiana, the PPP had ideas on how to use the land better and was interested in furthering workers' rights, as were other British colonies. This was enough for the British to feel their economic interests were threatened, and for the United States to worry the country would enter the Soviet sphere of influence.[48]

Even with the removal of PPP members, the accusations kept coming. Minutes from a Cabinet meeting in October 1953 recorded that 'elected Ministers in British Guiana, who were under strong Communist influences, were taking every opportunity to undermine the constitution and to further the Communist cause'. There had been a recent strike in the sugar industry and the minutes said the PPP was 'evidently seeking to establish a totalitarian dominance over the territory by penetrating the trade unions and local government'.[49]

A state of emergency followed the election, and Burnham and Jagan were put under travel bans and their movements monitored. Jagan was quick to contravene this, and he found himself sent to a prison in Guiana's remote outback for six months in 1954. A few years later, and under mounting political tensions, Burnham split from the PPP and formed the People's National Congress in 1957; with that, the racial loyalties divided, too. Another election was permitted and called that year, and this time the racial lines were clear even before the ballots were cast. The unity of the PPP had been shattered; Jagan represented the Indian vote, Burnham the African, and small parties represented groups such as the Portuguese. Yet the PPP won in 1957. A letter between US diplomatic officials about Jagan's upcoming visit to Washington in 1959 noted, 'Although Jagan is probably a communist, he has behaved responsibly since his election in 1957. In any event, he is certainly the strongest popular leader in Guiana at present. Under the circumstances, we feel we should deal with him but without a great show of friendliness.'[50] But before long this unfriendliness would turn into violent hostility. By the early 1960s the US was claiming that the PPP was receiving funding from communist sources, and that party members were visiting communist countries. The US placed Jagan under intense scrutiny, especially because of actions like his talks with Cuba for a loan, with one 1960 US report about this ending with the line 'Dr. Jagan and his wife have communist connections of many years standing.'[51] To the consternation of Britain and the US, the PPP won the 1961 elections as well.

By this point, political violence had spilled onto the streets, some of it covertly funded and organized by the United States, which had also been pressuring Britain to delay Guianese independence until Burnham could be put in power.[52] A wave of violence washed over the country in the years following the 1961 election; there were bombs in the streets, and those who could do so began to leave the country in droves, heading for the United States or Britain. Security services monitored politicians and activists from the country, at home and abroad.

One US dispatch reported an interview requested by a young Guianese lawyer, Vernon Bhairan, who went to the US embassy in London in 1964 claiming to be close to Jagan and asking if the embassy was 'aware that Jagan had sent a telegram to Prime Minister Wilson ... alleging that the CIA was actively fomenting and bore the responsibility for all the violence in British Guiana'.[53]

The British came up with a plan to implement proportional representation in the next election, which they thought would put a coalition headed by Burnham into power. They were correct, and in 1964 Burnham won with around 40 per cent of the vote; in conjunction with smaller parties, he was able to take office. The objectives of the British and United States now satisfied, the colony itself in tatters, and the public well aware of the political and diplomatic manoeuvrings, Guiana was given permission to press ahead with independence, which was granted in 1966.

In the same year, Venezuela chose to seize the river port of Ankoko. This was not completely out of the blue, as there had been a long-running dispute between Guiana and Venezuela over this stretch of land to the south and west of Guiana, but the Venezuelans certainly picked a moment when Guiana was otherwise engaged. The dispute dated to the 1880s, with the Venezuelans charging that the British were overstepping their sovereignty in the region. By 1895 the US president, Grover Cleveland, ordered arbitration to clear up the matter. A tribunal followed, comprising two Britons, two Americans to represent Venezuelan interests, and a Russian, presumed to be neutral, as chairman. After deliberation, Britain was awarded the territory.[54] However, in 1949, papers belonging to one of the lawyers representing Venezuela, Severo Mallet-Prevost, which surfaced after his death, caused the issue to be reopened. In them, he made clear he believed the Russian chairman had had a vested interest in helping Britain after all, in exchange for some support in Central Asia, and that the land should belong to Venezuela. Although there have been temporary accords, the dispute between Guyana and Venezuela continues.

The decades that followed Guyanese independence might have seemed – to Britain and the United States – a cruel irony, as Burnham turned out to be more of a problem than either could have imagined. He nationalized the sugar trade and bauxite mines. He established relations with the Soviets and even allowed Cuba to refuel its planes en route to Angola during the war there in the 1960s. Of course, it was far worse for the people who had to live through those years. The infrastructure crumbled on his watch, and the economy all but collapsed. Surrounding this was a regime of corruption and violence; yet he was able to rig the elections and stay in power until his death in 1985. The PNC continued as the ruling party until 1992, when Jagan, who had been in opposition for so many years, finally had his turn as prime minister, dying in office in 1997.

In British Honduras, renamed Belize in 1973, there was one very large problem blocking its path to independence: Guatemala.[55] Belize's neighbour had never recognized its sovereignty, much as Spain had quibbled over British claims to the coast in the colonial era. Over the course of the nineteenth century, the Miskito territory was ceded back to Nicaragua, and the British claim – a small sliver of land between Guatemala and the sea, with Mexico to the north – was only officially made a colony in 1862.

Guatemala based – and continues to base – claims to Belize on an 1859 boundary treaty. So while the British government was, by the early 1960s, in favour of independence, Belize's leaders realized it had to tread carefully, lest its neighbour rush in. George Price, the Honduran prime minister, led the colony in this delicate dance.[56] Price could not have been more different from his political contemporaries in the islands. He was neither Oxford educated, nor from a trade union background. Rather, he spent some of his formative years at a seminary in Mississippi from 1936 to 1940, intending to become a priest, and later spent a year in Guatemala City as part of his studies. Unlike many leaders, he continued to live, if not a monastic life, an austere one, and he never married or had children.

When he returned to British Honduras around 1947, he soon became involved in politics, and was one of the founding members of the People's United Party (PUP) in 1950. He saw the country as part of Central America, a view not shared by Guatemala. Britain granted British Honduras home rule in 1964, and Price became premier. During the decades that followed he began negotiations with Britain, the United States, and a number of international bodies such as the United Nations, CARICOM, the Commonwealth, and the Non-Aligned Movement to come to some sort of agreement, but none was reached. Instead, by 1980 Britain was pressing for independence without a settlement with Guatemala, and the following year, with assurances from the US that it would provide necessary security were Guatemala to take action, Belize became an independent nation, with Price as its prime minister.[57] The dispute lingers, even though Guatemalans continually cross the border looking for work.

*

Central American nations, too, would be unable to escape the influence of the United States. The establishment of the United Fruit Company along the Caribbean, and later Pacific, coast in Costa Rica, Nicaragua, Honduras, and Guatemala opened the door to unfair and humiliating treatment. Known as 'banana republics' in the United States, these countries and their leaders were seen as compliant to – or bribable by – the wishes of foreign corporations. United Fruit was quick to buy or control land and build infrastructure for its own use. Because so many of its employees were foreign, little of the profits earned went to locals. The United States spent decades meddling in the affairs of these countries, claiming that it was only protecting its interests; but with the onset of the Cold War, this took an even more menacing turn. Costa Rica managed to escape the period with a stable democracy but its neighbours were not so fortunate. This is not to say that the US did not reach into Costa Rica as well. Indeed, in a memo from the US ambassador, Whiting Willauer, to the assistant secretary of state, Thomas Mann, Willauer noted, 'As you know, I have always felt that Costa Rica was a good "pilot" country for proving out new changes in policy. All such changes need practical experience to "work the bugs out of them." If the bugs cannot be worked out in Costa Rica, then there is little hope in other countries. However, if they can be worked out, the example of Costa Rica will give concrete demonstrations which other foreign enterprises in other countries would be more likely to accept.'[58] And although the United States interfered in the politics of different regimes throughout Central America at varying junctures, its meddling in Guatemala and Nicaragua remains the starkest example of the excesses of that period.

Jorge Ubico was the last in a long line of dictators in Guatemala. He became president in 1931 and set about guarding the interests of the nation's coffee-planting elite, as well as those of United Fruit. He oppressed workers, kept wages low, and became very unpopular with most of the country. But by 1944, there was a growing resistance to his rule, and that year he was overthrown in a pro-democracy 'October revolution', confirmed by an election that voted reformist Juan José Arévalo Bermejo into power. The United States grew increasingly concerned by the new government's measures, particularly the land reforms which angered United Fruit. In 1951 Arévalo was succeeded by another reformer, Jacobo Árbenz Guzmán, who continued to redistribute land to peasants and enact reforms such as allowing trade unions to organize. He was vocal in his dislike of United Fruit and was soon denounced by the United States as a communist.

US President Eisenhower needed little persuasion to take action, and in 1953 approved a plan to topple the Guatemalan president. As it happened, the secretary of state at the time, John Foster Dulles, had once been a lawyer for United Fruit, while his brother, the CIA director Allen Dulles, sat on the company's board. Even Eisenhower's personal secretary was married to the chief lobbyist for United Fruit.[59] Árbenz did not stand a chance.

By July 1954, the US had their man in office, Colonel Carlos Castillo Armas, who immediately rolled back the previous decade of reform. Not long after, United Fruit was hit by an anti-trust suit; as the Cold War intensified its aggressive breed of capitalism was at odds with the image the US was trying to present to the world. By 1970, United Fruit's Guatemalan holdings were gone.[60] The politics of Guatemala were as disposable as one of its many banana peels. The nation sank into a civil war that lasted from 1960 until 1996, leaving tens of thousands dead and thousands more living abroad. The US had been involved in that long dispute, too, with the CIA training and providing equipment to the Guatemalan army during the war, despite being aware of the massacres that were taking place.[61] And although the fighting has stopped, Guatemala today remains racked by poverty, political oppression, and violence. The CIA School of the Americas, set up in 1946 to train Latin American security forces, both military and civil, became a byword for an institution offering its students detailed lessons in torture techniques and mobilizing death squads. While ostensibly protecting US interests throughout the region, the school appeared to provide dictators with ruthless armies and police forces, trained in brutality under the guise of preparation for the fight against communism. Now called the Western Hemisphere Institute for Security Cooperation (WHISC), it continues to train Latin American soldiers at the US base in Fort Benning, Georgia.[62]

Further south, Nicaragua also felt the blunt end of US intervention. Its taste of US military might began much earlier than in Guatemala; American troops were sent in after a coup in 1912. As in Haiti and the Dominican Republic, the US created and trained an army and police force, so when the US pulled out in 1933, it left a vacuum that was soon filled by Anastasio Somoza García, who took power after a coup in 1937. His family, propped up by the National Guard, controlled the nation for more than forty years. During this time, the Somoza family were willing allies of the United States, and much of the National Guard continued to receive its training from the US military.[63] The country was devastated by an earthquake on 23 December 1972 which reduced much of the capital, Managua, to rubble. In the years that followed, opposition in the form of the Frente Sandinista de Liberación Nacional (FSLN), or the Sandinistas, began to threaten the Somoza dynasty. The politics turned bloody as the recovery efforts lagged and the public grew angry. The then-president Anastasio Somoza Debayle left for Miami in 1979, and the Sandinistas took control. Their platform of wealth redistribution, land reforms, and other policies would fail to endear them to the United States. Coming as this did amid heightening

Cold War tensions, the United States refused to let them go ahead without a fight. When Ronald Reagan took office in 1981 he immediately supported efforts to overthrow the regime, giving the CIA nearly $20 million to train counter-revolutionaries, known as the Contras. The United States also convinced Honduras to allow Contras to attack from Honduran locations. When Congress tried to cut the programme's budget around 1985, it later emerged that the president had simply turned to Colonel Oliver North and others, resulting in what was later known as the Iran–Contra affair, a messy covert deal that involved the United States breaking an arms embargo to sell weapons illegally to Iran in exchange for hostages and money that would later be used to continue to fund the Contras.

The Sandinista victory in 1984, with Daniel Ortega winning office, further annoyed the United States, but the conflict began to wind down in the second half of the 1980s. In the 1990 elections, opposition leader Violeta Chamorro won, with US support for her campaign. The civil war had finally ended, with well over 30,000 people dead. Ortega returned to office in 2007, where he remains.[64]

While there are a number of differences between what happened on the banana fields and on the sugar plantations in the Caribbean, the parallels are many. Bananas are not a complete luxury as they have nutritional value, unlike sugar. And they were grown under a system of wage labour, not slavery, though often the conditions would have been little better. The United States brought an explosive mixture to the region, fuelled by limitless resources and unshakeable political beliefs, and its impact in these years reverberates to this day in Central America. The informal empire that interwove commercial and political interests was a murky business, and the relentless pursuit of self-interest left a pile of bodies in its wake.

*

Elsewhere in the Caribbean, independence assumed a very different character. The question of nationalism, or something larger, such as pan-Africanism, anti-colonialism, or a type of international Negritude, was one that preoccupied French islanders such as Frantz Fanon of Martinique. He was born on the island on 20 July 1925 to a black middle-class family – his father was a customs official. He fought for the Free French in 1943 when he was eighteen, and he stayed in France to study medicine and psychiatry in Lyon. He practised as a psychiatrist, during which time he began to write about the emotional realities of race and the colonial condition, publishing the ground-breaking *Peau Noire, Masques Blancs* (Black Skin, White Masks) in 1952, in which he observed,

> Every colonized people – in other words, every people in whose soul an inferiority complex has been created by the death and burial of its local cultural originality – finds itself face to face with the language of the civilizing nation; that is, with the culture of the mother country. The colonized is elevated above his jungle status in proportion to his adoption of the mother country's cultural standards. He becomes whiter as he renounces his blackness, his jungle.

The following year Fanon went to work at a hospital in Algeria, where, in 1954, he saw the eruption of the Algerian War of Independence. He quit his job and joined the Algerians' fight. But his health was poor, and the final months of his life were spent finishing his anticolonial masterpiece *Les Damnés de la Terre* (The Wretched of the Earth), published in 1961. France, like Britain, looked to its colonies to help rebuild after the war, and the movement of people between colony and capital often provoked resentment at their treatment. But in the case of France, this led to the islands being granted more liberties and autonomy.[65] In 1946, Martinique, Guadeloupe, and Guyane were made official *départements* and thus were considered part of, rather than satellites of, France. Martinicans had been citizens since 1848, but this new arrangement would put the island on a par with Paris or the Gironde. The poet and politician Aimé Césaire became the mayor of Fort-de-France in 1945 after running on a Communist Party ticket, and he served as a deputy in the French National Assembly. He set up the Martinican Progressive Party in 1950, which concentrated on the island's autonomy rather than independence. Others, like the influential Martinican Édouard Glissant, looked beyond the nation, at the larger process of creolization in the Americas, and embraced *créolité*, a critique of the other competing schools of thought that argued that French islanders should look to Africa for their cultural heritage.

France struggled with its other colonies, from Algeria to Indo-China to Madagascar, whose desire for liberation was far clearer. In the French islands, there was debate interspersed with some bouts of unrest, but nothing changed the system. There were nationalists in Guadeloupe and Martinique, but many people agitated for greater local autonomy rather than outright independence. Alongside this, islanders hoped that with more political recognition they would soon be on an equal footing with citizens in France itself.[66]

The Netherlands followed a path between that of Britain and France when, in 1954, it made its islands part of the kingdom of the Netherlands, giving the islands and Suriname such a degree of autonomy that the following year they were taken off the United Nations list of non-self-governing territories.

Puerto Rico was granted the status of Commonwealth (*estado libre asociado*) by the US in 1952, having first elected a governor, Luis Muñoz Marín, in 1948. In the same year, 'Operation Bootstrap' began, with the aim of stimulating economic growth. Mainland US firms were lured to the island through tax breaks, while infrastructure improvements were also made. The aim was to transform the economy away from agriculture and over-reliance on the monocrop of sugar, which made the island's fortunes too dependent on the fluctuations of the international market. The resulting industrialization also brought people into the cities, swelling the population of San Juan, and changing the rural–urban balance. Soon manufacturing jobs outpaced those in sugar and other agriculture, and there was a push to increase tourism. Critics claimed that by eradicating longer peasant agrarian traditions, the scheme made Puerto Ricans dependent on US capital and companies, but others on the island thought the investment was both necessary and worthwhile.

Meanwhile, in the Sierra Maestra mountains of Cuba, another sort of independence battle had begun, a battle that would grab the world's attention.

Chapter Eleven

THE COLD WAR IN THE TROPICS

In a quiet neighbourhood in the eastern suburbs of Santiago de Cuba sits an ochre multi-storeyed building with battlements along the rooftop. Around it and an adjacent field is a wall, in the same style, with occasional gates framed by towers that look like oversized chess rooks. It is perhaps appropriate that the young radical lawyer Fidel Castro made his opening move here, in the Moncada Barracks, the first in a decades-long tactical match pitting him against much more powerful enemies. On the morning of 26 July 1953, Castro and around 150 others, wielding shotguns and whatever weapons they could scrounge, attacked the barracks, which was at the time a regional military centre for President Fulgencio Batista's troops. Castro's rebels were no match for the soldiers; eight were killed, and more than seventy were taken to prison. Castro may have been idealistic enough to think he could have won against the more numerous and better-equipped troops, but he also had another motive: he wanted to send a message to Cubans that a fight was about to begin.

Batista was no stranger to the island's highest office; he had been president in 1940–44, but had risen to power earlier, in a 1933 coup. Under US pressure he allowed elections, putting puppet candidates in office until 1940. He returned to public life in 1952 when he campaigned for president in the upcoming election; when it became clear he was failing to mobilize support, he staged a coup and retook power that way instead. This ushered in the era of Cuba at its most infamous – the casinos, the nightclubs, the gangsters, the glamour. Fragments remain today, mostly in the hotels near the waterfront Malecón, such as the Habana Riviera, a 1950s modernist block with a neon sign reading 'Riviera' on the roof, that would not have looked out of place had it been plucked from Havana and dropped into the Las Vegas desert. People from the United States had long been coming to Havana, but the party was really swinging by the late Batista period. Cuba, like the Bahamas, had an initial tourist boost in the 1920s from Prohibition in the US, and even when that ended, many people continued to visit the island. It did not take long for the Mafia to cross the Florida Straits, build hotels, casinos, nightclubs, and racetracks, and bring with it the usual mix of drugs, prostitutes, guns, and corruption. Boats ran between Miami and Havana, and there were direct flights from major US cities. Batista was happy to do business with known gangsters such as Meyer Lansky and 'Lucky' Luciano. For wealthy visitors, Havana was a sensual, exotic paradise. For Cubans, it was a city starting to boil with anger and resentment. The disparity of wealth was glaring, and the poverty of the countryside grating, even as the output of sugar – often by US-owned firms – was at a healthy level. Indeed, within days of Batista's return to power, university students staged a protest in which they held a four-day wake for the 1940 constitution and buried it.[1]

Castro, meanwhile, escaped following the Moncada attack, although he turned himself in after being assured of a fair trial, which took place in September 1953. During the trial, Castro made the famous declaration – 'La historia me absolverá,' history will absolve me – and made clear his intentions to overthrow the regime. He was sentenced to fifteen years' imprisonment and sent to the Isle of Pines, off the mainland south of Havana, along with his brother, Raúl, and more than twenty others. From there they continued to make plans for their 26 July Movement, named for the event that landed them in prison.

In 1955 Batista granted amnesty for all political prisoners, including Castro, who fled with Raúl to Mexico, where they met and enlisted the Argentine revolutionary Ernesto 'Che' Guevara. Together, the men planned their next attack, rallying support from the Cuban exile community in Mexico and the United States. On 25 November 1956 a small vessel named Granma, overloaded with eighty-two men – at least six times its intended capacity – set out from Tuxpam, Veracruz, in Mexico, for the Oriente province of Cuba. Castro and his men were hit by storms almost throughout the consequently prolonged and very rough trip. The yacht ran aground off the coast of Cuba on 2 December, by which point they had missed their entrance. (They had intended to coincide with an uprising in Santiago a few days earlier; the uprising went ahead but was soon stifled.) The military was on the lookout. Reports circulated that the Cuban air force had destroyed the *Granma*, killing Castro and all his men, but they were mistaken. The rebels went ashore and were attacked a few days later, and only about twenty survived, including the Castro brothers and Guevara. They headed for the Sierra Maestra mountains, a terrain that had a long history of rebellions and armed struggle. There had been fighting there in the Ten Years War, but even before that the hills had offered refuge for runaway slaves and maroon colonies. Still, with limited resources and almost no supplies, Castro and his men had nothing but challenges ahead.

At first they had to rely on peasants in the mountains simply to survive; almost all their supplies had been destroyed. Castro began to plan: they would attack government troops in mountain outposts in order to build up stocks of guns and ammunition, and they would also need a public relations campaign. Castro quickly realized that without press coverage, support for the 26 July Movement might never go beyond the mountains. He knew reports of his death had been broadcast on the radio, and he wanted the island to know that he and his struggle had not been killed so easily. A short while later, a contact gave the *New York Times* correspondent Ruby Hart Phillips the story of the year – the young rebel Fidel Castro was not only alive, he was in the Sierra Maestra and wanted a US journalist to interview him. Hart Phillips knew the assignment was not right for her – not only was it risky for a woman to try sneaking past army checkpoints, but she also feared alienating her sources. She had good connections with Cuban officials and with Batista, and she had her doubts about Castro. Instead, leader-writer Herbert Matthews was sent from New York. After making his way to the mountain hideout, Matthews reported that Castro was 'alive and fighting', and his story included a picture of the rebel leader standing in the shade, holding a gun and sporting a beard.[2] The beards, born of necessity in the mountains, soon became a symbol of the revolution. Matthews reported breathlessly that 'no one connected with the outside world, let alone with the press, has seen Señor Castro, except this writer'.[3] The world was soon dazzled by this daring young man, waging war against a dictator. Matthews described his first impression of Castro:

Taking him, as one would at first, by physique and personality, this was quite a man – a powerful six-footer, olive-skinned, full-faced, with a straggly beard. He was dressed in an olive grey fatigue uniform and carried a rifle with a telescopic sight, of which he was very proud . . . The personality of the man is overpowering. It was easy to see that his men adored him and also to see why he has caught the imagination of the youth of Cuba all over the island.[4]

Little was known about Castro's background outside Cuba, but many people would have been surprised to discover that he did not come from a long line of freedom fighters, but was rather the son of a Spanish veteran who fought against Cuban rebels in 1895. Ángel Castro y Argiz was an impoverished peasant from Galicia, Spain, who had been conscripted into the army and sent to the island. Once his service was over and he returned to Spain, he decided his prospects were better back in Cuba than in his poor Galician village. He returned in 1899, and gradually built up a large sugar estate in Birán, in the east of the island, near present-day Holguín. Ángel Castro also accumulated a large family, with five children by his first wife and seven by his second. While married to his first wife, he began an affair with one of his estate's servants, Lina Ruz González, who was nearly thirty years his junior. She bore him Fidel in 1926, and six others out of wedlock, though they later married. Castro grew up amid the sugar fields and would have known some of the Haitians who cut his father's cane. His later education took him to Havana, where he enrolled at the university and got his start in politics.

Students played an important role in the revolution, and those years were formative for Castro. While he and his men were launching guer-rilla raids on the army, young rebels in cities were setting off bombs and protesting. There were also strikes throughout this period, from 1954 onwards. In retaliation, the government arrested their political opponents. This only led to more bombings and protests, prompting Batista to declare a state of emergency more than once. The United States suspended military aid to Cuba, concerned about reports of repression by the regime. By the end of 1958 fighting had intensified in Oriente, which was almost cut off from the rest of the island, as the rebels continued to attack supply lines. By the end of the year Batista knew his time was up; in the early hours of 1 January 1959 he left the island. Castro and his band of rebels were victorious. A brief period of uncertainty followed over who was to be installed as president, and Castro called a strike – which lasted until one of Castro's allies, Manuel Urrutia Lleó, was allowed to take office. He was made president, though the two fell into disagreement. Castro was the one with the power, even if he was not yet president.

On 2 January the rebels arrived in Havana, where, Hart Phillips observed, 'the trucks, filled with long-haired, bearded youths called *barbudos* could hardly move through the streets because of the cheering populace that swarmed around them'.[5] The strike soon ended, and on 8 January Castro rode into Havana. 'Never in the history of Cuba,' wrote Hart Phillips, 'has anyone received such a welcome. The ovation was of such magnitude that it was a little frightening.'

Castro and his men set up a temporary headquarters in the gleaming modern Havana Hilton, which had been open for less than a year; by 1960 it would be renamed the Habana Libre. In April of 1959 Castro made an unofficial visit to the US. He received an enthusiastic welcome in New York, with a crowd of two thousand cheering him and waving Cuban flags.[6] He also met with officials in Washington, including Vice-President Richard Nixon, and reassured the US that neither he nor anyone else in his government was a communist – there had been some concern about Raúl's Eastern Bloc visit in 1953. Castro also expressed hopes for a friendly relationship with the United States. Such goodwill did not last long.

By 1960 Castro had made an agreement with the Soviet Union to export 5 million tons of sugar over five years in exchange for money, oil, and other goods, which was the first in decades of trade deals that saw the Soviets subsidizing Cuba through buying varying amounts of sugar. The United States responded with a series of trade blockades that persist to the present day. When US refineries on the island refused to process the Soviet oil, Castro seized them, embarking on a programme of nationalization of foreign-held property and businesses, such as banks and sugar mills. Meanwhile, by the end of 1960 some 14,000 Cuban children were sent unaccompanied to the United States, in what was called Operation Pedro Pan, organized by the Catholic Welfare Bureau in the US, with the permission of the US State Department, which had granted visa waivers for the children, and Cubans on the island who were able to negotiate the necessary papers and transport for the children. When these children arrived in the US, many of them had to wait in shelters for their parents to tie up their affairs or obtain visas to join them. Thousands of Cubans were fleeing the island. Many were fearful of the growing body count during this period; former members of Batista's regime were being summarily executed, as, increasingly, were former members of the revolution, accused of treachery or disloyalty. Press restrictions mounted, and Hart Phillips, who was never as taken with Castro as her *New York Times* colleague, left the island in 1961. But these domestic matters were soon overshadowed by global events.

*

Under President Eisenhower, there had been plans for a US invasion of Cuba, although it never materialized, and indeed the press even reported on the camps in Guatemala where Cuban dissidents were training. Taking further action fell to Eisenhower's successor, John F. Kennedy. In this version, CIA-trained Cubans would land on a remote beach in the south of the island, and start a counter-revolution from there. The earlier plan had been to infiltrate the mountains, a long-standing tradition of Cuban warfare. However, the isolation of this new attack location probably ensured the plan's failure – there was only a sleepy village nearby. The Bahía de Cochinos, or Bay of Pigs, as the invasion site has since become known, is in the rural Matanzas province in the south. Nearly cut off from the rest of the island by poor roads, the desolate strip of sand seems an unlikely place to launch an offensive. On 15 April 1961, US B-26 bombers left Nicaragua and attacked Cuba's bases, but many missed their targets, leading a jumpy Kennedy to cancel a second round of air raids. Two days later, a force of 1,400 Cubans, many of whom had been trained at CIA camps in Guatemala, landed on the beach. Castro had heard through the exile networks in Miami that something was being planned, and he was ready for the attack. The Cuban air force was quick to land a number of tactical air strikes on two transport ships, and within a few days it was all over, with Castro taking more than 1,000 prisoners, with just under 300 people killed on both sides. Castro held the exiles hostage for months, humiliating them in show trials, before he finally released them in exchange for more than $50 million worth of food and medicine. Soon after the invasion was over, Castro wasted no time declaring his revolution 'socialist'. The Cold War had arrived in the Caribbean. Kennedy launched the covert Operation Mongoose, in which the US spent millions trying to bring down Castro any way it could, including an alleged CIA plot involving an exploding cigar.

Just over a year later, the international spotlight would again focus on the island. Tensions had been running high in the Cold War; the Berlin Wall went up in September 1961, and the Soviets started testing nuclear weapons again. They also sent troops to Cuba, ignoring the long-held Monroe Doctrine, declared dead in 1960 by the Soviet leader Nikita Khrushchev, who added that it should be buried, too, 'so that it does not poison the air by its decay'.[7] Along with troops, Soviet scientists brought missiles and nuclear technology to the island, news of which was passed to the White House. By the middle of 1962, U-2 spy planes had taken photos of what looked like missiles. Khrushchev denied the US allegations, but Kennedy chose to believe the photographic evidence and demanded the USSR remove the weapons from the island. He also implemented a blockade that would stop and search any ship en route to Cuba, feeling that this move might be less likely than an air strike to trigger Soviet retaliation. Kennedy went on television to inform the US public on 22 October, though little did they realize that the White House had put security at DEFCON 2, one step below what could have spelled nuclear war. Castro declared that if the United States launched air strikes, Cuba and Russia should retaliate with a nuclear strike. Fortunately, Khrushchev did not solicit Castro's advice, and the Soviet leader agreed to remove the weapons if the US pledged not to attack Cuba. A covert deal was also reached to remove US nuclear missiles from a base in Turkey, and by 28 October the crisis was over.

*

The revolution in Cuba and the island's subsequent involvement in the Cold War had won Castro fans around the world. His refusal to bow to the United States resonated in those parts of Latin America that had been on the blunt end of US force, not least in Central American nations like Nicaragua. Likewise, supporters of communism throughout the world admired Cuba and what Castro was doing there. Despite the embargo, Castro and his government implemented significant improvements to education and housing. But many Cubans left the island in this period, mostly for the US and mostly those who had been wealthy and powerful under the old regime. Some feared for their lives; others opposed the new order. People were not permitted to leave the island with any assets, and were often forced to start again in the US having surrendered their homes and livelihoods on the island. Many of the refugees went to Miami, joining the already sizeable Cuban community there, which would continue to grow in the decades that followed, transforming the city and creating a powerful anti-Castro base in the US.

Some Caribbean leaders, while concerned about US power in the region, were wary of Cuba's example. Eric Williams wrote in 1963 that,

> In the world of 1963 the Caribbean insists on not being ignored. America's Cuban colony, as it was described in the '30s, has become the Russian satellite of the '60s ... The Caribbean has become a happy hunting ground for Castro's declared policy of encouraging subversive movements in neighbouring countries. In 1963 the alternatives for the Caribbean are either Castroism or something else. It is the claim of Trinidad and Tobago that Trinidad and Tobago is that something else.[8]

While Williams remained an admirer of Castro's anti-colonial struggle, he was far more circumspect about the daily running of the island's politics and economy. Despite their differences, however, Trinidad and Tobago, along with Barbados, Jamaica, and Guyana, gave diplomatic recognition to Cuba, defying the US and the Organization of American States. Williams visited the island in June 1975, and, during a speech on the Isle of Pines, Castro thanked him, saying, 'your fatherland, Trinidad-Tobago, and all the fraternal Caribbean countries will always have the solidarity, respect and the most profound friendship of our people'.[9] The next Caribbean visitor, however, would show far more enthusiasm for Castro and the Cuban revolution. Jamaican Prime Minister Michael Manley and Castro had met on a flight to Algiers in 1973, en route to a Non-Aligned Movement Summit in the Algerian capital. Manley, son of Norman Manley, had been elected leader of the People's National Party (PNP) in 1969, and won the 1972 election, campaigning with enthusiasm for 'democratic socialism' to flourish on the island. Manley had been vocal in his admiration of the Castro regime and critical of its treatment by the United States.

As Manley stepped on to the runway in Havana on 9 July 1975, he gave a clenched fist salute while crowds cheered below, including shouts of ¡Viva Manley!' After what was described as a 'lengthy bear-hug', Manley and Castro began five days of talks and cultural events.[10] Upon his return to Kingston, Manley said, 'Cuba and Jamaica have both been destroyed by capitalism but now we are building bridges to unite our two peoples.'[11]

Although the Cuban example inspired many, some Jamaicans proved more disgruntled. A 1977 letter to the Daily Gleaner, signed by 'Pragmatist', asked 'why is the Government going to bed so much with Cuba and that International Imperialist exploiter Russia at the expense of learning practically from China, America and Japan, etc.?' before going on to declare, 'Jamaica will necessarily have to learn from China's hard experience and discipline. A tripartite relationship between America, China and Japan is the answer.'[12] Castro returned the visit in 1977, but his reception by Jamaicans was not quite so enthusiastic. Before his arrival, the opposition Jamaica Labour Party (JLP) issued a statement saying that its members would boycott Castro's visit because the party had not been formally told about it. There had been rumours of a visit, but the six-day event had been kept secret until the last minute, ostensibly because of Castro's security concerns. The statement claimed that 'the handling of the visit was an insult to the democratic process and the people of Jamaica when it is well known that the majority of the people of Jamaica feel a deep abhorrence and a profound distrust of communism in any form'.[13] There was much grumbling, too, about the extensive security provided to the Cuban leader. Of course, the JLP were playing politics more than debating the merits of implementing a Cuban ideology in Jamaica. In the end, Castro was greeted by what was reported to be a 'large turnout', with some members of the crowd saying the Cuban leader's visit was the 'best thing to happen to Jamaica since independence', and 'now the people have the opportunity of seeing for themselves President Castro in person, they will have a new understanding of him'.[14]

Manley struggled to implement his vision for Jamaica. He had famously declared 'We are not for sale' in 1976, but soon had to look for help from outside the island. He managed to bring in some changes, such as a minimum wage, free secondary education, and land reforms, but towards the end of his first term, the island's economy grew worse.

Before long Manley was hamstrung by the International Monetary Fund, which offered a high-interest loan on the condition that the island institute 'structural reforms', cutting government programmes that unravelled many of his plans.[15]

Cuba, meanwhile, stayed afloat with Soviet money. Castro's admirers in decolonized developing countries grew – Cuba could even afford to send troops to aid the MPLA in Angola's civil war in the 1970s – while the revolution at home continued, though economic pressures persisted. Castro remained a thorn in the side of the United States, undertaking manoeuvres like the Mariel boatlift in 1980, when he announced that any Cuban who wished to could leave the island from the port of Mariel. The US tried to blockade the arrivals but was eventually overwhelmed as more than 100,000 people in flotillas reached Florida. While many of those who left in the 1960s were wealthy and powerful the boatlift was an effort to get rid of people Castro deemed undesirable: criminals, homosexuals, disabled people, and some political dissidents. But the island's status quo could not persist, and less than a decade later, Castro's world would be turned upside down.

*

The Dominican Republic was also ensnared by the Cold War. Rafael Trujillo was assassinated on 30 May 1961, when his car was ambushed by a group of men. The president, Joaquín Balaguer, who had been installed by Trujillo, continued in his post, while Trujillo's son Ramfis became head of the army. The United States, having had enough of the Trujillo family, told Ramfis to step down, and when he failed to do so it sent a warship to the capital. Elections were called in 1962 – the first in more than thirty years – and the surprise winner was the leader of the opposition Dominican Revolutionary Party (PRD), Juan Bosch. Bosch had spent the better part of his political career organizing opposition to Trujillo outside the island, in exile in Cuba and Costa Rica for many years, after being forced to leave the Dominican Republic in 1938.

Once in power, Bosch began a series of reforms seemingly designed to guarantee that the United States would brand him a communist – not least his willingness to tolerate a branch of the Communist Party. He also redistributed land and tried to enact other social reforms. By September 1963 the military – whose powers Bosch had also tried to curb – arrested him and sent him to Puerto Rico. The domestic situation descended into civil war by 1965, as Bosch's supporters and the military took up arms. US President Lyndon Johnson feared that it was highly probable that the Dominican Republic could become communist, and he was not going to allow a 'second Cuba' anywhere near the United States. Once again, an invasion force was sent, more than 20,000 troops staying for almost a year until an agreement could be reached. In 1966 Balaguer had returned as president, and would remain in office until 1978. His victory did not put an immediate end to violence, though this time much of it was directed at repressing and punishing the people who had fought against the military in 1965.

In 1970, a more embittered, cynical Bosch returned and founded a new party, the Dominican Liberation Party, which would reflect his growing Leninist beliefs. By the 1970s the PRD had a viable candidate for president, Antonio Guzmán, who won the 1978 election. Under US pressure, Balaguer had to admit defeat. However, corruption and bribery infiltrated the PRD and such charges may have played a role in Guzmán's suicide in July 1982, after the party and its candidate, Salvador Jorge Blanco, had won the elections that May. The economy flatlined in the late 1980s, and there was unrest in the streets and within the party. Balaguer used this to his advantage to help him win the presidency once again in 1986, and he would stay in office for another ten years.

On the other side of the island, the Haitians were ruled by another diminutive, bespectacled, inscrutable man: François Duvalier. His innocuous beginnings did little to betray the tyrant he would become. He was born into a middle-class family and studied medicine in the United States. In the 1930s and 1940s he was involved in numerous public health campaigns and later became the minister for health. He was also a vocal proponent of the study of Haiti's African roots and the island's voodoo traditions. The interest in voodoo was particularly significant. Previous rulers of the country at various points had tried to ban its practice, and on paper the island was officially Catholic. Voodoo practices in Haiti, however, were still alive and well when African-American anthropologist Zora Neale Hurston visited the island in 1936–7. 'Under the very sound of drums, [the] upper class Haitian will tell you that there is no such thing as Voodoo in Haiti', Hurston observed. 'He knows this is not so and should know that you know it is not true.'[16] For Duvalier to express positive opinions and interest in voodoo was surprising – and pleasing – to many Haitians, especially the black peasants whose support he courted.

Duvalier wrote articles about various aspects of black culture – *noirisme* – and cultivated the air of a scholarly doctor, reflected by his nickname – 'Papa Doc'. By the 1950s he had become involved in politics, winning the 1957 election. He initially maintained his popularity, especially among black Haitians, not least by putting more blacks, rather than mulattos, into ministerial posts. The US supported him, too, though mostly because he was not a communist; in 1959, when some Cuban-trained communists tried to infiltrate the country, he drove them off. Duvalier also survived coup attempts between 1957 and 1959, but cracks in the facade began to appear. In 1960 the new US ambassador to Haiti, Robert Newbegin, wrote to Norman Warner at the Department of State, with a few preliminary observations about the island, including its leader. 'My impressions of President Duvalier are anything but favourable,' he said. 'As far as his regime is concerned, it strikes me as one of the worst dictatorships with which I have come in contact . . . It is indeed unfortunate that we should be in the unhappy position of having to support a regime headed by such a man.'[17] Unfortunate it might have been, but the US continued to do so. Duvalier won the 1961 election by fraud, and followed it with another in 1964 when he was elected president for life. To back up his claims to power, he built a private security force, known as the Tonton Macoute. The name comes from a fairy-tale character, Uncle Sack (or Gunnysack), who kidnaps children. Such dark humour was all many Haitians had left as the island plunged into worsening poverty; the Duvalier family, fortified by the brutality of the Macoute, controlled the economy. Over the years, Duvalier's appearance began to take a subtle and sinister turn. He was always turned out in neat black suits, horn-rimmed glasses, and sometimes a hat, not unlike one of the most powerful, and feared, voodoo gods, Baron Samedi. This particular *lwa* is related to death and resurrection and can be found around cemeteries; he is depicted as wearing a dinner jacket, glasses or sunglasses, a top hat, and carrying a cane or smoking a cigar. Duvalier was often rumoured to be a voodoo priest, and his similarities to the Baron could not have been entirely coincidental. He knew what a powerful image it was. His regime became a byword for torture, and his opponents were silenced with murder. One of the best-known English works about this period

17. An English portrait from 1802 of Toussaint Louverture, the Saint-Domingue general who fought to free the island's slaves. He was imprisoned by the French and died before the republic of Haiti was established in 1804.

18. The burning of Le Cap, Saint-Domingue – the port city faced numerous attacks throughout the Haitian revolution, including a devastating one in 1793.

19. George Cruikshank's 'The New Union Club' (1819) evokes the worst nineteenth-century stereotypes about black people, and the work parodies the aim of white abolitionists who expressed their desire to 'civilize' slaves and ex-slaves.

20. Abolitionist William Wilberforce, who campaigned to end the slave trade, which became law in 1807. He died in 1833, only a few days after an act to free slaves in the British Empire passed the House of Commons.

21. Agostino Brunias's 'A Linen Market' depicts the world of the free people of colour in the British Windward Islands c. 1780.

22 & 23. Costumes worn during the 1837 'Christmas Amusements' in Jamaica, as captured by the artist Isaac Mendes Belisario. Left: Jaw-Bone, or House John-Canoe, donned by former and soon-to-be-freed slaves. Right: Queen or 'Maam' of the Set-Girls.

24. Banana workers cutting fruit on a plantation in Costa Rica, c. 1910.

25. A hut belonging to Indian (also called 'coolie') indentured labourers, in Jamaica. Many people from India and China arrived in the Caribbean for work, from the mid-1850s onwards, mostly settling in Jamaica, Cuba, Trinidad, and Guiana.

26. Sugar workers in Yabucoa, Puerto Rico gather at a meeting in support of a strike at the sugar mill, in 1941.

27. Marcus Garvey c. 1924, around the time the success of the Jamaica-born Universal Negro Improvement Association founder began to unravel and he was sentenced for mail fraud in the United States.

28. RAF airman Carl Aitken, from Jamaica, was one of thousands of men from the West Indies to volunteer to fight in the Second World War. Sally Lopez, also from Jamaica, volunteered to join the Women's Auxiliary Air Force.

29. Fidel Castro and Che Guevara in Havana, Cuba in 1958 – the following year Castro would be in charge of the island, with Guevara as one of his top ministers.

30. Dr Eric Williams in 1961, the year before Trinidad and Tobago was granted its independence and he became Prime Minister, a role he kept until his death in 1981.

31. A 1950s travel poster – the onset of the jet age meant that people from Europe and the US could travel to the Caribbean in far less time, and some of the islands were quick to develop a tourism industry.

32. A tourist in Kingston, Jamaica poses with locals around the turn of the twentieth century.

33. Port-au-Prince, Haiti, 2012, two years after the cataclysmic earthquake that caused thousands of deaths and nearly destroyed the capital. In the background is the National Palace, which was razed later that year rather than repaired.

34. The courthouse in Plymouth, Montserrat, after the Soufrière Hills volcano erupted in 1995, destroying much of the island.

is Graham Greene's 1966 novel *The Comedians*, set in the Haiti of Papa Doc. For a new edition in 1976, Greene wrote a short introduction in which he discusses his last trip there before writing the novel, recalling, 'what I wanted most was to get away from the stifling nightmare city [Port-au-Prince] where a few weeks after I left all the schoolchildren were forced to attend the execution of two captured guerrillas in the cemetery, a scene repeated every night on local television'.[18]

By the time of his death in 1971, Papa Doc had established a stranglehold on the country, and his son, Jean-Claude, took over as leader. Chubby-faced 'Baby Doc', as he was called, was as bad as his father, and the Macoute continued their work for another fifteen brutal years, while the president raided the country's coffers. Haiti was pushed further and further into poverty, and many Haitians went to the Dominican Republic – despite the antagonism and racism often inflicted on them – to cut cane on woeful wages during the harvest season. To add insult to injury, Papa Doc had long been skimming off part of the salaries that the Dominican Republic paid Haiti for these workers. This was in addition to ongoing contracts between the two countries that paid the government $1 million to send some 20,000 cane-cutters over, though many were ignorant of this additional level of exploitation. But human-rights groups in the 1980s had become aware of what was going on and attempted to highlight the situation. In 1985–6 reports that cane workers had been robbed of their wages at the border crossing at the end of the previous season made people more wary about going over, and the Dominicans could not find enough domestic labour. In early 1986, with a harvest looming, desperate Dominican officials flew to Haiti with $2 million in cash in exchange for 19,000 workers. When this news came to light a few days later, violence erupted among the Haitian peasants. Troops were sent in, but the situation was out of control. The army seized on the protest as a means of ousting Baby Doc and on 7 February 1986 Duvalier and his light-skinned, glamorous, and publicly hated wife Michèle fled, still holding on to the Dominican cash.[19]

*

Although the emperor of Ethiopia, Haile Selassie I, was aware of his role in the larger black world, as articulated by Pan-Africanists like Marcus Garvey, he probably did not quite expect the welcome he got when he arrived in Jamaica in 1966, while stopping over on a regional tour. A newspaper report gave a vivid, enthusiastic account of this historic moment:

> His Imperial Majesty, Haile Selassie I, Emperor of Ethiopia, King of Kings, Conquering Lion of Judah, arrived in Jamaica yesterday to a welcome of superlatives. And he wept. He cried as he stood on the steps of an aircraft of Ethiopian Airlines which had brought him from Trinidad and Tobago to Jamaica and surveyed the vast and uncontrollable crowd which had gathered at the Palisadoes Airport to greet him. The tears welled up in his eyes and rolled down his face. It will perhaps never be known whether he cried in sorrow at the uncontrollableness of the vast throng of Jamaicans who had gathered to meet him, or out of pure joy, but whatever it was, it was an emotional reaction to a highly emotional welcome.[20]

The reason for this outburst of affection was that Selassie was a living god to the followers of the Jamaican religion Rastafarianism. This was a more recent addition to the pantheon of Caribbean religions, and it took shape in the early 1930s. It was around this time that Leonard Howell and his fellow believers took the message to the world that Selassie – the Ras Tafari – was, indeed, a god, and that the promised land was Ethiopia. They offered a spiritual realm outside that of white churches, and white Christianity.[21] It began as a niche religion, and officially remains so – in the Jamaican census of 2001 only around 24,000 people officially affiliated themselves with it.[22] But over the course of the 1930s through the 1960s it attracted more and more followers, although it was either ignored or condemned by the wealthy elite, which might explain why the airport was taken by surprise in 1966.

The people were so emotional that one of the senior Rasta leaders, Mortimer Planno, had to walk up the steps to the plane and ask everyone to calm down and allow the emperor to move through the crowd. Some Rastas were wearing the symbolic colours of red, green, and yellow, and shouting 'lamb of God' and 'black man time now'.[23] Followers of Rastafarianism had come from all over the island – walking, taking buses, hitching rides – in order to greet Selassie at the airport. According to the *Gleaner*, the unprecedented scale of arrivals caused problems with the official programme, and 'people were not presented; the red carpet was ignored; anthems were not played'. Indeed, the emperor was rushed off in a car.[24] Although much of his visit involved official functions, Selassie met with some Rastas – besuited in the newspaper photos – at a reception at the Sheraton where 'the Lion, a symbol associated with The Emperor, was created from ice to adorn a table at the reception'.[25]

Nothing, perhaps, could be further from Rasta ideology and practices than something as decadent, or 'Babylon', as a lion carved out of ice. Rastafarianism is a complex set of beliefs – there is great use of passages from the Old Testament – which emerged out of the unique mix of elements that only Jamaica could provide: the Pan-Africanism of Marcus Garvey and an anti-authoritarianism that was born out of a long tradition of Africans who rebelled or became maroons. Rasta beliefs tend towards millennialism, drawing from Christian and Jewish scriptures. They often use *ganja* to achieve higher spiritual states to commune with Jah, or the higher divinity, and to inspire 'groundings' or intense spiritual and philosophical conversations, or to focus on the spiritual self, often expressed as the 'I'. Many Rastas wear their hair in dreadlocks and wear beards, to show that they have eschewed the ways of Babylon by following an Old Testament edict to let 'no razor come upon his head' (Numbers 6:5), and they often follow a meat-free, natural, or Ital, diet. However, there is an enormous amount of variation. While there are many writings about Rastafarianism, it has no written creed, nor any organized places of worship. More of a problem for outsiders was the Rasta view of 'Babylon', or the secular world and its 'politricks', which often led to clashes with the authorities and campaigns of repression. Indeed, a few years before Selassie's visit, in 1963, there had been a violent battle between Rastas and police, in what was later known as the Coral Garden massacre. It started as an apparently unprovoked attack on some bearded men thought to be Rastas, and ended with people being killed. The police rounded up Rastas in the region around Montego Bay and sent them to prison on trumped-up charges. Other Rastas managed to escape by quickly chopping off their dreadlocks. The suppression continued well into the 1960s and 1970s. It was not until a Rasta called Robert Nesta Marley came along that the group's image would go global, and the official pressure would ease off in the face of rising popularity.

*

As unlikely as it may seem, Bob Marley and his band, the Wailers, were partly the product of experimental urban planning. In the 1930s,

Jamaica's Central Housing Authority had been set up to alleviate conditions among the squatter communities, many of which were in western Kingston, including a plot of land known as Trench Town – named for Daniel Power Trench, who had owned the land in the 1700s. Construction began there in the 1940s. The idea was based on a then-popular 'township' model which provided housing and other facilities, such as community centres, for poor Jamaicans. The housing comprised single-storey, multi-family units around a common courtyard, with shared kitchens and bathrooms.[26] There was running water and electricity, something most squatters did not have. Each family lived in one room of around 3m square (10ft × 10ft), which meant that most people lived their life in the courtyard. People slept outside, or at the very least spent days and evenings in these 'government yards', socializing and playing music. Demand far outstripped supply, and soon squatters had set up around the new developments. Within a short time, it was clear that these yards were nurturing some of the island's most creative output. In the late 1950s and early 1960s the Jamaican music scene exploded with upbeat ska and rocksteady songs by musicians from Trench Town, which also began to make their way to Britain to be listened to on sound systems in West Indian neighbourhoods. The young Marley, who spent time living in Trench Town, met and started to collaborate with fellow musicians Bunny Wailer, Peter Tosh, and others. They cut ska and rocksteady tracks, scoring a hit with 'Simmer Down' in 1964. Marley and the Wailers would move on to a reggae sound, and later global fame. But this period of his life was later commemorated in his 1974 hit 'No Woman, No Cry', in which he sings about the times 'we used to sit in the government yard in Trench Town'. The yards were also where Mortimer Planno lived, and functioned as the main meeting place for Rastafarians. And it was in the yards that Marley was introduced to the religion that would influence the direction his life would take and which his music would introduce to the world.[27]

These government yards soon became overrun with drugs and violence. Even in the 1960s, the cracks were showing, as political clientelism seeped into these poor communities. Political patronage was bought and sold, and soon tracts of ghetto were either PNP or JLP. By the 1970s political violence became so prevalent that Marley held a One Love Peace Concert on 22 April 1978 to ease tensions – by the

1980 election some 800 people had been killed. By this point the 'garrison constituencies' that persist today had coalesced (they are called 'garrison' because the police have to 'garrison' themselves in secure stations). Local 'dons' reign, and the situation is beyond the control of the police.[28] The more conservative JLP, led by Edward Seaga, took power in 1980 and stayed in office until 1989, when he was defeated by the PNP led by Michael Manley, who, having realized he no longer had the money to pay for extensive social reforms, had considerably toned down his rhetoric; Manley retired and handed power over to P. J. Patterson in 1992. Patterson and the PNP led the island until 2006. But the damage was done, and the yards of Trench Town and other poor neighbourhoods remain blighted by violence, exacerbated by the arrival of the drug trade in the 1970s and '80s. In addition, the fingerprints of the CIA were on the shipments of guns, and the unrest that unseated the Manley government in 1976.[29]

*

When Dr Walter Rodney tried to return to Kingston, Jamaica, from a black writers' conference in Montreal, Canada, he met with a nasty surprise. Rodney, a Guyanese academic, had recently taken up a post at the relatively new University of the West Indies, Mona, in 1968 to teach African history. But that life came to an abrupt end on 15 October when he was barred from re-entering the country, on the orders of the Prime Minister, JLP leader Hugh Shearer. The following day the students at UWI began a protest that would paralyse Kingston and spread throughout the city, leaving death and damage in its wake. It may seem an extreme chain of events, but Rodney was no ordinary historian. A gifted scholar who wrote a PhD dissertation on the slave trade at the School of Oriental and African Studies in London, he was also engaged with the radical thinking of the period. He spoke out about the oppression of the black poor, took an interest in the Rastafarian community in Jamaica, and was a supporter of Castro. He held 'groundings' with the Rastas, and his activism alarmed Shearer. The riots were the worst in Jamaica since the 1930s, but Shearer did not relent, claiming Rodney was a threat to national security.*

---

* Rodney travelled to Cuba and back to Tanzania, where he had taught previously. In 1974, he returned to Guyana, then under Forbes Burnham's rule, and continued

These protests became known as the 'Walter Rodney riots', and were a significant moment in the rise of Black Power movements in the Caribbean, mobilizing people throughout the region, especially in the former British islands, but also among the diaspora in the United States, Canada, and Europe.[30] Rodney later wrote that he was not surprised by the ban because, although the government is black 'they are all white-hearted. These men serve the interests of a foreign, white capitalist system and at home they uphold a social structure which ensures that the black man resides at the bottom of the social ladder.'[31]

Indeed, the trigger for what became known as the 'February Revolution' in Trinidad started far away from the island, at Sir George Williams University in Montreal. Some Trinidadian students were protesting about what they considered unfair treatment by taking over the university's computer lab in 1969. Eventually, some of the students were expelled for their participation in the protests, and there was much anger in the island over the affair. Added to the mix was the influence of the Black Power movement in the United States and the lingering anger that the government continued to ban the entry of Trinidad-born, US-educated Black Power leader Stokely Carmichael. At the same time, many people were disgruntled with Eric Williams and his People's National Movement (PNM). The government could not but notice the resentment – it had been put on parade. During the Carnival celebrations on 9 February 1970, some of the revellers had dressed in outfits evoking political themes such as slavery and Black Power, visibly communicating their dissatisfaction. Feeling the tension, Williams tried to address concerns in a statement to the nation, while the party claimed that it would begin to focus on 'black dignity' and attempt to tackle economic inequality among the island's different groups.[32] But it was too little, too late.

After about 200 students set off on 26 February 1970 to demonstrate against the sentencing of students involved in the Montreal protest in Canada, they were quickly joined by other groups and the protest swelled – on 6 March between 14,000 and 20,000 people headed from the capital to San Juan, about five miles away.[33] The movement was heavily African – the old hostilities made the East Indian com-

---

his political activism, setting up and leading the Working People's Alliance party until his life was cut short by an assassin's bomb on 13 June 1980.

munity wary of joining. On 26 March thousands of blacks went to Caroni, deep into sugar cane country in the centre of the island, in an attempt to recruit East Indians, but few joined in.[34]

The disturbances caused Eric Williams to declare a state of emergency on 21 April 1970 and arrest more than a dozen purported Black Power leaders. At the same time, the army refused to participate, its leaders claiming they did not want to take up arms against fellow black people, and also working on the premise that the government had lost its legitimacy.[35] But Williams stayed at the helm in Trinidad and Tobago. Britain was quick to send two warships, partly over concern for the two thousand Britons living there and the estimated £150 million investment it had made on the island. In the end, the protest was suppressed, and with the arrest of the leaders the movement was finished. Williams stayed on as prime minister and the island soon received a financial boost in the form of soaring oil revenues,[36] which saw a tenfold rise in price in the mid-1970s, due in large part to the OPEC embargo on the US in 1973, and which helped Williams to cement his position as leader.[37]

Williams and Shearer were not the only prime ministers to show a marked antipathy towards Black Power radicals – almost all the English-speaking islands' governments were hostile to their revolutionary message. Barbados introduced a Public Order Act in 1970 that clamped down on suspected leaders, increasing surveillance on them.[38] Indeed, this island, too, had trouble with Carmichael. When he arrived at Bridgetown airport in May 1970, the immigration official asked Carmichael for his signature on the landing card. What he got was: 'In order to free OUR land, we have to KILL.'[39] The Barbados Cabinet had been vacillating about allowing Carmichael to enter; in the end, Prime Minister Errol Barrow relented. Carmichael was allowed to land and have a brief visit as long as he did not speak or attend any public meetings. Instead, he went to a friend's house and his supporters followed him there, but there was little the police could do to stop the seventy or so people who showed up. He was reported to have said that 'the only action could be blood', but the rest of his trip went without incident.[40]

Meanwhile, as the disturbances in Trinidad continued there were some small-scale protests in Jamaica criticizing the Trinidadian government. In a memorandum to London, the British High Commissioner

·in Jamaica, Nick Larmour, reported that 'Jamaicans are apt to say that Black Power is a misnomer because in this country power is already firmly in Jamaican hands and Government largely in black hands.'[41] He added, however, that the real issue was social inequality: 'Black Power in Jamaican terms is not really a matter of politics. It is a matter of economics and of ensuring that black men get their fair or more than their fair share of what is going.'[42] He enclosed a report with the letter, titled 'A Post-Trinidad Assessment of Jamaican Stability', and focusing on the University of the West Indies at Mona, said, 'Although it is nowadays probably one of the most stable and trouble-free campuses in the whole of the Western Hemisphere, it is regarded with considerable apprehension by the Establishment in Jamaica.'[43] The British observer, however, thought the campus was under the 'illusion of ferment but [they] can in fact rarely penetrate or stir up the leaden lower middle-class lump of the student population'. Nor did the report find the Black Power movements on that island threatening, though he said 'it would certainly be a great mistake to write off the Black Power movement in Jamaica', and that the high unemployment rate (23 per cent) continued to make Jamaica ripe for unrest.[44]

In St Lucia, still under British control, the authorities were keeping close watch on a Black Power meeting on the island in December of 1970. One of the organizers, George Odlum, denied any connection to communism 'or any other -ism' and the island had been chosen for the conference because it had yet to ban anyone from entry, which was fast becoming a problem. In addition to the Carmichael ban in Trinidad, Dominica and Montserrat – the latter two also still British colonies – had prohibited him, too, while Barbados had banned Trinidadian activists Clive Nunez and Geddes Granger. Dominica had also banned Dr Walter Rodney.[45] In the end there were delegates from only Grenada, Trinidad, Guyana, St Vincent, and Jamaica.[46] The Black Power movement in the Caribbean shared many similarities with the struggle for racial equality and empowerment in the US, not least the constant surveillance and harassment from authorities. That this continued to be the case in Caribbean nations – almost all of them majority black nations – also illustrates the complexity of post-independence national unity. There was a fear that the movement would undermine the region's stability, and Trinidad was a worrying example of this. No doubt the pan-African consciousness in the movement also discomfited some, as it had done decades before when Marcus Garvey was preaching his pan-African message. For as much as Black Power expressed a wider global unity among people of African origin, it also exposed some of the differing attitudes and priorities of officials and others across the islands.

In Dominica, the premier, Patrick John, for instance, declared war on the island's more politicized adherents of Rastafarianism, the 'dreads', in 1974, intending to make it illegal for them to grow their hair in locks, as well as to maintain an 'unkempt' appearance. A critical piece from the Barbados Advocate News, reproduced in the Dominican newspaper the Star, noted that 'Premier John is not the first leader to arbitrate in regard to dress, although he may be the first to take his stand on hygienic and aesthetic grounds; not on moral principles.'[47] The Dreads Act passed the House of Assembly in November.[48] By the following week, John had linked the Dreads and Black Power with communism, saying 'International Communist organisations in North America and Cuba have recruited into their orbit Dominicans formerly resident abroad', and, according to the report in the Star, 'he added that they sought to destroy the State and its system through artificial race conflict and a black power cult'.[49]

By December, the action had intensified, with recent attacks on white tourists blamed on men thought to be involved with Black Power groups. The House of Assembly that month approved emergency legislation allowing judges to order the destruction of Black Power literature, and to dock the pay of any civil servant involved with a 'banned' group, i.e. the Dreads, who were now said to be engaging in 'guerrilla' behaviour.[50] Police raids and attempts to disband the groups soon followed. The measures – which also included the legal right to kill a Dread found in a private home – soon alarmed human rights groups. The Dreads, for their part, were said to have wanted the banking system nationalized and the land given over to common ownership, and one Dread, who spoke to a New York Times reporter, said they were 'disenchanted with political, economic and educational directions that have failed to improve the life of the average poor West Indian'.[51] From across the Atlantic, there were concurring voices. A former administrator on the island from 1952 to 1959, Sir Laurence Lindo, wrote a letter to *The Times* of London arguing that the 'basic cause of the present unrest in Dominica lies in the fact that there are virtually no jobs available for school-leavers. This inevitably leads to frustration and disillusion, and has resulted in lawlessness and violence among young people.'[52] The island was still under British administration at this point, a few years away from its independence.

In Grenada, however, a very different story was unfolding.

*

Perched above the town of St George's, Grenada, is a grey, weathered fort. The vistas are stunning, with the surrounding hills, colourful rooftops, harbour and azure sea in plain sight all around. The French thought it an ideal spot to start building a defence, which they did around 1705, calling it Fort Royal. With the onset of British control in 1763, it became Fort George. Today, some of its buildings are in a state of disrepair due to hurricane damage, and the police use some of the others. Colonial cannons still line sections of the ramparts, and weeds sprout from crumbling battlements. Inside the fort, two buildings and two parts of a wall create a courtyard, which has faintly visible lines marking out half of a basketball court, complete with a backboard and rim in place, though the net is long gone. On one wall hangs a weather-worn plaque commemorating the death of sixteen people who 'have gone to join the stars and will forever shine in glory'. One of them was the former prime minister, Maurice Bishop. He was executed there, under the basketball hoop, on 19 October 1983, along with seven of his ministers. Eight others also died on that tumultuous day.

The execution shocked the Caribbean and the world. Bishop, a lawyer who had trained in London, returned to the island in 1970 and quickly became a popular and charismatic leader. His socialist party, the New Jewel (Joint Endeavour for Welfare, Education, and Liberation) Movement, had been set up in 1973 and staged a coup on 13 March 1979, burning down an army barracks and taking power with little resistance. The previous regime, led by Eric Gairy, had grown increasingly violent and repressive, especially after independence from Britain in 1974. Gairy's henchmen, known as the Mongoose Gang, attacked opposition members, and there were also fraudulent elections in the period leading up to the coup.

Bishop and his party were inspired by Cuba, and looked to it and the USSR for support in its early days, angering the United States and causing concern in other Caribbean islands. They immediately suspended the constitution and set up the People's Revolutionary Army, and the fort was even renamed Fort Rupert in honour of Bishop's father. Bishop also tried to implement social reforms, and Cuba was quick to help. By 1983, it had given the island money and sent workers over to improve the Point Salines airport, including extending its runway, arousing US suspicions that armed Soviet and Cuban planes were going to use it.

However, the party began to unravel, and by September 1983 Bishop was facing an internal crisis. Bishop's deputy Bernard Coard and other members of the central committee had begun to criticize his softening stance toward the United States and the failure of his economic reforms, and were demanding he share the leadership. A radio broadcast by General Hudson Austin on 16 October tried to reassure the public but placed the blame on Bishop, saying, 'the truth is that during the past year, our party has faced the serious problem of the constantly growing desire of Comrade Maurice Bishop to exercise sole and exclusive power and authority'.[53]

By 19 October, a group of supporters had freed Bishop from house arrest, and the crowd marched upon Fort Rupert to take back control from the army. They were met with a hail of bullets, and Bishop and his Cabinet members were taken to the courtyard, where they were executed. General Hudson went on air again to explain what had happened, claiming 'Maurice Bishop and his group fired on the soldiers killing two members of the PRA . . . The Revolutionary Armed Forces were forced to storm the fort.'[54] Fears were expressed by the US and other Caribbean islands, even Cuba, which had released a statement on 15 October to report that Castro had 'deep concern over the fact that the split which had developed could considerably damage the image of the revolutionary process in Grenada within the country and abroad'.[55]

Less than a week after the executions, on 25 October the United States sent in the marines, accompanied by troops from other eastern Caribbean islands. President Ronald Reagan told the public in a televised address that the US had received 'an urgent' request from the Organization of Eastern Caribbean States for assistance 'in a joint effort to restore order and democracy on the island of Grenada'.[56] He claimed also to be protecting the thousand or so American residents, including students at the St George's University School of Medicine.

Over the next few weeks, some 6,000 troops were sent to the island, and Operation Urgent Fury was conducted under a press blackout during the initial days of the invasion.[57] There was international condemnation of the attack, which some argued was really undertaken to destroy the work Cubans were doing on the airport. Indeed, the workers there were stuck in the crossfire, and some were killed and others captured by the marines. Castro issued an angry statement decrying the fact that the attack on Cubans was without any warning.[58]

The anger spread well beyond the Caribbean. In Britain, Socialist Action circulated a pamphlet that claimed, 'Crocodile tears spilt for Maurice Bishop are unconvincing given that the CIA tried to assassinate him in 1981. Neither were the lives of American medical students in danger until the 4,000 US special forces arrived on 25 October.'[59] The US Anti-Imperialist League protested that 'Grenada, a liberated Black country in the Caribbean, now finds itself invaded by the same government that has historically distinguished itself as the main prop of racism and national chauvinism in the world', and that 'racism plays a central role in the US government's Caribbean policy'.[60] Even Reagan's staunchest Cold War ally, British Prime Minister Margaret Thatcher, was angered by the invasion plans – Britain had not even been consulted, and the island was a member of the Commonwealth.[61]

It was a short operation, officially ending on 13 November, with the dead numbering eighteen Americans, forty-two Cubans, and twenty-one Grenadians.[62] Elections were later held, and the island returned to democracy. 'The pros and cons of the action of the Caribbean governments will long be debated. So will those of President Reagan in coming to our aid,' said Barbados Prime Minister Tom Adams. 'But I think that history will agree with the verdict of public opinion in the eastern Caribbean.'[63] Global opinion differed; Operation Urgent Fury was heavily criticized at the UN, and the Security Council approved a resolution 'deeply deploring' the invasion as a 'flagrant violation of international law', with a vote of eleven for and one (the US) against, with Britain, Togo, and Zaire (Congo) abstaining.[64]

Today, there is a prominent war memorial, commemorating the

US soldiers who died in action there. A small plinth sits under four graceful arches that connect directly above it, with benches to rest on, and framed by landscaping. It is one of the first things visible on the road leading out of Maurice Bishop International Airport.

*

Although Eric Williams had ended the Black Power protests and remained in office, Trinidad would face another series of events that would leave it shaken. Williams died in 1981, and the PNM stayed in power for another five years. There continued to be disturbances during this period, and in the 1986 election the PNM was trounced by the opposition, the National Alliance for Reconstruction led by Arthur Robinson. There was a considerable amount of tension on the island owing to economic problems, including costly foreign debt payments and painful restructuring programmes as well as high unemployment. Around the same time, there had been changes within the Black Power movement, as some of its adherents had converted to Islam, inspired by the Nation of Islam movement in the United States. One such convert was Lennox Phillip, who became known as Yasin Abu Bakr.[65] He, with the help of around 130 men, would hold the island hostage for six days in July 1990, in what was called the Muslimeen Coup.

On the evening of 27 July 1990, journalists in the Trinidad & Tobago Television building heard shots. When they peered through the windows, they saw armed men in mufti entering the building. One of the hostages, Verne Burnett, who was news director at Radio Trinidad, later recalled, 'because of the way they were dressed, I first thought they were Libyans, but when they began to criticise the government, I realised they were locals'.[66]

Bakr – who was rumoured to have links to Libyan leader Muammar Gaddafi – had attacked the state-run TV station because he wanted to announce that the 'government of Trinidad and Tobago was overthrown'; masked and armed members of his militia stood behind him when he did so.[67] They also stormed the Red House parliament building, taking Robinson and others hostage, while other men bombed the police station. They beat Robinson and shot him in the leg after he ordered the army to attack. Bakr called for elections to take place in ninety days, and they also demanded Cabinet posts. However, they had little popular support. The intellectual community was horrified, as was the traditional Islamic community. Bakr realized that without the mobilization of more people, they were doomed. They agreed to negotiate with the government, and the coup attempt ended on 1 August and the hostages were freed.

Ismail Abdullah Muhammad, one of the men who participated, claimed they did not plan to kill anyone, nor to loot. 'This statement [Bakr on TV], to my knowledge, was not a signal to loot. What I do know is that there were some followers of the Jamaat Al Muslimeen who used to come off and on to the Mosque to worship who were not real Muslims but had knowledge of our plans.'[68] But looting and rioting followed in the wake of the announcement, and martial law was declared. In the end some twenty-four people were killed, and more than five hundred injured. The riots destroyed many buildings in central Port of Spain, and many shops belonging to Chinese, Indian, and Syrian owners were damaged or ruined.

Bakr and others who were arrested were granted amnesty as part of their deal and were released from prison in 1992. He was later arrested on the charge of trying to buy weapons in Miami. His estimated worth is more than $6 million.[69] In the following round of elections in 1991, the PNM were returned to power.

*

The second half of the twentieth century was a time of enormous transition in the Caribbean. With the arrival of communism in Cuba, and the independence of the British islands, it became clear that there was little uniformity across the region. As the reception of Black Power on some of the islands indicated, building unity – or indeed, accepting that things were not as harmonious as people would have liked them to be – in some of these new nations was going to be a challenge: Walter Rodney wrote that 'since "Independence", the Black police force of Jamaica have demonstrated that they can be as savage in their approach to black brothers as the white police of New York, for ultimately they serve the same masters'.[70] US interference perhaps reached its apogee in this period, with the Cold War as a pretext for seemingly incessant meddling. Fidel Castro, despite all efforts to topple and kill him, survived and his regime still endures, under the leadership of his brother, Raúl. But many of the scars from this time have not healed, and they are still visible.

Chapter Twelve

ISLAND LIFE

On the breezy late afternoon of 12 January 2010, normal life in the Haitian capital of Port-au-Prince came to an abrupt end. Buildings collapsed into rubble under the force of the 7.0-magnitude earthquake, and a city with a large population already living in shanty towns found itself faced with a tragedy of unparalleled proportions. The epicentre was only about ten miles from the capital, and the aftershocks that continued for days compounded the damage in Port-au-Prince and the surrounding area.

Most of the islands – except Cuba and the Bahamas – sit on the Caribbean plate, which moves around 20mm a year, but there had not been any significant seismic activity for almost two centuries.[1] Haiti, long the poorest nation in the western hemisphere, had no building codes, so where a more prepared city might have withstood the force of the earthquake, Port-au-Prince was barely left standing. Nothing symbolized this more than the photos beamed around the world of the National Palace: its elegant facade resembled a sad, collapsed tier of a wedding cake. The remnants of this century-old building in the centre of the capital were a painful reminder of the tragedy, and the whole palace was demolished in 2012. Some, however, believed that the ruins were part of Haiti's national heritage and, as such, should have been preserved. But that is a minor question in comparison with the thousands of people still living in tents who need rehousing. And, just to add to the island's troubles, the UN Stabilization Mission in Haiti (MINUSTAH) troops brought a biological stowaway with them – a strain of cholera from Nepal. In a city ravaged by the earthquake and already lacking decent sanitation, the disease spread rapidly, killing more than 7,000 people and causing more than half a million more to be ill. The death toll from the earthquake is still uncertain; the numbers range from the official Haitian tally of 316,000 to much lower estimates of 46,000, and it is far from clear exactly how the government arrived at its figures, which has become a matter of concern for aid agencies and other NGOs working on the island.[2]

The reconstruction continues, and aid agencies permeate the capital. UN 4x4s fight for space in the crowded streets, along with colourful tap-tap buses, pedestrians, and roadside vendors. Indeed, the government, according to an investigation in the *Nation* magazine, has no idea how many NGOs there are in Haiti – estimates range from 560 to 10,000. Some groups, of course, had been there well before the earthquake.[3] Yet by the end of 2012 only around half of the $9.3 billion in aid pledged to the country had been delivered. No one is sure where the rest is, nor when it will be paid. There has been much recrimination and finger-pointing, and political unrest to boot, putting pressure on pop-star-turned-president Michel Martelly, also known as Sweet Micky.

The years between the end of the Duvalier regime in 1986 and the earthquake were restless and violent. Constitutional reforms were enacted in 1987 to prevent a future dictatorship, but it did not lead to peace or stability. Leslie Manigat, General Henri Namphy, and Prosper Avril all came and went as president. The United States began to put pressure on the island to reform its disruptive politics, and in 1990 there were elections to replace the interim government of Ertha Pascal-Trouillot, in which a former Salesian priest named Jean-Bertrand Aristide won office. Aristide's outspoken, fiery sermons won him a large following among the poor, known as the Lavalas (flood) movement. Expelled from the order in 1988, he turned to organized politics, running for president as the candidate for the National Front for Change and Democracy (FNCD), and winning the 1990 election. He did not last a year. But his enemies were quick to try to run him out of office, which they succeeded in doing on 30 September 1991, and the United States immediately protested and then enacted an embargo. Aristide fled to Venezuela and later Washington, DC. Tens of thousands of Haitians followed, trying to get out the country any way they could, most often in flimsy dinghies or overcrowded rafts, hoping they would survive the trip to Florida. President George H. W. Bush demanded that Aristide be returned to the island, and the Haitian president won supporters in the US and Europe, not only in politics but also in celebrity circles in Hollywood and New York.

In 1993 the new administration of US President Bill Clinton put further pressure on Haiti, and soon the military agreed to let Aristide return. Aristide brought the US Marines with him, as Clinton created Operation Uphold Democracy in 1994 to oversee the transition. For some Haitians, this would be the second time that they had witnessed the large-scale arrival of US soldiers. Aristide resumed office, disbanded the army, and set up a national police force the following year.

The next election, in 1995, was won by René Préval, with Aristide's support – Haiti's constitution prohibits a president from serving consecutive terms. However, Préval quickly implemented IMF-related structural reforms, angering Aristide and others, though Aristide had himself signed off on a rice deal in 1994 that slashed tariffs on imported US rice and wrecked the livelihoods of thousands of Haitian farmers. He split from his former party and formed the Fanmi Lavalas party. Aristide returned to office in 2000, but there were growing suspicions about his abuse of power, not least his use of personal footsoldiers called Chimères, or ghosts. This period was marred by political violence, and Aristide was driven out of office and once more fled into exile in 2004.[4] Préval was running the island when the earthquake struck.

As Haiti struggles to rebuild its present, it is haunted by its past. Not only did Baby Doc return to the country in 2011 after twenty-five years of exile, so, too, did Aristide. Rumours about Baby Doc's return ranged from political involvement with the then ongoing elections to it being a homecoming because he was terminally ill. And although a tiny faction of Duvalier supporters still exists, the authorities have brought corruption charges against the former dictator, and he remains on the island under house arrest, though he is frequently seen out in public. Haiti's appeals court ruled in February 2014 that he could face charges of crimes against humanity. Many Haitians, meanwhile, want to see the political return of Aristide, who also still commands some international support. He did not make any public appearances until 2013, when he was summoned to a courtroom to answer questions from the inquiry into the assassination in 2000 of the high-profile journalist Jean Dominique.[5]

*

Although the Haitian earthquake remains one of the worst natural disasters in Caribbean history, the twentieth century has been marked by a regular onslaught of hurricanes inflicting damage. Every island has buildings bearing reminders of hurricanes past, though many new construction projects use reinforced concrete, and early warning systems mean the storms no longer bring the death tolls they used to. But reconstruction is a long, expensive process; Grenada, for instance, continues to rebuild after the devastation of Hurricane Ivan in 2004. Bluefields, on the Nicaraguan coast, lost everything – including most of its archival holdings – in Hurricane Joan in 1988. The town, which could be reached only by air or river from Managua, first received aid from Cuba, as it could land planes there.

Volcanoes also continue to erupt, sometimes with extreme consequences, as the people of Montserrat know all too well. In June of 1995, the dormant Soufrière Hills volcano rumbled back to life and has been active ever since. The capital, Plymouth, lies buried under ash and mud, and the southern part of the tiny island is uninhabitable. Steeples and roofs poke out of the packed ash, adding to the eerie landscape. Only about a third of the population remains, with some 10,000 people having left the island. Because it was still a British dependency at the time of the disaster, many islanders took refuge in the UK, where they continue to live. Although there is little that can be done about such natural phenomena, environmental problems that may be linked to human activity plague the region, too. The changing climate has made the recent summer storm seasons more erratic, while rising sea levels and flooding brought about by melting ice caps are causing concern. Trinidad was hit by severe floods in 2012, while coastal regions of Colombia experienced almost non-stop rains. Enriquillo and Azuei, neighbouring lakes in the Dominican Republic and Haiti, respectively, have swelled to record levels, and after more than a dozen villages were flooded the resulting submergence of land has forced families to leave the area.[6]

Haiti has long been criticized for its deforestation, the result of which is obvious from the air. The mountains are folds of brown, rather than green; at ground level, the poorest people are left at risk of seasonal landslides. It is not a government policy to chop down trees, but rather the last resort of the rural poor, who use the roots as cooking fuel.

Many islands are concerned, too, about the health of coral reefs and marine life, also under threat from the changing climate and humans' further encroachment. The ability of each island to respond to these needs varies by income, but environmental problems are becoming an increasing priority.

*

Like the ever-present threat of natural disaster, another shared feature of Caribbean life is a sharp disparity between rich and poor. While islands like Barbados and the Dutch Antilles have a larger social safety net and a sizeable middle class, the differences elsewhere can be striking. Nowhere, perhaps, is the gulf so deep and wide as in Haiti. Not far from the Karibé hotel, where rooms start at US$150 a night, sits a tent city, where people displaced by the earthquake continue to wait for a home. The gulches in the city do not flow with water, but with styrofoam, plastic bottles – and foraging pigs.[7] Pigs are, in a literal sense, currency for many people. A group of friends or family will chip in to buy one, and then share the meat when it is slaughtered, usually to mark a wedding or a funeral. While the disparity is greatest in the capital, it extends throughout the country. Piled in a corner of the ruins of the Sans-Souci palace are bottles bearing the unmistakable orange label of Veuve-Clicquot, left over from a society wedding in 2012. The spirit of Henri Christophe lives on. These images might be at odds with those of poor peasants and suffering earthquake victims, but the number of world-class restaurants in the Port-au-Prince suburb of Pétionville and plans for luxury hotels in the city point to a very different reality. Much of the money is foreign, brought in by wealthy Haitians from abroad, or by the aid industry and the UN, whose logistical needs fund a wide network of drivers, translators, and landlords, in addition to hotels and restaurants.

The poor – and that is the majority of the people on the island – still face the challenges that have confronted them for decades, if not centuries. Illiteracy runs at well over 50 per cent, and land disputes often hinder the rural peasantry from prospering. Indeed, this has led to a sort of internal slavery. The poorest children are frequently sent to work for families – often wealthier relatives – who can at least feed them. Known as *restaveks*, these children are regularly denied schooling and are also abused and overworked. It is a complex and often brutal response to dire poverty.

In contrast to this is Cuba. The type of deprivation seen in Haiti is almost unknown there, though these are perhaps the two polar examples. There is enough food for everyone because of a rationing system – but many complain about both the quality and the paucity of choice – as well as a world-famous state-run health-care system, universal education, and housing for all. However, the government has struggled to pay for these social services since the collapse of communism. Once the wall came down in Berlin, so, too, did the Soviet subsidy crumble away. Cuba entered what was called the 'special period', a terrible time of shortages and uncertainty. Thousands tried to leave the island; by 1994 so many Cubans were trying to get into the United States that it agreed to hand out 20,000 visas, but also warned that any Cuban caught at sea would now be returned to the island. Castro had nowhere to turn but inwards, and so, with some reluctance, he opened Cuba's doors to tourists. But revolutionary slogans still abound, and there are no bill-boards advertising Coca-Cola just yet. Everywhere there are images of José Martí and Che Guevara, and the post-1959 patrimony is as well preserved as it can be for the moment.[8]

By the 2000s, Cuba was trading doctors for oil from Venezuela, though with the death of Venezuelan president Hugo Chávez, the future of the programme is uncertain. Cuba receives an estimated $6 billion for the services of the 40,000 medical and other professionals working in Venezuela. The two countries also have joint ventures in hotels and manufacturing. Other Cuban doctors are scattered around the region, in places such as Belize, where they help prop up the health-care system, and Haiti, where they are helping the relief effort. For others, it is more difficult to leave Cuba. Economic opportunity within is changing, but the average state salary still only works out to about US$18 a month. The standard of living appears low, and even im-poverished, to visitors, yet Cuba is far more egalitarian than other Caribbean societies. In addition, Cubans do not usually pay rent, or for health care, and some food and public transport is subsidized. Personal income has long been propped up by remittances sent from Cubans living abroad, although that money is heavily taxed. Tourism, in the end, has proved an economic godsend, but it has also brought numerous problems with it, not least sex tourism. The government permitted people to open private guest houses and small restaurants, which have been successful. In 2012 there was an easing of restrictions on exit visas, too, which means Cubans will be able to travel and live abroad more freely.

The journalist John Jeremiah Sullivan, who is married to a Cuban and has travelled there many times, wrote in a 2012 article about his most recent trip, noting that before he even got out of Miami airport, it was clear that things had changed:

> There were other post-Bush differences in the direct-to-Cuba zone. The lines had grown fewer and shorter. Most noticeable, the Cubans on our flight – a mixture of Cuban-Americans and returning Cuban nationals who had been in Florida or D.C. on visas of their own (some people do move back and forth) – weren't carrying as much stuff. Last time, people had multiple pairs of shoes tied around their necks by the laces. Thick gorgets of reading glasses. Men wearing 10 hats, several pairs of pants, everybody's pockets bulging. Everybody wearing fanny packs. The rule was, if you could get it onto your body, you could bring it aboard.[9]

There is a rising level of prosperity, but it threatens the socialist nature of the revolution. People who have family abroad can collect the capital necessary to run a B&B or restaurant, which in turn will give them an income well above the state salary. By running a business catering to tourists, these Cubans have more access to goods that are hard to come by on the island, as well as hard currency. Cuba replaced the US dollar – which is used throughout the West Indies – with a closed currency, known as the CUC, which is equal in value to the US dollar. To add to the confusion, there is also a national currency (*moneda nacional*, or *pesos*) in which Cubans receive their salary and in which they pay for certain subsidized goods. For instance, tickets to the national ballet in Havana cost 20CUC for visitors, i.e., $20, but for Cubans it is 20 *pesos*, less than $1.

Although the island is free to trade with other nations, it continues to feel the pain of the ongoing US embargo – but some food and medicine is allowed in. Also, US travel restrictions keep potential tourists out; however, though they are permitted to visit through official channels such as organized tours or family visits. The question that remains for Cubans is whether it can continue its experiment in equality in the face of growing tourism and migration, as well as political change. In 2013 Raúl Castro, who became president after Fidel stood down in 2008, announced he would leave office at the end of his term, in 2018, when he will be eighty-seven years old. In addition, restrictions on allowing Cubans to leave the country – getting the right paperwork was an often fraught, expensive task – have recently been eased, though the impact has not yet become clear. The cracks in the old system are showing, but by many socio-economic measures, such as access to health care and education, Cuba still is one of the most equitable places in the West Indies, if not the world, and the question now is how much longer such a system can last. Reforms to loosen up the many restrictions on daily life, however, have been slow – Cubans were only recently permitted to own mobile phones and use the internet, and the relatively high price for such services there means that while there is permission on paper, in practice it remains difficult for Cubans to communicate with the outside world, while the rest of the Caribbean becomes increasingly wired up and reliant on mobile phone technology.

The other islands fall somewhere between Haiti and Cuba. The French colonies are supported by tourism and subsidies, sometimes a cause of friction. In Guadeloupe there was a forty-four-day strike in 2009 over the discrepancies between pay on the island and in metropolitan France. Some forty-eight unions were involved – for a population of about 460,000 – and they put a number of demands to the government, not least of which was a $250 rise in the monthly minimum wage.[10]

Other subsidies are not so generous. Puerto Rico, according to the 2010 census, lags far behind Mississippi, the poorest US state, where 26.6 per cent of people live below the poverty line of $22,881 for a family of four. In Puerto Rico, 45.6 per cent live below the poverty line.[11] Although there have been attempts to woo business to the island through tax breaks, and there is a tourism economy, the island relies on US funding and remittances from family members in the mainland states or elsewhere.

Overall, all the islands struggle. Some are heavily hamstrung by the repayments on their debts to the IMF. The high cost of debt not only hinders the development of social services but can also cause financial problems and lead to policies such as currency devaluation, or leave people in even more poverty. Some of the Caribbean islands suffer debt-to-GDP ratios of more than 100 per cent, including St Kitts and Nevis (153 per cent), Jamaica (138 per cent), and Barbados (117 per cent).[12] Crime also continues to be a problem – the murder rates in Jamaica, Honduras, and Puerto Rico are among the highest in the world.

*

The summer of 2012 was an exciting one for Jamaica and Trinidad, as both islands were celebrating fifty years of independence. Bunting was out, flags were flying, and billboards and advertisements proclaimed their pride in the island nations. Indeed, Jamaica received a special present in the form of medal-winning performances in athletics during the 2012 Summer Olympics. Jamaican runners brought home four gold, four silver, and four bronze medals – including two personal and one relay gold for sprinter Usain Bolt – helping to place the island eighteenth in the medal table. Trinidad and Tobago was not left out either; it came back with one gold and three bronze medals. Athletes from Cuba, the Dominican Republic, the Bahamas, Grenada, and Puerto Rico added another twenty medals to the overall Caribbean count.

In the fifty years since those islands won their independence, most of the other British West Indian colonies have followed suit, but a few chose to remain as British overseas territories: Anguilla, the British Virgin Islands, Montserrat, the Turks and Caicos, the Cayman Islands, and Bermuda. That has been no guarantee of ease or tranquillity, and these small islands have had their share of problems. In 2012, the premier of the Cayman Islands, McKeeva Bush, was arrested on suspicion of theft in connection with financial irregularities within the government, and his administration was given a vote of no confidence, though as of January 2013 no charges have been filed. In the Turks and Caicos, former premier Michael Misick was arrested under an Interpol warrant in Rio de Janeiro over an ongoing investigation into corruption. The Turks have had their own government since 1976, so when Whitehall decided to reassert direct rule in 2009 in an attempt to end financial irregularities and corruption, many people were outraged. Indeed, Premier Galmo Williams said they were being 're-colonised by the United Kingdom'.[13]

The French overseas territories, meanwhile, have seen few changes in their relationship with France. In 2007, St Martin and St Bart's voted to continue as *collectivités d'outre-mer*, which meant that these smaller islands would no longer be administered by Guadeloupe, but by Paris. Guadeloupe, Martinique, and Guyane became official *départements et territoires d'outre-mer* (DOM-TOM) in the 1980s, giving them equal status with the other *départements* in mainland France.[14] In 2010, the French President Nicolas Sarkozy held a referendum on the level of autonomy the islands wanted; Martinique voted against any further self-governing powers.

The Netherlands Antilles was officially dissolved in 2010. Aruba had become a separate territory in 1986, and now Curaçao and Sint Maarten have similar status, while Bonaire, Saba, and Sint Eustatius are special municipalities of the Netherlands. Suriname was the only colony to become fully independent, which it did in 1975. In the 1970s, much like Guiana, it had been divided between black, Indian (there known as Hindustani), and Javanese communities. The Hindustani community supported continued Dutch rule. The Dutch legislature granted sovereignty to Suriname in 1971 but it did not take effect until 1975; in the interim anyone who wanted to take advantage of their Dutch citizenship to move to the Netherlands could do so, and so thousands of Hindustani people began to leave.[15]

Five years after independence, in 1980, an army sergeant named Desi Bouterse and sixteen officers staged a coup. At first it had popular support. In December 1982 fifteen prominent intellectuals who were critical of Bouterse and his regime were imprisoned, tortured, and later executed, a crime known as the 'December murders'. In retaliation, the Dutch cut off all aid. Bouterse himself soon faced a coup, led by Ronny Brunswijk, a member of the Ndyuka maroon colony. Brunswijk was able to gather money and support from the exile community and triggered a civil war.[16]

Bouterse not only resisted the attempt to topple him, he also managed to avoid extradition over international charges of drug smuggling, bringing to the country Colombian drug-trafficking business that kept his pockets lined and voters bought, with enough money to pay off his rivals, too: in 2008 he was seen 'rubbing shoulders' with Brunswijk. Indeed, two years later, Brunswijk supported Bouterse's successful presidential campaign, and he remains in office.[17] In 2012 a law was passed granting him amnesty in respect of murder charges relating to the events of 1982.

The remaining Dutch territories, meanwhile, are usually far more tranquil. But in May 2013 a prominent politician from Curaçao, Helmin Wiels, was shot dead. He was an outspoken opponent of corruption – the island suffers, like many in the Caribbean, from drug trafficking – and an advocate of full independence from the Netherlands. No suspect has yet been found, but the island was left stunned after the attack.

In US-controlled Puerto Rico, while the world was watching the outcome of the US presidential election in 2012, islanders were also casting a significant ballot. Although they cannot vote in US presidential elections, they were voting on a referendum to become the fifty-first state of the US. Puerto Ricans are already US citizens and have US passports. The question posed first was whether people were happy with the 114-year-old relationship with the US. Some 54 per cent, or 970,910 people, said no. Then there was a second question on the ballot of what should replace the status quo, with the options being statehood, independence, or 'sovereign free association'. There were 834,191 votes for statehood; 454,768 for sovereign free association; and 74,895 for independence. To complicate matters, on the second question there were 498,604 ballots left blank. The statehood option was chosen on 44 per cent of the ballots cast, but – with the huge number of blanks disregarded – won 61 per cent of the valid votes. Despite the ambiguity of the result, the pro-statehood regarded this as a clear majority. The US, while considering the results, is unlikely to take any action in the immediate future. The island has a population of about 3.6 million, though many more people of Puerto Rican ancestry live in the US. It has its own legislature and governor, Alejandro Padilla, but like most colonies, the final decisions are made or funded by the United States. The island would get at least $20 billion more in federal funding as a state. However, the tax-free status of the island – there is no federal income tax or corporate tax – would be lost. And the cost of making the transition to statehood would be high for the US, which is in recession; the fifty-first state could be a long way off.

*

Efforts to unite the region, especially in trade, have had mixed results. There is CARICOM, but it is often criticized for not being effective enough in extending free trade and free movement to its members. Indeed, its membership does not include every island – with the exception of Haiti and Suriname, all the members are from the English-speaking islands. In 2001 a Caribbean Court of Justice was set up, and it is now the legal arm of CARICOM. The English-speaking islands and Haiti are also members of the Caribbean Development Bank, established in 1969. Mexico, Colombia, and Venezuela are regional members but are not allowed to borrow funds, and Canada, China, Germany, Italy, and Britain are non-borrowing members with voting rights in the organization. In an attempt to widen West Indian cooperation to non-English-speaking islands, the Association of Caribbean States was set up in 1995, with twenty-five members from the islands and Central America, and Mexico. Like CARICOM, the emphasis is on economic issues. These remain influential organizations, but the effort to bring so many islands with such divergent needs to agreement remains a challenge.

Although official cooperation can be limited, regional migration is a force that has altered the dynamic of many of the islands. People from Colombia and Venezuela have come to Curaçao, whose streets are now full of restaurants serving *empanadas* and other South American fare. Spanish is now heard in Dutch St Eustatius as well, to which people from the Dominican Republic have come to work. The Dutch islands also have the added inducement of the potential for an EU passport, as do the French territories. There is movement from Suriname to French Guiana, too. Migration, so much a part of West Indian life, continues apace.

*

About half the territories are now independent nations, but some colonial hangovers endure. All the islands reflect decades of European control through language and culture, at least to a degree. At the same time, the ongoing influence of the United States means North American culture has seeped into the islands as well. Teenagers listen to rap, while their parents buy imported US junk food. Yet there is a more pernicious residue. In the Dominican Republic, racist attitudes toward Haitians – who continue to arrive to cut cane – persist. Although on paper the population is around 65 per cent mulatto, 15 per cent white, and 15 per cent black, these numbers and categories have little meaning when, as David Howard has pointed out in his work on the island, 'what to one person may be *mulatto*, will be *negro* to another'.[18] Indeed, some people claim to be *indio* or Taino, and draw their identity from the island's indigenous past. To invoke the *indio* is often to disavow the black, and the politics of race in the Dominican Republic remain complex. The presidential election of 1996 was an extreme example of this. The leader of the Dominican Revolutionary Party (PRD), José Francisco Peña Gómez, a black Dominican, adopted as a baby by a farming family after his birth parents fled to Haiti during the *perejil* massacre of 1937, was running for president for the third and final time. His opponents had for years made absurd claims that, were he elected, he would turn the country over to Haiti. In the 1996 campaign Peña Gómez went so far as to hire a historian to research his family's genealogy and prove that they were indeed Dominican. At the same time the Dominican Liberation Party (PLD) – whose candidate Leonel Fernández eventually won the race – claimed that hundreds of thousands of Haitians were going to use fake IDs to vote. The police began to ask dark-skinned people for their papers, hoping to deport anyone who was there illegally. Nearly sixty years after the events of 1937, the ghost of Trujillo still haunted the island.[19]

In Cuba, the revolution banned racial discrimination, but with that any discussion of areas of lingering prejudice. According to the Afro-Cuban writer Roberto Zurbano, the issues surrounding this silence are manifold but impossible to discuss: 'To question the extent of racial progress was tantamount to a counterrevolutionary act. This made it almost impossible to point out the obvious: racism is alive and well.' One of the problems is that white Cubans are still the more economically well off because they are more likely to have relatives who left the island and so can send money. In addition, Zurbano said black people have been excluded from much of the lucrative work in the tourist industry.[20] Meanwhile, Haiti's black–mulatto tensions run through its twentieth-century politics, and the divides between Indian and black communities in Trinidad and Guiana have not entirely healed either.

Another aspect of the colonial past is a virulent strain of homophobia, with British anti-sodomy laws staying on the books in many of the independent nations in the Anglophone Caribbean. As same-sex marriage has become legal in a growing number of European nations and in US states, many islands remain resolute in their outlawing of homosexual relations, despite welcoming thousands of gay tourists. Jamaica is the most infamous. Some of the music of its dancehall scene rails against gay men, or 'batty boys'. Buju Banton penned a song in 1988 called 'Boom Bye Bye', which spoke of shooting gay men. Banton was later acquitted of charges that he and other men assaulted a group of gay men. Prison did not elude him, however, and he was arrested in the United States on drug charges in 2009, was subsequently convicted, and will not be released until 2019. Likewise, the homophobic lyrics of Beenie Man came under scrutiny in 2004 for songs about the killing of gay people. In 2006 a UK concert was cancelled and he was banned from performing in many international venues. In 2012 he appeared to change his view and attempted to apologize via a video he released to the gay community. But attacks on gays and lesbians continue. Jamaica also has anti-sodomy laws – article 76 of Jamaica's Offences Against the Person Act mandates a punishment of up to ten years' imprisonment for 'buggery', and article 79 carries up to two years in jail for any sort of physical intimacy between men. There have been growing calls for the island to address homophobia, and the Prime Minister Portia Simpson-Miller called for a review of the anti-buggery law, but as of 2013 nothing has changed. Another colonial-era law – that prescribing flogging as a punishment for sodomy – was amended in 2012. Although human rights activists welcomed the change, sodomy remains illegal.

Dominica's government also refuses to budge on the issue, and in fact recently announced a task force to deal with homosexuality and other 'deviant' behaviour in its schools. Homosexuality is still illegal in the country, which also has anti-sodomy laws.

Trinidad and Tobago has an entry ban on gay people – section 8 of its Immigration Act prohibits the entry of 'prostitutes, homosexuals or persons . . . coming to Trinidad and Tobago for these or any other immoral purposes' – which the activist Maurice Tomlinson plans to challenge in the Caribbean Court of Justice.[21] Tomlinson is also going to take action against Belize, which has a similar law. In Puerto Rico, there is social homophobia – there are no laws against it, but there are hate crimes against the gay community. Nearly two dozen members of the gay community were murdered between 2009 and 2011.[22]

Elsewhere there have been some positive changes, especially in Cuba. Although in the 1970s and 1980s Fidel Castro had been known to imprison homosexuals – and many fled – the island has had a volteface, some say due to Raúl Castro's daughter, Mariela, who is a gay rights activist. It has come a long way from the world of the 1993 hit Cuban film *Fresa y chocolate*, which was the story of the friendship of two men during the dire economic 'special period', one of whom was gay, and many interpreted the movie as a plea for more tolerance of homosexuals, aside from the film's other political critiques. Now, the island is one of the most progressive places in the region on the question of sexuality. Cuba has one of the best AIDS prevention programmes in the Americas, if not the world, good birth control, and a growing culture of open sexuality. Transsexuals walk the streets of Havana, and gay couples are spotted on the beach. In Jamaica, that could mean a death sentence.

Cuba made further Caribbean history when forty-eight-year-old Adela Hernández became the first transgender person elected to public office in 2012, winning a seat on the municipal government in the town of Caibarién in Villa Clara. Remarkably, in the 1980s she was one of those sent to prison by the regime for her 'dangerousness', and her family disowned her.[23] Hernández has not yet had a sex-change operation, but in 2007 such surgery began to be offered by Cuba's health-care system. Wendy (born Alexis) Iriepa was part of the pilot programme for gender reassignment surgery, and in 2011 celebrated her wedding to Ignacio Estrada – although same-sex marriage is not yet permitted.[24]

Bermuda recently announced plans to amend laws that discriminate against non-heterosexuals. And the Dutch island of Saba now permits gay marriages, as same-sex unions for the islands were passed by the House of Representatives in October 2012, although they have been legal in the Netherlands since 2001. The other islands have to recognize same-sex marriages because they are governed by Dutch law, but are not bound to legalize it themselves.

*

Although the exploding cigars and blatant regime toppling in the region have, for the time being, come to an end, the Caribbean has provided a training ground of sorts, helping the US build a case for intervention and protection of its interests well beyond the boundary of the Monroe Doctrine. The early twentieth century was particularly instructive: the CIA learned what to do (Guatemala) and what not to do (the Bay of Pigs) when intervening militarily. There are traces of these misadventures, no doubt, in more recent operations, not least the invasion of Iraq and the overthrow of Saddam Hussein, as well as events in Afghanistan. And the Caribbean continues to play a role in these wider geopolitical confrontations through the US military base in Guantánamo Bay, Cuba, which is still in use even though all other precepts of the Platt Amendment have long since lapsed. The base currently serves as a prison for more than 150 men captured during the 'war on terror'. Human rights groups have made allegations of torture and abuse at the base, but despite a move by US President Barack Obama in 2009 to close the facility, and high-profile hunger strikes by inmates, it remains open.

And although the Cold War is long over, communism is still a presence in the Caribbean, in the form of Chinese interest in the region. While China has not provoked the political stand-offs of the Soviet years, the US and the rest of the world are watching its rise with concern. The booming Chinese economy and China's seemingly insatiable need for natural resources has led it all over the globe – and China's links with the Caribbean are long-standing. China–Caribbean Economic and Trade Cooperation Forums have been held in Trinidad, and according the Chinese vice-premier Wang Qishan, who spoke at the forum in 2011, Chinese investment in the Caribbean by that point had reached $400 million.[25] Other pledges included providing $1 billion in loans in support of local economic development, and a donation of $1 million to the CARICOM Development Fund. The Chinese also promised training and study options for people in the Caribbean to go to China, and cooperation on cultural exchanges, tourism, environmental protection, and agriculture.[26]

Chinese-funded projects dot the islands, not all of them without controversy, such as the State House in Dominica, which is part of a $14 million loan deal that also includes the construction of Dominica State College.[27] In Antigua, the Chinese are providing $45 million for a new airport terminal. China has shown interest in Caribbean timber and in bauxite and minerals, although to a lesser degree than in its controversial and – to some – neo-imperialist mining projects in Africa. But China's interest in the West Indies is, in some respects, related to a problem closer to home: Taiwan.

Taiwan, which has long struggled against prevailing Chinese rule, was expelled from the UN in 1971 when the Republic of China was granted membership. This small island has subsequently spent millions trying to build alliances among the UN membership, especially with those who might be willing to vote in the UN against China.[28] Twenty-three nations now recognize Taiwan, many in the Caribbean: Belize, Dominican Republic, Guatemala, Haiti, Honduras, Nicaragua, Panama, St Kitts and Nevis, St Lucia – which had switched allegiance from China to Taiwan in 2007 – and St Vincent and the Grenadines. China has ties to Costa Rica, Cuba, Antigua and Barbuda, the Bahamas, Barbados, Guyana, Jamaica, and Trinidad, along with Dominica, Grenada, and Suriname.

The Caribbean is one of the few public areas where the fight between China and Taiwan is still enacted – and some of the islands have supported both sides. For instance, when China pledged millions more in aid to Dominica in 2004, the prime minister, Roosevelt Skerrit, cut relations with Taiwan. Grenada, too, switched sides a year later because it was crippled by debt, and found itself red-faced after its Royal Grenada Police Band played Taiwan's national anthem in front of Chinese officials during a ceremony to inaugurate a $40 million Chinese-funded cricket stadium in 2007.[29] Some of China's major construction projects include the prime minister's official residence in Trinidad, a sugar factory in Guyana, a 20,000-seat stadium in Antigua, and a port in the Bahamas.[30] It has been paving roads in Suriname and handing over low-interest loans, and its embassy estimates there are some 40,000 Chinese living there – out of a population of about 400,000.[31]

Such economic might is hard to match. Chinese firms invested $7 billion in 2009 across the region, though much of that was in tax havens in places like the Caymans.[32] Such investment with so little return – Caribbean countries account for less than 0.001 per cent of imports to China – is economically puzzling at least.[33] However, China is able to both outspend the troublesome Taiwan and encroach on an area thought to be dominated by the United States. As the axis of global power begins to tilt to the east, the Caribbean islands still find themselves in a strategic position.

Chapter Thirteen

Import/Export

The Caribbean has always been a region of flux; ships arrive, people leave, and vice versa. Islanders go to the mainland looking for work, mainlanders come to the islands for a holiday. This give and take applies at all levels throughout the Caribbean, from people to controlled substances. The Caribbean as a drugs transshipment point – or indeed a place to indulge – is not a recent phenomenon. Drugs legislation in the British West Indies was updated as early as the 1930s to include the control and restriction of the 'production, possession, sale or distribution of Opium in the Turks and Caicos Islands and the Cayman Islands', as well as morphine, heroine, and cocaine.[1] One US report from this period discussed a man named Frederick Allen, whom the consul in Jamaica suspected of being an opium dealer because he had been making suspicious runs to the Bahamas. He noted that Allen 'goes from time to time to Ragged Island in a motor launch named "OLGA" which belongs to a pilot named Wells at Port Antonio carrying rum, coconut oil and other products, and returning with salt'.[2] Another US report noted that Barranquilla, a port city on Colombia's Caribbean coast, had for 'some time past' been the source of opium, cocaine, and morphine, which had been smuggled into Jamaica and possibly other islands. It quoted an article in the Jamaica *Gleaner* about a recent bust: 'it is reported on good authority that the Chinese are the major dealers, and are being run a good second by the Syrians'.[3] The Caribbean has always provided good cover for illicit activities.

The sea was crucial to the smuggling, as it had been since the Europeans first arrived. Even in the twentieth century, seemingly legitimate ships could be harbouring people working in the shadows. A Mexican, Cesario Riviera, later reported as 'age 26, height 5 feet 7 inches,

weight 150 pounds', was working as cook's mate on the US steamer
Santa Marta, along with Manuel Pérez, a twenty-nine-year-old Spaniard,
'height 5 feet 9 inches, weight 165 pounds', who was on board as an
endman, when they were arrested in Kingston on 12 January 1933 for
breaching the island's drugs law.[4] Indeed, even United Fruit Company
vessels were not above suspicion, and Britain and the United States
exchanged reports on seamen aboard their ships who were suspected
of smuggling narcotics.[5]

The drugs trade grew throughout the twentieth century, especially
with the growth of the Colombia cocaine cartels in the 1970s and 1980s.
The islands were close to the US, which was one of the main destinations for the drugs, and the islands' long history of smuggling meant
there were plenty of willing people who knew how to move contraband
without detection. However, violence was also quick to follow.

Jamaica, perhaps more than any of the other islands, is associated
with marijuana use. Collie, as it is also called there, is a valuable cash
crop, albeit an illegal one. In an island with deep pockets of poverty,
drugs provided – and continue to provide – economic opportunity.
There is also a long association with its use in Rastafarianism, which
at times gave the police yet another reason to attack and arrest Rastas
during the long-running period of unrest between their community
and the government. Reggae music was quick to denounce oppressive
policies, as encapsulated in the title of the 1976 Peter Tosh album
Legalize It. Just to drive the point home, the cover photo shows Tosh
smoking a pipe while sitting in a field of marijuana plants.

Or there is the 1983 single, 'Police in Helicopter', by John Holt,
with its lyrics:

> Police in helicopter, a search fi marijuana.
> Policemen in the streets, searching fi collie weed.
> Soldiers in the field, burnin' the collie weed.
> But if you continue to burn up the herbs, we gonna
>   burn down the cane fields.

Marijuana growing continues throughout the Caribbean, for
export and domestic consumption. However, the real drug traffic is
now cocaine. Colombia and other Andean countries still produce it,
but its distribution has been taken over by Mexican cartels, which has
led to thousands of deaths on the US–Mexico border over the past

decade. However, drugs still move through the Caribbean as well, and the violence that follows the trade has caused the murder rate to soar in Honduras and Guatemala, as well as some of the islands.

In May 2010 Kingston was brought to a standstill as gang and drug 'don' Christopher 'Dudus' Coke and his supporters battled the Jamaica Defence Force in Tivoli Gardens. The previous year, Jamaica had received an extradition request from the US government. The prime minster, the JLP's Bruce Golding, initially refused the request, but in May 2010, as the matter threatened to turn into a diplomatic crisis with the US, Golding relented. When the news reached Tivoli Gardens that Coke was, indeed, going to be sent to the US, people erected barricades, and waited for a battle, which began on 23 May. Days of fighting followed, security forces were sent in, and a state of emergency was declared. Seventy-three people died, though many questions remain over how many were innocent victims killed in error by the army.[6] Coke, however, was not caught until a month later, on 22 June, at a roadblock, where the police were not fooled by his disguise as a woman. When he arrived in the US, he pleaded guilty to drugs trafficking charges. The court heard about his network, which spanned Jamaica, Miami, and New York, and he was sentenced to twenty-three years in a US prison. Coke's family had reigned over the Tivoli Gardens neighbourhood – one of the poorest in the city – for more than thirty years, and it was assumed he was protected by politicians.

Tivoli Gardens had not only been long controlled by the Coke family, but in the garrison politics of Jamaica it was also JLP territory since the housing was built over former squatter sites in the 1960s. Like many of the other poor neighbourhoods, it suffered the terrible gun violence that plagued the island in the 1970s and 1980s. Coke was also said to have his own army of 200 soldiers, and a penal system in which he was judge, jailer, and possibly executioner.[7] Indeed, it was claimed the police needed his permission to enter Tivoli Gardens.[8] Although Coke omits such details in a letter to the judge who was sentencing him, he describes at length his role in the community, pointing out that he 'did a lot of charitable deeds and social services . . . I was involved in community development, where I implemented a lot of social programs that the residents from my community could better their lives, programs that teach them about self-empowerment, education and skills training'. He went on to list nearly three pages of good works, including an Easter party for elderly people in the community; giving books and school supplies to children; hosting a neighbourhood party in December; and giving local children Christmas presents.[9] Dons like Coke earned the loyalty of their community through such largesse, funding it with the profits of the drug trade. Although Coke is now serving a federal prison sentence in the United States, drug-fuelled garrison violence continues in the poorest parts of Kingston.

Drugs are a problem throughout the region, although the trade does contribute an estimated $3 billion every year to the Caribbean economy. The 'war' on drugs led by the US is ongoing, and the governments of most islands cooperate to some degree with US measures to curb the trade. Illegal substances and the violence associated with them have resulted in a regional homicide rate of 30 people per 100,000 per year, making the Caribbean one of the most violent parts of the world.[10] Where drugs go, so also do corruption and money laundering. Perhaps it is no coincidence that there has been a rise in financial services in the Caribbean as well.

*

The Bahamas were the first islands in the Caribbean to welcome the financial services sector, in 1936, and they were later joined by the Caymans, Barbados, Antigua, Nevis, and Dominica. Many offices sprang up in the 1970s, when the IMF was offering loans on the condition that the islands move away from traditional agriculture to mass tourism and financial services, which was also just around the time that the cocaine trade was booming. In addition, tax legislation and changes to banking in the United States and Europe meant more people were looking to invest in offshore accounts, which are both untaxed and discreet. The Caymans are now the sixth largest financial centre in the world – with $1.6 trillion on the books in assets. Although only 56,000 people live across the three islands, more than 92,000 companies are registered there.[11] (One of these is Bain Capital, the corporation founded by 2012 US presidential candidate Mitt Romney, who, during his losing campaign, was photographed on a yacht flying the Cayman flag, which did little to endear him to the recession-weary US voters.) However, because these firms pay no tax – the incentive that lures them to the Caribbean in the first place – the islands are struggling in the economic downturn, and some are considering introducing a levy on these corporations to raise much-needed revenue.[12]

There is also offshore gambling, with many islands hosting firms that offer online gaming. In 2000, the industry employed 3,000 people and made $1 billion, though the Unlawful Internet Gambling Enforcement Act (UIGEA) of 2006 banning most US citizens from gambling online devastated it.[13] Antigua demanded $3.4 billion in compensation from the United States, even petitioning the World Trade Organisation when the US offered only around $500,000.[14] Antigua's fortunes were not helped by the collapse of the financier Allen Stanford's empire in 2009. His Stanford International Bank had been the island's largest private employer.[15] However, in January 2013 the WTO made a surprise ruling allowing Antigua to sell US media downloads – such as music or films – without paying royalties to their creators, which in effect suspends US intellectual property rights on the island. This would allow the island to recoup some of the losses it sustained from UIGEA.[16]

Some islands have turned to raising money through economic citizenship. For instance in St Kitts, for a real estate investment of $400,000 – e.g. buying a holiday condominium – you can also receive a passport, a fact eagerly promoted on billboards around the island. Dominica charges $100,000 for citizenship, and many eager buyers are taking up the offer, especially those who have been affected by the turmoil of the Arab Spring. Middle Easterners have been quick to invest in the islands, including Palestinians, whose nationhood is not recognized by many countries. A Dubai-based company has even set up in St Kitts to allow investors to buy property and a passport at the same time, though the island closed the programme to Iranians in 2011 after the British embassy was stormed in Tehran.[17] In 2001 after the 11 September attacks in the United States, Grenada suspended its programme of selling passports for $40,000. However, it announced in 2013 that it was going to restart the scheme. Such programmes have made the United States nervous, fearing that terrorists wishing to attack the US could make their plans very close to home.[18]

*

The sugar economy struggles on, having weathered numerous rounds of protectionist legislation, though some islands have given up the cane fields for tourist sun loungers. Trinidad and St Kitts have closed their state-run operations, but there is still production in Jamaica, Barbados, Belize, and Guyana, where labour costs remain low, as well as Cuba, Puerto Rico, and the Dominican Republic. However, the industry continues to face challenges.[19]

Coffee is still an important export as well; Jamaican Blue Mountain coffee is particularly valuable, fetching high prices in the global coffee market. The Dominican Republic, Cuba, Puerto Rico, most of Central America, and Haiti are also producers. But competition and protectionism threaten all Caribbean commodities. This has especially been the case with bananas. Tensions flared once again over this fruit in the 1990s when the US was pushing a free-trade agenda through its North American Free Trade Agreement and there was considerable pressure to 'liberalize' trade markets.

Behind the cheerful, if not outdated, blue Chiquita sticker of a woman wearing a basket of fruit on her head in the style of Carmen Miranda, there has been a ruthless pursuit for market share. In the mid-1990s, Chiquita launched a suit through the World Trade Organisation claiming that European quotas provided to small growers in the Caribbean contravened fair trade rules. This claim was made despite the fact that the quota concerned less than 10 per cent of the market – the rest of, course, was provided by US firms through their Latin American providers, as no bananas are grown in the United States. Chiquita won, and in 1997 the EU was forced to drop the provision. But the suit rumbled on and it was not until 2012 that the matter was finally settled, when the EU pledged to gradually reduce the tariff placed on bananas imported from Latin America until it was in line with the small Caribbean producers. The 1975 Lomé Convention had outlined special trade provisions for the African, Caribbean, and Pacific states (ACP) to help develop their economies, though this recent change in banana tariffs may put all of this in jeopardy for the small islands. An equalization of tariffs will cause the price of Latin American bananas to drop, eroding the advantage enjoyed by fruit growers in Dominica, St Vincent, and other Windward Islands, and potentially ending their livelihood as they are priced out of the market.

Another trade war is looming, too: at stake is a market worth $500 million for the rum-producing islands. US rum producers receive an indirect subsidy that gives them an advantage over small producers.

Rum distillers in the US Virgin Islands and Puerto Rico receive almost all the money that an excise tax on rum sold in the US generates; these islands turn the money over to producers as a subsidy for giant firms such as Bacardi in Puerto Rico, and Cruzan in the Virgin Islands, which is owned by Beam Inc., the makers of Jim Beam bourbon and other spirits. In 2009 this attracted Diageo, the UK makers of Captain Morgan rum, to set up in St Croix – the excise tax revenue it is projected to receive is $2.7 billion over thirty years, while Bacardi was given $95 million to renovate its plants. Smaller distillers in Barbados, Jamaica, and elsewhere are fearful that such advantages will allow the competition to force them out of business.[20] CARICOM has begun to make a case to the WTO that these subsidies violate fair trade, but so far there has been no ruling.

Domestic food production is racked with problems as well, partly because the WTO has over the years convinced many of the islands that it is preferable to import food, especially surpluses from the United States, so soft drinks, processed foods, and cheap meat and grain-dumping replaced traditional, island-grown agriculture because it was no longer cost-effective. These measures have not been universally popular. In the Dominican Republic, for instance, there have been numerous rumours about 'gringo' (i.e. imported or raised with US feed) chicken meat: that it had worms, that it caused AIDS, that it contained hormones, or that it caused infertility in women and men.[21] Now the CARICOM nations alone are saddled with an import food bill of $3.5 billion a year, and little has replaced the void created by the ending of agricultural jobs. Grocery stores are stocked with US imports – sugary cereals, crisps, sodas – fuelling a health crisis in the Caribbean similar to the one that the US is experiencing. Despite the fertility of the islands, most are now net food importers. Fishing, too, has dropped off, because large-scale trawling is putting small fishermen out of business, and pollution and environmental problems are harming stocks.

*

One of the Caribbean's most valuable exports in the twentieth century has been not its food or drugs, but its people. Although many were forced out in search of a better life, or at least better pay, the people have contributed to their host countries in manifold ways.

During the *Windrush* years and into the 1950s, some 150,000 West Indians arrived in the UK in the 1950s and another 168,000 before the Commonwealth Immigrants Act in 1962 restricted settlement.[22] These years, however, were often difficult. By the 1970s there was an established West Indian community in Britain, one that often faced persecution from racist groups as well as aggression from the police. Riots fuelled by these issues broke out in Notting Hill, London, as early as 1958, and again in 1976; these were followed by further episodes of unrest and anger directed at the police, including in Bristol in 1980, and in Brixton, London; Toxteth, Liverpool; and Handsworth, Birmingham, in 1981. Mistrust continues to be a problem between the Afro-Caribbean community and the British police.

Other emigrants opted instead for the United States. At first, immigration was limited by the McCarran–Walter Act of 1952, which brought in restrictions and quotas, at a time when many people were going to Britain. But the US loosened these rules in 1968 and by the 1980s more than 60,000 people a year arrived from the English-speaking islands alone. There are West Indian communities throughout the country, but sizeable ones in New York, Washington, DC, and Miami. Canada also changed its immigration restrictions in 1967, and many West Indians braved the cold in search of employment and education opportunities. Today Canada's Caribbean-born population is around 300,000, many of them in Toronto and Quebec, with Haitians keen to take advantage of their access to French-speaking areas.[23] Throughout the tumult of the 1990s Haitians also made their way to the United States, and by the 1990s there was a community of about 200,000 people, and in Miami 'Little Haiti' soon sprang up.[24]

Cubans, because of their unique predicament, had fewer restrictions placed on them, leading to hundreds of thousands of emigrants, with a large community in the US, although some emigrants went to Spain and Latin America. In the 1950s and '60s, around 470,000 people from Puerto Rico went to the US, especially New York.[25] Dominicans, meanwhile, went not only to New York and Miami, but also to Curaçao, St Martin, and even St Eustatius. Some 200,000 people in the Netherlands Antilles and Suriname had left for the Netherlands by the 1980s,[26] and some 300,000 people in Holland now claim Surinamese descent.[27] And by the middle of the 1980s, there were some 80,000 French Antilleans in France.[28] Other economic migrants are now turning their back on the United States and Europe – there are not enough jobs, and the cost of living is high – and seeking opportunities in Brazil, where the economy is growing.

But the direction of travel is two-way; many migrants have returned to their islands, and not all because they want to. The British government tries to send back people from the Caribbean who over-stay their visas. Indeed, in the case of Jamaica, the Foreign Office has taken extra measures, including a Rehabilitation and Reintegration programme, put together jointly with the island's government, that includes a video shown to those being repatriated, entitled 'Coming Home to Jamaica'.[29] Coming home, even for people not forced to leave, can be a fraught business. Many people left their original communities and stayed away for twenty or thirty years. Places like Mandeville in Jamaica, which sits up in the mountains where the breezes are cooler, have seen an influx of returnees of retirement age, and new houses are dotted around the town. Some people there welcome it, as the bauxite industry which made the town prosperous for decades has recently collapsed. But while the returnees bring many benefits to the commu-nity, not least through economic spending power, there are often complications as well. From a distance of thousands of miles it is easy to romanticize the past, or not be aware of the changes of the present. Not everyone who has returned to the islands has had the easiest time.

Jean Popeau left Dominica in 1957 at the age of eleven and returned to live there in 2008. Popeau's family were small farmers, but poverty drove his father to try to live in England. 'We knew that it was cold in England though and that there was prejudice,' he recalled. 'The stories filtered back.' Popeau paid his first return visit to Dominica in 1974, and took his own family back for a visit in 1992, which marked the point at which he 'came to terms with the assumption my children will identify with British culture . . . there's a new generation of kids who are creating a new culture in which all sorts of inter-cultural interchanges are taking place . . . It's a completely different world to the one I emigrated to.' After retiring from thirty years in teaching, he returned to the island for good, bought land, and built a house. He says his experience has mostly been positive, but others who went back to communities where they no longer had family or connections were more isolated. Being able still to speak the island's Creole language helped, too: 'If I came back with a Yankee accent and no Creole, it would have been much more difficult.' But as well as charges of being 'English' or 'Yankee', despite having been born in the islands, the returnee still has to contend with claims that he or she is far better off than locals who never left.[30] The range of experience varies, but the comings and goings of people from the West Indies has shaped not only the islands' modern identity, but the places in Europe and the Americas where they have chosen to live. Displacement remains part of the Caribbean story.

Music, literature, and art have come from the islands, and often been fashioned in the interchange across the Atlantic, from the earliest times to the present day. The Spanish islands gave the world salsa, and the more modern (and often controversial) hip-hop style reggaeton, which was forged between the islands and Miami. Its violent and often misogynistic lyrics have caused the Cuban government to declare it unsympathetic to the revolution and attempt to ban it – though at various points the revolution tried to ban rock and jazz as well. Puerto Rican star Daddy Yankee had a crossover hit with 'Gasolina' in 2004, introducing reggaeton to a wider English-speaking audience. Jamaica gave the world reggae, as well as rocksteady and ska, and the newer (and also often controversial) dancehall. Trinidad's calypso, soca, and steelpan drumming also appeal to music fans the world over.

Novelists such as Dominica's Jean Rhys and Phyllis Shand Allfrey, Trinidad's Nobel Prize-winning V. S. Naipaul, and Haiti's Edwidge Danticat have a global readership. Caribbean art enjoys a wide following, especially the work of Haitian painters. And among Haiti's biggest exports, though not one that makes any money for Haiti itself, are voodoo and zombies, or the 'living dead'. The zombie – supposedly a person locked between life and death who can be controlled and used in nefarious ways – has been immortalized, and misrepresented, by films such as *The Serpent and the Rainbow*, or the James Bond story *Live and Let Die*. The fascination with zombies shows no sign of abating, with television shows like *The Walking Dead* and contemporary films like *Shaun of the Dead* taking the idea of the Haitian undead and placing it in a white, suburban setting, following in the footsteps of *The Night of the Living Dead* and subsequent zombie films directed by George A. Romero. One of the earliest examples of the genre, the 1943 black-and-white *I Walked with a Zombie*, used traditional voodoo motifs to great effect. The film is set on a nameless Caribbean island, and involves a white woman under a zombie curse who is taken by her nurse to be healed at a dramatic voodoo ceremony. Although these films often misrepresent actual practices – especially in the case of the modern zombie film – it does mean that voodoo has become increasingly well known outside the Caribbean. In Haiti itself, however, voodoo is, not for the first time, under the legal spotlight. Recent legislative changes have resulted in the repeal of provisions in the religious freedom legislation that permit voodoo. This effectively reinstates a 1935 law punishing those who practise voodoo, or other 'superstitious practices', and it remains uncertain how the religion, so long liberalized now, will be affected.[31] The embracing and public acceptance of these syncretic practices have a wider significance than simple religious tolerance; they also indicate an appreciation and validation of cultural uniqueness, whether from Haiti, or Cuba, or any of the other islands.

This spills over into language policy as well. For a long time Jamaican patois was considered to be no more than uneducated slang, rather than what it really is – a distinct language that blends African and English words and grammar, among other influences. There is a growing acceptance of its use, and even the Bible is being translated into Jamaican patois, rendering this passage from the Gospel of Luke: 'And having come in, the angel said to her, "Rejoice, highly favoured one, the Lord is with you: blessed are you among women"' into: 'De angel go to Mary and say to 'er, me have news we going to make you well 'appy. God really, really, bless you and him a walk with you all de time.' It is, perhaps, inevitable that there are those who disapprove of the translation.[32] On the Dutch islands, many people speak Papiamento, which blends Dutch, English, Portuguese, and Spanish, and has evolved for centuries in Aruba, Bonaire, and Curaçao. It has been officially recognized, and now foreigners who come to live in the islands must be able to pass a Papiamento test as well as a Dutch one when applying for citizenship.

Another cultural hybrid celebrated in the Caribbean is Carnival. Trinidad is one of the few islands that still holds the event in line with the Catholic calendar, with the days of greatest celebration falling on the Monday and Tuesday before the start of Lent. Every year photographs of Trinidadians decked out in vivid costumes, feathered and sequinned headdresses, and often scanty bikinis, appear in newspapers around the world, alongside those of celebrations in Brazil and New Orleans. Other islands, such as Barbados, celebrate harvest-related festivals like Cropover, which was linked to the sugar cycle, rather than the Church. It, too, is a time of celebration and extravagant costumes, but it takes place in the summer months. Cuba, once host to a significant pre-Lenten Carnival, now limits itself to a summer celebration in July in Santiago de Cuba, timed to celebrate the anniversary of the revolution, rather than the cane crop, or Lent, which was the original reason for it.

Carnivals can be traced back to ancient times. Over the centuries, such celebrations became interlinked with Christian rituals, specifically Easter. Before the forty-day Lenten season of prayer and fasting begins on Ash Wednesday, everyone is given an opportunity to free themselves from all sinfulness. Indeed in some cultures this period begins almost three months before Lent. From 6 January – Twelfth Night, or Epiphany – cultures that observe Carnival can engage in weeks of balls, parties, and feasting. This was very much the case in colonial Trinidad, as it still is today. However, in earlier times the revelry was mostly confined to the white population. Free people of colour were excluded from most of the events, but they were allowed to 'mask' or go in costume. Slaves, of course, were left out altogether.[33] But they created their own processions, lit by flaming sugar cane stalks, known as *canboulay*. After emancipation, the former slaves could bring their customs to the celebration. Indeed, the whites felt this was so threatening that the authorities tried to outlaw 'masking', first in 1846, and again in 1849, limiting celebrations to two days. Every year brought some degree of tension, and in 1881 police and revellers ended up in a battle. Throughout these years, and against a backdrop of an ailing sugar industry and poor economy, the authorities continued to try to clamp down on everything from the flaming torches to the drumming, even Carnival itself. But this was also the period that most influenced Trinidad's modern Carnival, as all members of the community began to participate, not just the planters.[34]

Today, it is a rum-soaked extravaganza, with elaborate costumes involving few clothes and many feathers for women, which no doubt would have horrified the prudish Victorian administrators. Calypsonians prepare songs and compete against each other, and steelpan bands perform as well. Steelpan drums come from Trinidad and Tobago, where they evolved from old oil drums. Parts of the drums are hammered into a bowl shape, with different sections tuned to produce a range of notes. They are now used throughout the Caribbean, but especially in Trinidad. Everyone dances, sings, and – most important of all – lets off steam. Carnival is a safety valve of sorts, a time when people from all backgrounds across the island can get together and put past grievances aside. But it does not fade once the party is over. People in Trinidad talk about next year's plans throughout the year and popular calypso and soca songs about Carnival are played on the radio all year round.

In Britain, this tradition has fed into the pan-West Indian Notting Hill Carnival in August. While it is not linked to a liturgical calendar, it is timed to take advantage of a public holiday and the best of what little hot weather there is in England. Its popularity has grown in the past decades, and more than a million people pile into the streets of West London to watch the parades, listen to the steel drums and booming sound systems, and enjoy some jerk chicken.

In November 2012 there was even a 'Caribbean Carnival' event in Dubai, with Jamaican-American rapper Sean Kingston headlining a concert in the Arab state. Billed as 'family-oriented', it no doubt was free of rum and scanty costumes, but it is almost certain to have been the first major celebration of Caribbean-related events in the Arabian desert.

Perhaps the most important cultural phenomenon of all, beyond literature and art, or even Carnival, is something akin to a religion: cricket. Cricket remains enormously popular at home and among the diaspora. As Trinidadian historian C. L. R. James wrote in his book about cricket, *Beyond a Boundary*, 'My father had given me a bat and ball, I had learnt to play and at eighteen was a good cricketer. What a fiction! In reality my life up to ten had laid the powder for a war that lasted without respite for eight years, and intermittently for some time afterwards – a war between English Puritanism, English literature and cricket, and the realism of West Indian life.'[35] The West Indian cricket team – one of the few remnants from the era of federalization – has a global following. Players come from around the Anglophone cricket-playing islands, and the West Indian side reached a zenith from the 1970s to the 1990s, as its fast bowlers dazzled spectators from England to Australia.[36] But those years were marked with scandal, too, not least when the West Indian side toured apartheid South Africa in the 1980s. Despite this, and the fact that their superiority could not last for ever, the Windies, as they are often known, are a much-loved side. In 2007 the cricket World Cup was hosted in the Caribbean, and matches were played in Jamaica, Barbados, St Lucia, Trinidad, Guyana, Antigua, Grenada, and St Kitts. Although it has been a while since the West Indian side has been on a long winning run, the sport remains popular and the fan base loyal at home and abroad.

The other great ball sport is, of course, *el béisbol*. Cuba, Puerto Rico, and the Dominican Republic are all baseball powerhouses, and some of the sport's greatest players have come from these islands. The fortieth anniversary of Roberto Clemente's 3,000th hit was in 2012, and even though he died in 1972 – in a plane crash helping a relief effort after the earthquake in Nicaragua – his memory and accomplishment are still celebrated. Many of the current players in US Major League Baseball come from the Caribbean, such as Dominican Robinson Canó. Other retired greats, like fellow Dominican Sammy Sosa, are heavily involved in promoting young players on the island through baseball programmes and building local playing facilities. As a result, large numbers now come from places such as San Pedro de Macorís on the south coast of the Dominican Republic, which has sent dozens of players to the major leagues in the US. The baseball season in the Caribbean runs through the winter – which is the opposite of the season in the US – so scouts can watch and recruit players from the islands. And there are the more unlikely sportsmen of the Caribbean, such as the Jamaican bobsled team in the 1988 Winter Olympics, immortalized in the 1993 film *Cool Runnings*. Even more recently, a skiing slalom event in 2013 saw Jamaican Michael Elliot Williams pip Haitians Jean-Pierre Roy and Benoit Etoc in a qualifying run, though Williams took twice as long as the Finnish race winner.[37]

Beyond the arts, culture, and sport there is one place where the Caribbean now reigns supreme – as the ideal holiday destination.

Chapter Fourteen

INVENTED PARADISE

With the development of mosquito eradication programmes and improving public health, by the early twentieth century it had become safer for people to visit the Caribbean for leisure. And around the same time, there had been a complete volte-face and some of the islands were being vaunted for their health-giving properties. Promotional literature for a 1905 passage from Bristol to Jamaica claimed, 'The island possesses great natural beauty, and its warm healthy climate is recommended by the medical faculty.'[1] A Barbados tourism guide from 1914 went further, boasting:

> Barbados is undoubtedly the most healthy of the West India Islands, and is a favourite resort for families of the North and South American Continents. There are numerous hotels and bay houses along the Windward Coast . . . where the ozone from the breakers greatly contributes to recuperation from any ailment . . . The Island has within recent years become so popular that the hotels have all increased their accommodation of which there are several along the sea coast, and bay houses along the Hastings and St. Lawrence Coast are being continually erected to meet the demand caused by families from the South American continent spending several months here for the benefit of their health.[2]

In the 1920s tourism in the British islands and elsewhere was still small-scale, and as a source of revenue still well behind bananas, sugar, and coffee.[3] Cuba was an early recipient of tourists, no doubt from the glowing reports North Americans were sending back from the island after US firms began to set up there in the early 1900s, and a National Tourist Commission was established in 1919. Wealthy North

Americans began to look south, rather than to Europe, for their holidays, and soon steamships were running from Key West to Cuba, and
were later joined by planes from the east coast. In Cuba, the number
of US visitors leapt from 90,000 in 1928 to 178,000 in 1937.[4] This near
doubling of tourists no doubt owed a lot to thirsty Americans during
the Prohibition years.[5] But the numbers did not dip, and by 1957 had
soared to 356,000, many lured by the idea that they could holiday
without inhibition as gambling, booze, sex, and the sea were all on
offer.

The British, too, began to think of some of these tropical colonies
as ideal holiday destinations – Ian Fleming, the creator of James Bond,
had his Jamaican house, Goldeneye, and Princess Margaret was photo-
graphed at parties on the private Grenadine island of Mustique, bought
by Colin Tennant for £45,000 in 1958. Islands are still up for sale –
Richard Branson now owns Necker Island, in the British Virgin Islands;
the whole island can be rented out, starting at around $42,000 a night.
Early holidays in the Caribbean were often limited to the wealthy until
after the Second World War, when the proliferation of jet travel and rise
in personal income propelled many more people to visit. The resorts
were ready to provide them with the kind of luxury they thought the
wealthy and the famous enjoyed on these islands. All-inclusive accommodation meant visitors did not need to think about money; they had
food and drink, as well as excursions, organized and prepaid. A BOAC/
BWIA promotional film from about 1960 – 'Flying Visit to the Caribbean' – exhorts the viewer to fly above the 'path Columbus took', adding
that it is the 'modern way to the Caribbean' before cutting to a man in
a straw hat playing a drum in Trinidad who is later joined by an African
dancer. The narrator goes on to declare that the island is near the South
American mainland but 'centuries away in its traditions'. It is a Techni-
color tour of beaches and happy 'natives'. The islanders are all depicted
as black fishermen or agricultural workers, dancers, or hotel staff – no
Indians appear in the section on Trinidad – while white tourists frolic
on the beach, in boats, or swim in the water. Besides a shot of basket-
sellers in Bridgetown, there is little depiction of city life; the film instead
focuses on palm trees and sandy beaches. Such promotional material
was common in this period to entice people to the islands, and the
stereotypes stuck. People who lived on the islands were reduced to
caricatures of what a West Indian was supposed to be.

Cruises, too, expanded in this period. The earliest ones were some-what less comfortable than today's super-liners – in the 1890s they were on banana boats.[6] Such ships ran passengers from Philadelphia, Baltimore, and New York to Portland, Jamaica, on the north coast of the island. It added little to their overheads, and on the island it began to fuel a demand for hotels and restaurants. As cruising evolved, the ships became bigger and the passengers slept on board so that they could call at more places, taking business away once more. Being on board and calling into ports also did little to reduce the stereotyping of the island, as ports turned into market-places of basket-sellers, and islanders in many places had little choice but to play the role.

*

V. S. Naipaul was one of many Caribbean writers to articulate the deep unease that came with the arrival of mass tourism, calling it a 'new slavery'. Certainly in the Anglophone islands the reality of tourism meant that black people served white people in an uncomfortable echo of a not-forgotten past. Grenada's former prime minister Maurice Bishop was explicit about this in a 1979 speech, saying, 'It is important for us to face the fact that in the early days and to some extent even today, most of the tourists who come to our country happen to be white, and this clear association of whiteness and privilege is a major problem for Caribbean people just emerging out of a racist colonial history where we have been so carefully taught the superiority of things white and the inferiority of things black.'[7]

Fidel Castro, too, was against tourism, having already been exposed to its effects in 1950s Cuba. He said in a 1977 press conference that the Revolution did not want tourists in Cuba: 'Before the Revolution, we exported to the United States not only sugar. True, there was tourism, a tourism based on gambling casinos and prostitution on many occasions. We do not want that type of tourism and we will not accept it.'[8] However, he was forced to relent once the Soviet era ended: although there are still no casinos, there are large all-inclusive resorts on the north of the island full of package-holidaymakers from colder climates. But perhaps Cuba's antipathy is palpable, as it has a very low rate of 'repeat tourism', meaning thousands of visitors have little wish to return.[9]

Not everyone was opposed to tourism – in the face of declining agriculture and the prospect of emigration, tourism provided the promise of local jobs. Indeed, during the independence period, tourism was touted as a way to 'modernize', and the World Bank and other international lending institutions helped finance the construction of hotels and resorts. These ideas were not imposed on the islands – the West Indian Commission endorsed them, too.[10] Yet not all islands developed equally. Jamaica, with its many hundreds of miles of beaches, had more to offer developers than Dominica, which is mostly mountainous and has few beaches. A satirical poem in its *Star* newspaper (edited at that time by Phyllis Shand Allfrey) made barbs at the promise of tourism gold:

> Who say Tourist Board working well?
> Dey's travel plenty but dey can't sell,
> the special package that they promise to –
> 'Cinderella island – land of Sisserou,'
> or else it have a jinx on Dominican sun,
> and State of Emergency ain't help we none . . .
> all that bad publicity it really stick,
> everybody think is the DOMINICAN Republic![11]

Dominica's flagging tourist economy was dealt a further blow when a US visitor to the island was fatally shot in the abdomen in March 1974, while the same night four Americans camping near Marigot were attacked and one was left with knife injuries, and visiting white Carnival revellers were reported to have been pelted with stones.[12] In November that year, two Canadians who had retired from the cold north and settled in the warmth of Pond Cassé returned home from what would be their last shopping trip: they were murdered and their house set on fire.[13] A couple of years earlier, in 1972, six black gunmen attacked patrons at the Fountain Valley Golf Course clubhouse in St Croix, robbing sixteen people and killing eight of them.[14] Yet these incidents were isolated to Dominica, and did little to stop the march of the Caribbean tourist industry. Crime against tourists continues throughout the islands but incidents are rare. Indeed in 2012, Haiti was named one of the safest destinations in the Americas, with a violent death rate of 6.9 per year out of 100,000, which puts it on the same level as Long Beach, California.[15]

Tourism is one of the world's largest industries, generating $34 billion a year by the end of the twentieth century.[16] The Caribbean's slice was only around 2.5 per cent in 2000, which is small overall but significant for the islands. In 2012, some 18 million people stayed on one or other of the islands, and another 17 million cruise passengers called in.[17] Those are significant numbers for a region with a population of around 40 million. Many islands see a tourist population far higher than the number of permanent residents: on the Bahamas, population just over 320,000, around 1.4 million people visited and more than 4 million stopped while on a cruise. The recession has done little to dent tourism over the past few years – 35 million people were reported to have visited the islands in 2012, up 5 per cent from 2011, spending $27 billion.[18] Most visitors to the West Indies are from the US and Canada, though there are a considerable number of Europeans as well. In 2002, for instance, of the 4.5 million Europeans who visited the Caribbean, 1.5 million were French, 1 million British, 320,000 Spanish, and 244,000 Dutch. But in comparison, New York City alone gets more than a million British tourists a year, and around 10 million international visitors in total.

Despite their geographic diversity, many of the tourists are alike: they have to be reasonably well-off to holiday in the islands in the first place. Cuba is the only island that offers an affordable and extensive B&B system. Hotel rooms in many islands cost in excess of $100 a night. And the backpacker culture found elsewhere in the world, such as Thailand, scarcely exists. Younger people are put off by the high prices; their parents are more likely to go on a cruise or stay in a resort. And while local people work in the resorts, they are often owned by foreign companies and the profits do not stay on the island. There is little tourist infrastructure for the independent traveller – European-style youth hostels are virtually non-existent, and poor public transport makes it difficult to get around. It is often impossible to go between neighbouring islands without flying well out of the way. For instance, LIAT (Leeward Islands Air Transit, or Luggage In Another Terminal, as locals joke) flights travel around the Lesser Antilles but do not connect with Cuba, and neither does Caribbean Airways, which covers Jamaican and Trinidadian routes. Cuba's carrier Cubana does not connect to those islands. And the French islands offer only limited flights between

themselves and a few connections on LIAT. The European carriers tend
to go to former colonies, with British Airways to Jamaica and Barbados,
while KLM goes to Suriname and Curaçao, Air France to Martinique,
and there used to be an Iberia flight to Cuba. The US airlines go to the
major holiday destinations, such as the Dominican Republic and
Jamaica, while also offering an increasing number of special charter
flights to Cuba. Sea routes are not extensive or coordinated either, with
only two public ferries: one between the Dominican Republic and
Puerto Rico and one that runs Guadeloupe–Dominica–Martinique.
The lack of joined-up transportation hinders wider regional exploration and connections, and the hassle involved makes potential travellers more likely to stay in one place. It is also somewhat symbolic of
the persistence of colonial linguistic and cultural divisions.

Central America has emerged as a more popular budget destination. Accommodation and food are far cheaper, and there is a good
regional bus network for exploring. Although few island tourist boards
might bemoan the lack of students travelling on the cheap, what it
means is that the same type of wealthy, older tourist goes to the Caribbean, and there is little engagement between the locals and visitors,
except the people who work in the tourist industry. But the trend
continues for high-end experience. There is money to be made in
luxury tourism, even when it seems absurd. In 2012 the Best Western
chain announced plans to build a 'Premier' range hotel in the Port-au-
Prince suburb of Pétionville, with 105 rooms and a spa. This is the part
of Haiti's capital that is the most upscale, and where most foreign
nationals work. Marriott is opening a hotel there, too, and the expensive Karibé is also planning an expansion. And then there is the Royal
Oasis, a five-star hotel with 128 rooms, five restaurants and bars, and
shops, paid for with $7.5 million from the World Bank, and $2 million
from the Clinton Bush Haiti Fund. As journalist Amy Wilentz pointed
out, 'The Royal Oasis is one of the few post-quake projects that have
come to fruition, unlike dozens of housing and school construction
projects.' This is while more than 300,000 people remain in post-
earthquake camps.[19]

Although Haiti is one extreme, these expensive hotels are frequently
born of lucrative deals involving tax breaks, so the revenue generated
from the cruise ports and the all-inclusive resorts does not often filter

into local pockets. For instance, in Jamaica, home to large resorts, the World Bank has estimated that as much as 80 per cent of the money made from tourism does not stay on the island.[20] Other islands, such as Dominica, have begun to go down a different route by eschewing the all-inclusive culture, and focusing instead on the island's natural resources: eco-tourism. Indeed, the environmental costs of large-scale tourism are high: food is often imported, and scarce water supplies are used up. Eco-tourism at the very least tries to address the high consumption that resort culture entails. And yet, many people go to the Caribbean not to be reminded of poverty or climate change, but to escape. Palm trees and sand have become shorthand for paradise, and it is a most modern equation, and quite a turnaround for a region that not so long ago was considered a death trap for Europeans.

*

In the 1970s a common refrain throughout some of the islands was that 'Tourism is whoreism'. It was a double-edged barb – residents did not want to see their country sell out, nor did they want to watch the arrival of sex tourists. But it has become part of the allure, though it is difficult to generalize across the islands. The 'exotic' beauty of people there has been written about for centuries. For instance, Moreau St Méry, in his 1789 book on Saint-Domingue, wrote of mulatto women:

> The entire being of a *mulâtresse* is dedicated to sensual pleasure and the fire of that goddess burns in her heart until she dies . . . There is nothing that the most passionate imagination can conceive that she has not already sensed, foreseen, or experienced. Her single focus is to charm all the senses, to expose them to the most delicious ecstasies, to suspend them in the most seductive raptures.[21]

Such exoticism now goes the other way as well, and white women and black men walk hand-in-hand on a beach in the Dominican Republic while elsewhere middle-aged European or American men might buy drinks for Dominican or Haitian women young enough to be their daughters, enjoying a short-lived holiday romance. For many of these local men and women, this offers a reasonable living, if not a shot at a ticket to Europe or the United States. But in the Dominican Republic, it is a grey area. The Dominican Republic is the most visited country in the Caribbean, with 4.6 million visitors a year, and it is estimated that some 60,000 to 100,000 women work in the sex trade.[22] Yet prostitution has no legal status – it is not condoned or regulated, but neither is it illegal. It leaves the women vulnerable but not on the wrong side of the law.

Other islands are more pragmatic. The Netherlands Antilles follow the spirit of Dutch law, and allow for controlled, legal prostitution and regulation to monitor the safety and health of the women. There are legal brothels in St Maarten (Seaman's Club) and Curaçao (Campo Alegre), established on the basis that by permitting such institutions, prostitution would be kept out of sight. But apart from these two brothels, there are strip bars and other places where sex is traded. By the very nature of sex work, there are still many problems, not least human trafficking. And if a woman is there illegally – many undocumented Colombians and Venezuelans are thought to work in the industry – then she is not regulated and is thus at greater risk. But throughout the islands there is still the standard model of prostitution as well, with women under the control of pimps.

In Cuba, prostitution is not legal, yet *jineterismo* is rife. The word comes from *jinete*, which means jockey, but in this context it signifies a man or woman who will engage in a relationship of some sort with a tourist and get what they can from it. It might be a man who marries a tourist and leaves the islands; or a woman who charges a visitor for sex; or even something as simple as someone offering their services as a 'guide' in exchange for a tip and a free lunch. Not all sex tourists are men seeking younger women; women also arrive looking for young gigolos, whom they may financially support between visits, as captured in the film *Heading South*, in which a New England schoolteacher played by Charlotte Rampling makes annual trips to then-stable Haiti, until the changing politics of the country disrupt her amorous routine. There is also gay sex tourism in Cuba, but rampant homophobia in the Caribbean makes it a risky proposal in just about every other island.

*

When the gloss of the tourism industry is stripped off, it seems almost a wilful act of the imagination to consider any part of the West Indies a 'paradise'. The only reason people can go there in the numbers they do and come away relatively untouched by the reality that surrounds them is the warm bubble of the resort and cruise industry. Of course, this is not the case for every traveller, and in some ways the responsibility lies with each country itself: what image is it trying to promote? There was a row over an advertisement for Volkswagen in the 2013 US Super Bowl that featured an average-looking white man who, when he opened his mouth, spoke with a 'Hey, Mon' stereotypical Jamaican accent, his laid-back, cool ways courtesy of the laid-back, cool car he was driving. Some Jamaicans found it funny, others bemoaned the continuation of a lazy cliché.

The rise of tourism has placed many islands in a bind. They are forced to play up long-standing images such as the 'Hey Mon' Jamaican in order to do what they think will make money, often under international pressure. Yet when people arrive demanding to see the 'authentic' island – it almost produces a paralysis of sorts. The 'real' Jamaica becomes a place of dreadlocked spliff-smokers, not one where most people work in offices, pay high electricity bills, wait for the bus to go home, and Skype their relatives in the US. Or it becomes the Cuba of cigars, salsa, and Havana Club rum, and not shortages and sex tourism. This even has a sartorial level: tourists wander the streets of cities and towns throughout the islands in their shorts and flip-flops, oblivious to the fact that many people in the West Indies do not dress as if they were on the beach, but wear shoes, trousers, and long-sleeved shirts, going about their daily routine. Indeed, on some islands it is frowned upon for women to wear skimpy or revealing clothing, or for men to wear shorts in public places like clubs or smart restaurants, though tourists often do. The locals, after all, are not on vacation; life for them is not a permanent party. Antiguan author Jamaica Kincaid expressed the disconnect between local and tourist in her 1988 memoir *A Small Place*:

> That the native does not like the tourist is not hard to explain. For every native of some place is a potential tourist, and every tourist is a native of somewhere. Every native everywhere lives a life of overwhelming and crushing banality and boredom and desperation and depression . . . Every native would like to find a way out, every native would like a rest . . . But some natives – most natives in the world – cannot go anywhere. They are too poor . . . They are too poor to escape the reality of their lives; and they are too

poor to live properly in the place where they live, which is the very place you, the tourist, want to go – so when the natives see you, the tourist, they envy you, they envy your ability to leave your own banality and boredom.[23]

The West Indies, as they are known and understood today, started out as a different type of European fantasy – they held the riches of the East, the cities of gold. That dream was a nightmare for the persecuted Amerindians and enslaved Africans, yet instead of these islands being accepted for what they are now, as distinct from what people wish them to be, the fantasy persists. Now they offer the ultimate 'experience': what is more indulgent to the harried, exhausted office worker than the idea of a week on a beach, staring at the sea, beer in hand? Free time is now the luxury, not sugar, or coffee, or mahogany, or indigo, or any of the goods that delighted the fickle tastes of Europeans. Such goods are now taken for granted – they came with a price, too, though that has long been forgotten. And while there is nothing wrong with wanting a break, with loving the sea, with enjoying a cold beer, there is often – though not always – a hidden price tag in the Caribbean, one most tourists do not and cannot see. As with sugar, someone somewhere else is paying for it. Yes, some of these islands' modern problems can be blamed on short-sighted governments, or greedy corporations, or unbending pressure from international organizations, but the rise of tourism and the perpetuation of the paradise myth has a long genealogy; it is nothing new. It has been there from the beginning.

St Lucian poet Derek Walcott wrote in his 1992 Nobel Lecture about the enthusiasm of the tourist:

What is hidden cannot be loved. The traveller cannot love, since love is stasis and travel is motion. If he returns to what he loved in a landscape and stays there, he is no longer a traveller but in stasis and concentration, the lover of that particular part of earth, a native. So many people say they 'love the Caribbean', meaning that someday they plan to return for a visit but could never live there, the usual benign insult of the traveller, the tourist. These travellers, at their kindest, were devoted to the same patronage, the islands passing in profile, their vegetal luxury, their backwardness and poverty . . . What is the earthly paradise for our visitors? Two weeks without rain and a mahogany tan, and, at sunset, local troubadours in straw hats and floral shirts beating 'Yellow Bird' and 'Banana Boat Song' to death. There is a territory wider than this – wider than the limits made by the map of an island – which is the illimitable sea and what it remembers. All of the Antilles, every island, is an effort of memory; every mind, every racial biography culminating in amnesia and fog. Pieces of sunlight through the fog and sudden rainbows, *arcs-en-ciel*.[24]

From the village of Labadie on the northern coast of Haiti, the Royal Caribbean cruise liner docked at the far end of the bay overwhelms the horizon and dwarfs the small fishing boats. With its on-board air conditioning, satellite TV, restaurants, bars, and room for 5,000 passengers, the liner is a far cry from the breeze-block houses in the village across the water, most of which lack a steady supply of electricity. Although the village is poor, it is surrounded by a rich landscape of blue waters and green hills. And it is generally far easier to glide into the village from the sea because the mountainous road from the regional capital of Cap Haïtien takes a bumpy hour, which feels like much longer. When the road dead-ends at the waterfront, small launches run passengers to the village itself. Tourists paying thousands of dollars to relax do not necessarily want to be confronted with the realities of the Haitian infrastructure, so Royal Caribbean decided it would be easier to create its own Labadie.

In the 1980s, Royal Caribbean leased a small, idyllic bit of land near the village. The company erected a fence, built a port, set up some buildings, and installed what it says is the 'longest zip line in the Americas' where a guest can enjoy 'breathtaking views, as you zip down the flight line at speeds of 40–50 mph'. It is not the real Labadie, which lies at the end of the bay, but rather a construct, based on what planners and tourist boards think the Caribbean ought to be like. Indeed, in the past the cruise line had been criticized for using the name Hispaniola in its promotional literature at a time when the island was going through a period of unrest, though now it is clear from its website that the ships go to Haiti. While the cruisers zip along, in the actual village trouserless children wander up and demand 'Gimme a dollar' in a perfect imitation of an American accent. Royal Caribbean paraphernalia abounds in the real Labadie: plastic cups, T-shirts, baseball caps are scattered about, brought home from family members who have a job seeing to the tourists, being paid to be professional locals.

Royal Caribbean also leased a neighbouring bay, where it set up 'Paradise Beach'. Tourists are spirited from the main dock in small boats to this sandy bay, with its sparkling water and nearly white sand. There are sun loungers and a bar with cold drinks. For the energetic, there is a small nature trail that takes you through a bit of flora and fauna, while also passing Haitians engaged in so-called traditional practices, such as cooking cassava. It is a far cry from the rubbish-clogged bay in Cap Haitïen or Port-au-Prince. It is paradise.

Paradise, however, can only allow in a select few. The main Labadie compound is surrounded by a perimeter fence and patrolled by local security guards when a ship is in port. Paradise Beach can be reached only by boat. While there are tourists present, a few hundred approved Haitians are allowed on the site to sell handicrafts. Royal Caribbean and others that favour this sort of development argue that it is better than nothing at all, especially as they pay millions in tax to the Haitian government. They argue that they have helped the community, and the village would be much worse off without it. Some of the villagers are grateful for a job, no doubt, and even if they did not enjoy the work they would be loath to say so. As the green light blinks from the end of the Royal Caribbean dock every night, it is hard to know what Haitians in Labadie looking out across the water must think about the 600,000 or so passengers who visit this part of the island every year, staying on their side of the fence.

Conclusion

It was on the edge of evening when I heard the drums and the horns, coming from the far end of Plaza José Martí, in Cienfuegos, Cuba. It was the sort of dusk that I associate with the Caribbean. Soft, fading light, a gentle breeze, a walk around the old port and customs house along the waterfront. I had stopped for a rest in the plaza, sitting on a bench watching the world go by, when the music started, so I strolled over to have look. By the row of benches lining the path through the square were musicians: a group of men, young and old, with a variety of drums, a battered trombone, an instrument that looked like two frying pans turned upside down, and even a cowbell. I started to focus the lens of my camera to grab a photo while the light was good, but at that moment they started playing in earnest, and I put down the camera before taking even one shot. They were making an almighty racket with those drums and horns and rusty pans, but it all fell together, it *worked*. The wild, diverging sounds were harnessed by a rhythm that somehow managed to corral the notes together. The teen-agers, boys and girls, milling around the musicians began a coordinated dance routine. As it turned out it was a practice session for an upcoming performance. It was quite a sight, and judging by the crowd of locals and tourists who began to gather, I was not the only one impressed. Not having a musicologist or ethnologist by my side, I had to trust my instinct that the drumming and the dancing was coming out of the Afro-Cuban tradition. The teachers clapped the counts for the dancers, who strutted up and down the plaza, shaking, turning, chanting. While they were a spectacle in themselves, there was another reason to observe – the range of colour among the teens ran from a very light olive to a deep brown. The musicians, too, were a multi-hued lot. The dancing and the music seemed to say that the island's Afro-Cuban heritage was part of everyone's life. The crowd was smiling, people were clapping and cheering. Then again, it is easy to idealize such serendipitous moments. Was I seeing the real Cuba, such as it is, or how I would like it to be?

In the past twenty years or so, new theories in cultural studies and history have developed to articulate ways of thinking about and characterizing the Caribbean. According to historian B. W. Higman, two of the most important are the idea of the slave society and that of the creole society. The difference between them is significant. Many societies, such as that of the Romans, could be considered slave societies, from ancient times onwards. Yet the idea of a creole society is unique to the Caribbean, and Higman argues that this model 'places emphasis on complex and subtle cultural interactions between peoples and the creativity that existed within and in spite of the brutality and exploitation of plantation slavery'.[1] It is an optimistic characterization, and not one that everyone would necessarily buy into. But sitting in that plaza in Cuba, more than a hundred years after the end of slavery, and more than fifty years after the beginning of the Cuban revolution, I felt as if I was watching this theory in motion, a creolized world of people from many backgrounds making what they could out of the bad and good they had been dealt, in the context of a world that had given them more than their fair share of hardships.

*

In his 1962 Caribbean travelogue *The Middle Passage* V. S. Naipaul made the infamous claim that 'history is built around achievement and creation; and nothing was created in the West Indies'.[2] However he meant it – with irony, or with serious intent – this line was received with seriousness and, for some, offence. Yet, in the context of the tourism industry, maybe he was right. Virgin beaches, 'unspoilt' paradise. It is much easier to imagine a West Indies without history. Then you don't have to understand why there is poverty or inequality, but rather it is easy to think the palm trees have always swayed in the breeze, and that there has always been someone to refresh your glass of rum punch. But in our post-colonial, postmodern world, such a notion seems completely anachronistic. The idea of what history is has been dissected and picked over for the past fifty years, while the study of West Indian

history has come into its own, with research now ranging from archaeology of the earliest inhabitants to musicology of twenty-first-century
dancehall. Indeed, when thinking about it, this seems the wrong away
round: *everything* was created in the West Indies. The Europe of today,
its financial foundations built with sugar money and the factories and
mills built as a result of the work of slaves thousands of miles away;
the idea of true equality as espoused in 1794 Saint-Domingue; and
even globalization and migration, with the ships passing to and fro
taking people and goods in all possible directions, hundreds of years
before the term 'globalization' was coined. The Caribbean contains all
this. 'That is the basis of the Antillean experience, this shipwreck of
fragments, these echoes, these shards of a huge tribal vocabulary, these
partially remembered customs, and they are not decayed but strong,'
Derek Walcott wrote. 'They survived the Middle Passage and the *Fatel
Razack*, the ship that carried the first indentured Indians from the port
of Madras to the cane fields of Felicity, that carried the chained Cromwellian convict and the Sephardic Jew, the Chinese grocer and the
Lebanese merchant selling cloth samples on his bicycle.'[3]

There is no easy time ahead in paradise. The islands all face a
number of challenges that will shape the future: ecological concerns,
immigration issues, poverty, political instability, to name but a few.
These, of course, are not for the Caribbean to shoulder alone. At the
time of writing, many of Europe's economies were in meltdown, the
United States was in a recession, and China was facing unprecedented
environmental problems. There is a tremendous amount of uncertainty
in the powerful nations, as well as in the weaker ones. Opinion varies
over which is the world's true 'superpower' – the United States or
China? And what about the countries on the rise, like India or Brazil?
Little is known for certain about who, if anyone, will next call the
shots, or control the resources, or start the wars, but whichever way
the axis of power tilts for the foreseeable future, the Caribbean remains
in the middle of it all, a crossroads connecting the world as it has done
for more than five hundred years.

Timeline: Key Events in the Caribbean

1492–1600

1492 Columbus lands in Caribbean on his First Voyage (1492–3)

1493 Columbus's Second Voyage (1493–6)

1494 Treaty of Tordesillas splits spheres of influence in this 'New World' between the Spanish and Portuguese

1497 John Cabot finds a route between Bristol and Newfoundland

1498 Vasco da Gama finds route to India; Columbus embarks on Third Voyage (1498–1500)

1502 Bartolomé de las Casas arrives in Hispaniola; Columbus goes on fourth and final voyage (1502–4)

1506 Columbus dies in Spain

1508 Settlement established on Puerto Rico

1509 Settlement established on Jamaica

1511 Settlement established on Cuba

1518 First official shipment of African slaves to Hispaniola

1586 English privateer Francis Drake attacks Santo Domingo, Cartagena, and St Augustine, Florida

1600–99

1609 Grotius publishes his *Freedom of the Seas*

1612 Dutch put settlements on Tortola

1623 English begin to settle St Kitts

1625–7   French share St Kitts with English

1627   England establishes a colony on Barbados

1628   England claims Nevis

1629   English Providence Island Company arrives in the Caribbean to set up a colony

1632   England claims Antigua and Montserrat

1634–6   The Dutch claim Curaçao, Aruba, and Bonaire

1635   France claims Guadeloupe and Martinique

1646   Spanish destroy Dutch settlement on Tortola

1648   France claims St Barthélemy; France and the Dutch share St Martin; the Dutch claim St Eustatius; Treaty of Westphalia puts an end to Thirty Years War in Europe

1649   France claims Grenada

1650   England claims Anguilla; France settles St Lucia

1651   English Navigation Acts

1655   England's Oliver Cromwell launches ill-fated attack on Santo Domingo, but comes away with island of Jamaica

1668–9   Henry Morgan makes raids on Cuba, Panama, and Venezuela

1671   Morgan raids Panama City; English and Spanish sign Treaty of Madrid recognizing England's Caribbean possessions

1672   England takes control of Virgin Islands (Tortola, Jost Van Dyke); Danish settle St Thomas

1692   Severe earthquake destroys Port Royal, Jamaica

1697   Treaty of Ryswick cedes the western third of Hispaniola to France, and it is given the name Saint-Domingue

1700–99

1733   Six-month slave insurrection on Danish St John's (settled in 1710); Molasses Act enacted on British colonies

1739   War of Jenkins' Ear begins

1754   The French and Indian War begins in North America

1756	France and Britain declare war and the Seven Years War begins
1760	Tacky's Rebellion in Jamaica
1763	Seven Years War ends; slave uprising in Berbice (Guyana)
1764	British Sugar Act
1772	Somerset Ruling in Britain
1773	Boston Tea Party
1776–83	War for American Independence
1784	James Ramsay publishes *An Essay on the Treatment and Conversion of African Slaves in the British Sugar Colonies*
1787	The Society for Effecting the Abolition of the Slave Trade set up in Britain
1788	*Société des amis des Noirs* set up in France
1789	French Revolution begins; Olaudah Equiano publishes his autobiography
1791	The Bois Caïman ceremony in Saint-Domingue which starts the slave uprising
1792	Denmark announces plans to abolish the slave trade in ten years' time
1793	Britain sends troops to Saint-Domingue
1794	France abolishes slavery
1795	The Treaty of Basle cedes the eastern, Spanish side of Hispaniola to the French

1800–99

1802	French troops arrive in Saint-Domingue to wrest control from Toussaint Louverture; slavery reinstituted in French colonies
1803	Toussaint Louverture dies in France; French forces surrender to Jean-Jacques Dessalines
1804	The Republic of Haiti is established

1807   Slave Trade Act ends Britain's participation in the slave trade;
        the US also bans the importation of slaves

1833   Slavery Abolition Act passed in Britain, though there is to be
        an apprenticeship period until 1838, when full emancipation
        occurs

1847   Slavery abolished in Danish and Swedish islands

1848   France abolishes slavery in all its colonies

1851   Slavery abolished in Colombia

1854   Slavery abolished in Venezuela

1861–65 US Civil War; slavery abolished at the end

1863   Dutch outlaw slavery

1867   Cuba ends slave trade

1868   Rebellion in Lares, Puerto Rico; rebellion in Yara, Cuba,
        which turns into a war for independence (Ten Years War)

1886   Slavery ends in Cuba

1888   Brazil is the last country in the Americas to abolish slavery

1895   Cuban War of Independence begins in February; José Martí
        killed in May

1898   On 15 February the USS Maine is blown up in Havana
        harbour; war concluded by July, with control of Puerto Rico
        and the Philippines going to the US and a nominal
        independence under US administration for Cuba

1900–99

1902   Mt Pelée erupts in Martinique, destroying the capital,
        St Pierre; La Soufrière volcano erupts in St Vincent

1912   Violent suppression in Cuba of the first black political party
        in the west, Partido Independiente de Color

1914   Marcus Garvey sets up the Universal Negro Improvement
        Association (UNIA) in Jamaica; Panama Canal opens

1915   British West Indies Regiment set up during First World War;
        US Marines occupy Haiti

1916	US Marines occupy the Dominican Republic
1930–39	Strikes and labour unrest throughout the region
1937	Some 25,000 Haitians are massacred in the Dominican Republic in October
1938	West India Royal Commission set up to investigate living conditions on the British islands
1939–45	Second World War
1957	François 'Papa Doc' Duvalier takes power in Haiti
1958	West Indies Federation set up, comprising ten British West Indian territories
1959	Fidel Castro takes power in Cuba
1961	Bay of Pigs invasion in Cuba
1962	Cuban missile crisis; West Indies Federation disbands in May; Jamaica and Trinidad become independent in August
1964	Forbes Burnham becomes prime minister in Guiana after Britain changes the voting system
1966	Guiana becomes independent; Barbados becomes independent
1973	Bahamas becomes independent
1974	Grenada becomes independent
1978	Dominica becomes independent
1979	St Lucia and St Vincent and the Grenadines become independent
1981	Belize becomes independent
1986	President of Haiti Jean-Claude 'Baby Doc' Duvalier flees
1983	St Kitts and Nevis becomes independent; US launches Operation Urgent Fury in Grenada
1990	Jean-Bertrand Aristide is elected president in Haiti but is forced out in a coup months later
1994	US military sent to Haiti after Aristide is allowed to return and resume office

1995   Montserrat residents forced to leave after dormant Soufrière
        Hills volcano becomes active again

2000 onwards

2008   Fidel Castro cedes Cuba's presidency to his brother, Raúl

2010   Earthquake devastates Haiti

2013   Raúl Castro announces he will stand down as president of
        Cuba in 2018

Gazetteer: The Caribbean (and surroundings)

Anguilla – Settled by English planters from nearby St Kitts in 1650. Was initially administered as part of the Leeward Islands. In the nineteenth century it was put under rule from St Kitts and by 1967 it was placed in a union with St Kitts and Nevis. It tried to become independent, which led to direct British control in 1971. Today it is an overseas territory of the United Kingdom.

Antigua & Barbuda – Antigua was visited by Christopher Columbus in 1493, though not colonized until 1632 by English settlers, as was neighbouring Barbuda in 1678. Barbuda was granted to the Codrington family in 1685, and by the nineteenth century was administered as part of Antigua. The islands became the independent nation of Antigua and Barbuda in 1981.

Aruba – Initially claimed by Spain, the island was settled by the Dutch, who took it in 1636. Today the island is an autonomous state of the Netherlands, a status it secured in 1986.

Bahamas – Christopher Columbus is thought to have first set foot in the Americas on one of the islands, San Salvador, in 1492. Spain claimed but did not settle. The English began to colonize in the 1640s, with a group of settlers arriving in 1648 to set up plantations. It remained under British rule until 1973, when the independent Commonwealth of the Bahamas was established.

Barbados – Explored by the English around 1625, and the first settlers arrived in 1627. Continued under British rule until 1966, when it became independent.

Belize – English pirates, buccaneers, and log-cutters settled along the coastal region throughout the latter part of the 1600s, but treaties with Spain, which had initially claimed the territory, to formalize the boundaries were not signed until 1763. It was officially given the name British Honduras in 1862 and became a crown colony in 1871. It became independent in 1981.

Berbice – see Guyana.

Bermuda – Although not technically in the Caribbean, it was part of the early colonization of the Americas. English settlers landed there in 1609 after being blown off course during a storm, and initially named it Somers Isles. It was administered by the crown from 1684 and it continues to be an overseas territory of the United Kingdom.

Bonaire – Settled by the Dutch around 1636. Became part of the Netherlands Antilles in 1954, which was dissolved in 2010. Today the island is a special municipality of the Netherlands.

British Guiana – see Guyana.

British Honduras – see Belize.

British Virgin Islands (Tortola, Virgin Gorda, Anegada, and Jost Van Dyke) – Tortola was initially settled by the Dutch around 1648. The English took it in 1666 and by 1672 it was part of England's Leeward islands. Virgin Gorda, Anegada, and Jost Van Dyke were settled by the English throughout the later decades of the seventeenth century. The islands are administered together and remain an overseas territory of the United Kingdom.

Cayman Islands (Grand Cayman, Little Cayman, and Cayman Brac) – Thought to be first sighted by Columbus; ceded to England in 1670. The population was mostly pirates and sailors, with a few plantation settlers. It had been governed from Jamaica, but after Jamaican independence in 1962 it returned to direct rule. The islands remain an overseas territory of the United Kingdom.

Colombia – Santa Marta, on the Caribbean coast, was settled by Spain in 1525 and Cartagena in 1533, and the territory was part of Spain's Viceroyalty of New Granada. After independence it was known as Gran Colombia, along with what is now Panama, Venezuela, and Ecuador (1819–30), established by Simón Bolívar. It became a republic after the union dissolved.

Costa Rica – Visited by Columbus on his final voyage, but not settled by Spain until around the 1560s; administered by the vice-royalty of New Spain. It became independent in 1821 and joined the United Provinces of Central America, which it stayed part of until 1838, when it became fully independent.

Cuba – Visited by Columbus in 1492, and settled by the Spanish in 1511. Havana was briefly under British control, in 1762–63. The island remained under Spanish control, despite many attempts at independence, until Spanish-American War of 1898. Cuba was occupied by the United States twice from the end of the war until 1909, and US influence persisted until the Revolution led by Fidel Castro in 1959. Castro's brother, Raúl, is currently president.

Curaçao – Initially claimed by the Spanish, but settled by the Dutch around 1634. Brought together with other Dutch islands as part of the Netherlands Antilles in 1845, which was disbanded in 2010. The island is now a country within the kingdom of the Netherlands.

Demerara, Berbice, and Essequibo – see Guyana.

Dominica – First settled by the French in the 1630s. Ceded as neutral territory to the native peoples under the terms of the 1748 Treaty of Aix-la-Chapelle, though this did not stop British and French settlers. The island was passed between the two colonial powers until it was formally ceded to Britain in 1763 in the aftermath of the Seven Years War. The French captured it once again in 1778, and the British took it back in 1783 and from that point fended off further French incursions. The island achieved full independence in 1978.

Dominican Republic – Site of Columbus's first settlement in the Americas and known as Santo Domingo. The western third of the island was ceded to the French in 1697 under the Treaty of Ryswick and became Saint-Domingue. Santo Domingo continued under Spanish rule until 1795, when it was ceded to France until 1809. From 1822 it was under Haitian control, until it established its independence in 1844.

Essequibo – see Guyana.

French Guiana – French merchants settled it in 1620, though it was not an official territory until 1667. It became a department of France in 1946, a region in 1974, and today it is known as the Overseas Department of French Guiana.

Gran Colombia – see Colombia.

Grenada – Initially French; a settlement was built in St George's in the 1650s. It was captured by the British in 1762 during the Seven Years War and ceded the following year. In 1779, the French recaptured it, but it was returned to Britain in 1783. It became fully independent from Britain in 1974.

Guadeloupe – Columbus visited in 1493, though its native people fought off Spanish settlers in the early decades of the 1500s. However, the Spanish managed a settlement by the 1620s, though they were driven out again, this time by the French. It became a colony under the French crown in 1674. The British occupied it in 1759, but it was returned to France in 1763. Britain invaded again in 1794, and in 1810 once again occupied the island, though it was given back to France in 1816. In 1946 it was given department status, and region status in 1974, and today is known as the Overseas Department of Guadeloupe.

Guatemala – Settled by the Spanish in the sixteenth century. Became independent of Spain in 1821 and joined the United Provinces of Central America. It remained a member until the federation began to dissolve around 1838, after which it was an independent republic.

Guiana – see French Guiana.

Guyana – Spotted by the Spanish, but settled by the Dutch in the late 1500s. During the war-torn years of 1792 to 1815 in Europe, the colony changed hands between the Dutch, British, and French a number of times. However, in 1814 the British purchased the territory then known as Demerara, Berbice, and Essequibo, which in 1831 was renamed British Guiana. It remained under British rule until 1966, when it gained its independence and changed its name to Guyana.

Haiti – Initially part of Spanish Hispaniola, until the western third of the island was ceded to France in 1697 and named Saint-Domingue. A slave rebellion starting in 1791 and lasting thirteen years finally secured the colony's freedom – and that of its slaves – and the republic of Haiti was established in 1804.

Hispaniola – The first Spanish colony. The western part became French Saint-Domingue in 1697, and later independent Haiti in 1804. The eastern part, Santo Domingo, passed through French rule from 1795 until 1809, and then Haitian rule from 1822 until 1844, becoming the independent Dominican Republic in that year.

Honduras – Occupied by the Spanish in the 1500s, becoming independent in 1821. It joined the United Provinces of Central America until its collapse, and became fully independent in 1838.

Jamaica – Initially settled by the Spanish in 1509, but captured by the British in 1655 and ceded by Spain. It was a founding member of the short-lived West Indies Federation in 1958, and the first to leave it in 1961. It became independent in 1962.

Martinique – Sighted by Columbus in 1493, but occupied by the French starting in 1635, and put under the French crown in 1674. It was captured by the British in 1762 and returned to France the following year. The British took it again in 1794, occupying it until 1802 and then on and off until they recaptured it in 1809. It was once again returned to France in 1814. In 1946 it was made a department, in 1974 a region, and today it is the Overseas Department of Martinique.

Jost Van Dyke – see British Virgin Islands.

Mexico – Invaded by the Spanish in 1518, and put under Spain's control by 1521, eventually establishing it as the viceroyalty of New Spain. It remained under Spanish rule until its independence in 1821.

Montserrat – Sighted by Columbus in 1493 but occupied by English settlers from St Kitts in 1632, as well as Irish Catholics sent there. France took the island in 1664 and 1667, but it was returned to England. France re-captured it in 1782, but it was given back to Britain the following year. It was administered as part of the Leeward Islands, and later, after it joined the short-lived West Indian Federation, it did not opt for independence. Today it is an overseas territory of the United Kingdom.

Netherlands Antilles – A Dutch Caribbean state that was disbanded in 2010. It comprised Aruba, Bonaire, Curaçao, Sint Maarten, Saba, and Sint Eustatius.

Nicaragua – Settled by the Spanish by 1524, and remained under Spain until independence in 1821. It then joined the United Provinces of Central America, but left in 1838, becoming fully independent.

Panama – Spanish settlements were established in 1510, and it remained part of Spain's American territories until independence in 1821, when it joined Gran Colombia. Once that broke down, Panama became a state within Colombia. By the turn of the twentieth century, the US wanted to build a canal across the isthmus, a project started by the French in the 1880s. Colombia rejected the US canal deal, and by 1903 pro-independence Panamanians, with the support of the United States, broke away from Colombia and established an independent republic, which allowed the US plans to go ahead.

Puerto Rico – Colonized in 1508, it continued under Spanish rule until the Spanish-American War of 1898. It was ceded to the United States in that same year, and continues under US rule to the present day as the Commonwealth of Puerto Rico (Estado libre asociado de Puerto Rico).

Saba – The Dutch settled in 1632, and it continues under Dutch rule. After the Netherlands Antilles was broken up in 2010, Saba became a special municipality of the Netherlands.

St Barthélemy – Colonized by the French around 1648, it was sold to Sweden in 1784. Just under a century later, in 1877, it was returned to France. It has been administered from Guadeloupe, but in 2007 it became an overseas collectivity.

St Croix – see US Virgin Islands.

Saint-Domingue – see Haiti.

St Eustatius – First settled by the English; the Dutch took control in 1632, and the island continued to change hands throughout the seventeenth century. It was captured by the British in 1781, though later returned to the Dutch. The island was part of the Netherlands Antilles, and after 2010 became a special municipality.

St John – see US Virgin Islands.

St Kitts & Nevis – Called St Christopher by Columbus, English settlers shortened the name after they began to arrive in 1623. St Kitts was shared with the French, and the two sides often fought, though the French were later driven out. The 1713 Treaty of Utrecht ceded St Kitts to the British. The French briefly captured it in 1782–83. Nevis was colonized by the English in 1628. The two islands were united, along with Anguilla, in

1882. By 1967, Anguilla had left the federation and its union with the other two islands ended in 1980. St Kitts and Nevis stayed together, and became a fully independent nation in 1983.

St Lucia – Attempts to settle the island were not successful until around 1650, when the French made peace with the hostile indigenous people. The English took it in 1664, but it was returned to France three years later. Under the 1748 treaty of Aix-la-Chappelle, the British and French agreed it was to be neutral, however Britain captured it again in 1762, but returned it to France. The remaining decades of the eighteenth century saw the island oscillate between the two powers until it was Britain's under the terms of the 1814 Treaty of Paris, where it remained until it became independent in 1979.

St Martin – The northern part of an island shared with the Dutch (see also Sint Maarten), which was partitioned in 1648 after French and Dutch settlers began to colonize the island. Today it is an overseas collectivity of France.

St Thomas – see US Virgin Islands.

St Vincent and the Grenadines – Settlement did not begin until the 1700s because of the fierce resistance of the indigenous people. Initially the settlers were French, but in 1763 Britain gained control of the island under the Treaty of Paris. It lost the island to the French in 1779, but regained it in 1783. Full independence was granted in 1979.

San Salvador – see Bahamas.

Santo Domingo – see Dominican Republic.

Sint Maarten – The southern portion of an island shared with the French (see also St Martin), which was partitioned in 1648 after French and Dutch settlers began to colonize the island. It was part of the Netherlands Antilles until it disbanded in 2010, and today is a country within the kingdom of the Netherlands.

Suriname – Initially settled by English planters but taken by the Dutch in 1667, it was later officially ceded to them in exchange for New Amsterdam (New York City). However, it returned to British rule briefly in 1799–1802 and 1804–15, but both times was returned to the Netherlands. Suriname became independent in 1975.

Tobago – see Trinidad & Tobago.

Tortola – see British Virgin Islands.

Trinidad & Tobago – Trinidad was colonized by the Spanish, with settlements appearing in the 1590s, though there was a significant influx of French planters in the mid-eighteenth century. In 1797, Britain attacked the island and took it from Spain, which was made official in 1802. Meanwhile, Tobago saw the arrival of Dutch, Baltic Kurlanders (briefly), French and British settlers in the seventeenth and eighteenth centuries, and Britain and France both controlled it, until it was finally given to the British in 1814. The two islands were brought together in 1889 and became independent in 1962.

Turks & Caicos Islands – European colonizers did not arrive until the 1670s, and some of the settlers were from nearby Bermuda. Initially annexed by the Bahamas, the Turks were later granted their own charter in 1848, though in the 1960s the islands were again under the administration of the Bahamas. After its independence, the Turks did not follow, and today they are an overseas territory of the United Kingdom.

US Virgin Islands (St Thomas, St John, St Croix) – St Croix was settled by the Dutch and English first, in the early 1600s, though the Spanish intervened before the island ended up under French rule. It was sold to the Knights of Malta in 1651 who later sold it back. It became a colony of France in 1674, and was bought by Denmark in 1733. Likewise, St Thomas was colonized by the Dutch and Danish, and became the territory of the Dutch West India Company in 1685, and the crown around 1754. The British took the island from 1807 until 1815, but it was given back to Denmark. St John was settled in 1717, when planters from St Thomas arrived, and the island came under Danish control. Denmark sold the three islands to the United States in 1917. Today they are classified as an organized, unincorporated territory of the United States.

Venezuela – Colonized by the Spanish in 1523, and remained under Spain's control until it declared its independence in 1811 and was part of Gran Colombia in 1819. It left that union in 1829 and became fully independent.

Acknowledgements

This book is not mine alone – it is the product of the efforts and generosity of many people on both sides of the Atlantic. First, I would like to thank my editor, Georgina Morley, for her unflagging enthusiasm for this project. Thanks also go to my agent, Bill Hamilton, for his support when this book was still little more than a conversation. I'm also grateful that Jamison Stoltz at Grove Atlantic in the US was eager to come on board, and my work benefited in infinite ways from the careful attention of all three.

Although any errors are my own, Juan José Ponce-Vázquez provided thoughtful comments; Juan Fernando Cobo Betancourt helped me think through my ideas; and Rory Foster made sure the details were straight. At the production stage, Trevor Horwood's copy-editing and Anthony Hippisley's proofreading helped me avoid a number of pitfalls. Martin Lubikowski provided elegant maps, and the team at Pan Macmillan made the whole process as painless as possible.

This book relied on two crucial things: a rich body of historical work to engage with, and eager librarians and archivists who could point me in the necessary directions. I was fortunate enough to have this in abundance across Britain, the United States, and the Caribbean, and am very grateful. Members of the academic community provided enlightening discussion and encouragement for my project wherever I went, from conversations with colleagues from my Ph.D. days to those with new aquaintances at the Institute of Americas in London, or in Miami, Havana, and beyond.

On the road I totted up a number of debts. In the US, Jane Landers, Brooke Wooldridge, Sherry Johnson, Michael Deibert, and Sandra de Marchena kindly took time to speak with me. In Haiti, Jacqui Labrom helped me get my bearings. In Jamaica, Antonia Graham and Roger

Drinkall opened their doors to a grateful traveller, Christopher Whyms-Stone explained the origins of Trench Town, and Andrine Cover showed me Mandeville. In Dominica Polly Pattullo invited me for a memorable lunch. Antigua would not have been the same without Matteo Cavazos and Kristal Gaston. In Trinidad I experienced the generosity of Sharon Millar (thanks to Ted Davis for the introduction), Sarojini Ramnarain, Valerie Kelsick, and Gregory George. In Cuba it was a pleasure to spend time with Assad Shoman (thanks to Dylan Vernon for putting us in touch), Jorge Renato Ibarra Guitart, Jorge Ibarra Cuesta, and Elena Schneider.

Thanks also go to my friends in Britain, the US, and further afield who had either a ready sofa, an open bottle, or a willing ear – or any combination of the three: Andrea Acle-Kreysing and Moritz Kreysing, Lisa Bachelor and Simon Hill, Tiffany Ferris and Chris Hall, Vicky Frost and Anthony Pickles, Crystal Paulk-Buchanan and Teague Buchanan, Anne-Isabelle Richard and Alexandre Afonso, Jennifer Vanden Bosch and Dana Burleson, David Batty, Mark Berry, Benjamin Carr, Mike Carter, Steve Cushion, Stefanie Gänger, Mariama Ifode, Simon Pirani, and Yvonne Singh. At the *Guardian* and *Observer*, colleagues always welcomed me back after long sojourns away, with special thanks going to Nigel Willmott on the *Guardian* Letters desk, as well as the team on Comment. In the US, my parents, brothers, and extended family gave their usual patient and enthusiastic support for my work, though a special thanks goes to my cousin Laura Groth, who hosted me while I was researching in Washington, DC.

And finally, my most heartfelt thanks go to Chris Stanford. Although this project started without him, it is impossible to contemplate how I would have completed it without his generosity, patience, and love.

Selected Bibliography

I have only included here some more recent books that I consulted and that might be of interest for the non-specialist reader. For a full list of primary and secondary sources used in this work, see *carriegibson.co.uk*.

Abulafia, David. *The Great Sea: A Human History of the Mediterranean*. London: Allen Lane, 2011.

—— *The Discovery of Mankind: Atlantic Encounters in the Age of Columbus*. New Haven, CT: Yale University Press, 2009.

Adams, William Howard. *On Luxury a Cautionary Tale, a Short History of the Perils of Excess from Ancient Times to the Beginning of the Modern Era*. Washington, DC: Potomac Books, 2012.

Ayala, César Jacques. *American Sugar Kingdom: The Plantation Economy of the Spanish Caribbean, 1989–1934*. Chapel Hill: University of North Carolina Press, 2003.

Barringer, T. J., Gillian Forrester, and Barbaro Martinez-Ruiz. *Art and Emancipation in Jamaica: Isaac Mendes Belisario and His Worlds*. New Haven, CT: Yale Center for British Art in association with Yale University Press, 2007.

Bailyn, Bernard, and Patricia L. Denault. *Soundings in Atlantic History: Latent Structures and Intellectual Currents, 1500–1830*. Cambridge, MA: Harvard University Press, 2009.

Bayly, C. A. *The Birth of the Modern World, 1780–1914: Global Connections and Comparisons*. Oxford: Blackwell, 2004.

Beckles, Hilary McD. *A History of Barbados* (2nd edn). Cambridge: Cambridge University Press, 2006.

—— *White Servitude and Black Slavery in Barbados, 1627–1715*. Knoxville: University of Tennessee Press, 1989.

Berg, Maxine. *Luxury and Pleasure in Eighteenth-century Britain* (illus., repr. edn). Oxford: Oxford University Press, 2007.

Berry, Christopher J. *The Idea of Luxury: A Conceptual and Historical Investigation*. Cambridge: Cambridge University Press, 1994.

Bethell, Leslie. *Cuba: A Short History*. Cambridge: Cambridge University Press, 1993.

Bethencourt, Francisco, and Diogo Ramada Curto. *Portuguese Oceanic Expansion, 1400–1800*. Cambridge: Cambridge University Press, 2007.

Bindman, David, and Henry Louis Gates (eds). *The Image of the Black in Western Art* (new edn). Cambridge, MA: Belknap Press of Harvard University Press in collaboration with the W. E. B. Du Bois Institute for African and African American Research and the Menil Collection, 2010.

Blackburn, Robin. *The Making of New World Slavery: From the Baroque to the Modern, 1492–1800*. London: Verso, 2010; originally published 1997.

—— *The Overthrow of Colonial Slavery 1776–1848*. London: Verso, 1988.

Block, Kristen. *Ordinary Life in the Caribbean: Religion, Colonial Competition, and the Politics of Profit*. Athens: University of Georgia Press, 2012.

Bolland, Nigel O. *The Formation of a Colonial Society: Belize, from Conquest to Crown Colony*. Baltimore: Johns Hopkins University Press, 1977.

—— *On the March: Labour Rebellions in the British Caribbean, 1934–9*. London: Ian Randle, 1995.

Boxer, C. R. *The Portuguese Seaborne Empire 1415–1825*. Manchester: Carcanet in association with the Calouste Gulbenkian Foundation, 1991.

Braudel, Fernand. *The Mediterranean and the Mediterranean World in the Age of Philip II* (trans. Siân Reynolds). London: Collins, 1972.

Brereton, B., G. Carrera Damas, P. C. Emmer, J. Ibarra Cuesta, B. W. Higman, F. Knight, K. O. Laurence, J. Sued-Badillo, (eds) *General History of the Caribbean*, vols 1–6 (London: Unesco, 1997–2011).

Brion Davis, David. *Inhuman Bondage: The Rise and Fall of Slavery in the New World*. Oxford: Oxford University Press, 2008.

Buck-Morss, Susan. *Hegel, Haiti, and Universal History*. Pittsburgh: University of Pittsburgh Press, 2009.

Bulmer-Thomas, Victor. *The Economic History of the Caribbean Since the Napoleonic Wars*. Cambridge: Cambridge University Press, 2012.

Bulmer-Thomas, Victor, John Coatsworth, and Roberto Cortés-Conde (eds). *The Cambridge Economic History of Latin America*. Cambridge: Cambridge University Press, 2006.

Carrington, Selwyn H. H. *The Sugar Industry and the Abolition of the Slave Trade, 1775–1810*. Gainesville: University Press of Florida, 2003.

Childs, Matt D. *The 1812 Aponte Rebellion in Cuba and the Struggle against Atlantic Slavery*. Chapel Hill: University of North Carolina Press, 2006.

Chomsky, Aviva. *West Indian Workers and the United Fruit Company in Costa Rica, 1870–1940*. Baton Rouge: Louisiana State University Press, 1996.

Colby, Jason M. *The Business of Empire: United Fruit, Race, and U.S. Expansion in Central America* (illus. edn). Ithaca: Cornell University Press, 2011.

Corwin, Arthur F. *Spain and the Abolition of Slavery in Cuba, 1817–1886*. Austin: Published for the Institute of Latin American Studies by the University of Texas Press, 1967.

Crosby, Alfred W. *The Columbian Exchange: Biological and Cultural Consequences of 1492*. Westport, CT: Greenwood, 2003.

Curran, Andrew S. *The Anatomy of Blackness: Science and Slavery in An Age of Enlightenment*. Baltimore: Johns Hopkins University Press, 2011.

Curtin, Philip D. *The Atlantic Slave Trade: A Census*. Madison: University of Wisconsin Press, 1969.

Dando-Collins, Stephen. *Tycoon's War: How Cornelius Vanderbilt Invaded a Country to Overthrow America's Most Famous Military Adventurer*. Cambridge, MA: Da Capo Press, 2009.

Darwin, John. *After Tamerlane: The Global History of Empire Since 1405*. London: Allen Lane, 2007.

Davies, Martin. *Columbus in Italy: An Italian Versification of the Letter on the Discovery of the New World: With Facsimiles of the Italian and Latin Editions of 1493*. London: British Library, 1991.

Deibert, M. *Notes from the Last Testament: The Struggle for Haiti*. New York: Seven Stories Press, 2011.

Drayton, Richard. *Nature's Government: Science, Imperial Britain, and the 'Improvement' of the World*. New Haven, CT: Yale University Press, 2000.

Dubois, Laurent. *Haiti: The Aftershocks of History*. New York: Picador/ Metropolitan Books, 2013.

—— *Avengers of the New World: The Story of the Haitian Revolution*. Cambridge, MA: Belknap Press of Harvard University Press, 2004.

—— *A Colony of Citizens: Revolution & Slave Emancipation in the French Caribbean, 1787–1804*. Chapel Hill: University of North Carolina Press, 2004.

Edmonds, Ennis Barrington, and Michelle A. Gonzalez. *Caribbean Religious History: An Introduction*. New York: New York University Press, 2010.

Elliott, John Huxtable. *Empires of the Atlantic World: Britain and Spain in America, 1492–1830*. New Haven, CT: Yale University Press, 2006.

Eltis, David. *The Rise of African Slavery in the Americas*. Cambridge: Cambridge University Press, 2000.

Eltis, David, and Stanley L. Engerman. *The Cambridge World History of Slavery*, vol. 3: *AD 1420–AD 1804*. Cambridge: Cambridge University Press, 2011.

Emmer, Peter. *The Dutch in the Atlantic Economy, 1580–1880: Trade, Slavery and Emancipation*. Aldershot: Ashgate, 1998.

Engerman, Stanley, and Robert Paquette (eds). *The Lesser Antilles in the Age of European Expansion*. Gainesville: University Press of Florida, 1996.

Fernández-Armesto, Felipe. *1492: The Year the World Began*. London: HarperCollins, 2009.

———— *Pathfinders: A Global History of Exploration*. Oxford: Oxford University Press, 2006.

———— *Columbus and the Conquest of the Impossible*. London: Orion, 2000.

———— *Before Columbus: Exploration and Colonisation from the Mediterranean to the Atlantic, 1229–1492*. Philadelphia: University of Pennsylvania Press, 1987.

———— *The Canary Islands after the Conquest: The Making of a Colonial Society in the Early Sixteenth Century*. New York: Oxford University Press, 1982.

Fernández Olmos, Margarite, and Lizabeth Paravisini-Gebert. *Sacred Possessions: Vodou, Santería, Obeah, and the Caribbean*. New Brunswick, NJ: Rutgers University Press, 1997.

Fick, Carolyn E. *The Making of Haiti: The Saint Domingue Revolution from Below*. Knoxville: University of Tennessee Press, 1990.

Fradera, Josep Maria. *Colonias para Después de un Imperio*. Barcelona: Edicions Bellaterra, 2005.

Fraginals, Manuel Moreno. *El Ingenio: El Complejo Económico Social Cubano del Azúcar*. Havana: Editorial de Ciencias Sociales, 1978.

Geggus, David Patrick. *Haitian Revolutionary Studies*. Bloomington: Indiana University Press, 2002.

———— *The Impact of the Haitian Revolution in the Atlantic World*. Columbia: University of South Carolina Press, 2001.

———— *Slavery, War and Revolution: The British Occupation of Saint Domingue, 1793–1798*. Oxford: Clarendon Press, 1982.

Gill, Lesley. *The School of the Americas: Military Training and Political Violence in the Americas*. Durham, NC: Duke University Press, 2004.

Goldish, Josette C. *Once Jews: Stories of Caribbean Sephardim*. Princeton, NJ: Markus Wiener, 2009.

Goslinga, Cornelis Ch. *The Dutch in the Caribbean and in Surinam, 1791*. Assen: Van Gorcum, 1990.

Gott, Richard. *Cuba: A New History*. New Haven, CT: Yale University Press, 2005.

Grant, Colin. *I&I: The Natural Mystics: Marley, Tosh, and Wailer*. London: Jonathan Cape, 2011.

———— *Negro with a Hat: The Rise and Fall of Marcus Garvey*. Oxford: Oxford University Press, 2011.

Helg, Aline. *Our Rightful Share: The Afro-Cuban Struggle for Equality, 1886–1912*. Chapel Hill: University of North Carolina Press, 1995.

Heuman, Gad. *The Killing Time: The Morant Bay Rebellion in Jamaica*. London: Macmillan, 1994.

Higman, B. W. *A Concise History of the Caribbean* (Cambridge: Cambridge University Press, 2011).

Honychurch, Lennox. *The Dominica Story: A History of the Island*, 3rd edn. Oxford: Macmillan Education, 1995.

Hopkins, A. G. *Globalization in World History*. London: Pimlico, 2002.

Howard, David. *Coloring the Nation: Race and Ethnicity in the Dominican Republic.* Oxford: Signal Books, 2001.

Hulme, Peter, and Neil L. Whitehead. *Wild Majesty: Encounters with Caribs from Columbus to the Present Day: An Anthology.* New York: Oxford University Press, 1992.

Hurston, Zora Neale. *Tell My Horse: Voodoo and Life in Haiti and Jamaica.* New York: Perennial Library, 1990; originally published 1938.

James, C. L. R. *The Black Jacobins: Toussaint L'Ouverture and the San Domingo Revolution.* London: Penguin, 2001; originally published 1938.

———— *Beyond a Boundary.* Durham, NC: Duke University Press, 1993.

Johnson, Sherry. *Climate and Catastrophe in Cuba and the Atlantic World in the Age of Revolution.* Chapel Hill, University of North Carolina Press, 2011.

———— *The Social Transformation of Eighteenth-century Cuba.* Gainesville: University Press of Florida, 2001.

Karras, Alan L. *Smuggling: Contraband and Corruption in World History.* Lanham, MD: Rowman & Littlefield, 2010.

Klein, Herbert S. *The Atlantic Slave Trade.* Cambridge: Cambridge University Press, 1999.

———— *Slavery in the Americas: A Comparative Study of Virginia and Cuba.* Oxford: Oxford University Press, 1967.

Knight, Franklin W. *The Caribbean: The Genesis of a Fragmented Nationalism.* New York: Oxford University Press, 1990.

Kritzler, Edward. *Jewish Pirates of the Caribbean: How a Generation of Swashbuckling Jews Carved Out an Empire in the New World in Their Quest for Treasure, Religious Freedom – and Revenge.* New York: Knopf Doubleday, 2009.

Kriz, Kay Dian. *Slavery, Sugar, and the Culture of Refinement: Picturing the British West Indies, 1700–1840.* New Haven, CT: Yale University Press, 2008.

Kurlanksy, Mark. *Salt: A World History.* London: Jonathan Cape, 2002.

Lamming, George. *The Pleasures of Exile.* London: Pluto Press, 2005.

Landers, Jane G. *Atlantic Creoles in the Age of Revolutions* (illus. edn). Cambridge, MA: Harvard University Press, 2010.

Lasso, Marixa. *Myths of Harmony: Race and Republicanism During the Age of Revolution, Colombia, 1795–1831.* Pittsburgh: University of Pittsburgh Press, 2007.

Latimer, Jon. *Buccaneers of the Caribbean: How Piracy Forged an Empire.* Cambridge, MA: Harvard University Press, 2009.

Lazo, Rodrigo. *Writing to Cuba: Filibustering and Cuban Exiles in the United States.* Chapel Hill: University of North Carolina Press, 2005.

Lester, Toby. *The Fourth Part of the World: The Race to the Ends of the Earth, and the Epic Story of the Map that Gave America Its Name.* New York, Free Press, 2009.

Lewis, Gordon K. *Main Currents in Caribbean Thought: The Historical Evolution of Caribbean Society in Its Ideological Aspects, 1492–1900.* Lincoln: University of Nebraska Press, 2004.

Linebaugh, Peter, and Marcus Rediker. *The Many-Headed Hydra: Sailors, Slaves, Commoners and the Hidden History of the Revolutionary Atlantic*. Boston: Beacon Press, 2000.

Mann, Charles C. *1493: Uncovering the New World Columbus Created*. New York: Vintage Books, 2012.

Mawby, Spencer. *Ordering Independence: The End of Empire in the Anglophone Caribbean, 1947–1969*. Basingstoke: Macmillan, 2012.

May, Robert E. *The Southern Dream of a Caribbean Empire, 1854–1861*. Baton Rouge: Louisiana State University Press, 1973.

McNeill, J. R. *Mosquito Empires: Ecology and War in the Greater Caribbean, 1620–1914*. Cambridge: Cambridge University Press, 2010.

Midlo Hall, Gwendolyn. *Social Control in Slave Plantation Societies: A Comparison of St. Domingue and Cuba*. Baton Rouge: Louisiana State University Press, 1996.

Moya Pons, Frank. *The Dominican Republic: A National History*. New Rochelle, NY: Hispaniola Books, 1995.

Musgrave, Toby, and Will Musgrave. *An Empire of Plants: People and Plants that Changed the World*. London: Cassell, 2000.

Muthu, Sankar. *Enlightenment against Empire*. Princeton, NJ: Princeton University Press, 2003.

Nicholls, David. *From Dessalines to Duvalier: Race, Colour and National Independence in Haiti*. Warwick University Caribbean Studies. London: Macmillan, 1996.

Norton, Marcy. *Sacred Gifts, Profane Pleasures: A History of Tobacco and Chocolate in the Atlantic World* (illus. edn). Ithaca: Cornell University Press, 2010.

O'Shaughnessy, Andrew Jackson, *An Empire Divided: The American Revolution and the British Caribbean*. Philadelphia: University of Pennsylvania Press, 2000.

Pagden, Anthony. *Lords of All the World: Ideologies of Empire in Spain, Britain and France c.1500-c.1800*. New Haven, CT: Yale University Press, 1995.

Palmié, Stephan, and Francisco A. Scarano. *The Caribbean: A History of the Region and Its Peoples*. Chicago: University of Chicago Press, 2011.

Paquette, Robert L. *Sugar Is Made with Blood: The Conspiracy of La Escalera and the Conflict Between Empires over Slavery in Cuba*. Middletown, CT: Wesleyan University Press, 1988.

Parker, Matthew. *The Sugar Barons: Family, Corruption, Empire and War*. London: Hutchinson, 2011.

—— *Panama Fever: The Battle to Build the Canal*. London: Hutchinson, 2007.

Pattullo, Polly. *Last Resorts: The Cost of Tourism in the Caribbean* (London and New York: Latin America Bureau, 2005).

Pestana, Carla Gardina. *Protestant Empire: Religion and the Making of the British Atlantic World*. Philadelphia: University of Pennsylvania Press, 2009.

Phillips, William D. *The Worlds of Christopher Columbus*. Cambridge: Cambridge University Press, 1992.

Popkin, Jeremy D. *Facing Racial Revolution: Eyewitness Accounts of the Haitian Insurrection*. Chicago: University of Chicago Press, 2007.

Preston, Diana, and Michael Preston. *A Pirate of Exquisite Mind: Explorer, Naturalist, and Buccaneer: The Life of William Dampier.* New York: Berkeley Publishing Group, 2004.

Rediker, Marcus. *Villains of All Nations: Atlantic Pirates in the Golden Age.* London: Verso, 2004.

Reid, Basil A. *Myths and Realities of Caribbean History* (illus. edn). Tuscaloosa: University of Alabama Press, 2009.

Renda, Mary A. *Taking Haiti: Military Occupation and the Culture of US Imperialism, 1915–1940.* Chapel Hill: University of North Carolina Press, 2001.

Restall, Matthew. *Seven Myths of the Spanish Conquest.* New York: Oxford University Press, 2003.

Rodney, Walter. *A History of the Upper Guinea Coast, 1545–1800.* Oxford: Clarendon Press, 1970.

Rogozinski, Jan. *A Brief History of the Caribbean.* New York: Plume, 1999.

Russell, P. Edward. *Prince Henry 'the Navigator': A Life.* New Haven, CT: Yale University Press, 2000.

San Miguel, Pedro L. *The Imagined Island: History, Identity, and Utopia in Hispaniola.* Chapel Hill: University of North Carolina Press, 2005.

Scarano, Francisco A. *Sugar and Slavery in Puerto Rico: The Plantation Economy of Ponce, 1800–1850.* Madison: University of Wisconsin Press, 1984.

Schama, Simon. *Rough Crossings: Britain, the Slaves and the American Revolution.* London: HarperCollins, 2006.

Schmidt-Nowara, Christopher. *Empire and Antislavery: Spain, Cuba and Puerto Rico, 1833–74.* Pittsburgh: University of Pittsburgh Press, 1999.

Shoman, Assad. *Belize's Independence and Decolonization in Latin America: Guatemala, Britain, and the UN* (illus. edn). New York: Macmillan, 2010.

—— *13 Chapters of a History of Belize.* Belize City: Angelus Press, 1994.

Shovlin, John. *The Political Economy of Virtue: Luxury, Patriotism, and the Origins of the French Revolution* (illus. edn). Ithaca: Cornell University Press, 2007.

Simms, Brendan. *Three Victories and a Defeat: The Rise and Fall of the First British Empire, 1714–1783.* New York: Basic Books, 2008.

Smith, Godfrey P. *George Price: A Life Revealed: The Authorized Biography.* Kingston: Ian Randle, 2011.

Stearns, Peter N. *Globalization in World History.* London: Routledge, 2010.

—— *Consumerism in World History: The Global Transformation of Desire.* London: Routledge, 2006.

Striffler, Steve, and Mark Moberg. *Banana Wars: Power, Production, and History in the Americas.* Durham, NC: Duke University Press, 2003.

Thornton, John. *Africa and Africans in the Making of the Atlantic World.* Cambridge: Cambridge University Press, 1998.

Von Tunzelmann, Alex. *Red Heat: Conspiracy, Murder, and the Cold War in the Caribbean*. New York: Henry Holt, 2011.

White, Ashli. *Encountering Revolution: Haiti and the Making of the Early Republic*. Baltimore: Johns Hopkins University Press, 2010.

Wilentz, Amy. *Farewell, Fred Voodoo: A Letter from Haiti*. New York: Simon & Schuster, 2013.

Williams, Eric Eustace, *Capitalism and Slavery*. Chapel Hill: University of North Carolina Press, 1994.

—— *From Columbus to Castro: The History of the Caribbean, 1492–1969*. New York: Vintage Books, 1984.

Wilson, Andrew (ed.), *The Chinese in the Caribbean*. Princeton, NJ: Markus Wiener, 2004.

Wilson, Samuel M. *The Archaeology of the Caribbean*. New York: Cambridge University Press, 2007.

Wucker, Michele. *Why the Cocks Fight: Dominicans, Haitians, and the Struggle for Hispaniola*. New York: Hill and Wang, 2000.

Zahedieh, Nuala. *The Capital and the Colonies: London and the Atlantic Economy, 1660–1700*. Cambridge: Cambridge University Press, 2010.

Notes

Introduction

1 Anthony Trollope, *The West Indies and the Spanish Main* (London: Chapman & Hall, 1859), p. 55.
2 Derek Walcott, Nobel Lecture: 'The Antilles: Fragments of Epic Memory', www.nobelprize.org/nobel_prizes/literature/laureates/1992/walcott-lecture.html (accessed 12 July 2013).
3 Stuart Hall, 'Cultural Identity and Diaspora', in Patrick Williams and Laura Chrisman (eds), *Colonial Discourse and Post-Colonial Theory: A Reader* (Columbus University Press, 1994), chapter 2, p. 296.
4 Ennis Barrington Edmonds and Michelle A. Gonzalez, *Caribbean Religious History: An Introduction* (New York University Press, 2010), p. 13.
5 George Lamming, *The Pleasures of Exile* (Pluto Press, 2005), p. 16.
6 Fernand Braudel, *The Mediterranean and the Mediterranean World in the Age of Philip I*, trans. Siân Reynolds (Collins, 1972), vol. 1, p. 16.

One – A Passage to the Indies

1 The surviving account of the expedition was written by court chronicler Gomes Eanes de Zurara, an admirer of his patron. Zurara witnessed the attack on Ceuta and wrote about it thirty-four years after the event. An English translation can be found in Edgar Prestage (ed.), *The Chronicles of Fernão Lopes and Gomes Eannes de Zurara* (Watford, 1928).
2 P. E. Russell, *Prince Henry 'the Navigator': A Life* (Yale University Press, 2000), p. 31.
3 Ibid., pp. 33–4.
4 Much of the biographical information on Henry comes from Russell, *Prince Henry*, chapter 1.

5   David Abulafia, *The Great Sea: A Human History of the Mediterranean* (Allen Lane, 2011), pp. 393–5.

6   B. W. Higman, *A Concise History of the Caribbean* (Cambridge University Press, 2011), p. 57.

7   See George D. Winius (ed.), *Portugal, the Pathfinder: Journeys from the Medieval toward the Modern World 1300–ca.1600* (Hispanic Seminary of Medieval Studies, 1995).

8   Toby Lester, *The Fourth Part of the World: The Race to the Ends of the Earth, and the Epic Story of the Map that Gave America Its Name* (Free Press, 2009), p. 31.

9   For a discussion on map-making see Felipe Fernández-Armesto, 'Exploration and Discovery', in Christopher Allmand (ed.), *The New Cambridge Medieval History* (Cambridge University Press, 1998), and Fernández-Armesto, *Pathfinders: A Global History of Exploration* (Oxford University Press, 2006).

10   See Jalil Sued Badillo, 'From Tainos to Africans in the Caribbean: Labour, Migration, and Resistance', in Stephan Palmié and Francisco Scarano (eds), *The Caribbean: A History of the Region and Its Peoples* (University of Chicago Press, 2011), pp. 103–9.

11   Luis Adão da Fonseca, 'The Discovery of Atlantic Space', in Winius, *Portugal, the Pathfinder*, p. 15.

12   *The Travels of Marco Polo* (Oliver & Boyd, 1845), p. 117.

13   See, for instance, Fernández-Armesto, *Pathfinders*, and Steven Epstein, *Genoa and the Genoese, 958–1528* (University of North Carolina Press, 1996).

14   Epstein, *Genoa*, p. 267.

15   John E. Kicza, 'Patterns in Early Spanish Overseas Expansion', *William and Mary Quarterly* 49, 2 (1992), pp. 231–2.

16   Epstein, *Genoa*, pp. 268–9.

17   Juan Gil (trans.), *The Book of Marco Polo: Copy with Annotations by Christopher Columbus Which Is Conserved at the Capitular and Columbus Library of Sevilla* (Testimonio Compañia Editorial, 1986), p. 84.

18   Ibid., p. 103.

19   David Abulafia, *The Discovery of Mankind: Atlantic Encounters in the Age of Columbus* (Yale University Press, 2009), p. 25.

20   William D. Phillips, *The Worlds of Christopher Columbus* (Cambridge University Press, 1992), p. 110.

21   Phillips, *Columbus*, p. 121.

22   John Huxtable Elliott, *Imperial Spain, 1469–1716* (Penguin, 2002), p. 61.

23   Phillips, *Columbus* p. 140.

24   Martin Davies, *Columbus in Italy: An Italian Versification of the Letter on the Discovery of the New World: With Facsimiles of the Italian and Latin Editions of 1493* (British Library, 1991).

25   Higman, *A Concise History*, p. 33.

26   Davies, *Columbus in Italy*.
27   Matthew Restall. *Seven Myths of the Spanish Conquest* (Oxford University Press, 2003), pp. 108–11.

Two – Stepping Stones to the New World

1   Felipe Fernández-Armesto, *Before Columbus: Exploration and Colonisation from the Mediterranean to the Atlantic, 1229–1492* (University of Pennsylvania Press, 1987), p. 153.
2   Ibid., p. 176.
3   The source for the retelling of this expedition in this section is Pierre Bontier and Jean Le Verrier, *The Canarian or Book of the Conquest and Conversion of the Canarians in . . . 1402, by J. De Béthencourt*, ed. and trans. Richard Henry Major (Hakluyt Society, 1872).
4   At around 3,718m (12,200ft), Mount Teide is so high it is usually snow-capped in the winter.
5   Bontier and Le Verrier, *The Canarian*, p. 9.
6   Some accounts put his death at 1422.
7   Bontier and Le Verrier, *The Canarian*, p. xxxiii.
8   Felipe Fernández-Armesto, *The Canary Islands after the Conquest: The Making of a Colonial Society in the Early Sixteenth Century* (Oxford University Press, 1982), p. 7.
9   Ibid., p. 13.
10   Leonara de Alberti and A. B. Wallis Chapman, 'English Traders and the Spanish Canary Inquisition in the Canaries During the Reign of Queen Elizabeth', *Transactions of the Royal Historical Society* 3 (1909), p. 245. Charles V made a grant in 1538 to English merchants, but this was often overshadowed by the ongoing Anglo-Spanish rivalry. The islands would come under attack by the English navy commanded by Sir Walter Raleigh in 1595.
11   Russell, *Prince Henry*, p. 85.
12   William D. Phillips, Jr, 'Old World Precedents: Sugar and Slavery in the Mediterranean', in Palmié and Scarano, *The Caribbean*, p. 77.
13   See Stewart B. Schwartz, 'The Economy of the Portuguese Empire', in Francisco Bethencourt and Diogo Ramada Curto (eds), *Portuguese Oceanic Expansion, 1400–1800* (Cambridge University Press, 2007).
14   Robin Blackburn, *The Making of New World Slavery: From the Baroque to the Modern, 1492–1800* (Verso, 1997), 2010 edn, p. 109.
15   Russell, *Prince Henry*, p. 101.
16   Schwartz, 'The Economy of the Portuguese Empire', p. 24.
17   Though in the case of Cape Verde, the fort on Ribeira Grande was not

built until the reign of Spain's Philip II (when Portugal and its territories were part of the Iberian Union).

18   C. Jane, and E. G. R. Taylor (eds), *Select Documents Illustrating the Four Voyages of Columbus* (Hakluyt Society, 1929), p. 24.

19   Davies, *Columbus in Italy*, pp. 49–51.

20   Jane and Taylor, *Select Documents*, p. 28.

21   See for instance Maximilian C. Forte, 'Extinction: The Historical Trope of Anti-Indigeneity in the Caribbean', *Issues in Caribbean Amerindian Studies* 6, 4 (2004), pp. 1–24. Certainly words have survived as well, not least *huracán* (or hurricane), barbecue, and hammock, among many others.

22   Basil A. Reid, *Myths and Realities of Caribbean History* (University of Alabama Press, 2009).

23   Samuel M. Wilson, *The Archaeology of the Caribbean* (Cambridge University Press, 2007).

24   Reid, *Myths*, see chapter 2.

25   Wilson, *The Archaeology of the Caribbean*, pp. 1–2.

26   Reid, *Myths*. Reid himself admits that the term 'Carib' 'is a product of European cultural biases, but Caribbean archaeologists will continue to use it, given the lack of a better alternative' (p. 11).

27   Wilson, *The Archaeology of the Caribbean*, p. 144.

28   Reid, *Myths*, p. 58.

29   Daniel Defoe, *The Life and Adventures of Robinson Crusoe*.

30   Jean-Baptiste Labat, *Memoirs of Père Labat, 1693–1705* (Constable, 1931), p. 102.

31   Higman, *A Concise History*, p. 35.

32   Restall, *Seven Myths*, p. 32.

33   Robin Law, 'Horses, Firearms, and Political Power in Pre-Colonial West Africa', *Past & Present* 72 (1976), pp. 112–32.

34   Lennox Honychurch, *The Dominica Story: A History of the Island*, 3rd edn (Macmillan, 1995), p. 21.

35   Gert Oostindie and Bert Paasman, 'Dutch Attitudes Towards Colonial Empire, Indigenous Cultures, and Slaves', *Eighteenth-Century Studies* 31, 3 (1998), p. 353.

36   Restall, *Seven Myths*, pp. 72–3.

37   Matthew Restall, 'Black Conquistadors: Armed Africans in Early Spanish America', *The Americas* 57, 2 (2000), pp. 171–205.

38   Frank Moya Pons, *The Dominican Republic: A National History* (Hispaniola Books, 1995), p. 30.

39   Jane and Taylor, *Select Documents*, pp. 50–51.

40   Higman, *A Concise History*, p. 63.

41   Luis N. Rivera-Pagán, 'Freedom and Servitude: Indigenous Slavery and the Spanish Conquest of the Caribbean', in Jalil Sued Badillo (ed.), *General*

History of the Caribbean, vol. 1: *The Autochthonous Societies* (Unesco, 1997), p. 322.

42 There are some discrepancies regarding the date of his birth, which could be as early as 1474 or as late as 1484. See Franklin Knight (ed.) and Andrew Hurley (trans.), *Bartolomé de las Casas, An Account, Much Abbreviated, of the Destruction of the Indies* (Hackett, 2003).

43 Rivera-Pagán, 'Freedom and Servitude', p. 325.

44 C. R. Johnson, 'Renaissance German Cosmographers and the Naming of America', *Past & Present* 191, 1 (2006), pp. 3–45.

45 Knight and Hurley, *Bartolomé de las Casas*, p. 89.

46 Sued Badillo, 'From Tainos to Africans', p. 105.

47 Restall, *Seven Myths*, p. 56.

48 Ibid., p. 54.

49 Higman, *A Concise History*, pp. 78–9.

50 Knight and Hurley, *Bartolomé de las Casas*, p. 7

51 Ibid., p. 9.

52 Rivera-Pagán, 'Freedom and Servitude', p. 345.

53 Molly A. Warsh, 'Enslaved Pearl Divers in the Sixteenth Century Caribbean', *Slavery & Abolition* 31, 3 (2010).

Three – Pirates and Protestants

1 Jon Latimer, *Buccaneers of the Caribbean: How Piracy Forged An Empire* (Harvard University Press, 2009).

2 See chapter 1 of Linda Colley, *Captives: Britain, Empire, and the World, 1600–1850* (Pantheon, 2002).

3 See Introduction in Charles Mann, *1493: Uncovering the New World Columbus Created* (Vintage Books, 2012).

4 D. O. Flynn and A. Giráldez, 'Born with A "Silver Spoon": The Origin of World Trade in 1571', *Journal of World History* 6, 2 (1995), p. 201.

5 Isaac Curtis, 'Masterless People: Maroon, Pirates and Commoners', in Palmié and Scarano, *The Caribbean*, p. 153.

6 Its Castilian title was somewhat more scientific: *Primera y segunda y tercera partes de la historia medicinal de las cosas que se traen de nuestras Indias Occidentales que sirven en medicina* (First, Second, and Third Parts of the Medicinal History of the Goods Brought from Our West Indies Serving in Medicine).

7 See 'Of Tobaco', in Nicolás Monardes, *Joyfull Newes Out of the Newe Founde Worlde*, original translation by John Frampton (1577), and edited by Stephen Gaselee (AMS Press, 1967), vol. 2.

8 Ibid.

9   Iain Gately, *Tobacco: The Story of How Tobacco Seduced the World* (Grove Press, 2001), p. 3.

10   Monardes, 'Of Tobaco'.

11   Gately, *Tobacco*, pp. 2–5.

12   Monardes, 'Of Tobaco'.

13   Ibid.

14   Gately, *Tobacco*, p. 23.

15   Ibid., p. 8.

16   Ibid., p. 44.

17   James I, *A Counterblaste to Tobacco* (1604), italics in original.

18   Ibid.

19   Gately, *Tobacco*, pp. 50–57.

20   Ibid., p. 114. The connection between Seville and tobacco was further – and much later – enshrined by the Georges Bizet opera *Carmen* (1874).

21   Ibid., p. 72

22   William Alexander, *An Encouragement to Colonies* (1624), p. 27.

23   J. P. Knox, *A Historical Account of St. Thomas, WI: With Its Rise and Progress in Commerce . . . And Incidental Notices of St. Croix and St. John's* (Charles Scribner, 1852), p. 35.

24   On Protestant settlement, see Carla Gardina Pestana, *Protestant Empire: Religion and the Making of the British Atlantic World* (University of Pennsylvania Press, 2009); Kristen Block, *Ordinary Life in the Caribbean: Religion, Colonial Competition, and the Politics of Profit* (University of Georgia Press, 2012).

25   In the Caribbean there would be no commercial banks until after 1830. Most goods were bartered or paid for in commodities such as sugar. See Higman, *A Concise History*, p. 175.

26   Juan José Ponce-Vázquez, 'Social and Political Survival at the Edge of Empire: Spanish Local Elites in Hispaniola, 1580–1697' (unpublished PhD thesis, University of Pennsylvania, 2011), pp. 31–2.

27   Moya Pons, *The Dominican Republic*, p. 45.

28   For an in-depth account of these events, as well as an analysis of where it fits into the wider narrative of Dominican history, see Ponce-Vázquez, 'Social and Political Survival', pp. 44–135.

29   Jon Miller, 'Hugo Grotius', in Edward N. Zalta (ed.), *The Stanford Encyclopedia of Philosophy* (Fall 2011 edn), http://plato.stanford.edu/archives/fall2011/entries/grotius/ (accessed 10 July 2013).

30   Lauren Benton, 'Legal Spaces of Empire: Piracy and the Origins of Ocean Regionalism', *Comparative Studies in Society and History* 47, 4 (2005), p. 703.

31   Ibid., p. 705.

32   Ibid., p. 707.

33   Ibid., p. 705.

34   John C. Appleby, 'An Association for the West Indies? English Plans for

a West India Company 1621–9', *Journal of Imperial and Commonwealth History* 15, 3 (1987), p. 213.

35 Jack Beeching, 'Introduction', in A. O. Exquemelin, *The Buccaneers of America . . .*, trans. Alexis Brown (Folio Society, 1972), p. 8.

36 Appleby, 'An Association for the West Indies?', p. 215.

37 This section is indebted to Karen Ordahl Kupperman, *Providence Island, 1630–1641: The Other Puritan Colony* (Cambridge University Press), 1993, pp. 1–24.

38 Ibid., pp. 153–72.

39 Ibid., pp. 336–8.

40 Hilary McD. Beckles, *White Servitude and Black Slavery in Barbados, 1627–1715* (University of Tennessee Press, 1989), pp. 14–16.

41 John Oldmixon, *The British Empire in America: Containing the History of the Discovery, Settlement, Progress and Present State of All the British Colonies, on the Continent and Islands of America*, 2nd edn (1741), p. 6.

42 Beckles, *White Servitude*, pp. 1–2.

43 Ibid., p. 10.

44 John Cordy Jeaffreson (ed.), *A Young Squire of the Seventeenth Century from the Papers (AD 1676–1686) of Christopher Jeaffreson* (Hurst & Blackett, 1878), p. 19.

45 B. Dyde, *Out of the Crowded Vagueness: A History of the Islands of St Kitts, Nevis & Anguilla* (Macmillan, 2005), pp. 18–26. See also Matthew Parker, *The Sugar Barons: Family, Corruption, Empire and War* (Hutchinson, 2011), pp. 20–22.

46 Honychurch, *The Dominica Story*.

47 Jeaffreson, *A Young Squire*, p. 192.

48 Ibid., pp. 210–11.

49 Ibid., p. 216.

50 Ibid., pp. 254–60.

51 Ibid., p. 192.

52 Mark Kurlanksy, *Salt: A World History* (Jonathan Cape, 2002), p. 6.

53 New York State Archives, Curaçao Papers, 1640–1665. trans. and ed. Charles T. Gehring, New Netherland Research Center, 2011, pp. 3–5, www.newnetherlandinstitute.org/research/online-publications/curacao-papers/ (accessed 28 February 2013).

54 Ibid., p. 18.

55 Ibid., pp. 120–21.

56 Ibid., p. 23.

57 Isaac Samuel Emmanuel, 'New Light on Early American Jewry', *American Jewish Archives* 7, 1 (1955), pp. 20–21.

58 Curaçao Papers, pp. 51–4.

59 Emmanuel, 'New Light', pp. 20–21.

60 Ross Jamieson, 'The Essence of Commodification: Caffeine Dependencies in the Early Modern World', *Journal of Social History* 24, 2 (2001), p. 275.

61   Mark Pendergrast, *Uncommon Grounds: The History of Coffee and How It Transformed Our World*, 2nd edn (Basic Books, 2010), pp. 1–17.

62   John Garrigus, 'Blue and Brown: Contraband Indigo and the Rise of a Free Colored Planter Class in French Saint-Domingue', *The Americas* 50, 2 (1993), p. 238.

63   Frederick Harold Smith, *Caribbean Rum: A Social and Economic History* (University Press of Florida, 2005), p. 21.

64   Jeaffreson, *A Young Squire*, pp. 269–70.

65   Nuala Zahedieh, *The Capital and the Colonies: London and the Atlantic Economy, 1660–1700* (Cambridge University Press, 2010), p. 259. For currency values, I used the 'real price' calculation of worth. See www.measuringworth.com/ukcompare/relativevalue.php

66   Wim Klooster, 'Communities of Port Jews and Their Contacts in the Dutch Atlantic World', *Jewish History*, vol. 20, no. 2, 2006, pp. 129–45.

67   David Armitage, 'The Cromwellian Protectorate and the Languages of Empire', *Historical Journal* 35, 3 (1992), p. 532.

68   J. Eric S. Thompson (ed.), *Thomas Gage's Travels in the New World* (Greenwood, 1981).

69   Quoted in Armitage, 'The Cromwellian Protectorate', p. 538.

70   Thomas Gage, 'Some Briefe and True Observations Concerning the West-Indies, Humbly Presented to His Highness, Oliver, Lord Protector of the Commonwealth of England, Scotland, and Ireland', in Thomas Birch (ed.) *A Collection of the State Papers of John Thurloe, Esq.* (1742), pp. 59–60.

71   C. H. Firth (ed.), *The Narrative of General Venables* (Longmans, Green, 1900), p. 29.

72   Ibid., p. 29.

73   Ibid., p. 35.

74   Armitage, 'The Cromwellian Protectorate', pp. 538–40.

75   Ibid., p. 542.

76   Klooster, 'Communities', p. 140.

77   Beeching, 'Introduction', p. 8.

78   Exquemelin, *The Buccaneers of America*, p. 49.

79   Ibid., p. 59.

80   Indeed, in Bluefields, now in Nicaragua, non-Spanish traditions persist, such as the month-long celebration around the maypole, a remnant of more English times.

81   Exquemelin, *The Buccaneers of America*, p. 114.

82   For money conversions see www.measuringworth.com/ukcompare/relativevalue.php

83   Exquemelin, *The Buccaneers of America*, p. 187.

84   Ibid., p. 200.

85   Ibid., p. 207.

86   William Dampier, *Voyages and Descriptions*, 2nd edn (1700), p. 208.

87   Biographical sketch from Diana and Michael Preston, *A Pirate of Exquisite Mind: Explorer, Naturalist, and Buccaneer: The Life of William Dampier* (Berkeley Publishing Group, 2004).

88   J. R. McNeill, *Mosquito Empires: Ecology and War in the Greater Caribbean, 1620–1914* (Cambridge University Press, 2010), p. 108.

89   Mann, *1493*.

90   See account in Matthew Parker, *Panama Fever: The Battle to Build the Canal* (Hutchinson, 2007).

91   McNeill, *Mosquito Empires*, pp. 113–15.

92   Ibid., p. 119. For currency calculation see www.measuringworth.com/ukcompare/relativevalue.php

93   Jesse Cromwell, 'Life on the Margins: (Ex) Buccaneers and Spanish Subjects on the Campeche Logwood Periphery, 1660–1716', *Itinerario* 33, 3 (2009), p. 47.

94   Dampier, *Voyages and Descriptions*, p. 218.

95   Ibid., p. 280.

96   Frank Griffith Dawson, 'William Pitt's Settlement at Black River on the Mosquito Shore: A Challenge to Spain in Central America, 1732–87', *Hispanic American Historical Review* 63, 4 (1983), p. 677. Unfortunately there is no evidence of the two Pitts ever meeting.

97   Cromwell, 'Life on the Margins', p. 43.

98   Dawson, 'William Pitt's Settlement', p. 680.

99   Ibid.

100   Ibid., p. 683.

101   Ibid., p. 684.

102   The National Archives, London (hereafter TNA), Colonial Office (CO)123/1, The Declaration of Edward King of Mosquito Indians in the Presence of God under the British Standard.

103   TNA CO/123/1, Letter to Captain Hodgson, 5 October 1749.

104   TNA CO/123/1, The First Account of the State of That Part of America Called the Mosquito Shore in the Year 1757, 30 August 1759.

105   Ibid.

106   Nigel O. Bolland, *The Formation of a Colonial Society: Belize, from Conquest to Crown Colony* (Johns Hopkins University Press, 1977), chapter 3.

107   Jennifer L. Anderson, 'Nature's Currency: The Atlantic Mahogany Trade and Commodification of Nature in the Eighteenth Century', *Early American Studies*, vol. 12 no. 1, Spring 2004, pp. 47–80.

108   Marcus Rediker. *Villains of All Nations: Atlantic Pirates in the Golden Age* (Verso, 2004), p. 10.

109   Ibid., p. 29.

Four – Sugar

1   The background on sugar for this section uses detail from from Toby Musgrave and Will Musgrave, *An Empire of Plants: People and Plants that Changed the World* (Cassell, 2000), chapter 2.

2   Frank Moya Pons, 'The Establishment of Primary Centres and Primary Plantations', in P. C. Emmer and Germán Damas Carrera (eds), *General History of the Caribbean*, vol. 2: *The Caribbean in the Long Sixteenth Century* (Unesco, 1999), pp. 66–7.

3   Bethencourt and Curto, *Portuguese Oceanic Expansion*, p. 25.

4   Moya Pons, 'The Establishment', pp. 66–7.

5   For a brief summary, see Matthew Parker, 'Barbados: Cavaliers of the Caribbean', *History Today* 61, 7 (2011), www.historytoday.com/matthew-parker/barbados-cavaliers-caribbean

6   Richard Ligon, *A True & Exact History of the Island of Barbados* (1657), pp. 2–22.

7   Ibid., p. 46.

8   Ibid., p. 85.

9   Quoted in Oldmixon, *The British Empire in America*, p. 7.

10   'A German Indentured Servant in Barbados in 1652: The Account of Heinrich von Uchteritz', *Journal of the Barbados Museum and History Society* 33, 3 (1970), pp. 92–3.

11   Oostindie and Paasman, 'Dutch Attitudes Towards Colonial Empire', p. 352.

12   *Curaçao Papers*, p. 145.

13   Hans Sloane, *A Voyage to the Islands Madera, Barbados, Nieves, S. Christophers and Jamaica* (1707), p. xiv.

14   This section is particularly indebted to the first part of Mann, *1493*.

15   See Chapter 3 in Mann, *1493*.

16   Ibid. and Reinaldo Funes Monzote, 'The Columbian Moment: Politics, Ideology, and Biohistory', in Palmié and Scarano, *The Caribbean*, p. 91.

17   Mann, *1493*.

18   Hilary McD. Beckles, 'The Economics of Transition to the Black Labor System in Barbados, 1630–1680', *Journal of Interdisciplinary History* 18, 2 (1987), pp. 227–8.

19   Ibid., p. 230.

20   Ibid., p. 242.

21   These calculations come from Voyages: The Trans-Atlantic Slave Trade Database, www.slavevoyages.org (accessed 4 March 2012). This accessible database is open to the public and is an excellent resource for anyone interested in the slave trade.

22   Beckles, 'The Economics of Transition', p. 226.

23   See Philip Morgan, 'Slavery in the British Caribbean', in David Eltis and

Stanley L. Engerman (eds), *The Cambridge World History of Slavery*, vol. 3: *AD 1420–AD 1804* (Cambridge University Press, 2011), p. 380; see also Matthew Parker, *The Sugar Barons* (Windmill, 2012).

24 Voyages: The Trans-Atlantic Slave Trade Database, www.slavevoyages.org

25 Edward Littleton, *The Groans of the Plantations: Or, A True Account of Their Grievous and Extreme Sufferings by the Heavy Impositions Upon Sugar, and Other Hardships Relating More Particularly to the Island of Barbados* (1698), p. 17.

26 Musgrave and Musgrave, *An Empire of Plants*, provides a clear description of the techniques.

27 Campbell, *Candid and Impartial Considerations on the Nature of the Sugar Trade* (1763), pp. 22–3.

28 Ibid., p. 26.

29 Littleton, *The Groans of the Plantations*, p. 23.

30 Ibid., p. 1.

31 Richard S. Dunn, 'The Barbados Census of 1680: Profile of the Richest Colony in English America', *William and Mary Quarterly*, vol. 26 no. 1 (Jan. 1969), p.4.

Five – The Rise of Slavery

1 Sloane, *A Voyage*, p. xlvii.

2 David Wheat, 'The First Great Waves: African Provenance Zones for the Transatlantic Slave Trade to Cartagena De Indias, 1570–1640', *Journal of African History* 52, 1 (2011), pp. 1–22.

3 See Peter Emmer, 'Slavery and the Slave Trade of the Minor Atlantic Powers', in Eltis and Engerman, *The Cambridge World History of Slavery*, vol. 3, pp. 457–9.

4 Curaçao Papers, pp. 109–11.

5 This section is indebted to Emmer, 'Slavery and the Slave Trade', p. 471.

6 Ibid.

7 His actions are said to have laid the foundation for the Johnkankus/ Junkanoo carnivalesque masquerades found among slave communities near Christmas in Jamaica, the Bahamas and coastal North Carolina and Virginia. See Emmer, 'Slavery and the Slave Trade', p. 471.

8 Voyages: The Trans-Atlantic Slave Trade Database, www.slavevoyages.org

9 Carl Wennerlind, *Casualties of Credit: The English Financial Revolution, 1620–1720* (Harvard University Press, 2011), p. 222.

10 John Thornton, *Africa and Africans in the Making of the Atlantic World* (Cambridge University Press, 1998), pp. 73–7.

11 Ibid., pp. 86–99.

12 This and the quotes that follow come from Paul Erdmann Isert, *Letters on*

West Africa and the Slave Trade: Paul Erdmann Isert's Journey to Guinea and the Caribbean Islands in Columbia (1788), trans. and ed. S. Axelrod Winsnes (Sub-Saharan Publishers, 2007), pp. 31–252.

13   Olaudah Equiano, *The Interesting Narrative of the Life of Olaudah Equiano, or Gustavus Vassa, the African. Written by Himself*, 9th edn (1794; originally published 1789).

14   Recent scholarship suggests Equiano may have been born in North America and invented his African past in order to lend weight to his tract. Even if that were the case – and the jury is still out – his story still represents the experiences of people he would have known and spoken to, and remains valid. See Vincent Carretta, *Equiano, the African: Biography of a Self-made Man* (University of Georgia Press, 2005.)

15   For this and the subsequent passages, see Equiano, *Interesting Narrative*, pp. 32–49.

16   Voyages: The Trans-Atlantic Slave Trade Database, www.slavevoyages.org

17   Mary Prince, *The History of Mary Prince: A West Indian Slave* (London, 1831), available at Project Gutenberg (2006), www.gutenberg.org/files/17851/17851-h/17851-h.htm (accessed 19 December 2012), p. 4.

18   B. W. Higman, 'The Development of Historical Disciplines in the Caribbean', in P. C. Emmer, B. W. Higman and Germán Carrera Damas (eds), *General History of the Caribbean*, vol. 6: *Methodology and Historiography of the Caribbean* (Unesco, 1999), p. 31–2.

19   Sloane, *A Voyage*, p. xlvii.

20   John Stewart. *An Account of Jamaica and Its Inhabitants by a Gentleman Long Resident in the West Indies* (Longman, Hurst, Rees, and Orme, 1808), p. 236.

21   Ibid., p. 247.

22   A discussion of slavery in the Iberian world should make reference to the Tannenbaum debate: see Frank Tannenbaum, *Slave and Citizen: The Negro in the Americas* (Knopf, 1946), in which he argues that the emancipation had a different tenor because the Iberian system of slavery had different contours to the French and British, for example the right of slaves to buy their freedom. Since the work's reception in 1946 it has been a subject of controversy, with his thesis falling in and out of fashion. See, for instance, Alejandro de la Fuente, 'Forum: What Can Frank Tannenbaum Still Teach Us About the Law of Slavery?', *Law and History Review* 22, 2 (2008), pp. 339–71.

23   For an English translation of the code, see http://chnm.gmu.edu/revolution/d/335/ (accessed 4 March 2012).

24   Gwendolyn Midlo Hall, *Social Control in Slave Plantation Societies: A Comparison of St. Domingue and Cuba* (Louisiana State University Press, 1996), p. 95.

25   St Bart's slave code (in French) can be found at Le Code Noir suédois de Saint-Barthélemy, www.memoirestbarth.com/st-barts/esclavage/archives-code-noir-suedois (accessed 19 December 2012).

26   See Morgan, 'Slavery in the British Caribbean', p. 390.

27 Malick W. Ghachem, 'Prosecuting Torture: The Strategic Ethics of Slavery in Pre-Revolutionary Saint-Domingue (Haiti)', *Law and History Review* 29, 4 (2011), p. 993.

28 For a full account see ibid., pp. 985–1029.

29 Ibid., p. 1003.

30 Prince, *A West Indian Slave*, p. 7.

31 Bryan Edwards, *The History, Civil and Commercial, of the British Colonies in the West Indies*, 2 vols, 1806 edn (1801), vol. 2, bk 4, pp. 203; 343–55.

32 Ibid., pp. 204–7.

33 Ibid, p. 209.

34 Kay Dian Kriz, *Slavery, Sugar, and the Culture of Refinement: Picturing the British West Indies, 1700–1840* (Yale University Press, 2008), pp. 37–8.

35 Ibid., p. 38.

36 See Morgan, 'Slavery in the British Caribbean', p. 392.

37 This passage is based on Guillaume Aubert, 'The Blood of France: Race and Purity of Blood in the French Atlantic World', *William and Mary Quarterly* 61, 3 (2004), pp. 446–55.

38 Garrigus, 'Blue and Brown', p. 247.

39 Ibid., p. 239.

40 This sketch of the Raimond family comes from ibid., pp. 248–51.

41 Matt D. Childs, *The 1812 Aponte Rebellion in Cuba and the Struggle against Atlantic Slavery* (University of North Carolina Press, 2006), pp. 18, 98–100.

42 Ibid., pp. 102–3.

43 Jane G. Landers, *Atlantic Creoles in the Age of Revolutions* (Harvard University Press, 2010), pp. 147–8.

44 Margarite Fernández Olmos and Lizabeth Paravisini-Gebert, *Sacred Possessions: Vodou, Santería, Obeah, and the Caribbean* (Rutgers University Press, 1997), p. 5.

45 Ibid., p. 12.

46 Edwards, *The History*, vol. 2, bk 4, p. 302.

47 Knox, *A Historical Account*, p. 78.

48 TNA CO 71/10, Governor Orde to Whitehall, 6 February 1786.

49 TNA CO 260/4, Valentine Morris to Lord George Germain, 25 March 1777.

50 Knox, *A Historical Account*, p. 69.

51 Ibid., p. 70.

52 Sloane, *A Voyage*, p. lvii.

53 Michel de Montaigne, 'Of the Cannibals', in Derek Hughes (ed.), *Versions of Blackness: Key Texts on Slavery from the Seventeenth Century* (Cambridge University Press, 2007), p. 288.

54 Ibid., p. 289.

55 John Locke, *Two Treatises of Government* (1821), pp. 205–8.

56 See, for instance James Farr, 'Locke, Natural Law, and New World Slavery', *Political Theory* 36, 4 (2008), pp. 495–552.

57 Locke, *Two Treatises*, p. 213.
58 On the subject of improvement, see Richard Drayton, *Nature's Government: Science, Imperial Britain, and the 'improvement' of the World* (Yale University Press, 2000).
59 T. Fiehrer, 'Slaves and Freedmen in Colonial Central America: Rediscovering a Forgotten Black Past', *Journal of Negro History* (1979), p. 53.
60 James H. Sweet, 'The Iberian Roots of American Racist Thought', *William and Mary Quarterly* 54, 1 (1997), p. 145.
61 Eric Williams, *Capitalism and Slavery* (University of North Carolina Press, 1944) 1994 edn, p. 7.
62 Sloane, *A Voyage*, p. lv.
63 David Eltis, Frank D. Lewis, and David Richardson. 'Slave Prices, the African Slave Trade, and Productivity in the Caribbean, 1674–1807', *Economic History Review* 58, 4 (2005), p. 678. For money conversions see www.measuringworth.com/ukcompare/relativevalue.php. I used the factor 'income value' in assessing the worth.
64 Ron Chernow, *Washington: A Life* (Penguin, 2010), p. 106.
65 Ibid.
66 Christopher J. Berry, *The Idea of Luxury: A Conceptual and Historical Investigation* (Cambridge University Press, 1994), p. xii.

Six – A World at War

1 As might be imagined, there are numerous versions of this tale – in some he brought the ear, in others he did not; the ear was in a box, the ear was in a jar, etc.
2 Edward Lawson, 'What Became of the Man Who Cut Off Jenkins' Ear?', *Florida Historical Quarterly* 37, 1 (1958), p. 33.
3 Ibid.
4 Ibid., p. 34.
5 Ibid., p. 35.
6 For a detailed account of the European power struggles during this period, see Brendan Simms, *Three Victories and a Defeat: The Rise and Fall of the First British Empire* (Basic Books, 2008).
7 Kathleen Wilson, 'Empire, Trade and Popular Politics in Mid-Hanoverian Britain: The Case of Admiral Vernon', *Past & Present* 121 (1988), p. 81.
8 Montesquieu, *The Spirit of the Laws*, ed. Anne Cohler, Basia Miller and Harold Stone (Cambridge University Press, 1989), p. 259.
9 Christopher Miller, *The French Atlantic Triangle: Literature and Culture of the Slave Trade* (Duke University Press, 2008), p. 65.
10 Montesquieu, *The Spirit of the Laws*, p. 263.

11 Miller, *The French Atlantic Triangle*, p. 66.

12 David Hume, *Political Essay*, ed. Knud Haakonssen (Cambridge University Press), 1994, p. 86.

13 Louis Jaucourt, 'Slave Trade', in *The Encyclopedia of Diderot & d'Alembert Collaborative Translation Project*, trans. Stephanie Noble (University of Michigan Library, 2007), http://hdl.handle.net/2027/spo.did2222.0000.114 (accessed 7 March 2103).

14 Ibid.

15 Adam Smith, *Lectures on Jurisprudence*, ed. R. L. Meek, D. D. Raphael, and P. G. Stein (Liberty Classics, 1982), p. 185.

16 Susan Buck-Morss, *Hegel, Haiti, and Universal History* (University of Pittsburgh Press, 2009), p. 85.

17 Montesquieu, *The Spirit of the Laws*, pp. 246–8.

18 Antonio Sánchez Valverde, *Idea del Valor de la Isla Española*, ed. Emilio Rodríguez Demorizi and Fray Cipriano de Utrera (Editora Nacional, 1971), pp. 33–4.

19 Jean Rhys, *Wide Sargasso Sea* (Penguin, 1997), p. 40.

20 Sankar Muthu, *Enlightenment against Empire* (Princeton University Press, 2003).

21 Adam Smith, *The Wealth of Nations* (Viking Penguin, 2000; originally published 1776), p. 138.

22 For an extensive explanation of the debate about luxury, see István Hont, 'The Early Enlightenment Debate on Commerce and Luxury', in Mark Goldie and Robert Wokler (eds), *The Cambridge History of Eighteenth-Century Political Thought* (Cambridge University Press, 2006), p. 379.

23 Jean-François Saint-Lambert, 'Luxury', in *Encyclopedia of Diderot & d'Alembert*.

24 Ibid.

25 Berry, *The Idea of Luxury*, pp. 155–6.

26 John Shovlin, *The Political Economy of Virtue: Luxury, Patriotism, and the Origins of the French Revolution* (Cornell University Press, 2007), pp. 5–6.

27 Montesquieu, *The Spirit of the Laws*, pp. 403–4.

28 José del Campillo y Cossío, *Nuevo sistema de gobierno económico para la América* (Madrid, 1798), p. 33.

29 Íñigo Abbad y Lasierra, *Historia geográfica, civil y natural de la isla de San Juan Bautista de Puerto Rico* (San Juan, 1971), p. 179.

30 Archivo General de Indias, Seville (hereafter AGI), Santo Domingo, legajo 2395 *Comisión dada al Mariscal de Casupo Don Alejandro Orreli para la vista de aquella Ysla*, 1765.

31 Douglas Salisbury (attrib.), *A Letter Addressed to Two Great Men, on the Prospect of Peace; And the Terms Necessary to Be Insisted Upon the Negociation*, 2nd edn (1760), p. 4; pp. 30–35.

32 Anon., *Remarks on the Letter Addressed to Two Great Men* (1760), p. 14.

33 Ibid., p. 17.

34 Douglas Hamilton, 'Rivalry, War and Imperial Reform in the 18th-century Caribbean', in Palmié and Scarano, *The Caribbean*, p. 265.

35 Sherry Johnson, *Climate and Catastrophe in Cuba and the Atlantic World in the Age of Revolution* (University of North Carolina Press, 2011), pp. 41–7.

36 Patrick Mackellar, *A Correct Journal of Landing His Majesty's Forces on the Island of Cuba* (1762).

37 McNeill, *Mosquito Empires*.

38 Cuban and British historians had long claimed some 10,700 slaves were brought in during the occupation, but later the figure was revised to 4,000. For more detail on this, see Steve Cushion, 'Using the Transatlantic Slave Database to Shed More Light on a Historiographical Debate' (paper delivered at the Society of Caribbean Studies annual conference, 2013, caribbeanstudies.org.uk).

39 Francisco López Segrera, 'Dependence, Plantation Economy, and Social Class, 1762–1902', in Manuel Moreno Fraginals, Frank Moya Pons, and Stanley L. Engerman (eds), *Between Slavery and Free Labor: The Spanish-speaking Caribbean in the Nineteenth Century* (Johns Hopkins University Press, 1985), p. 81.

40 Allan J. Kuethe, *Cuba, 1753–1815: Crown, Military, and Society* (University of Tennessee Press, 1986), pp. 33–8.

41 Ibid., pp. 68–9.

42 This section is based on the more extensive account in E. Rothschild, 'A Horrible Tragedy in the French Atlantic', *Past & Present* 192, 1 (2006), pp. 67–108.

43 Ibid., p. 76.

44 One of these would later be known as Devil's Island and turned into a penal colony.

45 Rothschild, 'A Horrible Tragedy', p. 77; on the issue of disease in the colony, see also McNeill, *Mosquito Empires*.

46 T. D. Allman, *Finding Florida: The True History of the Sunshine State* (Atlantic Monthly Press, 2013), pp. 52–3.

47 Andrew Jackson O'Shaughnessy, *An Empire Divided: The American Revolution and the British Caribbean* (University of Pennsylvania Press, 2000), p. 64.

48 Ibid., p. 81.

49 Musgrave, 'An Empire of Plants', p. 90.

50 Ibid., pp. 93–4.

51 O'Shaughnessy, 'An Empire Divided', p. 143.

52 Ibid., pp. 146–54.

53 Johnson, *Climate and Catastrophe*, p. 148.

54 See Mann, *1493*, chapter 3.

55 Dawson, 'William Pitt's Settlement', p. 698.

56 O'Shaughnessy. *An Empire Divided*, p. 213.

57 Janet Schaw, *Journal of a Lady of Quality, Being the Narrative of a Journey from Scotland to the West Indies, North Carolina, and Portugal, in the Years 1774 to 1776*, ed. Evangeline Walker Andrews and Charles McLean Andrews (University of Nebraska Press, 2005), pp. 135–7.

58 O'Shaughnessy, *An Empire Divided*, p. 214.

59 TNA CO 111/1, Edward Thompson to Lord George Germain, 22 April 1781. See www.measuringworth.com/ukcompare/relativevalue.php, using 'historic standard of living' calculation.

60 Hamilton, 'Rivalry, War and Imperial Reform', p. 268.

61 Ibid. According to Hamilton this tactic was later put to good use by Admiral Horatio Nelson during the Battle of Trafalgar. Also see O'Shaughnessy, *An Empire Divided*, pp. 226–37.

62 Maya Jasanoff, *Liberty's Exiles: American Loyalists in the Revolutionary World* (Knopf, 2011), pp. 6–8.

63 See Jasanoff, *Liberty's Exiles*, and Simon Schama, *Rough Crossings: Britain, the Slaves and the American Revolution* (HarperCollins, 2006).

64 TNA CO 71/10, Petition of His Majesty's faithful American subjects, 16 April 1786.

65 TNA CO 71/10, Alex Stewart and Thomas Beech to the King, 17 April 1786.

66 See Jasanoff, *Liberty's Exiles*, p. 272.

67 O'Shaughnessy, *An Empire Divided*, p. 238.

68 The following passage is taken from James Ramsay, *An Essay on the Treatment and Conversion of African Slaves in the British Sugar Colonies* (1784), pp. 62–114.

69 Ibid., p. 63.

70 Equiano, *Interesting Narrative*, p. 357.

71 For a fuller account see Schama, *Rough Crossings*, pp. 37–55.

72 Morgan, 'Slavery in the British Caribbean', p. 385.

73 T. Clarkson, *An Essay on the Impolicy of the African Slave Trade in Two Parts*, 2nd edn (1788), pp. 9–10.

74 William Fox, *An Address to the People of Great Britain, on the Consumption of West-India Produce* (1791), pp. 2–11.

75 For the following, see Anon., *A Vindication of the Use of Sugar, the Produce of the West India Islands* (London, 1792), pp. 8–21.

76 Blackburn, *The Making of New World Slavery*, p. 403; Voyages: The Trans-Atlantic Slave Trade Database, www.slavevoyages.org.

77 AGI, Santo Domingo, legajo 954, Commander Vicente to Joaquín García, 5 November 1790.

78 For an English translation see http://avalon.law.yale.edu/18th_century/rightsof.asp

79 John Lynch, *Bourbon Spain* (Basil Blackwell, 1993), pp. 378–9.

80   AGI, Caracas, 153, 27 January 1790.

81   Julien Raimond, *Observations on the Origin and Progression of the White Colonists' Prejudice against Men of Colour* (1791), quoted in Laurent Dubois and John D. Garrigus (eds), *Slave Revolution in the Caribbean, 1789–1804:*
A *Brief History with Documents* (Palgrave Macmillan, 2006), p. 80.

82   Médéric-Louis-Eli Moreau de Saint-Méry, *A Civilization that Perished: The Last Years of White Colonial Rule in Haiti*, ed. Ivor D. Spencer (University Press of America, 1985), p. 76.

83   Stewart R. King, *Blue Coat or Powdered Wig: Free People of Color in Pre-Revolutionary Saint Domingue* (University of Georgia Press, 2001), p. 42.

84   C. L. R. James, *The Black Jacobins: Toussaint L'Ouverture and the San Domingo Revolution* (Penguin, 2001; originally published 1938). p. 59. See also Laurent Dubois, *A Colony of Citizens: Revolution & Slave Emancipation in the French Caribbean, 1787–1804* (University of North Carolina Press, 2004) for more about the debates over slavery and *gens de couleur* in the National Assembly, and for events in the neighbouring French sugar island of Guadeloupe. Also see Carolyn E. Fick, *The Making of Haiti: The Saint Domingue Revolution from Below* (University of Tennessee Press, 1990).

85   Vincent Ogé to the Count de Peinier, 21 October 1790, quoted in Dubois and Garrigus, *Slave Revolution in the Caribbean*, p. 76.

86   Dubois and Garrigus, *Slave Revolution in the Caribbean*, p. 18.

87   AGI, Santo Domingo, legajo 1028, Pedro Catani to Floridablanca, 29 December 1790.

Seven – Haiti, or the Beginning of the End

1   This section quotes Baron de Wimpffen (Francis Alexander Stanislaus), *A Voyage to Saint Domingo, in the Years 1788, 1789, and 1790* (1817 translation; originally published 1797), p. 51.

2   Ibid., p. 108.

3   Ibid., p. 201.

4   Ibid., p. 206.

5   Ibid., pp. 216–17.

6   Ibid., pp. 111–12.

7   Ibid., pp. 265–6.

8   Ibid., p. 333.

9   There is a large degree of mystery over these events, as, for obvious reasons, there was no note-taker present. For a discussion of the date

of this event and the larger use of voodoo in the incitement in Saint-Domingue, see David Patrick Geggus, *Haitian Revolutionary Studies* (Indiana University Press, 2002); and Robin Blackburn, 'Haiti, Slavery, and the Age of Democratic Revolution', *William and Mary Quarterly*, 63, 4 (2006), pp. 643–74. Antonio Benítez-Rojo has argued that voodoo was an integral part of not only the start of the Haitian Revolution, but that it was the central ideological force that propelled and sustained the slaves' fight. See his work, *The Repeating Island* (Duke University Press, 2005), pp. 159–66. See also James, *Black Jacobins*, pp. 69–71, and Laurent Dubois, *Avengers of the New World: The Story of the Haitian Revolution* (Belknap Press of Harvard University Press, 2004), pp. 94–102.

10 TNA CO 37/43, no. 218, Council Chamber of Bermuda to Henry Hamilton, 17 January 1792.

11 TNA CO 71/20, Orde to Lord Grenville, 3 February 1791.

12 TNA CO 71/20, The Examination of Polinaire: A Free Mulatto Man, 7 February 1791, p. 2. Italics in original.

13 For more on this incident, see Honychurch, *The Dominica Story*, pp. 100–103.

14 TNA CO 71/20, Bertrand to Orde, 17 February 1791.

15 Honychurch, *The Dominica Story*, pp. 100–103.

16 TNA CO 71/20, Adjournment of the King's Bench, 1 March 1791.

17 AGI, Papeles de Cuba, legajo 1434, Juan Bautista Vaillant to Luis de las Casas, 20 August 1790.

18 Voyages: The Trans-Atlantic Slave Trade Database, www.slavevoyages.org

19 Althea De Parham (ed. and trans.), *My Odyssey: Experiences of a Young Refugee from Two Revolutions, by a Creole of Saint Domingue* (Louisiana State University Press, 1959).

20 Ibid., p. 32.

21 Herbert S. Klein, *Slavery in the Americas: A Comparative Study of Virginia and Cuba* (Oxford University Press, 1967), p. 217.

22 Conde de Floridablanca to Luis de las Casas, 26 November 1791, Archivo Nacional de Cuba (hereafter ANC), legajo 42, no. 7, Correspondencia de los Capitanes Generales, in José Luciano Franco (ed.), *Documentos para la historia de Haití en el Archivo Nacional* (Comisión Nacional de la Academia de Ciencias, 1954), p. 67.

23 For more on Toussaint Louverture, his leadership of Saint-Domingue and his historical depiction, see James, *Black Jacobins*; Sibylle Fischer, *Modernity Disavowed: Haiti and the Cultures of Slavery in the Age of Revolution* (Duke University Press, 2004); David Scott, *Conscripts of Modernity: The Tragedy of Colonial Enlightenment* (Duke University Press, 2004); Dubois, *Avengers of the New World*.

24 For more on the life of Georges Biassou, see Landers, *Atlantic Creoles*; on

Toussaint, see James, *Black Jacobins*; Dubois; *Avengers of the New World*; Madison Smartt Bell, *Toussaint Louverture* (Vintage, 2008).

25 AGI, Papeles de Cuba, 1434, 15 September 1792.

26 Francisco de Arango y Parreño, 'Discurso sobre la agricultura de la Habana y medios de fomentarla', in *Obras*, vol. 1 (1888), pp. 62–3.

27 Manuel Moreno Fraginals, *El Ingenio: El Complejo Economico Social Cubano del Azucar* (Editoral de Ciencias Sociales, 1978).

28 Francisco de Arango y Parreño, 'Representación hecha á S.M. con motivo de la sublevación de esclavos en los dominios franceses de la Isla de Santo Domingo', 20 November 1791, *Obras*, vol. 1 (1888), pp. 48–9.

29 Dale Tomich, 'The Wealth of Empire: Francisco Arango y Parreño, Political Economy, and the Second Slavery in Cuba', in Christopher Schmidt-Nowara and John M. Nieto-Phillips (eds), *Interpreting Spanish Colonialism: Empires, Nations, and Legends* (University of New Mexico Press, 2005).

30 Chernow, *Washington*, p. 710.

31 For more on the fate of the refugees who went to the US, see Ashli White, *Encountering Revolution: Haiti and the Making of the Early Republic* (Johns Hopkins University Press, 2010).

32 Ashli White, 'The Politics of "French Negros" in the United States', in Alyssa Goldstein Sepinwall, *Haitian History: New Perspectives* (Routledge, 2012), chapter 5.

33 For more on Guadeloupe see Dubois, *A Colony of Citizens*.

34 Geggus, *Haitian Revolutionary Studies*, p. 13.

35 De Parham, *My Odyssey*, p. 91.

36 David Patrick Geggus, *Slavery, War and Revolution: The British Occupation of Saint Domingue, 1793–1798* (Clarendon Press, 1982), pp. 105–8.

37 Geggus, *Haitian Revolutionary Studies*, p. 180.

38 Gabriel Esteban Debien, 'Les colons de Saint-Domingue réfugiés à Cuba 1793–1815', *Revista de Indias* 54–6 (1953), pp. 11–37. He argues that there was a first wave lasting until 1798, which was followed by an evacuation from 1798 to 1802, and a great exodus in 1803–4, and then another triggered by events of 1808.

39 William Walton, *Present State of the Spanish Colonies; Including a Particular Report of Hispañola, of the Spanish Part of Santo Domingo; With A General Survey of the Settlements on the South Continent of America* (1810), p. 187.

40 For a detailed account, see Geggus, *Haitian Revolutionary Studies*, pp. 179–203.

41 AGI, Caracas, legajo 153, 'Estado de población y agricultura', 1795.

42 They were later tricked into a deal, and 600 were sent to Nova Scotia. See Higman, *A Concise History*, p. 142.

43 Seymour Drescher, 'The Long Goodbye: Dutch Capitalism and Antislavery in Comparative Perspective', *American Historical Review* (1994), pp. 58–9.

44 Johanna von Grafenstein, *Nueva España en el circuncaribe, 1779–1808: revolución, competencia imperial y vínculos intercoloniales* (Universidad Nacional Autónoma de México, 1997), pp. 252–3; AGI, Caracas, legajo 426, Expediente sobre la sublevación de los Negros de Coro, 12 June 1795.

45 AGI, Estado, legajo 5A, no. 15, Luis de las Casas to Eugenio Llaguno, 18 August 1795. See also, David Geggus, 'Slave Resistance in the Spanish Caribbean', in *A Turbulent Time: The French Revolution and the Greater Caribbean* (Indiana University Press, 1997), pp. 133–6.

46 There would be numerous other conspiracies on the island blamed on the 'francés' of Saint-Domingue. See Guillermo A. Baralt, *Esclavos rebeldes: Conspiraciones y sublevaciones de esclavos en Puerto Rico (1795–1873)*, 2nd edn (Ediciones Huracán, 1985).

47 ANC, Asuntos Políticos, legajo 255, sig 29, Conde de Santa Clara, 28 January 1799.

48 See Geggus, 'Slave Resistance', pp. 145–9, for more on the different types of revolts.

49 The Black Caribs are thought to be the ancestors of the Garifuna people who live along the Caribbean coast of Central America. See Michael Craton, 'The Black Caribs of St Vincent', in Stanley Engerman and Robert Paquette (eds), *The Lesser Antilles in the Age of European Expansion* (University Press of Florida, 1996), pp. 71–84.

50 Geggus, *Slavery, War and Revolution*, p. 192.

51 Geggus, *Haitian Revolutionary Studies*, p. 22.

52 Marcus Rainsford, *A Memoir of Transactions That Took Place in St. Domingo, in the Spring of 1799* (1802), pp. 6–7; 22–9.

53 He soon followed that up with a more substantial history of the island in 1805, *An Historical Account of the Black Empire in Hayti*.

54 For a clear summary of this very complicated period, see chapter 3 of Jeremy Popkin, *A Concise History of the Haitian Revolution* (Wiley, 2011).

55 This was reported in the newspapers, including the *General Advertiser*, Philadelphia, 16 March 1801, www2.webster.edu/~corbetre/haiti/history/revolution/takes-dr.htm (accessed 12 March 2013).

56 AGI, Santo Domingo, legajo 1039, Juan Gonzales Ferino and Juan de Lauastida to Miguel Cayetano Soler, 13 March 1801.

57 AGI, Caracas, legajo 148, Migares to Antonio Cornél, 24 February 1801.

58 AGI, Caracas, legajo 148, Suplica of Pedro Sánchez Valverde, 21 March 1801.

59 Ibid.

60 Haiti: The 1801 Constitution (English translation), The Louverture Project, Haitian Constitution of 1801, last updated 11 October 2007, http://thelouvertureproject.org/index.php?title=Haitian_Constitution_of_1801_(English) (accessed 10 March 2013). On the issue of Haitian constitutions, see Julia Gaffield, 'Complexities of Imagining Haiti: A

Study of National Constitutions, 1801–1807', *Journal of Social History*, 41, 1 (2007), pp. 81–103.

61   Grafenstein, *Nueva España*, p. 205.

62   Frank Moya Pons, 'The Land Question in Haiti and Santo Domingo: The Sociopolitical Context of the Transition from Slavery to Free Labour, 1801–1843', in Moya Pons, Fraginals and Engerman, *Between Slavery and Free Labour*, p. 188.

63   Philippe Girard, 'Jean-Jacques Dessalines and the Atlantic System: A Reappraisal', *William and Mary Quarterly* 69, 3 (2012), p. 557.

64   Philippe Girard, 'Black Talleyrand: Toussaint Louverture's Diplomacy, 1798–1802', *William and Mary Quarterly* 66, 1 (2009), p. 93.

65   *English Poetry II: From Collins to Fitzgerald*. The Harvard Classics (P. F. Collier & Son, 1909–14), vol. 41; available at www.bartleby.com/41/ (accessed 22 December 2012).

66   McNeill, *Mosquito Empires*, p. 258.

67   Jasanoff, *Liberty's Exiles*, p. 273.

68   Lady Nugent, *Lady Nugent's Journal* (Institute of Jamaica, 1939).

69   Ibid., p. 242.

70   Quoted in Geggus, *Haitian Revolutionary Studies*, p. 27.

71   Haiti 1805 Constitution, www.webster.edu/~corbetre/haiti/history/earlyhaiti/1805-const.htm (accessed 13 March 2013).

72   'American Papers', *The Times*, 11 July 1806.

73   Data from Voyages: The Trans-Atlantic Slave Trade Database, www.slavevoyages.org. It should also be noted that the database puts 'Danish/Baltic' together.

74   AGI, Estado, legajo 2, exp 43, Marqués de Someruelos to Pedro Ceballos, 20 December 1803; Emilio Bacardí y Moreau, *Crónicas de Santiago de Cuba* (Carbonell y Esteva, 1909), p. 45.

75   Debien, 'Les colons de Saint-Domingue', pp. 11–37.

76   Bacardí y Moreau, *Crónicas*, p. 46.

77   ANC, Asuntos Políticos, legajo 255, sig 36, Sebastián Kindelán, 7 July 1803.

78   Josep Maria Fradera, *Colonias para después de un imperio* (Barcelona, 2005), p. 705; Fraginals, *El Ingenio*.

79   Archivo General de Puerto Rico (hereafter AGPR), Fondo Gobernadores Españoles, Asuntos Políticos y Civiles, caja 174, Toribio Montes, 8 August 1808.

80   AGI, Santo Domingo, legajo 1042, Proclamation, General Louis Ferrand, 9 August 1808.

81   AGI, Santo Domingo, legajo 1042, Juan Sánchez Ramírez, 'Diario de las operaciones practicadas para la reconquista de la parte española de Santo Domingo', May 1808.

82   Moya Pons, *The Dominican Republic*, p. 114.

83　C. Armando Rodríguez (trans.), *Diario histórico (guerra domínico-francesa de 1808) por Gilbert Guillermin* (Santo Domingo, 1938), p. 60.

84　AGI, Santo Domingo, legajo 1042, Juan Sánchez Ramírez, March 1809.

85　Ibid.

86　Walton, *Present State*, p. 255.

87　Bacardí y Moreau, *Crónicas*, pp. 56–7.

88　Thomas Jefferson to James Madison, 19 April 1809, Library of Congress, Jefferson papers, http://memory.loc.gov/ammem/collections/jefferson_papers/ (accessed 10 March 2013).

89　ANC Cuba, Asuntos Políticos, legajo 142, no. 108, Lieutenant Governor of Holguín to Governor, 7 September 1808.

90　Debien, 'Les colons de Saint-Domingue', p. 18.

91　Archivo Histórico Provincial de Santiago de Cuba, Protocolos Notariales Escribanos de Santiago de Cuba; Escribanes Giro, no. 240, 15 and 24 April 1809.

92　ANC, Asuntos Políticos, legajo 255, sig 41, Sebastián Kindelán, 10 April 1809.

93　Fraginals, *El Ingenio*, p. 41.

94　Alexander von Humboldt, *The Island of Cuba: A Political Essay* (Princeton University Press, 2001), pp. 166, 198.

95　Alexander von Humboldt, *Personal Narrative of Travels to the Equinoctial Regions of the New Continent During the Years 1799–1804*, vol. 7 (Longman, 1829), p. 8.

96　Ibid., p. 12.

97　Ibid., pp. 163–4.

98　Ibid., p. 16.

99　Ibid., pp. 100–104.

100　John Huxtable Elliott, *Empires of the Atlantic World: Britain and Spain in America, 1492–1830* (Yale University Press, 2006), see chapter 12.

101　See, for instance, James F. King, 'The Colored Castes and American Representation in the Cortes of Cadiz', *Hispanic American Historical Review* 33, 1 (1953), pp. 33–64; Marixa Lasso, *Myths of Harmony: Race and Republicanism During the Age of Revolution, Colombia, 1795–1831* (University of Pittsburgh Press, 2007); Mario Rodriguez, *The Cádiz Experiment in Central America, 1808 to 1826* (University of California Press, 1978).

102　Quoted in King, 'The Colored Castes', p. 41.

103　Ibid., see footnote 14 in the article.

104　Lasso, *Myths of Harmony*, pp. 42–3.

105　*Diario de las discusiones y actas de las Cortes*, 2 April 1811, vol. 4, p. 439.

106　Ibid., p. 443.

107　Ibid., pp. 444–5.

108　Expediente, 18 March 1812, in *El proceso abolicionista en Puerto Rico: documentos para su estudio* (University of Puerto Rico, 1974), pp. 125–56.

109   Childs, *The 1812 Aponte Rebellion*, pp. 2–4. See Childs's book for a comprehensive account of events and testimony surrounding the rebellion. Also see the first chapter of Sibylle Fischer, *Modernity Disavowed*, for an examination of the trial of Aponte and the larger meanings of his book.

110   Voyages: The Trans-Atlantic Slave Trade Database, www.slavevoyages. org/, accessed 10 March 2013.

111   Raymond A. Mohl, 'A Scotsman in Cuba, 1811–1812', *The Americas* 29, 2 (1972), pp. 235–6.

Eight – Cuba and the Contradictions of Freedom

1   AGPR, Fondo Gobernadores Españoles, Asuntos Políticos y Civiles, caja 174, Real Cédula, 10 August 1815.

2   Voyages: The Trans-Atlantic Slave Trade Database, www.slavevoyages.org/

3   Kenneth F. Kiple, *Blacks in Colonial Cuba, 1774–1899* (University of Florida Press, 1976), p. 3.

4   George Dawson Flinter, *An Account of the Present State of the Island of Puerto Rico* (1834), p. 206.

5   Pablo Tornero Tinajero, *Crecimiento económico y transformaciones sociales: esclavos, hacendados y comerciantes en la Cuba colonial (1760–1840)* (Ministerio de Trabajo y Seguridad Social, 1996), p. 174.

6   Manuel Barcia Paz, *Seeds of Insurrection: Domination and Resistance on Western Cuban Plantations, 1808–1848* (Louisiana State University Press, 2008), p. 34.

7   Midlo Hall, *Social Control*, pp. 55–6.

8   Luis Diaz Soler, *Historia de la esclavitud negra en Puerto Rico* (University of Puerto Rico, 1965), p. 213.

9   Paul Verna, *Petión y Bolívar: cuarenta años (1790–1830) de relaciones haitiano-venezolanos y su aporte a la emancipación de Hispanoamérica* (Ministerio de Educación [Venezuela], 1969), p. 92.

10   Ibid., p. 94.

11   Ibid., p. 148.

12   Grafenstein, *Nueva España*, p. 238.

13   'A Letter by Simón Bolívar', trans. Lewis Bertrand, in *Selected Writings of Bolivar* (The Colonial Press, 1951), http:// faculty.smu.edu/bakewell/ BAKEWELL/texts/jamaica-letter.html (accessed 13 March 2013).

14   William F. Lewis, 'Simón Bolívar and Xavier Mina: A Rendezvous in Haiti', *Journal of Inter-American Studies* 11, 3 (1969), p. 461.

15   Alexandre Pétion to Simón Bolívar, 18 February 1816 quoted in Verna, *Pétion y Bolívar*, p. 537.

16 Simón Bolívar to Alexandre Pétion, 4 September 1816, quoted in Lewis, 'Simón Bolívar and Xavier Mina', p. 460.

17 For more on this period see, John Lynch, *Simón Bolívar: A Life* (Yale University Press, 2006), pp. 97–102.

18 Quoted ibid., p. 109. The issue of manumission would plague Bolívar for many years. Even after mandating manumission in 1821, further decrees were issued in 1823, 1827, and 1828 due to pro-slavery groups ignoring previous laws. See Harold A. Bierck, Jr, 'The Struggle for Abolition in Gran Colombia', *Hispanic American Historical Review* 33, 3 (1953), p. 367.

19 Charles Wilson Hackett, 'The Development of John Quincy Adam's Policy with Respect to an American Confederation', *Hispanic American Historical Review* 8, 4 (1928), p. 514.

20 John Quincy Adams, 'State of the Union Address to US Congress', 6 December 1825, www.ushistory.org/documents/monroe.htm (accessed 22 May 2010).

21 On the issue of wider public reaction, see Frances L. Reinhold, 'New Research on the First Pan-American Congress Held at Panama in 1826', *Hispanic American Historical Review* 18, 3 (1938), pp. 342–63.

22 Ralph Sanders, 'Congressional Reaction in the United States to the Panama Congress of 1826', *The Americas* 11, 2 (1954), p. 143.

23 Ibid., p. 144.

24 Anon., *Spanish America: Observations on the Instructions Given By the President of the United States of America to the Representatives of That Republic, At the Congress Held At Panama in 1826* (1829), pp. 59–60.

25 Moya Pons, 'The Land Question in Haiti and Santo Domingo', pp. 182–4.

26 Thomas Clarkson to Baron Turik Lecisos, 11 March 1820, Letter no. 160, Fold 6, Thomas Clarkson Papers, St John's College, Cambridge.

27 Arthur O. White, 'Prince Saunders: An Instance of Social Mobility Among Antebellum New England Blacks', *Journal of Negro History* 60, 4 (1975), pp. 527–8.

28 Ibid.

29 Prince Saunders, *Haytian Papers: A Collection of the Very Interesting Proclamations and Other Official Documents; Together with Some Account of the Rise, Progress, and Present State of the Kingdom of Hayti* (1816).

30 White, 'Prince Saunders', p. 530.

31 Ibid., p. 532.

32 Ibid., p. 534.

33 AGI, legajo 970, Jean-Pierre Boyer to Sebastián Kindelán, 22 December 1820.

34 Emilio Rodríguez Demorizi, *Santo Domingo y la Gran Colombia* (Academia Dominicana de la Historia, 1971), p. 53.

35 Victor Bulmer-Thomas, *The Economic History of the Caribbean Since the Napoleonic Wars* (Cambridge University Press, 2012), p. 551.

36 Loring Daniel Dewey, *Correspondence Relative to the Immigration to Hayti of the Free People of Colour* (1824), p. 8.
37 White, 'Prince Saunders', p. 534.
38 John Candler, *Brief Notices of Hayti: With Its Condition, Resources, and Prospects* (T. Ward & Co., 1842), p. 6.
39 Ibid., pp. 26–7.
40 Ibid., p. 38.
41 Ibid., p. 83.
42 Ibid., pp. 90–105.
43 John Quincy Adams to Hugh Nelson, Washington, 28 April 1823, in Worthington Chauncey Ford (ed.), *Writings of John Quincy Adams*, vol. 7 (Norwood Press, 1917), pp. 374–5.
44 Ibid.
45 James Monroe, 'Seventh Annual Message to Congress', 2 December 1823, www.ushistory.org/documents/monroe.htm (accessed 22 May 2013).
46 Eleazar Córdova-Bello, *La independencia de Haití y su influencia en hispanoamérica* (Instituto Panamericano de Geografía e Historia, 1967), p. 151.
47 ANC, Primera pieza de la causa por la Conspiración de los Soles de Bolívar, quoted in Roque E. Garrigó, *Historia documentada de la conspiración de los Soles y rayos de Bolívar* (A. Muñiz and Bros, 1927), p. 170.
48 Josep Maria Fradera, *Colonias para después de un imperio* (Edicions Bellaterra, 2005), p. 56.
49 Francisco Morales Padrón, 'Conspiraciones y masonería en Cuba (1810–1826)', *Anuario de Estudios Americanos* 29 (1972), pp. 375–7.
50 AGI, Estado, legajo 96, no. 108, Conde de la Alcudia to Manuel González Salmón, 22 August 1828.
51 William Manning, *Diplomatic Correspondence of the United States Concerning the Independence of the Latin-American Nations* (Oxford University Press, 1925), pp. 230–31.
52 Robert Francis Jameson, *Letters from the Havana, During the Year 1820, Containing an Account of the Present State of the Island of Cuba, and Observations on the Slave Trade* (John Miller, 1821), p. 19.
53 Ibid.
54 Eric Williams, 'The British West Indian Slave Trade After Its Abolition in 1807', *Journal of Negro History* 27, 2 (1942), p. 178.
55 Meredith A. John, 'Communications: The Smuggled Slaves of Trinidad, 1813', *Historical Journal* 31, 2 (1988), p. 365.
56 Ibid., p. 371.
57 Gert Oostindie, '"British Capital, Industry and Perseverance" Versus Dutch "Old School"?: The Dutch Atlantic and the Takeover of Berbice, Demerara and Essquibo, 1750–1815', *Low Countries Historical Review* 127, 4

(2012), p. 35; Voyages: The Trans-Atlantic Slave Trade Database, www.slavevoyages.org

58 Michael Craton, 'Proto-Peasant Revolts? The Late Slave Rebellions in the British West Indies 1816–1832', *Past & Present* 85 (1979), pp. 101–2.

59 Ibid., pp. 103–4.

60 Knox, *A Historical Account*, p. 95.

61 See the excellent digital resource Legacies of British Slave-ownership to follow where the compensation money went: www.ucl.ac.uk/lbs/project/ (accessed 21 August 2013).

62 T. J. Barringer, Gillian Forrester, and Barbaro Martinez-Ruiz, *Art and Emancipation in Jamaica: Isaac Mendes Belisario and His Worlds* (Yale Center for British Art in association with Yale University Press, 2007), pp. 72–3.

63 Selwyn H. H. Carrington, *The Sugar Industry and the Abolition of the Slave Trade, 1775–1810* (University Press of Florida, 2003), pp. 284–6.

64 Parker, *The Sugar Barons*, p. 363.

65 Aline Helg, *Liberty & Equality in Caribbean Colombia, 1770–1835* (University of North Carolina Press, 2004), pp. 152–61.

66 Marixa Lasso, 'Haiti as an Image of Popular Republicanism in Caribbean Colombia Cartagena Province (1811–1828)', in David Geggus (ed.), *The Impact of the Haitian Revolution in the Atlantic World* (University of South Carolina Press, 2001), p. 183.

67 Knox, *A Historical Account*, p. 114.

68 Ibid., p. 115.

69 Calculated at www.measuringworth.com.

70 Rodrigo Lazo, *Writing to Cuba: Filibustering and Cuban Exiles in the United States* (University of North Carolina Press, 2005), p. 3.

71 Anon., *Filibustiero: A Life of General Lopez, and History of the Late Attempted Revolution in Cuba* (1851), p. 3.

72 Ibid.

73 Ibid., p. 4.

74 From Cuban Filibuster Movement, www.latinamericanstudies.org/ filibusters.htm (accessed 30 March 12).

75 Robert E. May, *The Southern Dream of a Caribbean Empire, 1854–1861* (Louisiana State University Press, 1973), p. 23.

76 Lazo, *Writing to Cuba*, p. 5.

77 May, *The Southern Dream*, p. 79.

78 See Stephen Dando-Collins, *Tycoon's War: How Cornelius Vanderbilt Invaded a Country to Overthrow America's Most Famous Military Adventurer* (Da Capo Press, 2009).

79 Ibid., p. 251.

80 *Harper's New Monthly Magazine*, quoted in Amy S. Greenberg, 'A Gray-Eyed Man: Character, Appearance, and Filibustering', *Journal of the Early Republic* 20, 4 (2000), pp. 674–83.

81　Charles Swett, *A Trip to British Honduras, and to San Pedro, Republic of Honduras* (1868), pp. 5–25.

82　Ibid., pp. 121–3.

83　'Proclamations of Col. Alexander McDonald, Superintendent of British Honduras on the Settlement of the Colony of British Honduras', National Library of Jamaica, MS 825, 2 November 1840.

84　Archibald Robertson Gibbs, *British Honduras: An Historical and Descriptive Account of the Colony from Its Settlement, 1670* (Low, 1883), p. 117.

85　Ibid., pp. 158–9.

86　It would go on in that status until 1860, then there was a Miskito Reserve until 1894, then an Incorporated Reserve until 1905, and then it became part of Nicaragua.

87　Trollope, *The West Indies*, p. 115.

88　Ibid., p. 116.

89　For an account of this period and the corresponding debates, see Nicholas Guyatt, 'America's Conservatory: Race, Reconstruction, and the Santo Domingo Debate', *Journal of American History* 97, 4 (2011), pp. 974–1000.

90　James Redpath (ed.), *Guide to Hayti* (1861), p. 5.

91　Ibid., p. 64.

92　Dubois, *Avengers of the New World*, chapter 4.

93　Philip Magness, 'The Île à Vache: From Hope to Disaster', *New York Times*, 12 April 2013, http://opinionator.blogs.nytimes.com/2013/04/12/the-le-vache-from-hope-to-disaster/

94　George Staunton, *An Authentic Account of An Embassy from the King of Great Britain to the Emperor of China: Taken Chiefly from the Papers of His Excellency the Earl of Macartney*, vol. 1 (London, 1797), p. 21.

95　Ibid., p. 21.

96　Ibid., p. 527.

97　Julia Lovell, *The Opium War: Drugs, Dreams, and the Making of China* (Picador, 2011), p. 3.

98　Ibid., p. 23.

99　Ibid.

100　Ibid., p. 2.

101　Edward Brown, *Cochin-China, and My Experience of It* (1861), pp. 42–3.

102　Susan Campbell, 'Carnival, Calypso, and Class Struggle in Nineteenth Century Trinidad', *History Workshop* 26 (1998), p. 4.

103　Ibid., p. 5.

104　Ibid., p. 6.

105　Higman, *A Concise History*, p. 171.

106　Thomas Hancock, *Are the West India Colonies to Be Preserved? A Few Plain Facts* (1840), p. 6.

107　Ibid., p. 8.

108　See Capt. & Mrs Swinton, *Journal of a Voyage with Coolie Emigrants from Calcutta to Trinidad* (1859), pp. 3–15.

109　TNA CO 318/165. Controlling Indian Emigration to Jamaica, British Guiana and Trinidad, 16 November 1844.

110　Rosemarijn Hoefte, 'A Passage to Suriname? The Migration of Modes of Resistance by Asian Contract Laborers', *International Labor and Working-Class History* 54, Fall (1998), pp. 19–39.

111　Stanley Engerman, 'Contract Labor, Sugar, and Technology in the Nineteenth Century', *Journal of Economic History* 43, 3 (1983), p. 642.

112　Ibid., p. 645.

113　Joseph Dorsey, 'Identity, Rebellion, and Social Justice Among Chinese Contract Workers in Nineteenth-Century Cuba', *Latin American Perspectives* 31, 3 (2004), p. 21.

114　Ibid.

115　*Immigration: A Series of Articles Upon the Benefits of Indian Immigration to Trinidad* (Mole Bros, 1893), pp. 4–5.

116　Ibid., p. 6.

117　Ibid., p. 7.

118　Alan L. Karras, *Smuggling: Contraband and Corruption in World History* (Rowman & Littlefield, 2010), p. 99.

119　Honychurch, *The Dominica Story*, pp. 127–8.

120　*Anti-Slavery Reporter*, London, 1865; see also Gad Heuman, *The Killing Time: The Morant Bay Rebellion in Jamaica* (Macmillan, 1994); B. A. Knox, 'The British Government and the Governor Eyre Controversy, 1865–1875', *Historical Journal* 19, 4 (1976), pp. 877–900; Gillian Workman, 'Thomas Carlyle and the Governor Eyre Controversy: An Account With Some New Material', *Victorian Studies* 18 (1974), pp. 77–102.

121　Eltis, Lewis, and Richardson, 'Slave Prices', p. 678.

122　Leslie Bethell, *Cuba: A Short History* (Cambridge University Press, 1993), p. 16.

123　Tornero Tinajero, *Crecimiento económico*, p. 390.

124　David Eltis, *Economic Growth and the Ending of the Transatlantic Slave Trade* (Oxford University Press, 1987), p. 284; see www.measuringworth.com for calculations.

125　Jameson, *Letters from the Havana*, p. 39.

126　Trollope, *The West Indies*, pp. 147–8.

127　Voyages: The Trans-Atlantic Slave Trade Database, www.slavevoyages.org

128　Midlo Hall, *Social Control*, p. 132.

129　Ibid., p. 133.

130　David R. Murray, *Odious Commerce: Britain, Spain and the Abolition of the Cuban Slave Trade* (Cambridge University Press, 1980), p. 273.

131　Bethell, *Cuba*, p. 16.

132　Voyages: The Trans-Atlantic Slave Trade Database, www.slavevoyages.org

133 Bethell, *Cuba*, p. 27.
134 José Martí, *Our America: Writings on Latin America and the Struggle for Cuban Independence*, ed. Philip Foner, trans. Elinor Randall (Monthly Review Press, 1977), pp. 312–13.
135 Bethell, *Cuba*, p. 28.
136 Martí, *Our America*, p. 26.

Nine – Banana Wars and Global Battles

1 'The Korona Brings Roraima Survivors', *New York Times*, 21 May 1902.
2 Ibid.
3 Ibid.
4 Ibid.
5 Ibid.
6 Stephen J. Randall, Graeme S. Mount, and David Bright, *The Caribbean Basin: An International History* (Routledge, 1998), p. 37.
7 'The Platt Amendment', in C. I. Bevans (ed.), *Treaties and Other International Agreements of the United States of America, 1776–1949*, vol. 8 (United States Government Printing Office, 1971), pp. 1116–17; www.fordham.edu/halsall/mod/1901platt.asp (accessed 16 March 2013).
8 Theodore Roosevelt, Fourth Annual Message to Congress, 6 December 1904, www.presidency.ucsb.edu/ws/index.php?pid=29545 (accessed 16 March 2013).
9 Cesar J. Ayala, 'The American Sugar Kingdom, 1898–1934', in Palmié and Scarano, *The Caribbean*, p. 435; J. H. Galloway, 'Botany in the Service of Empire: The Barbados Cane-Breeding Program and the Revival of the Caribbean Sugar Industry, 1880s–1930s', *Annals of the Association of American Geographers* 86, 4 (1996), p. 682.
10 Galloway, 'Botany', p. 684.
11 César J. Ayala, *American Sugar Kingdom: The Plantation Economy of the Spanish Caribbean, 1989–1934* (University of North Carolina Press), 2003, p. 5.
12 Ibid., p. 30.
13 For an examination of this period, see Jorge Renato Ibarra Guitart, *El Tratado Anglo-Cubano de 1905* (Editorial de Ciencias Sociales, 2006).
14 Aline Helg, *Our Rightful Share: The Afro-Cuban Struggle for Equality, 1886–1912* (University of North Carolina Press, 1995), p. 2.
15 Ibid., p. 225; Bethell, *Cuba*, p. 44.
16 Walter Rodney, *A History of the Guyanese Working People, 1881–1905* (Johns Hopkins University Press, 1981), pp. 190–96.
17 This article marks the 100th anniversary of this event, and its connection

to the present: www.stabroeknews.com/2013/features/in-the-diaspora/03/11/fatally-policed-protest-the-1913-rose-hall-uprising/

18 Rutherford B. Hayes: 'Special Message', 8 March 1880. See The American Presidency Project by Gerhard Peters and John T. Woolley, online at www.presidency.ucsb.edu/ws/?pid=68534 (accessed 21 August 2013).

19 Randall, Mount, and Bright, The Caribbean Basin, p. 39.

20 Ibid.

21 Ibid., p. 41.

22 For more on Panama and Barbados see Hilary McD. Beckles, A History of Barbados, 2nd edn (Cambridge University Press, 2006), pp. 208–11.

23 TNA CO 137/648, Edward Hudson to Claude Mallet, 11 November 1905.

24 Investigations of Panama Canal Matters: Hearings Before the Committee on Interoceanic Canals of the United States Senate, 4 vols (US Government Printing Office, 1908), vol. 1, p. 932.

25 TNA CO 137/648, Mallet to Lansdowne, 6 May 1905.

26 TNA CO 137/648, Mallet to Lansdowne, 9 May 1905.

27 Investigations of Panama Canal Matters, p. 52.

28 Ibid., p. 53.

29 Beckles, A History of Barbados, pp. 208–11.

30 Colin Grant, Negro with a Hat: The Rise and Fall of Marcus Garvey (Oxford University Press, 2011), p. 31.

31 John Soluri, 'Banana Cultures: Linking the Production and Consumption of Export Bananas, 1800–1980', in Steve Striffler and Mark Moberg (eds), Banana Wars: Power, Production, and History in the Americas (Duke University Press, 2003), p. 49.

32 Jason M. Colby, The Business of Empire: United Fruit, Race, and U.S. Expansion in Central America (Cornell University Press, 2011), p. 108.

33 'The Trade in Bananas', New York Times, 7 May 1882.

34 Frances Emery-Waterhouse, Banana Paradise (Stephen-Paul Publishers, 1947), p. 12.

35 Colby, The Business of Empire, p. 4.

36 See John Gallagher and Ronald Robinson, 'The Imperialism of Free Trade', Economic History Review 6, 1 (1953), pp. 1–15.

37 Nigel O. Bolland, 'Labour Protests, Rebellions, and the Rise of Nationalism during Depression and War', in Palmié and Scarano', The Caribbean, p. 465.

38 Barry Carr, 'Identity, Class, and Nation: Black Immigrant Workers, Cuban Communism, and the Sugar Insurgency, 1925–1934', Hispanic American Historical Review 78, 1 (1998), p. 90.

39 Ibid., p. 93.

40 Emery-Waterhouse, Banana Paradise, p. 12.

41 Colby, The Business of Empire, p. 126.

42 Ibid., p. 163.

43 Laura T. Raynolds, 'The Global Banana Trade', in Striffler and Moberg, *Banana Wars*, p. 27.

44 Ibid., p. 27.

45 'Siquirres Notes', Limón *Times*, 27 April 1911, in Robert A. Hill (ed.), *The Marcus Garvey and Universal Negro Improvement Association Papers: The Caribbean Diaspora, 1910–1920* (Duke University Press, 2011), p. 26.

46 Grant, *Negro with a Hat*, pp. 53–4.

47 Colby, *The Business of Empire*, p. 133.

48 Ibid., p. 122.

49 Quoted in Colby, *The Business of Empire*, p. 123.

50 TNA Cabinet papers (CAB)/24/125, 'A Monthly Review of Revolutionary Movements in British Dominions Overseas and Foreign Countries', 31 May 1921.

51 TNA CAB/24/89, 'Unrest Among the Negros', 7 October 1919.

52 Grant, *Negro with a Hat*, p. 2.

53 Nigel O. Bolland, *On the March: Labour Rebellions in the British Caribbean, 1934–9* (Ian Randle, 1995), pp. 27–8.

54 Ibid.

55 Ibid., p. 28.

56 Eric Jennings, 'Monuments to Frenchness? The Memory of the Great War and the Politics of Guadeloupe's Identity, 1914–1945', *French Historical Studies* 21, 4 (1998), p. 562.

57 US National Archives and Records Administration (hereafter NARA), Records of the Government of the Virgin Islands of the United States, 1917, RG55, 'Virgin Islands of the United States: general conditions, 1 August 1917'.

58 NARA RG59 844D.014/8, 'Not For Sale', *Daily Gleaner*, 10 July 1933.

59 Bethell, *Cuba*, p. 47.

60 Ayala, 'The American Sugar Kingdom', p. 442.

61 Bolland, 'Labour Protests', p. 463.

62 Ibid., p. 461.

63 Ibid.

64 Bolland, *On the March*, p. 27.

65 Randall, Mount, and Bright, *The Caribbean Basin*, p. 65.

66 Bolland, *On the March*, pp. 44–6.

67 NARA RG59 844C.504/1, 'Subversive movements in the British West Indies', 30 November 1935.

68 Barbados National Archives (hereafter BNA) GH/4/52, 'Position of British West Indians in Central and South American Countries', July 1933.

69 TNA FO 288/204, 'Draft confidential letter from J Crosby, British Legation to the Hon Marquis of Reading', 8 September 1931.

70 Ibid.

71 BNA GH/4/89, Josiah Crosby, British Legation, Panama, 15 June 1933.

72 BNA GH/4/89, Letter to Governor Young from St Lucia, 10 November 1935.

73 Bolland, *On the March*, pp. 70–72.

74 NARA RG59 844C.504/1, 'Subversive Movements in the British West Indies', 30 November 1935.

75 Bolland, *On the March*, p. 58.

76 NARA RG59 844D.504/10, George Alexander Armstrong to US Secretary of State, 19 April 1935.

77 BNA GH/4/60, Letter from Guiana to Governor Young, 25 September 1933.

78 Bolland, *On the March*, p. 112.

79 TNA CO 28/325/12, E. J. Waddington, 'The Necessity for Emigration from Barbados', 27 October 1939.

80 Ibid.

81 Bolland, *On the March*, p. 129.

82 '1000 Labourers Halt Tate and Lyle in Westmoreland', *Daily Gleaner*, 2 May 1938, p. 1.

83 '4 Dead! 9 In Hospital!! 89 in Jail!!', *Daily Gleaner*, 3 May 1938, p. 1.

84 'Intrepid Gleanerman Says: I was in the mob when "hell broke loose" at Frome', *Daily Gleaner*, 3 May 1938, p. 1.

85 TNA CAB 23/93, Cabinet 26 (38) Meeting of the Cabinet to be held at No. 10 Downing Street, SW1, on Wednesday 25th May, 1938, at 11.00am. Jamaica – ff.352–3.

86 NARA RG59 844D.5045/13, 'Disturbances in Kingston, Confidential report from Hugh Watson, American Consul General', 25 May 1938.

87 Bolland, *On the March*, pp. 173–5.

88 Carr, 'Identity, Class, and Nation', p. 89.

89 Higman, *A Concise History*, p. 202.

90 Mary A. Renda, *Taking Haiti: Military Occupation and the Culture of US Imperialism, 1915–1940* (University of North Carolina Press, 2001), p. 30.

91 Higman, *A Concise History*, p. 206.

92 Renda, *Taking Haiti*, p. 10.

93 Laurent Dubois, *Haiti: The Aftershocks of History* (Picador USA, 2013), see chapter 6.

94 Quoted in Renda, *Taking Haiti*, p. 31.

95 Ibid., p. 10.

96 Dubois, *Aftershocks of History*, chapter 6.

97 Renda, *Taking Haiti*, p. 10.

98 Ibid., p. 33.

99 Caribbean Documents Collection, University of Miami Special Collections Folder 22, Letters to Helen Esqueme From Edmond; Account of His Trip to Haiti, 28 August 1930.

100 Quoted in Renda, *Taking Haiti*, p. 34.
101 Ibid., p. 4.
102 Ibid., p. 34.
103 Higman, *A Concise History*, p. 204.
104 Ibid., p. 205.
105 Quoted in Richard Turits, *Foundations of Despotism: Peasants, the Trujillo Regime, and Modernity in Dominican History* (Stanford University Press, 2004), p. 162.
106 Ibid., p. 163.
107 Ibid., p. 161.
108 Quoted ibid., p. 167.
109 Ibid., p. 168.

Ten – The Road to Independence

1   TNA CAB 65/5/27, Conclusions of a Meeting of the War Cabinet held at 10 Downing Street, SW1, on Tuesday, January 30, 1940 at 11.30AM.
2   Ibid.
3   TNA CAB 65/5/42, Conclusions of a Meeting of the War Cabinet held at 10 Downing Street, SW1 on Thursday, February 15, 1940, at 11.30AM.
4   TNA CAB 66/61/21, War Cabinet: Publication of the West India Royal Commission Report, 27 January 1945.
5   Bolland, 'Labour Protests', p. 464.
6   NARA CP RG59 844C.4016/1. East Indians in the West Indies. 3 November 1939.
7   Ibid.
8   TNA CAB 67/4/45, War Cabinet: Recommendations of the West India Royal Commission, 13 February 1940.
9   Bolland, 'Labour Protests', p. 464.
10 TNA CO 28/332/4, Barbadian Affairs Intelligence & Situation Reports, 13 November 1944.
11 TNA CO 28/332/4, Bushe to Stanley, 11 July 1944.
12 TNA CO 28/332/4, Telegram No 388, 11 December 1944, Secretary of State for the Colonies to Barbados.
13 TNA CO 28/332/4, Barbadian Affairs Intelligence & Situation Reports, 13 November 1944.
14 Randall, Mount, and Bright, *The Caribbean Basin*, pp. 72–3.
15 V. S. Naipaul, *Miguel Street* (Penguin, 1987), p. 55.
16 Louis Nizer, *My Life in Court* (Doubleday, 1961), p. 236.
17 Ibid., p. 235.
18 Ibid., pp. 267–73.

19   Jennings, 'Monuments to Frenchness?', p. 561.

20   Randall, Mount, and Bright, *The Caribbean Basin*, p. 77.

21   Ibid., pp. 78–80.

22   TNA WO 106/2845, 'General Situation in Dominica', May 1943.

23   TNA WO 106/2845, Telegram no. 860, Sir A. Grimble to Secretary of State for Colonies, 28 July 1943.

24   TNA WO 106/2845, 'General Situation in Dominica', May 1943.

25   Ibid.

26   Angela Pidduck, 'Rotarians honour a Calypso Jew', *Trinidad and Tobago Newsday*, 29 July 2012, www.newsday.co.tt/features/0,164047.html (accessed 28 November 2012).

27   Hans Stecher, 'Historical Notes on the Jews in Trinidad' (1982), unpublished paper, West India Collection, University of West Indies, St Augustine, Trinidad.

28   Jean Rhys, *Voyage in the Dark* (Penguin, 2000; originally published 1934).

29   For a recent discussion of the state of this debate see Dale Tomich, 'Econocide? From Abolition to Emancipation in the British and French Caribbean', in Palmié and Scarano, *The Caribbean*, chapter 20.

30   Williams, *Capitalism and Slavery*.

31   See, for instance, Seymour Drescher, *Econocide: British Slavery in the Era of Abolition* (University of North Carolina Press, 2010); Hilary McD. Beckles, 'Capitalism, Slavery and Caribbean Modernity', *Callaloo* 20, 4 (1997), pp. 777–89; Selwyn H. H. Carrington, 'Capitalism & Slavery and Caribbean Historiography: An Evaluation', *Journal of African American History* 88, 3 (2003), pp. 304–12; Eltis, *Economic Growth*; Cedric J. Robinson, 'Capitalism, Slavery and Bourgeois Historiography', *History Workshop Journal* 23 (1987), pp. 122–40.

32   Colin A. Palmer, *Eric Williams and the Making of the Modern Caribbean* (University of North Carolina Press, 2008).

33   George Lamming, 'The Legacy of Eric Williams', *Callaloo* 20, 4 (1997), p. 731.

34   Spencer Mawby, *Ordering Independence: The End of Empire in the Anglophone Caribbean, 1947–1969* (Palgrave Macmillan, 2012), pp. 123, 180.

35   'Ministry Paper No. 32: Jamaica Independence Celebrations', 1962, National Library of Jamaica 31/1962.

36   Ibid., Annex V.

37   *Daily Gleaner*, 2 August 1962, p. 23.

38   *Daily Gleaner*, 5 August 1962, p. 5.

39   Ibid.

40   Dr Martin Luther King, Jr, 'The American Dream', http://mlk-kpp01. stanford.edu/index.php/encyclopedia/documentsentry/doc_the_

american_dream/ (accessed 21 March 2013). See also: Carter Mathes, 'Circuits of Political Prophecy: Martin Luther King Jr., Peter Tosh, and the Black Radical Imaginary', *Small Axe* 14, 2 (2010), pp. 17–41.

41 Barbados Independence Celebrations, 27 Nov.–4 Dec. 1966, West India Collection, UWI Cave Hill.

42 TNA FCO 141/40, Frank McDonald to Richard Nolte, report on Anguilla to the Institute of Current World Affairs, 17 March 1969.

43 *The Times*, 20 March 1969, p. 1.

44 *The Times*, 17 March 1969, p. 9.

45 Ibid.

46 BNA GH/3/6/5, MSS/G/2.

47 Richard Drayton, 'Anglo-American "Liberal" Imperialism: British Guiana, 1953–64 and the World Since September 11', in Wm Roger Louis (ed.), *Yet More Adventures with Britannia: Personalities, Politics, and Culture in Britain* (I. B. Tauris, 2005), p. 326.

48 Ibid., pp. 327–32.

49 TNA CAB 128/26, Conclusions of a Meeting of the Cabinet held at 10 Downing Street SW1 on Friday, 2nd October, 1953, at 11.30 am.

50 NARA RG59 Box 2, British Guiana, Confidential letter regarding impending visit of Dr Cheddi Jagan, 30 July 1959.

51 NARA RG59 Box 2, British Guiana, 'Confidential: Reported Cuban Loan to British Guiana', 15 September 1960.

52 Drayton, 'Anglo-American', p. 322.

53 NARA RG59 Box 2, British Guiana, General folder, 'Confidential Memorandum of Conversation', 21 October 1964.

54 Randall, Mount, and Bright, *The Caribbean Basin*, p. 33.

55 The definitive account of this period is by Assad Shoman, who was involved in the negotiations. See Assad Shoman, *Belize's Independence and Decolonization in Latin America: Guatemala, Britain, and the UN* (Palgrave Macmillan, 2010).

56 See Godfrey P. Smith, *George Price: A Life Revealed* (Ian Randle, 2011).

57 Shoman, *Belize's Independence*, p. 190.

58 NARA RG59, General Records of the Department of State, Bureau of Inter-American Affairs, Records relating to Costa Rica, 1958–62, Box 2, Whiting Willauer to Thomas Mann, 21 September 1960.

59 Colby, *The Business of Empire*, p. 204.

60 Ibid., p. 205.

61 Douglas Farah, 'Papers Show US Role in Guatemalan Abuses', *Washington Post*, 11 March 1999, p. 26.

62 Lesley Gill, *The School of the Americas: Military Training and Political Violence in the Americas* (Duke University Press, 2004).

63 John A. Booth, Thomas W. Walker, and Christine J. Wade (eds),

Understanding Central America: Global Forces, Rebellion, Change (Westview Press, 2010), pp. 83–4.

64 Ibid., p. 91.

65 James E. Genova, 'Constructing Identity in Post-War France: Citizenship, Nationality, and the Lamine Guèye Law, 1946–1953', *International History Review* 26, 1 (2004), p. 57.

66 Anne S. Macpherson, 'Toward Decolonization: Impulses, Processes, and Consequences since the 1930s', in Palmié and Scarano, *The Caribbean*, pp. 478–9.

Eleven – The Cold War in the Tropics

1 Ruby Hart Phillips, *Cuba: Island of Paradox* (McDowell, Obolensky, 1959), p. 262.

2 Herbert L. Matthews, 'Cuban Rebel Is Visited in Hideout', *New York Times*, 24 February 1957.

3 Ibid.

4 Ibid.

5 Hart Phillips, *Cuba*, pp. 400–404.

6 Philip Benjamin, 'Castro Gets a Noisy Reception Here', *New York Times*, 22 April 1959.

7 'US Stand against Reds in Cuba Has Its Roots in Monroe Doctrine', *New York Times*, 19 April 1961.

8 Eric Williams, 'International Perspectives for Trinidad and Tobago', 1964, UWI, SA, Eric Williams Memorial Collection, No. 644.

9 Speech by Cuban Prime Minister Fidel Castro at friendship rally at 14 June rural basic secondary school, Isle of Pines, in honor of Trinidad-Tobago Prime Minister Eric Williams, 20 June 1975, http://lanic.utexas.edu/project/castro/db/1975/19750720.html (accessed 23 March 2013).

10 'Manley gets warm welcome in Cuba', *Daily Gleaner*, 10 July 1975, p. 1.

11 'PM returns from Cuba', *Daily Gleaner*, 14 July 1975, p. 1.

12 Letter, *Daily Gleaner*, 29 September 1977, p. 8.

13 'JLP to boycott Castro's visit', *Sunday Gleaner*, 16 October 1977, p. 1.

14 'Castro Is Here: Security Tight for Cuba Head', *Daily Gleaner*, 17 October 1977, pp. 1–2.

15 There is an excellent documentary about this called *Life and Debt*; see www.lifeanddebt.org/

16 Zora Neale Hurston, *Tell My Horse: Voodoo and Life in Haiti and Jamaica* (Perennial Library, 1990; originally published 1938), p. 83.

17 NARA, RG59, Records Relating to Haiti, 1960–74, Container 2, Policy Papers, Haiti, Robert Newbegin to Norman Warner, 28 November 1960.

18   Graham Greene, *The Comedians* (The Bodley Head, 1976), p. x.
19   Michele Wucker, *Why the Cocks Fight: Dominicans, Haitians, and the Struggle for Hispaniola* (Hill and Wang, 2000), pp. 120–21.
20   'Wild Welcome for Negus – And the Emperor Wept', *Daily Gleaner*, 22 April 1966, p. 1.
21   Barrington and González, *Caribbean Religious History*, p. 186.
22   National Census Report Jamaica, www.caricomstats.org/Files/Publications/NCR%20Reports/Jamaica.pdf (accessed 9 July 2013).
23   *Daily Gleaner*, 22 April 1966.
24   Ibid.
25   'Selassie Leaves', *Sunday Gleaner*, 24 April 1966, p. 13.
26   Jacquiann Lawton, 'Social and Public Architecture in Kingston, Jamaica', *Docomomo* 33 (2005), pp. 58–9.
27   See chapter 6 of Colin Grant, *I&I: The Natural Mystics: Marley, Tosh, and Wailer* (Jonathan Cape, 2011).
28   Anthony Maingot, 'Independence and Its Aftermath: Suriname, Trinidad, and Jamaica', in Palmié and Scarano, *The Caribbean*, p. 533.
29   Richard Drayton, 'From Kabul to Kingston', *Guardian*, 14 June 2010, www.guardian.co.uk/commentisfree/2010/jun/14/jamaica-tactics-army-afghanistan (accessed 25 March 2013).
30   Brian Meeks, *Radical Caribbean: From Black Power to Abu Bakr* (University of the West Indies Press, 1996), p. 1.
31   Walter Rodney, *The Groundings with My Brothers* (Villiers, 1975), p. 60.
32   Quoted in Meeks, *Radical Caribbean*, p. 11.
33   Ibid., p. 19.
34   See Herman L. Bennett, 'The Challenge to the Post Colonial State: A Case Study of the February Revolution in Trinidad', in Franklin W. Knight and Colin A. Palmer (eds), *The Modern Caribbean* (University of North Carolina Press, 1989), chapter 6.
35   Meeks, *Radical Caribbean*, p. 30.
36   TNA CAB 128/45/18, 'Conclusions of a Meeting of the Cabinet held at 10 Downing Street, SW1, on Thursday, 23rd April, 1970'.
37   Maingot, 'Independence and Its Aftermath', p. 529.
38   Beckles, *A History of Barbados*, p. 282.
39   TNA FCO 63/443, 'Secret despatch re Stokely Carmichael', 15 May 1970.
40   Ibid.
41   TNA FCO 63/494, 'Confidential: Black Power EN Larmour to TRM Sewell', London, 29 May 1970.
42   Ibid.
43   TNA FCO 63/494, 'A Post-Trinidad Assessment of Jamaican Stability', 29 May 1970.
44   Ibid.
45   TNA FCO 141/50, Secret files on Black Power, 17 December 1970.

46 Ibid.
47 'Legislation Against Dreads, Advocate News, Barbados', *Star* (Dominica), 13 September 1974, pp. 1 and 3.
48 'Suppression of the Dreads Act Passed', *Star* (Dominica), 22 November 1974, p. 1.
49 'Premier on Dreads & Communism', *Star* (Dominica), 29 November 1974, p. 6.
50 'Dominica Is Given New Powers to Combat Black Guerrillas', *New York Times*, 7 December 1974, p. 8.
51 Robert Trimbull, 'Dominica's Harsh Law Against Black Guerrillas Stirs Concern', *New York Times*, 6 January 1975, p. 8.
52 Laurence Lindo, 'Unrest in Dominica', *The Times*, 9 July 1975, p. 15.
53 Sybil Farrell Lewis and Dale T. Mathews (eds), *Documents on the Invasion of Grenada* (Institute of Caribbean Studies, University of Puerto Rico, October, 1983), p. 5.
54 Ibid., p. 10.
55 Ibid., p. 41.
56 Ibid., p. 17.
57 'Grenada: Behind Reagan's propaganda victory: British and American press coverage', newspaper cuttings, University of Miami Special Collection, M0001, Caribbean and South American Ephemera Collection, Box 9.
58 Lewis and Mathews, *Documents on the Invasion of Grenada*, p. 51.
59 Socialist Action 'Hands Off Grenada!', University of Miami Special Collection, M0001, Caribbean and South American Ephemera Collection, Box 9.
60 US Anti-Imperialist League, 'The Invasion of Grenada'.
61 Lewis and Mathews, *Documents on the Invasion of Grenada*, p. 87.
62 Ibid., p. 107.
63 Ibid., p. 39.
64 Richard Bernstein, 'US Vetoes UN Resolution "Deploring" Grenada Invasion', *New York Times*, 29 October 1983.
65 Maingot, 'Independence and Its Aftermath', p. 530.
66 University of the West Indies (hereafter UWI), St Augustine MCD, Box 5, Folder 5, Statements from Witnesses, Verne Burnett, 29 September 1992.
67 UWI, St Augustine MCD, Box 6, Folder 1, *Financial Times* clipping, 3 August 1990.
68 UWI, St Augustine MCD, Box 5, Folder 5, Statements from Witnesses, Ismail Abdullah Muhammad, 28 February 1993.
69 Maingot, 'Independence and Its Aftermath', p. 530.
70 Rodney, *The Groundings with My Brothers*, p. 13.

Twelve – Island Life

1 Higman, *A Concise History*, p. 4.
2 'Two Years Later, Haitian Earthquake Death Toll in Dispute', *Columbia Journalism Review*, 12 January 2012, www.cjr.org/behind_the_news/one_year_later_haitian_earthqu.php?page=all (accessed 25 March 2013).
3 Kathie Klarreich and Linda Polman, 'The NGO Republic of Haiti', *The Nation*, 19 November 2012.
4 For a full account of this turbulent period, see Michael Deibert, *Notes from the Last Testament: The Struggle for Haiti* (Seven Stories Press, 2011).
5 See the 2003 documentary *The Agronomist* (available on DVD) for the story of Jean Dominique's extraordinary life and death in Haiti.
6 'Cries for help as Caribbean's largest lake continues mysterious growth', Caribbean 360, www.caribbean360.com/index.php/news/dominican_republic_news/656232.html#ixzz2IN7cGI9R (accessed 25 March 2013).
7 Haiti apparently passed a ban to begin 1 October 2012 on plastic bags and polystyrene containers, though it may take a while to see the effect.
8 See for instance, Nicola Miller, 'The Absolution of History: Uses of the Past in Castro's Cuba', *Journal of Contemporary History* 38, 1 (2003), pp. 147–62.
9 John Jeremiah Sullivan, 'Where is Cuba Going?', *New York Times*, 20 September 2012.
10 Humberto García Muñiz, 'The Colonial Persuasion', in Palmié and Scarano, *The Caribbean*, p. 548.
11 Census: PR poverty up, income down, 23 September 2012, http://caribbeanbusinesspr.com/news/census-pr-poverty-up-income-down-76580.html (accessed 12 January 2013).
12 Based on 2012 IMF figures, see www.imf.org.
13 Quoted in 'Islanders split as Whitehall takes over Turks and Caicos', *Guardian*, 16 August 2009, www.guardian.co.uk/politics/2009/aug/16/whitehall-takes-over-turks-caicos (accessed 12 January 2013).
14 García Muñiz, 'The Colonial Persuasion', p. 547.
15 Macpherson, 'Toward Decolonization'', pp. 483–4.
16 Maingot, 'Independence and Its Aftermath', pp. 525–7.
17 Ibid., pp. 526–7.
18 David Howard, *Coloring the Nation: Race and Ethnicity in the Dominican Republic* (Signal Books, 2001), p. 3.
19 Wucker, *Why the Cocks Fight*, pp. 185–94.
20 Roberto Zurbano, 'For Blacks in Cuba, the Revolution Hasn't Begun', *New York Times*, 23 March 2013.
21 'Activist to sue Trinidad and Tobago entry ban on gays', 27 November 2012, www.gaystarnews.com/article/activist-sue-trinidad-and-tobago-entry-ban-gays271112 (accessed 11 January 2013).

22 Joe Mirabella, 'Advocates Tell Puerto Rico: Do Not Eliminate Hate Crimes Protections', Huffington Post, 12 August 2011, www.huffingtonpost.com/ joe-mirabella/puerto-rico-hate-crimes-protections_b_1135384. html?ref=latino-voices&ir=Latino%20Voices (accessed 25 March 2013).

23 'Cuban transsexual elected to public office', Guardian, 18 November 2012, www.guardian.co.uk/world/2012/nov/18/cuban-transsexual-adela-hernandez-elected (accessed 11 January 2013).

24 Gay man weds transsexual woman in Cuba, 14 August 2011, Guardian, www.guardian.co.uk/world/2011/aug/14/gay-man-weds-trans-sexual-woman-cuba (accessed 11 January 2013).

25 'Remarks by Vice Premier Wang Qishan at the Opening Ceremony of the 3rd China–Caribbean Economic and Trade Cooperation Forum', 12 September 2011, http://tt.chineseembassy.org/eng/zt/3rdCNCForum/ t860706.htm (accessed 11 January 2013)

26 Ibid.

27 'Dominica Defends Relationship with China', Daily Gleaner, 26 October 2011, http://jamaica-gleaner.com/gleaner/20111026/business/business6. html (accessed 25 March 2013).

28 'Taiwan's "Caribbean headache"', BBC News, 30 March 2004, http://news. bbc.co.uk/2/hi/asia-pacific/3583733.stm (accessed 11 January 2013).

29 'Grenada: Bandleader Loses Job in Chinese Anthem Gaffe', New York Times, 8 February 2007.

30 Paper presented at the IMF/UWI Conference on 'The Caribbean Challenges after the Global Crisis', Barbados, 27–28 January 2011, www.imf.org/external/np/seminars/eng/2010/carib/pdf/bernal2.pdf (accessed 11 January 2013).

31 Simon Romero, 'With Aid and Migrants, China Expands Its Presence in a South American Nation', New York Times, 10 April 2011.

32 'Why is China spending billions in the Caribbean?', 22 April 2011, www.globalpost.com/dispatch/news/regions/americas/110325/ china-caribbean-investment-tourism (accessed 11 January 2013).

33 See note 30 above.

Thirteen – Import/Export

1 NARA RG59, Department of State, 844d.114, Narcotics, enclosure no. 9 to despatch no. 314 . . . on the subject of Laws and regulation relating to traffic in narcotic drugs, 29 October 1931.

2 NARA RG59, Department of State, 844d.114, Narcotics, Paul C. Squire to Fred D. Fisher, 27 June 1931.

3 NARA RG59, Department of State, 844d.114, Narcotics/27, Alfredo L. Demorest to US Secretary of State, 28 October 1932.

4 NARA RG59, Department of State, 844d.114, Narcotics/31, Gaston A. Cournoyer to US Secretary of State, 13 January 1933.

5 NARA RG59, Department of State, 844d.114, Narcotics/29, A. S. Jelf, Colonial Secretary, to W. W. Corcoran, US Consul in Jamaica, 12 January 1933.

6 Mattathias Schwartz, 'A Massacre in Jamaica', New Yorker, 12 December 2011.

7 Ed Pilkington, 'Christopher "Dudus" Coke handed 23-year US jail term for drug trafficking', Guardian, 8 June 2012, www.guardian.co.uk/world/2012/jun/08/christopher-dudus-coke-jail-term (accessed 25 March 2013); Mattathias Schwartz, 'As Jamaican Drug Lord is Sentenced, U.S. Still Silent on Massacre', 8 June 2012, www.newyorker.com/online/blogs/newsdesk/2012/06/christopher-coke-tivoli-massacre.html#ixzz2Ob7mYLgC (accessed 25 March 2013).

8 Schwartz, 'A Massacre in Jamaica'.

9 'Christopher Coke's Letter to Sentencing Judge', New York Times, 21 September 2011, www.nytimes.com/interactive/2011/09/21/nyregion/21coke-letter.html?ref=nyregion (accessed 25 March 2013).

10 Robert Goddard, 'Tourism, Drugs, Offshore Finance, and the Perils of Neoliberal Development', in Palmié and Scarano, The Caribbean, p. 576.

11 'Indebted Caribbean Tax Havens Look to Tax Foreign Investors', 26 November 2012, www.csmonitor.com/World/Americas/2012/1126/Indebted-Caribbean-tax-havens-look-to-tax-foreign-investors (accessed 12 January 2013).

12 Ibid.

13 'Antigua Declares Trade War on US', 9 December 2012, www.belfasttelegraph.co.uk/news/world-news/antigua-declares-trade-war-on-us-16248226.html?r=RSS (accessed 12 January 2013).

14 Ibid.

15 Ibid.

16 'WTO grants Antigua right to launch "pirate" site selling US media', Wired, 29 January 2013, www.wired.co.uk/news/archive/2013-01/29/antigua-legitimate-piracy (accessed 26 March 2013).

17 'Struggling Caribbean Islands Selling Citizenship', 12 February 2013, www.usnews.com/news/world/articles/2013/02/12/struggling-caribbean-islands-selling-citizenship?page=2 (accessed 25 March 2013).

18 'Caribbean Island of Grenada Plans to Revive Program Selling Citizenship to Global Investors', Washington Post, 27 March 2013, www.washingtonpost.com/business/caribbean-island-of-grenada-plans-to-revive-program-selling-citizenship-to-global-investors/2013/03/27/847fcc90–9705–11e2-a976–7eb906f9ed9b_story.html (accessed 27 March 2013).

19 Goddard, 'Tourism, Drugs', p. 580.

20 'US Rum Subsidies Hammer Caribbean Producers', 10 August 2012, http://finance.yahoo.com/news/us-rum-subsidies-hammer-caribbean-

producers-144901594--finance.html (accessed 12 January 2013).

21 Lauren Derby, 'Gringo Chickens with Worms: Food and Nationalism in the Dominican Republic', in G. M. Joseph, Catherine LeGrand and Ricardo Donato Salvatore *American Encounters/global Interactions* (Duke University Press, 1998).

22 Higman, *A Concise History*, p. 283.

23 Indeed, in 2012 the traditional chief of the Algonquian people symbolically adopted the Haitian community who live on their historic territory.

24 Higman, *A Concise History*, p. 284.

25 Christine M. Du Bois, 'Caribbean Migrations and Diasporas', in Palmié and Scarano, *The Caribbean*, pp. 586–8.

26 Higman, *A Concise History*, p. 283

27 Goddard, 'Tourism, Drugs', p. 590.

28 Higman, *A Concise History*.

29 FCO Blog, 'Coming Home to Jamaica', http://blogs.fco.gov.uk/ukinjamaica/2013/02/19/coming-home-to-jamaica/ (accessed 25 March 2013).

30 Interview taken from *Home Again: Stories of Migration and Return*, comp. Celia Sorhaindo and Polly Pattullo (Papillote Press, 2012).

31 Gina Athena Ulysse, 'Defending Vodou in Haiti', 18 October 2012, www.huffingtonpost.com/gina-athena-ulysse/defending-vodou-in-haiti_b_1973374.html (accessed 13 January 2013).

32 'Jamaica's Patois Bible: The Word of God in Creole, BBC News, 24 December 2012, www.bbc.co.uk/news/magazine-16285462, accessed 13 January 2103.

33 Campbell, 'Carnival, Calypso, and Class Struggle', p. 8.

34 Ibid., p. 10.

35 C. L. R. James, *Beyond A Boundary* (Serpent's Tail, 1994; originally published 1963).

36 See the excellent documentary *Fire in Babylon* for more on the glory days of international West Indian Test cricket.

37 Brian Homewood, 'Alpine Skiing – Jamaica Edge Haiti in Caribbean Slalom Duel', 16 February 2013, www.globalpost.com/dispatch/news/thomson-reuters/130216/alpine-skiing-jamaica-edge-haiti-caribbean-slalom-duel (accessed 25 March 2013).

Fourteen – Invented Paradise

1 Quoted in Polly Pattullo, *Last Resorts: The Cost of Tourism in the Caribbean* (Latin American Bureau, 2005), p. 13.

2 West India Collection, UWI Cave Hill, *Barbados Tourist Guide* (Hanschell & Co., 1914).

3 Goddard, 'Tourism, Drugs', p. 574.

4   Ibid., p. 572.
5   Ibid.
6   Ibid.
7   Quoted in Pattullo, *Last Resorts*, p. 81.
8   'Castro's Jamaica Press Conference 30/10/77', http://lanic.utexas.edu/project/castro/db/1977/19771030.html (accessed 11 November 2012).
9   Goddard, 'Tourism, Drugs', p. 573.
10   Pattullo, *Last Resorts*, p.6.
11   'Tourism: Ca Ka Fait?', *Star* (Dominica), 8 February 1974, p. 2.
12   'Shots and Chops', *Star* (Dominica), 1 March 1974, p. 1.
13   'Fire & Foul Play: Canadian Couple Killed', *Star* (Dominica) 29 November 1974, p. 1.
14   Goddard, 'Tourism, Drugs', p. 575.
15   'Haiti Among the Safest Destinations in the Americas', 4 January 2013, http://finance.yahoo.com/news/haiti-among-safest-destinations-americas-223000869.html (accessed 26 March 2013).
16   Pattullo, *Last Resorts*, p. 7.
17   Caribbean Tourism Organization: Latest Statistics 2012: 4 June 2012, www.onecaribbean.org/wp-content/uploads/June142013Lattab2012.pdf (accessed 15 July 2013).
18   'Dutch Caribbean 2012 Tourism Growth Beats Caribbean Average', 14 February 2013, www.curacaochronicle.com/tourism/dutch-caribbean-2012-tourism-growth-beats-caribbean-average/ (accessed 26 March 2013).
19   Amy Wilentz, 'Letter From Haiti: Life in the Ruins', *The Nation*, 28 January 2013.
20   World Bank, 'Jamaica – Country Economic Memorandum: Unlocking Growth', https://openknowledge.worldbank.org/handle/10986/2756 (accessed 26 March 2013).
21   Quoted in Dubois and Garrigus, *Slave Revolution in the Caribbean*, p. 59.
22   Ezra Fieser, 'In Dominican Republic Seaside Village, a Virtual Supermarket of Sex', *Miami Herald*, 2 February 2013, www.miamiherald.com/2013/02/02/v-fullstory/3214575/in-dominican-seaside-village-a.html#story (accessed 26 March 2013).
23   Jamaica Kincaid, *A Small Place* (Farrar Straus & Giroux, 1988).
24   'Walcott, 'The Antilles: Fragments of Epic Memory'.

Conclusion

1   Higman, *A Concise History*, pp. 137–9.
2   V. S. Naipaul, *The Middle Passage* (Picador, 2001; originally published 1962), p. 20.
3   Walcott, 'The Antilles: Fragments of Epic Memory'.

Index